An Asperger Dictionary of Everyday Expressions

of related interest

Asperger's Syndrome
A Guide for Parents and Professionals
Tony Attwood
Foreword by Lorna Wing
ISBN 1 85302 577 1

What did you say? What do you mean?
An Illustrated Guide to Understanding Metaphors
Jude Welton
Illustrated by Jane Telford
Foreword by Elizabeth Newson
ISBN 1 84310 207 2

Can I tell you about Asperger Syndrome?
A Guide for Friends and Family
Jude Welton
Illustrated by Jane Telford
Foreword by Elizabeth Newson
ISBN 1 84310 206 4

Freaks, Geeks and Asperger Syndrome
A User Guide to Adolescence
Luke Jackson
Foreword by Tony Attwood
ISBN 1 84310 098 3

Mind Reading
The Interactive Guide to Emotions
Based on research by Cambridge University, led by Simon Baron-Cohen
DVD-ROM ISBN 1 84310 214 5
CD-ROM Set ISBN 1 84310 215 3
Emotions Library ISBN 1 84310 216 1

Succeeding in College with Asperger Syndrome
A student guide
John Harpur, Maria Lawlor and Michael Fitzgerald
ISBN 1 84310 201 3

An Asperger Dictionary of Everyday Expressions

Ian Stuart-Hamilton

Jessica Kingsley Publishers
London and Philadelphia

First published in the United Kingdom in 2004
by Jessica Kingsley Publishers
116 Pentonville Road
London N1 9JB, UK
and
400 Market Street, Suite 400
Philadelphia, PA 19106, USA

www.jkp.com

Copyright © Ian Stuart-Hamilton 2004
Second impression 2005

Library of Congress Cataloging in Publication Data

Stuart-Hamilton, Ian.
    An asperger dictionary of everyday expressions / Ian Stuart-Hamilton.— 1st American
pbk. ed.
      p. cm.
    Includes bibliographical references.
    ISBN 1-84310-152-1 (pbk.)
    1. Asperger's syndrome—Patients—Language—Dictionaries. 2. English
language—Idioms—Dictionaries. I. Title.
RC553.A88S865 2004
616.85'88—dc22
                                  2004005451

British Library Cataloguing in Publication Data
A CIP catalogue record for this book is available from the British Library

ISBN-13: 978 1 84310 152 9
ISBN-10: 1 84310 152 1

Printed and Bound in Great Britain by
Athenaeum Press, Gateshead, Tyne and Wear

For Mark and Kate

Introduction

It is well documented that people with Asperger's syndrome and other autism spectrum disorders have difficulty interpreting everyday phrases that must be interpreted symbolically rather than literally. For example, a *little bird told me* literally implies that a bird assumed the powers of speech and gave information, whilst the symbolic meaning is of course rather different.[1] However, it is worth noting that *everyone* can have problems with dealing with phrases like this from time to time. In practical terms, the only difference between someone with Asperger's syndrome and someone without it is the frequency with which this occurs.

Dealing with this problem is itself difficult. The most obvious solution is to not interpret any phrase literally. However, not only is it the most obvious, it is also the most stupid. This would make unambiguous language impossible to understand. Advising people to use context to interpret the symbolic meaning of something that is nonsensical if interpreted literally is likewise unworkable, even for someone with very high linguistic skills.

Arguably the only practical solution is to use a dictionary such as this, which gives definitions of at least the commoner everyday phrases. The phrases I have chosen for inclusion are ones that appear to be the most often used amongst UK English speakers. There are a considerable number of common American English phrases, and some Australian phrases as well. Together, they cover the majority of the everyday phrases that are potentially confusing for English speakers in most countries. There are of course many other phrases that could have been included, but arguably this is a case of diminishing returns. In other words, it was either a dictionary this size or a truly enormous one (at least four times the size) with many of the phrases being very rare indeed. In making my selections, I chose not to include the following:

1. Contemporary slang, for the simple reason that most of it lasts a few months and then is replaced by other slang.

---

1   The meaning of a *little bird told me* and other phrases used in the Introduction are given in the dictionary.

2. A lot of classical and literary references, on the grounds that these cause *everybody* problems, and there is a large problem of where to stop. This is meant to be a dictionary of commonly used idiomatic phrases, not quotations. Where phrases that are in fact quotations (e.g. *salt of the earth*) are included, it is usually because they are such a part of everyday speech that most people are probably unaware that they are quotations.

3. Phrases that are largely historical and/or little used.

4. Specialist slang from occupations and professions, unless it is so common that it has entered everyday speech (e.g. *pyramid selling*).

5. Phrases which really are self-evident (e.g. 'fast as a hare' simply means fast).

6. Single ambiguous words (e.g. 'gay'), for the simple reason that about half the words in an ordinary dictionary fall into this category, and this is intended to be a relatively portable book!

Inevitably there will be phrases that have been missed from this dictionary that should have been included. This is the fate of every dictionary compiler in history. Future editions will attempt to amend wrongs, but please do not contact me with suggestions. This is not because I do not value readers' comments (far from it), but unsolicited suggestions create a difficult problem of copyright.

A detailed guide to using the dictionary is provided in the next section of this book. I have tried as far as possible to keep things simple and intuitive. Thus, phrases are usually listed as they are spoken, with key words from the phrase providing references back to the phrase.

In finishing this Introduction, I hope that this book is of use to people with Asperger's syndrome, or of course anyone else who is puzzled by an apparently nonsensical phrase.

Professor Ian Stuart-Hamilton
University of Glamorgan
December 2003

A guide to using the dictionary

(1) Absence of definite and indefinite articles
Entries are without definite and indefinite articles ('the', 'an', etc.). For example, 'the real McCoy' is entered as *real McCoy*.

(2) Phrases are usually listed as they are spoken
Entries are as far as possible done as they would be spoken. For example, 'after their blood' is entered as *after their blood*, not *blood, after their*. Where I have felt there could be difficulties in finding the phrase by this method, I have included directions to it using other key words (e.g. *walk on air* is also referenced under *air*).

(3) Key part of phrases
Where there are several similar variants of the same phrase, I have usually simply entered the key part of the phrase; for example, there are various phrases like 'a man after my own heart', 'a boy after their own heart', etc. The key part of the phrase is *after their own heart*, and this is the phrase that is provided by this dictionary.

(4) Use of *their*
Phrases usually can be used to describe or apply to a variety of people. For example, the phrase 'after their blood' can be used in the forms 'after his blood', 'after our blood', 'after my blood', 'after their blood', 'after her blood', 'after its blood', 'after one's blood' and 'after your blood'. Rather than have entries for each phrase, I have simply included one – namely, *after their blood*. In nearly all cases, I have used 'their' in preference to 'one', 'his', 'her', 'its', etc. This is because 'their' is arguably the most 'neutral' form. However, when 'their' is used, 'her', 'his', etc. can be substituted in. Where a phrase is given with something other than 'their' (e.g. *are you sitting comfortably?*) then this is because the phrase is usually only heard in this form.

A

A word The phrase 'a word' (sometimes accompanied by a visual signal to 'come here') means that the speaker wishes to discuss something or provide information.*

Above board Legal, usually with the implication of being honest and trustworthy. The phrase comes from card games – any manipulating of the cards under the table (i.e. below board) is likely to be an indication of cheating. Thus, keeping the hands and cards on the table (i.e. above board) is more likely to indicate an honest player.*

Above par Of good standard.*

Above their weight If someone performs 'above their weight', then they are performing at a higher standard than was predicted.*

Absence of mind Failure to remember and/or pay attention.*

Academic interest Something of 'academic interest' is of limited usefulness and may be considered an inconsequential detail.*

Acceptable face of… The best example of something that is generally seen as unattractive. The phrase can thus imply that what is being discussed is not very pleasant, and only looks good when compared to other members of the same category.*

Accident waiting to happen (1) A situation or set of circumstances in which an accident is far more likely to happen (e.g. waxing a wooden floor so it is very slippery and then putting a rug on it might be said to be 'an accident waiting to happen'). (2) A derogatory term for a person who through carelessness or lack of intelligence is likely to be the cause of accidents or other serious problems.*

Accidentally on purpose Something done 'accidentally on purpose' is done intentionally, but appears to be accidental.*

According to Hoyle In keeping with the rules and/or expectations. Hoyle was author of a standard reference book on card games, and the phrase spread from card players to the general public.*

Ace See *ace in the hole, ace up their sleeve, hold all the aces, play the ace* and *within an ace.*

Ace in the hole A hidden advantage; the term comes from a variant of the card game of poker, in which one card called the 'hole' is hidden from the players' view until betting is completed. Since an ace is a high-scoring card, finding an ace in the hole would be an advantage.*

Ace up their sleeve A hidden advantage. The term is derived from the concept of cheating at cards – keeping an extra ace card hidden to be added into a player's hand of cards at an advantageous moment. The term 'ace up my sleeve' usually does not imply cheating, however.*

Achilles heel A weakness in an otherwise strong system – it often refers more specifically to a character defect in an otherwise resilient person. The term derives from the ancient Greek legend of Achilles, who was immune to injury, save for a tiny spot on his heel. Guess how someone killed him…*

Acid test The definitive method of assessment (e.g. an 'acid test' of a new driving safety system might be if more lives are saved). The phrase is derived from the fact that gold is the only metal not to dissolve in many types of acid. Thus, dipping a piece of metal of unknown origin into acid is an acid test of whether it is gold.*

Across the board To apply in all situations or areas. The term is often used in describing changes in policy (e.g. 'these changes in management structure apply across the board').*

Act See entries below and: *balancing act, catch in the act, class act, clean up their act, get* *their act together, hard act to follow* and *in on the act.*

Act the can Means the same as *act the fool.*

Act the fool Behave stupidly and/or playfully.*

Act the goat Means the same as *act the fool.*

Act together See *get their act together.*

Act up To be awkward and/or refuse to cooperate.*

Action See *action stations, actions speak louder than words* and *piece of the action.*

Action stations A command to be prepared to do something. The phrase is generally used jokingly when expected visitors are seen approaching (e.g. 'action stations! – Auntie Mabel is walking up the drive'). The phrase was originally a command given in the navy just before battle commenced.*

Actions speak louder than words This has two principal meanings. (1) It is more effective to do something than just talk about it. Thus, a person is more likely to impress others with how skilful they are at decorating by actually decorating a room rather than just talking about how, one day, they will decorate a room. (2) People will be judged by what they do rather than what they say. Thus, an employer who claims to be egalitarian but who never actually employs people from ethnic minorities is likely to be judged as being racially biased.*

Adam See *don't know from Adam.*

Add fuel to the fire Means the same as *fan the flames.*

Add fuel to the flames Means the same as *fan the flames.*

Add insult to injury Make a bad situation worse.*

Admirable Crichton A person who is good at everything. Named after a character of such attributes in a play by J.M. Barrie.*

Adrift See *cast adrift.*

Afraid of their own shadow Very nervous or cowardly.*

After a fashion To some extent. The phrase is often used to describe something that is recognisable as what it is supposed to be, but it is not done very well.*

After all is said and done Means the same as *when all is said and done.*

After doing it Be about to start to do something.*

After the fact After something has happened. The phrase is often used to describe the events after a crime has occurred.*

After their blood Angry and seeking to have revenge and/or inflict punishment.*

After their head Means the same as *after their blood.*

After their own heart Something that pleases a person and is a good representation of their own wishes or ideas; possessing similar attitudes.*

After their time Describes something or someone who worked or lived in a place after another person was there (e.g. 'I never met Jane Smith – she was after my time in the office; I'd left and gone to another job before she arrived').*

Against the grain Against normal desired practice or inclination (e.g. if a person says they are doing something but that 'it goes against the grain' it means that they would prefer to be doing it in a radically different manner).*

Against the stream Means the same as *against the grain.*

Against the tide Means the same as *against the grain.*

Against the wind Means the same as *against the grain.*

Against their religion Against their beliefs or principles (not necessarily religious). The phrase is sometimes used jokingly to describe something that a person will not do because it would not be typical of their behaviour (e.g. a lazy person who will not do strenuous work because it is 'against their religion').*

Agony aunt A woman who acts as a counsellor or adviser in dealing with people's personal problems. The term originally referred to a person paid to run an advice service on personal problems in a newspaper. Originally all such people were women, but in recent times men have also taken on the role, and are known as *agony uncles.**

Agony uncle See *agony aunt*.

Agree to differ Agree to hold different opinions on something and not argue about it.*

Ahead of its time Highly innovative. There is often an implication that it is so innovative that contemporaries have difficulty understanding its true worth, which will only be properly appreciated by later generations.*

Ahead of the game More advanced and/or foreseeing further than others.*

Air See *air grievances, clear the air, hanging in the air, hot air, in the air, into thin air, out of thin air, up in the air* and *walk on air*.

Air grievances To tell someone the complaints about them or the institution they represent.*

Airs and graces A set of very formal manners and behaviours indicative of someone who is very 'upper class'. The term is usually reserved for people who are pretending to be socially superior and are thus said to *give themselves airs and graces* or *put on airs and graces*.*

Aladdin's cave Any place that is full of riches can be described as 'an Aladdin's cave'. The phrase is a shortening of a slightly longer phrase ('it's like an Aladdin's cave') that makes reference to the folk tale in which Aladdin found fabulous riches in a magically guarded cave.*

Alarm bells See *set alarm bells ringing*.

Alcohol talking Express opinions that are probably the result of inebriation rather than an expression of something genuinely believed or accurate.*

Alienate their affections Persuade someone to lose affection for someone.*

Alive and kicking To be alive and healthy. The phrase is sometimes used to emphasize that someone presumed dead or ill is not (e.g. 'I thought he'd died' – 'No, he's very much alive and kicking').*

All around Means the same as *all round*.

All bets are off The phrase means that the situation is unpredictable and it is impossible to foresee what will happen next.*

All-clear An indication that everything is all right and that something dangerous that was a threat is no longer a threat. The term comes from World War II, when an 'all-clear' signal was given after a bombing raid was finished.*

All done with mirrors Done by deception and/or illusion.*

All ears Very attentive. Often used to describe an attentive listener (e.g. 'he was all ears').*

All ends up Totally.*

All eyes Very attentive. Often used to describe someone who observes a lot (e.g. 'she was all eyes').*

All fingers and thumbs Clumsy.*

All gas and gaiters Pompous.*

All Greek to me Incomprehensible.*

All guns blazing See *with all guns blazing*.

All hands The total personnel working in a ship. The phrase is sometimes used to describe the total workforce in other areas of work.*

All he [or she] wrote See *that's all he [or she] wrote*.

All hell broke loose An exaggerated way of saying that there was a loud disturbance. The phrase is a quotation from Milton's poem *Paradise Lost*.*

All in a day's work What can be expected as part of the normal routine of a particular occupation.*

All in good time A phrase indicating that something will be done and that pestering about it is unnecessary.*

All mouth (1) Talkative. (2) Promises or threatens a lot of things verbally, but never actually does anything.** or ***
Note: this phrase is usually far more insulting when a person is told directly that they are 'all mouth' than when referring to someone who is not present at the time.

All mouth and no trousers Means the same as *all mouth* (definition 2). The phrase is often used to describe a boastful man.* or **
Note: like *all mouth*, more insulting when told to a person directly than when talking about someone not present at the time.

All of a dither In a confused and excitable state.*

All of a doodah Means the same as *all of a dither.*

All of a piece with... Consistent with... *

All over bar the shouting Almost finished and with a very predictable outcome.*

All over the lot Means the same as *all over the place.*

All over the map Means the same as *all over the place.*

All over the place (1) In describing a physical matter, 'all over the place' means scattered all around, in a disorganized manner. (2) The phrase can also mean 'disorganized' or 'very bad, with little coordination'.*

All over the shop Means the same as *all over the place.*

All over the show Means the same as *all over the place.*

All packaging Something that is superficially appealing but is in reality of poor quality.*

All roads lead to Rome A proverb expressing the belief that seemingly different events may have the same conclusion.*

All round (1) Fully comprehensive (e.g. 'an all round good person'). (2) For everyone (e.g. 'drinks all round').*

All singing, all dancing Used jokingly to describe any piece of equipment or technology that is the latest model and has lots of extra features. The item in question does not necessarily have to sing and dance. The phrase is probably derived from the rather exaggerated prose used to advertize new plays and movies ('All singing! All dancing! Cast of thousands!' etc.).*

All talk Means the same as *all mouth*.* or **
Note: generally less offensive than *all mouth*; level of politeness depends on context.

All that glistens The start of a proverb that ends 'is not gold'. The phrase means that not everything that appears valuable is actually valuable.*

All that jazz And other similar things. The phrase is often used in a dismissive sense to mean that the similar things are nonsense or of minor importance.*

All the rage Very fashionable.*

All the right buttons Someone who presses or operates 'all the right buttons' is competent at what they are doing.*

All their geese are swans People who believe that 'all their geese are swans' have an unrealistically good opinion of people or things. The phrase can denote either boasting or lack of critical faculties.*

All there Mentally sane and unimpeded by any intellectual handicap. *Not all there* means the opposite (though it is usually used to imply intellectual handicap rather than illness).*

All things being equal If nothing alters. Used to describe a calculation in which it is assumed that certain factors will not change, thus simplifying the calculation.*

All things to all people See *be all things to all people.*

All thumbs Means the same as *all fingers and thumbs.*

All to the good Good. Often used in the form 'that's all to the good, but', meaning 'what has been stated is good, but there are problems that have not been mentioned'.*

All up with All finished with.*

Along about Approximately.*

Alpha and omega (1) The most important aspects of something. (2) The first and the last. The phrase comes from the first (alpha) and last (omega) letters in the Greek alphabet.*

Alright on the night As in 'it'll be alright on the night'. The belief in theatrical workers that a bad final rehearsal will be followed by a successful first proper performance in front of a paying public. Thus, the belief that mishaps in rehearsing or preparing for any big event will not be repeated when the event itself is held.*

Altogether See *in the altogether.*

Amateur night Something done ineptly.*

Ambulance chasing Making financial gain out of other people's misery. The phrase often specifically refers to lawyers making money from representing accident victims in litigation cases.*

And a happy birthday to you too A sarcastic response to someone who has just shown a display of bad temper.*

And a merry Christmas to you too If said sarcastically, the phrase can be used as a response to a person who has just shown a display of bad temper. The phrase is intended as sarcastic, since a response such as 'and a merry Christmas to you too' would be a normal response to a pleasant greeting at Christmas time.*

And co. And the rest. The phrase is usually used after the name of one person – the 'and co.' refers to the people usually associated with him or her (e.g. 'John and co. were there').*

And no mistake A phrase added on to the end of a statement intended to emphasize the statement (e.g. 'Hitler was a bad person and no mistake').*

Angels See *on the side of the angels.*

Angry young man Phrase first used in the 1950s to indicate a young, usually idealistic person who was dissatisfied with the existing social and political system. It does not mean that the person is necessarily angry with everything.*

Ankle biter A small child.*

Another bite at the cherry Means the same as *second bite at the cherry.*

Another thing coming See *got another thing coming.*

Ante See *up the ante.*

Ants in the pants To have 'ants in the pants' is to be restless and/or to fidget a lot.*

Any day When following a statement of preference (e.g. 'give me the old boss any day'), a statement indicating that the stated preference is very strongly believed.*

Any day now Within a few days.*

Any minute now Soon.*

Any port in a storm The belief that in a crisis any source of relief and/or assistance is to be welcomed.*

Any time now Soon.*

Anything goes No restraints or restrictions.*

Ape (1) Copy. (2) A state of irrational rage or insanity (e.g. 'when he sees what you've done to his car he'll go ape').*

Apeshit Means the same as *ape*, definition 2, but not as polite.***

Apology for... A poor example of something (e.g. 'the meal Peter prepared was an apology for home cooking').*

Appeal from Philip drunk to Philip sober A request that someone reconsiders an earlier decision. It is usually implied that the earlier decision was capricious.*

Appeal to Caesar Make an appeal to the most important person or highest available authority.*

Apple See entries below and: *bad apple* and *upset the applecart*.

Apple of their eye In other words, their favourite. It is usually used about people rather than objects. The term is derived from the fact that in the past 'apple' meant the pupil of the eye.*

Apple pie order Everything is correct and neat.*

Apples and oranges Means the same as *apples and pears*, definition 1.

Apples and pears (1) Describes an unfair comparison because what are being considered are too fundamentally different for the comparison to make sense. Thus, comparing apples and pears is a foolish thing – they taste different and which one tastes nicer is a matter of personal opinion, not objective fact. (2) The phrase is also used as Cockney rhyming slang for 'stairs' (e.g. 'up the apples and pears to bed').*

Apron strings See *cut the apron strings* and *tied to the apron strings*.

Are there any more at home like you? This is usually used as a chat-up line, and indicates that the person asking the question likes the person they are addressing. If the tone of voice is sarcastic, however, it can be a mild rebuke to someone who is being a nuisance, meaning in essence, 'please tell me there *aren't* any more like you'.*

Are you sitting comfortably? This is typically followed by the phrase 'then I'll begin'. The phrase is used jokingly to mean that someone is about to tell a (usually lengthy or complex) piece of information. The phrase comes from children's TV and radio programmes where someone about to tell a story often begins with this phrase.*

Argue the toss Argue about a decision that has already been made.*

Ark See *out of the ark* and *went out with the ark*.

Arm and a leg See *cost an arm and a leg*.

Arm's length The term is used to denote lack of friendliness rather than a literal physical distance. Thus, *keep at arm's length* means to avoid being too friendly or communicative with someone (e.g. 'Paul remained polite to David but kept him at arm's length, and never discussed personal matters with him').*

Armchair critic A person who lacks any practical or applied knowledge of a subject, but based on reading about it they feel empowered to offer criticisms. The implication is that such a person knows too little about the subject, and instead of criticising they should be quiet. A prime example of an armchair critic is a physically unfit person who feels they have the right to judge the performance of sportsmen and sportswomen.*

Armed to the teeth (1) To possess a large quantity of weapons. (2) To be very well-prepared for presenting an argument. (3) To have a large quantity of equipment.*

Armpits See *up to the armpits*.

Army See *you and whose army?*.

Army marches on its stomach Workers need to be properly fed if they are to function efficiently.*

Around the clock Means the same as *round the clock*.

Arrow in the quiver A skill a person possesses.*

Arse The word means 'bottom'. It is rarely used in American English. The word is considered moderately rude. Note that most phrases containing 'arse' can substitute *ass*.***

Arse about face Back to front.***

Arse from their elbow See *don't know their arse from their elbow*.

Arse over tit To fall over. The phrase literally means 'bottom over chest', but the phrase is used for anyone falling over rather than almost turning upside down whilst falling.***

Arselicking Means the same as *ass licking*.

Art for art's sake The belief that something can be done just because it is pleasing, rather than for any practical purpose.*

Art form See *developed into an art form*.

Article of faith Something that is strongly believed and forms an important part of a person's general attitudes and behaviour.*

As easy as ABC Very easy.*

As easy as pie Means the same as *as easy as ABC*.

As every schoolchild knows Used to describe a piece of very basic information.*

As far as it goes To its limits.*

As good as (1) Of equivalent quality. (2) Almost (e.g. 'as good as done' means 'it has almost been completed').*

As much use as a chocolate fire screen Of no use.*

As much use as a chocolate teapot Of no use.*

As near as damn it Slightly ruder version of *as near as makes no difference*.**

As near as makes no difference Although not exactly the same, it is close enough for all practical purposes.*

As nice as pie Very pleasant.*

As sure as eggs is eggs In other words, with absolute certainty.*

As the crow flies In a straight line.*

As you do A sarcastic comment on an extravagant claim or description (e.g. 'we just had to have a three week holiday in Tibet this year' leading to a reply of 'as you do').* or **
Note: the phrase can be used as an insult as well as a humorous comment. As an insult, it is implying that someone is being pretentious or showing off.

Ask for it (1) To be deserving of punishment. Thus someone who gets bitten by a dog after taunting the poor creature for an hour or so might be said to have been asking for it. (2) There is an offensive sexist use of the term that 'justifies' rape by saying that a woman 'provocatively dressed' is making a sexual display and 'must' be 'asking for it' (i.e. wanting sex).* (1) or *** (2)

Ask for the moon Ask for something that is impossible to attain.*

Ask me another A joking reply to a question, that means 'I don't know'.*

Asking for trouble Behaving in a manner that greatly increases the probability of a problem or an argument being created.*

Asleep at the switch Means the same as *asleep at the wheel*.

Asleep at the wheel Inattentive to the job that is supposed to be done.*

Ass See *ass licking, bet your…, bust their ass, chew their ass, don't give a rat's ass, drag ass, get their…into gear, haul ass, kick ass, kick their ass, kiss ass, licking ass, pain in the ass, piece of ass, put their ass in a sling, tear ass* and *whip their ass*. Note that most phrases containing *arse* can subsitute 'ass' for 'arse'.

Ass licking Being obsequious to the point of stupidity – e.g. being helpful beyond any reasonable expectation, being far too polite and conciliatory and/or agreeing with everything a person more powerful in status says and does, regardless of whether it is correct. The phrase is most often used of someone behaving like this in the hope of gaining promotion at work.***

Ass on the line Ruder version of *head on the line*.***

At a canter Easily done.*

At a lick Rapidly.*

At a loose end Have nothing to do.*

At a low ebb In a poor condition. The phrase is used quite commonly to mean 'depressed'.*

At a pinch Describes something that will just about suffice for the task, but is not an ideal choice. See *in a pinch*.*

At a push Means the same as *at a pinch*.

At a rate of knots Moving rapidly.*

At a stretch (1) Something that can be done 'at a stretch' can be done, but not without greater effort than usual. (2) In a single period of time.*

At death's door Seriously ill, with a high probability of dying.*

At each other's throats Constantly attacking or criticising each other.*

At full cock With all strength and/or ability.*

At half cock Inadequately prepared or inept.*

At hand What has to be done now (e.g. 'the task at hand').*

At heel Under close supervision or control.*

At loose ends Means the same as *at a loose end*.

At sea To be confused and/or incapable of coping with a situation.*

At sixes and sevens To be in a state of confusion.*

At the…face A description of being at work within a particular profession (e.g. 'at the coalface' means working as a miner, 'at the chalkface' working as a teacher, etc.) *

At the bottom of it To be the original or most important cause (e.g. 'although several people were behind the rebellion, Jack was at the bottom of it').*

At the crossroads At a point of deciding between several options. The phrase generally implies that these choices are important ones.*

At the double Quickly.*

At the drop of a hat Describes a willingness to do something with very little encouragement.*

At the end of the day (1) Literally 'at the end of the day' or 'at the end of a work shift'. (2) What needs to be done after all things have been considered (e.g. 'at the end of the day the decision is yours').*

At the last minute With very little time to spare.*

At the touch of a button A phrase used to emphasize that an automated process or machine is very easy to use (e.g. 'you can have hot water at the touch of a button').*

At their beam-ends To be desperate; the phrase nearly always means that the cause of the desperation is a shortage of resources.*

At their fingertips Easily accessed.*

At their wits' end To have tried to deal with a problem logically and calmly but failed.*

Atmosphere that could be cut with a knife Describes the feeling of being in a tense or dangerous situation.*

Auld lang syne See *for auld lang syne*.

Avenue See *every avenue explored*.

Away with the fairies Daydreaming or absent-minded.*

Awkward age Adolescence; so called because it as an age at which many people behave awkwardly, question the relevance of society, etc., but also are awkward in performing adult tasks, such as courtship, assuming more responsibility and so forth.*

Awkward squad (1) A group of people who require further training before they will be competent to perform the tasks they have been assigned to do. (2) People who are predisposed to be uncooperative.*

Axe See *axe to grind* and *given the axe.*

Axe to grind This generally means one of two things: (1) being obsessed with a particular cause or argument; or (2) having a secret reason for wanting something as well as the reason given publicly.*

Ayes have it Meaning that the people who support a proposed change are in the majority, and thus the change will be made. The phrase comes from a method of voting (used in, e.g., the UK Parliament) in which people for a motion are called 'ayes' and those against are called 'noes'. Hence, the *noes have it* means that the majority are against change, and so things will stay as they are.*

B

Babes in the wood People who are innocent of what is going on around them. The phrase is often used of people who become involved in something they lack the experience to handle.*

Baby boomer Person born just after World War II. So called because there was a dramatic increase in the birth rate (a 'baby boom') in the late 1940s.*

Baby out with the bath water See *throw the baby out with the bath water.*

Back burner See *put on the back burner.*

Back door An unofficial method. Also see *in by the back door.**

Back down Allow something to happen or acknowledge an argument that had previously been opposed.*

Back in the swing of things Returned to normality after a period of absence or illness.*

Back into it See *put their back into it.*

Back is turned See *when a person's back is turned.*

Back number (1) An issue of a magazine or newspaper that was issued before the current issue. (2) A person whose skills and/or knowledge are not up to date.*

Back of a cigarette packet Follows the same meaning as *back of an envelope.*

Back of a fag packet Follows the same meaning as *back of an envelope.* 'Fag packet' means cigarette packet in UK English.*

Back of a lorry See *off the back of a lorry.*

Back of an envelope See *on the back of an envelope.*

Back of beyond Somewhere geographically distant; there is usually an implication that the place is also culturally unsophisticated.*

Back of Bourke Australian slang: means the same as *back of beyond.**

Back of the mind Something that is being thought about, but is not currently being concentrated upon.*

Back of their brain If a person says they have something 'at the back of their brain' then it means they feel they have a faint memory of something that they cannot quite recall.*

Back of their hand See *like the back of their hand.*

Back of their head Means the same as *back of their brain.*

Back off (1) A warning to stop interfering and/or to physically move further away. (2) Retreat.* (2) or ** (1)
Note: this is a phrase that if used in the sense of definition 1 usually does indicate that a person means it, no matter what their normal language is like.

Back out Withdraw from involvement in something.*

Back seat See entry below and: *take a back seat.*

Back seat driver A person not in a position of power who attempts to control the actions of a person in a position of power by telling them what to do. The phrase refers to a passenger telling the driver how he or she should be driving.*

Back story What has previously taken place. The phrase is often used for movie sequels, where knowledge of the 'back story' (i.e. what happened in the earlier movies) is necessary in order to understand fully the plot of the current movie.*

Back the wrong horse Make an inappropriate choice. The phrase often refers to choosing to support the person who turns out to be the loser in a struggle for power. *

Back to basics To reject complicated methods or details and return to a simpler method.*

Back to square one To go right back to the start. The origin of the phrase may refer to games such as snakes and ladders, where an unfortunate throw of the dice late in the game might result in landing on a snake and thus sending the player back to the start (i.e. 'square one'). Another explanation is that it refers to a system of describing the layout of a football field, and a ball sent back to square one was in essence the start of a new series of plays.*

Back to the drawing board To go right back to the start. The phrase derives from engineering designs that are so utterly wrong when put into practice that they have to be redesigned from the beginning (i.e. the point at which the first plans are produced on a drawing board). See *on the drawing board.**

Back to the jungle To return to a more primitive way of living. Based on the argument that our ancestors originally lived in jungles.*

Back to the wall To be in a difficult situation with little obvious chance of help.*

Back up Support. Also see *get their back up.*

Backbone See *put backbone into them.*

Backroom deal Secret negotiations.*

Backs to the wall In a difficult situation.*

Bacon See *bring home the bacon* and *save the bacon.*

Bad apple An unpleasant or immoral person. The term can be used to indicate that such people are inevitable (e.g. 'there's a bad apple in every bunch'). It can also imply that such a person is likely to corrupt those around them (in the same way that a bad apple stored with good apples will pass a rotting fungus to them and eventually destroy all the stored fruit).*

Bad blood Describes a state of hostility between two people or groups (e.g. 'there had been bad blood between the neighbours since the argument over the new fence').*

Bad business See *business.*

Bad form Something that is a breach of etiquette.*

Bad hair day A day when everything seems to be going wrong.*

Bad-mouthing Saying unpleasant things about something or someone.*

Bad news A person is said to be 'bad news' if they are likely to cause trouble or be a hindrance.*

Bad place See *in a bad place.*

Bad quarter of an hour A particularly unpleasant short period of time.*

Bad taste in the mouth An unpleasant feeling about an event or experience.*

Bag See *bag of tricks, in the bag, mixed bag, not my bag* and *pack their bags.*

Bag of tricks The term can either refer to a specialist collection of equipment (e.g. 'the technician came along with her bag

denotes level of impoliteness

of tricks and soon mended the computer') or the specialist skills of a person.*

Bail out (1) Abandon a failing enterprize (an analogy to bailing out of an aircraft about to crash). (2) Rescue someone and/or pay off their debts (an analogy to bailing a person out of jail).*

Bail up To physically corner someone.*

Baker's dozen Thirteen.*

Balanced personality Describes a person with no unusual behaviours. The phrase comes from the idea that some part of personality can be imagined to be like weights put on a balance. If one part of a personality is over-imposing, then it would be like a too-heavy weight that would not balance with the other weights available. See *unbalanced personality*.*

Balancing act (1) The process of trying to do several tasks within the same space of time (e.g. 'Jenny had a busy day – she had to do a tricky balancing act of taking the children to and from school, visiting the dentist's, dealing with her correspondence, and checking in with her office'). (2) Attempting to please several people, often with conflicting demands.*

Ball See entries below and: *behind the eight ball, crystal ball, crystal ball gazing, drop the ball, have a ball, have a lot on the ball, how long is a ball of string?, keep balls in the air, keep the ball rolling, keep their eye on the ball, new ball game, on the ball, play ball, set the ball rolling, pick up the ball and run with it, take the ball and run with it* and *whole ball of wax.*

Ball and chain A hindrance; something that restricts movements or activities. The phrase is sometimes used jokingly to refer to a husband or wife.*

Ball at their feet A person with the 'ball at their feet' has the best chance they will get of achieving what they want to do.*

Ball-breaker A person who takes perverse pleasure in giving work to someone else that is *ball-breaking*. To be called a

'ball-breaker' is insulting and usually implies the person is very angry with you, but in describing someone else the term (although very rude) may just indicate that they demand high standards.***

Ball-breaking Something is said to be ball-breaking if it is very troublesome, difficult and/or time-consuming. See *ball-breaker*.***

Ball is in their court In other words, the responsibility for doing something rests with them. The phrase comes from tennis – the ball cannot be played by someone until it is in their part of the court.*

Ball of fire A lively person. The phrase is often used sarcastically to mean someone who is dull (e.g. 'boy, he's a ball of fire' said in a sarcastic tone means that the person is boring).*

Ball of string See *how long is a ball of string?*

Ballistic See *go ballistic.*

Balloon's gone up Something important has started. The phrase probably derives from the twentieth-century use of barrage balloons (large balloons tethered to wires) that were raised as a primitive (but effective) defence against an incoming air attack.*

Ballpark See *ballpark figure, in the ballpark* and *in the same ballpark.*

Ballpark figure An estimate.*

Balls (1) Testicles. (2) An expression of disgust or denial (e.g. 'that's balls!' or 'that's a *load of balls!*'). (3) A synonym for courage (e.g. 'you've got a lot of balls to do something that brave').***

Balls-up A serious mistake.***

Banana oil Nonsense.*

Banana republic (1) A country of minor economic importance (almost always in Central America) whose economic fortunes depend on exporting a foodstuff (such as bananas). The term almost always has an additional supposition that the country has a corrupt government, police force, judiciary, etc., and is technologically backward. (2) The phrase is sometimes used to indicate a badly run company or office that is rife with corruption and inefficiency. Both definitions are insults.*

Note: For obvious reasons of politeness, the phrase 'banana republic' should not be used when speaking or writing to a person from a banana republic (either definition).

Banana skin See *slip on a banana skin*.

Band See *when the band begins to play*.

Bandwagon See *jump on the bandwagon*.

Bang for the buck Value for money.*

Bang goes... The term means 'this is the ruination of...' (e.g. 'When we heard about the opening of the toxic waste recycling plant next to our home, all I could think was "bang goes the neighbourhood"').*

Bang heads together Tell a group of people off. The phrase is usually used to describe telling off a group of people who have been arguing and squabbling between themselves.*

Bang on Absolutely correct.*

Bang their head against a brick wall Engage in a very frustrating task.*

Bang to rights An admission that an accusation is correct (as in 'you've got me bang to rights'). The phrase derives from a slang expression by criminals caught committing a crime. These days it is generally used more lightly to indicate that a person is admitting to making a mild error.*

Bank See entry below and: *break the bank, cry all the way to the bank* and *laugh all the way to the bank*.

Bank on it If a person feels that they can 'bank on it' then they feel certain that it will happen.*

Baptism of fire A first experience of something that is far more difficult or demanding than might be normally expected.*

Bar none With no alternatives or exceptions (e.g. 'she is the best bar none').*

Bare bones The simplest possible form of something which works or makes sense; in other words, something with no extraneous details.*

Bargepole See *wouldn't touch them with a bargepole*.

Bark at the moon Waste time on a protest that has no effect. Named after the phenomenon that dogs will sometimes bark at the moon in the night sky.*

Bark is worse than their bite The actual punishments a person makes are far less severe than their threats of punishment would have one expect. The phrase *bite is worse than their bark* means the opposite (i.e. their punishments are worse than their threats would suggest).*

Barking up the wrong tree To have arrived at an inaccurate conclusion. The phrase is derived from hunting – a dog following a scent trail that barked when it had 'found' its target hiding in one tree when it was in fact in another would of course be barking up the wrong tree.*

Barnstorming performance A display of great skill. The term is sometimes used more negatively to describe something not very subtle.*

Barrack room lawyer A non-lawyer who claims to know everything about a person's legal rights and entitlements and by extension what is and is not permissible. It is often implied that the person who is a troublemaker is anxious to provoke conflict over (often spurious) demands for 'legitimate rights'.*

Barrel See *barrel of laughs, give both barrels, on the barrel* and *over a barrel*.

Barrel of laughs Something very amusing. The phrase is more often used sarcastically (e.g. 'that funeral was a barrel of laughs').*

Base See *first base, off base, touch all the bases* and *touch base*.

---

* *denotes level of impoliteness*

Bash See *have a bash.*

Basket case In a poor state of health (typically the term describes mental ill health).**

Bat See *bat out of hell, go in to bat for them, not bat an eyelid, off their own bat, play with a straight bat* and *right off the bat.*

Bat out of hell Describes something moving very quickly (e.g. 'it set off like a bat out of hell and was soon out of sight').*

Baton See *pass the baton* and *pick up the baton.*

Bats in the belfry To be insane.*

Batten down the hatches Prepare for a difficult situation. The phrase refers to sealing hatches on a ship in preparation for stormy weather.*

Battle lines are drawn The principal causes of a conflict are established – i.e. all the sides in a conflict know what they will consider a successful conclusion.*

Battle of the bulge The psychological and physical effort involved in dieting and exercise in an attempt to lose weight. The phrase is a punning reference to the Battle of the Bulge, a key battle of World War II.*

Battle of the giants A contest between two people or groups who are notably skilful.*

Battle royal A vigorous (and often by implication vicious) contest. The term probably derives from a particularly barbaric version of cock fighting.*

Battle stations A warning to prepare for imminent combat. The phrase is often used jokingly when faced with a difficult situation (e.g. 'battle stations, everyone – the boss is on her way and she's in a bad mood').**

Bay See *bay for the moon, baying for blood* and *keep it at bay.*

Bay for the moon Means the same as *bark at the moon.*

Baying for blood Demanding punishment or revenge.*

Be a devil An encouragement to do something not quite correct, but which will be enjoyable or rewarding (e.g. encouraging someone on a diet to have a cream cake, saying 'be a devil – one cake won't harm your diet').*

Be all things to all people Be liked by everyone. The phrase often implies that the reasons why some people express a liking may be different from the reasons why other people express a liking.*

Be-all and end-all The most perfect form something can take. Hence, if something is *not the be-all and end-all* then it is not the only thing that might be of use.*

Be crook on Be angered by.*

Be expecting Be pregnant.*

Be in at the death Witness the end of an event (not necessarily a death).*

Be in good company Hold the same opinion as other, more exalted people (this does not guarantee that the opinion is correct, however).*

Be it on their head It is their responsibility.*

Be laughing Be in a state of contentment (e.g. 'you'll be laughing once the contract's accepted').*

Be my guest A phrase indicating permission to do something or to carry on doing something. The phrase is usually used as a reply to a question such as 'do you mind if I do this?'*

Be real Means the same as *get real.*

Be the death of … The cause of someone's ruination or death. The phrase is nearly always used in an exaggerated fashion to indicate that someone is being amusing.*

Be there for them Offer support and assistance for someone.*

Be there or be square A now rather dated phrase meaning 'unless you attend this event, you are very unfashionable'.*

Bead See *take a bead on.*

Beam-ends See *at their beam-ends.*

Bean See *bean counting, full of beans, how many beans make five?, not have a bean, not worth a hill of beans* and *spill the beans.*

Bean counting Derogatory term for: (1) being concerned with the facts and figures of something rather than its emotional consequences; (2) putting considerations of profit and business before moral or spiritual considerations; (3) occupations that involve working with numbers, such as statistics or accountancy.*

Bear See *bear with a sore head, do bears crap in the woods?* and *loaded for bear.*

Bear fruit Be successful.*

Bear the brunt Endure the majority of something unpleasant, such as a punishment.*

Bear with a sore head A person with a bad temper.*

Beat See entries below and: *chest beating, if you can't beat them join them, miss a beat, not miss a beat* and *off the beaten track.*

Beat a path Make a journey with great determination to reach the destination.*

Beat a path to their door Show great interest in a person. The phrase is usually used in the context of a group of people beating a path to someone's door after the person has done something that makes him or her famous.*

Beat a retreat Retreat or withdraw. The phrase comes from the army, when at one time the signal for troops to withdraw from the battlefield would be made by a drum beat.*

Beat about the bush Means the same as going *round the houses.*

Beat around the bush Means the same as going *round the houses.*

Beat at their own game Defeat a person at something they are skilled at doing.*

Beat swords into ploughshares Move from being aggressive to being peaceful.*

Beat the band Be better than everyone else.*

Beat the bejesus out Means the same as *beat the daylights out.*

Beat the bushes Try hard to achieve something.*

Beat the clock Work quickly.*

Beat the daylights out Physically assault with great severity.**

Beat the drum Actively and prominently support a cause or person.*

Beat the living daylights out Means the same as *beat the daylights out.*

Beat the meat Masturbate.***

Beat the pants off Prove to be far better than another person (e.g. 'Peter beat the pants off Richard').*

Beat the rap Evade punishment.*

Beat the system (1) Find a method of doing something that is supposedly forbidden by a set of rules and/or regulations. The phrase is more often heard in the form *you can't beat the system,* that argues that some regulations and institutions (particularly the legal system) cannot be defeated. (2) Find a method of defeating something elaborately structured and seemingly impossible to defeat.*

Beat them hollow Defeat decisively.*

Beat them to it Succeed in doing something before another person.*

Beat to a pulp Inflict severe damage.*

Beat to the punch Anticipate someone's choice of action.*

Beat to the world Means the same as *dead to the world.*

Beaten at the post Be defeated at the last moment.*

Beating the chest See *chest beating.*

Beautiful people People noted for their good looks, wealth, and belonging to a fashionable part of society. The term is often used sarcastically either about people who obviously *aren't* beautiful, fashionable or rich, or otherwise may be used as a negative comment about people who are beautiful, rich and fashionable, but are otherwise unappealing.*

Because it is there A reply given when questioned about the motivation to do something which is impractical and/or dangerous. The speaker is basically indicating that they want to do it simply because it is a challenge. The phrase was first used by a mountaineer called George Mallory, who was asked why he wanted to climb Mount Everest. It is perhaps worth noting that Mallory was killed trying to climb Mount Everest.*

Bed See *bed of nails, bed of roses, curious bed-fellows, get into bed with them, get out of bed on the wrong side, in bed with, put it to bed* and *they've made their bed they'd better lie in it.*

Bed of nails A disagreeable situation.*

Bed of roses An agreeable situation with no problems.*

Bedclothes See *born the wrong side of the bed-clothes.*

Bedside manner A medical doctor's or surgeon's skills at talking and listening to patients. The phrase usually is used in a more specific sense of how pleasant the patient finds the experience (e.g. a doctor good at diagnosing problems but who is rude to patients might be said to be 'a good clinician with a bad bedside manner'). The phrase is sometimes used to describe the communication skills of non-medical people.*

Bee in their bonnet Having a preoccupation about something (generally, something that is annoying rather than pleasant) – e.g. 'Sally has a bee in her bonnet about getting rid of the greenfly in the garden'.*

Bee's knees Joking term meaning 'the best'.*

Beef about Complain about.*

Beeline See *make a beeline.*

Been around If a person has 'been around' then they are experienced.*

Been in the wars Appearing damaged.*

Been there before Already have experience of an identical or very similar item or event.*

Been there, done that A jaded or contemptuous dismissal of a proposal to do something, because the person has already done it.*

Beer and skittles See *not all beer and skittles.*

Beer talking Means the same as *alcohol talking.*

Before the Flood A very long time ago.*

Before their time (1) Describing something that happened before a person was alive or before they were in a particular job (e.g. 'Smith worked here before my time'). (2) Describing someone who has ideas too advanced or modern for them to be accepted by their contemporaries (e.g. 'her ideas were before her time and it was another 50 years before their worth was appreciated').*

Before they could say... Followed by a word or phrase (a common one is 'Jack Robinson', but there are many others). Indicates that something happened very quickly.* or ** or ***
Note: politeness rating depends on the words used to finish the phrase. Most versions are innocuous.

Beg the question Make an argument without providing proof. Thus, a statement which 'begs the question' raises a logical point which needs an answer for the statement to make complete sense (e.g. the phrase 'I hate liver and onions and I ate a whole plate of it' begs the question 'why eat so much of something you hate?').*

Beggar belief Be so incredible (in the strict sense of the word, meaning 'beyond credence') that it is extremely difficult to believe it.*

Beggar on horseback A person who has acquired riches or power and has also become unpleasant.*

Begging See *going begging.*

Beginning of the end The start of a process that leads to the end of something. The phrase is nearly always used to describe something seen as the harbinger of something unpleasant.*

Behind closed doors In secret.*

Behind the eight ball To be in a difficult position. The term comes from the game of pool and refers to being in a position where it is very difficult to play a shot.*

Behind the scenes Secretly, or without widespread knowledge.*

Behind the times Lacking up-to-date information.*

Behind their back If something is done behind a person's back, it is done without them being aware of it. Usually it is implied that this is done in order to harm the person.*

Believe it or not The phrase indicates that what follows, although sounding incredible, is in fact true (e.g. 'believe it or not, people have gone to the Moon').*

Believe you me A statement stressing the truthfulness of what is being said (e.g. 'believe you me, this is an important issue').*

Bell See *bell the cat, bells and whistles, ring a bell, ring their bell, saved by the bell* and *set alarm bells ringing.*

Bell the cat Undertake a dangerous job on behalf of a group.*

Belle of the ball The most beautiful person at a social gathering.*

Bells and whistles Describes extra facilities that are provided with a piece of equipment or similar that generally are entertaining but provide no particularly useful practical purpose.*

Belly-up See *go belly-up.*

Bellyful See *have a bellyful.*

Below par Means the same as *under par.*

Below stairs (1) The area below street level in houses so equipped. (2) The servants in a (rich) household. This use of the phrase comes from the fact that the servants typically did a lot of their work (e.g. cooking) in the below stairs area. (3) The members of staff considered least important by the management of a company (in joking reference to definition 2).*

Below the belt Describes behaviour that is unfair, often with an implied sadistic intention (e.g. 'asking her about her recently deceased mother at the interview was below the belt'). The phrase comes from boxing – punches below the belt (i.e. that could hurt the genitals) are not allowed. Contrast with *under the belt.*

Below the salt Inferior social status.*

Belt and braces Having extra safety measures in place in case the primary set of safety measures fail. In other words, like wearing both a belt and braces (suspenders in US English) to prevent trousers falling down.*

Bend over backwards To do everything possible. The phrase is usually used to emphasize how hard the work has been (e.g. 'I've bent over backwards doing this project').*

Bend the elbow Drink alcoholic beverages.*

Bend their ear Talk to someone. The phrase usually indicates that this talk goes on too long and is far from relaxing.*

Bend their ear back Means the same as *bend their ear.*

Bend with the wind (1) Alter opinions to suit the prevailing mood. (2) Alter to adjust to changing conditions.*

Beneath them Describes something that is socially, intellectually and/or morally of such inferior status that it cannot be

---

* *denotes level of impoliteness*

imagined that the person being discussed would do it.*

Benefit of the doubt See *give them the benefit of the doubt.*

Benjamin's mess Means the same as *Benjamin's portion.*

Benjamin's portion The largest share. The phrase is from the Old Testament, in which Benjamin (Joseph's brother) receives a substantially larger proportion of food servings than his brothers.*

Bent out of shape Irritated and bad-tempered.*

Berth See *give them a wide berth.*

Beside themselves with anger To be very angry.*

Best bet The wisest option to choose (e.g. 'your best bet is to buy it now, because once the sale is over it will cost a lot more'.)*

Best bib and tucker The most formal, smartest clothes. The phrase does not imply baby clothes or overalls, but instead refers to items of clothing that were once part of formal women's wear.*

Best foot forward Make the best possible attempt at something. The phrase is probably an amendment of an earlier phrase 'best foot foremost', which would be appropriate advice in adopting, e.g., a fighting pose in facing an opponent in combat.*

Best of a bad lot Someone or something that is not very good, but was better than what else was available.*

Best of both worlds If something is the 'best of both worlds' then it combines the benefits of more than one thing.*

Best of British Short for 'the best of British luck', which means simply 'good luck'.*

Best will in the world See *with the best will in the world.*

Bet See *all bets are off, bet your…, best bet, don't bet on it, good bet, hedge their bets, I bet* and *safe bet.*

Bet your… Followed by the name of something precious to the person. This varies in politeness: e.g. 'you bet your life', 'you bet your bottom dollar' or 'you bet your last cent' (the latter two mean 'bet everything you have') are harmless. On the other hand, 'you bet your ass' is slightly ruder (the phrase refers to a part of the anatomy, not a donkey). The term means 'it's absolutely certain', the implication being that a person could wager something very precious to themselves on the outcome because it is an absolute certainty.* or ** or ***
Note: politeness rating depends on the word or words used to finish the phrase.

Better dead than red The slogan of right-wing members of NATO during the Cold War that it would be better to perish in a nuclear war than live under communist rule imposed by a victorious Warsaw Pact. This led to the riposte from anti-nuclear war campaigners that is was *better red than dead*, meaning that it was better to live, albeit under an unpleasant regime, than suffer a nuclear war. The phrases are sometimes more generally applied to situations where resistance to something unwelcome has considerable costs.*

Better half Joking term for partner (particularly husband or wife). The phrase was created by Sir Phillip Sydney, who meant it rather more seriously.*

Better late than never Phrase expressing the argument that it is better that something is done than it is not done at all (regardless of whether it is done punctually).*

Better nature A person's more gentle, accepting personality attributes.*

Better red than dead See *better dead than red.*

Better safe than sorry Phrase expressing the argument that it is better to be cautious and avoid injury than to be hasty and get hurt. The phrase is often used as a justification for doing something slowly but carefully, even if it puts things behind schedule.*

Better than a poke in the eye with a sharp stick Means that something, although not the best possible, is better than other far worse alternatives.*

Better the devil known Meaning that it is preferable to deal with an unpleasant person whose personality and tactics are known rather than someone unknown, who may be nicer, but who could also be far nastier. There are several permutations of this phrase.*

Betting is that It is anticipated that.*

Between a rock and a hard place Means the same as *between the Devil and the deep blue sea.*

Between the Devil and the deep blue sea Faced with choosing between two alternatives, both equally unattractive and dangerous.*

Between the eyes See *right between the eyes.*

Between the lines The true meaning of something as opposed to its superficial appearance.*

Between you, me and the bedpost Means the same as *between you, me and the gatepost.*

Between you, me and the gatepost A phrase indicating that what follows is confidential and should be told to nobody else.*

Between you, me and the wall Means the same as *between you, me and the gatepost.*

Betwixt and between Of uncertain identity.*

Beware of Greeks bearing gifts (1) A warning to be wary of a gift or other friendly act that is given for no logical reason. (2) A warning to be wary of enemies who suddenly begin acting in a conciliatory fashion. The phrase is derived from the story of the Trojan Horse, which was a gift from the Greeks to the Trojans, and which resulted in the fall of Troy.*

Beyond me See *it's beyond me.*

Beyond the black stump Lacking the amenities that are considered normal in an industrialized society.*

Beyond the grave If someone 'reaches from beyond the grave' it means that even after they have died, the effects of what they did whilst alive are still being experienced.*

Beyond the pale Denotes behaviour that is unacceptable by normal standards. The phrase derives from pales, which were English settlements in occupied countries. Within the pales English law was obeyed, but outside it was not. Hence, beyond the pale lay activities not controlled by English law and custom, which (in English eyes, if nobody else's) 'must' be uncivilized.*

Beyond their wildest dreams Something that exceeds all expectations.*

Bib See *best bib and tucker.*

Big... A person described as 'the big...' followed by a single word (e.g. 'fish', 'wheel', 'gun', 'noise') is likely to be the most important person in a particular group or organisation. However, context is vital in making this judgement. See *big cheese.*

Big ask A request that is difficult or will require more work or effort than usual to fulfil.*

Big bickies Australian colloquialism meaning 'lots of money'.*

Big boy (1) A man experienced enough to be able to cope (e.g. 'Brian is a big boy now, he can handle this problem by himself'). (2) A large muscular or fat man. There is often an innuendo that the man has a large penis.* (1) or ** (2)

Big Brother is watching you In other words, somebody is checking up on what you are doing. The phrase nearly always refers to the government or another

---

* *denotes level of impoliteness*

important organisation such as the police force or tax inspectors. It is derived from *1984*, a novel by George Orwell, in which everyone led a miserable life and where every activity was controlled by a government headed by a mysterious but ever-present man called 'Big Brother'.*

Big butter and egg man An insulting term describing a person who has become a success in a small town or country region who then moves to a big city to try to appear to be a big success there. There is usually an implication that such a person gets things hopelessly wrong, does not know the right social moves, etc.*

Big cheese The most important person in a group or organisation. The phrase is a corruption of an Urdu phrase meaning 'important thing'.*

Big Daddy The leader of a group.*

Big deal (1) An important event or thing. The phrase is often used in the question *what's the big deal?* (meaning, 'what is so important?'), asked when someone is making a fuss over something the speaker thinks is unimportant. (2) The phrase can be used in the negative (*no big deal*) to indicate that something is not important. (3) Used sarcastically, the phrase can mean 'who cares?' (e.g. 'big deal! – nobody's interested').*

Big E See *give the big E*.

Big enchilada Means the same as *big cheese*.

Big fish in a small pond A person or group who dominate a small set of people or groups. The implication is that if there were more people or groups, there would be a good chance that there would be other people/groups who would be more powerful.*

Big girl (1) A woman experienced enough to be able to cope (e.g. 'Berenice is a big girl now, she can handle this problem by herself'). (2) A woman with a curvaceous, muscular or fat figure. There is often an innuendo that the woman has large breasts.* (1) or ** (2)

Big girl's blouse The phrase is used to describe a male who is seen as cowardly.**

Big tick and a gold star A joking way of offering praise.*

Big white chief See *great white chief*.

Bill and coo Show affection. The phrase is often used of couples in the early stage of a relationship. The phrase is derived from the courtship behaviour of pigeons and doves.*

Bind hand and foot Limit activities and/or freedom of movement.*

Bird See *bird has flown, bird in the hand, bird of passage, bird's-eye view, birds and the bees, birds of a feather, do bird, early bird, eat like a bird, flip the bird, for the birds, get the bird, give them the bird, have a bird, kill two birds with one stone, little bird told them* and *rare bird*.

Bird has flown The statement 'the bird has flown' means that someone has disappeared or escaped.*

Bird in the hand The start of a saying – 'a bird in the hand is worth two in the bush' (i.e. a bird already captured is worth two birds a person has yet to capture; if the only place a captured bird can be kept is in the hand, chasing after more birds means having to put down the bird already caught, which would then escape). The saying implies that it is better to be content with what one has already got, since going after something better may mean losing what is already owned and without the guarantee of getting something else. Thus, a 'bird in the hand' is something that may not be the best available, but at least there is the certainty of owning something.*

Bird of passage A person who rarely stays in one place or job for very long.*

Bird's-eye view (1) The view from above (i.e. as a bird flying overhead would see it). (2) The phrase is sometimes used to mean an overview or summary, typically from someone who can offer an impartial judgement.*

Birds and the bees A euphemism for 'sexual intercourse'. Most often used when describing teaching a child the basic information about sex (e.g. 'John's mother told him about the birds and the bees').*

Birds of a feather People with similar interests or opinions. Shortened form of the saying 'birds of a feather stick together' (meaning: people of similar interests or opinions tend to be friendly with each other).*

Birthday suit Nakedness.*

Biscuit See *take the biscuit.*

Bit See entries below and: *champ at the bit, do their bit* and *get the bit between the teeth.*

Bit of a do A party (e.g. 'we're having a bit of a do on Saturday night – would you like to come?').*

Bit of a to-do An argument (e.g. 'Brian and Cathy's disagreement over the wedding plans led to a bit of a to-do between their respective families').*

Bit of all right Something or someone agreeable. A person considered 'a bit of all right' is usually being referred to as sexually desirable rather than for any other aspect of themselves.**

Bit of crackling An attractive woman. The term is dated and offensive.***

Bit of fluff A derogatory term for a woman, typically a girlfriend seen as being attractive but unintelligent. Although once considered acceptable, the term is now thought to be offensive and should be avoided.***

Bit of rough A person of coarse or unsophisticated manners and appearance. The phrase is nearly always used as a description of a sexual partner who is appealing to people with certain tastes because their coarseness and lack of sophistication are found sexually exciting. See *rough trade.****

Bit of skirt Means the same as *bit of fluff.*

Bit of stuff Means the same as *bit of fluff.*

Bit on the side (1) Secretly having sexual relations with someone other than an official partner. (2) A person who engages in this activity (e.g. 'he was her bit on the side'). (3) Money earned in addition to a salaried job (usually with the implication that this is illicit payment not being declared to the tax authorities).**

Bit rich A comment that someone is being hypocritical (e.g. 'it's a bit rich him complaining like that about Sue when his behaviour was just as bad').*

Bit thick (1) Slightly stupid. (2) Unfair. (3) Exaggerated or inaccurate.* (2 and 3) or ** (1)

Bitch goddess A person who 'worships the bitch goddess' is obsessed with making money and gaining status above considerations of friendship, compassion, etc.**

Bite at the cherry An opportunity to do something. See *second bite at the cherry.**

Bite is worse than their bark See *bark is worse than their bite.*

Bite me A general-purpose retort expressing displeasure with someone.*

Bite off more than they can chew To be over-ambitious and attempt something that is too difficult.*

Bite the big one Die.*

Bite the bullet Accept a punishment or difficult situation without complaining. The phrase comes from the fact that in the days before anaesthesia, soldiers being operated on on the battlefield were given a bullet to bite on, rather than cry out.*

Bite the dust Die, or be defeated. In spite of being a staple phrase of Westerns, the phrase is probably English in origin.*

Bite the hand that feeds Show ingratitude by offending or hurting a person who has shown kindness and/or offered monetary or other support.*

Bite their hand off Eagerly accept an offer.*

Bite their head off Respond in an unpleasant or aggressive manner. The phrase often implies an irrationally severe response.*

Bite their lip Suppress the urge to say something in the interests of keeping a secret or avoiding starting an argument. Refers to the action of pressing the teeth into the lower lip (without drawing blood) as a facial gesture indicating that a person could say something on the subject but is not going to.*

Bite their tongue Means the same as *bite their lip*.

Biter bit Describes a person coming to harm by the methods that he or she usually uses to do harm to others.*

Bits and bobs A collection of unimportant things.*

Bits and pieces Means the same as *bits and bobs*.

Bitten by the bug Gain a strong enthusiasm for something (e.g. 'she was bitten by the stamp collecting bug at an early age').*

Bitter end The very final section of something. If a person did something 'to the bitter end' it generally is implied that he or she did all that it was possible to do.*

Bitter pill Something that is accepted with difficulty. The phrase is nearly always used in the larger phrase 'a bitter pill to swallow'.*

Black See entries below and: *beyond the black stump, in the black* and *not as black as they are painted*.

Black and blue Severely bruised. Thus, 'beat someone black and blue' and similar phrases mean to hit someone hard and repeatedly.*

Black and white (1) Describes the opinions and thoughts of someone who thinks of things in terms of being totally right or totally wrong, and who does not recognize that some things are neither wholly right nor wholly wrong (e.g. 'he thinks of things in black and white – he can only perceive absolutes'). (2) Describes something that is very clearly described with no possibility of doubt (e.g. 'the matter is a simple black and white issue'). (3) Describes something printed or written so that there is no doubt of its existence (e.g. 'of course it's true – there it is in black and white in today's newspaper').*

Black books A list of people in disgrace, in debt, or similar. Hence to be in someone's black books is to be in disgrace. Not to be confused with *little black book*.*

Black box (1) A device whose contents are unknown, but that given a particular input is known to produce a particular output. More generally, any device that clearly does something, but whose internal workings are either unknown or are known but are too difficult to understand by non-experts. (2) A device (e.g. on aircraft) that records the mechanical performance of an aircraft along with bearing, altitude, etc., and if the plane crashes, can provide valuable information on what the plane was doing just before it crashed. This device is not coloured black (it is usually a bright orange colour) but its name is derived from the fact that pilots called it the 'black box' (using definition 1) because they claimed not to understand how it worked.*

Black dog Depression.*

Black look An expression of disgust or anger.*

Black mark The phrase is often used in a larger phrase such as 'a black mark against their name' or 'a black mark against someone'. It means that a person is noted for having done something that is disapproved of by other people.*

Black market The trade in illegal or stolen property (e.g. 'there is a thriving black market trade in counterfeit goods').*

Black sheep A person who differs from the rest of a group or family, and who is usually considered to lead a shameful or embarrassing life. The phrase comes from a superstition that black sheep were more aggressive or unpleasant than white sheep.*

Black spot An area with a reputation for something unpleasant (e.g. an 'accident black spot' is an area where there is a higher than usual proportion of accidents).*

Blank See *blank cheque, blank look, draw a blank* and *fire blanks.*

Blank cheque [or check] A promise to pay anything. If person B has a blank cheque from person A, it means that person A has authorized person B to buy whatever person B thinks is appropriate, and that person A will pay the bill.*

Blank look A facial expression indicating no recognition.*

Blanket See *born the wrong side of the blanket* and *wet blanket.*

Blarney stone See *kissed the Blarney stone.*

Blast from the past (1) Something capable of evoking clear memories of a past event. (2) Something that was very popular in the past (particularly a pop song or movie).*

Blaze See *blaze a trail* and *like blazes.*

Blaze a trail Be the first to do something that other people can then imitate and improve upon.*

Blaze a way Means the same as *blaze a trail.*

Bleed dry Make very weak. The phrase usually refers to someone who has to pay some large bills.*

Bleed white Means the same as *bleed dry.*

Bleeding hell Means the same as *bloody hell.*

Bleeding obvious Very obvious. The phrase usually denotes that something is so obvious that it did not have to be stated.**

Bless their little cotton socks A joking phrase of praise.*

Blessing in disguise Something which at first appears bad, but which may in fact be good. For example, *not* winning an elephant in a raffle.*

Blind See entries immediately following this one, and also *effing and blinding, flying blind, go it blind, play a blinder* and *rob them blind.*

Blind alley A piece of thinking that is wrong and has to be rejected. The term is often used in research and other forms of investigation where people must examine a wide range of ideas and theories, some of which are useful and some of which are 'blind alleys'.*

Blind as a bat To have poor eyesight.*

Blind bit of... The phrase emphasizes what follows (e.g. 'it won't make a blind bit of difference' emphasizes that it will have no effect).*

Blind date An arranged meeting (usually a 'date' in the sense of seeing someone with romantic intentions) for two people who do not know each other but whom a mutual acquaintance believes will find each other attractive.*

Blind leading the blind Poor leadership with underlings obediently following bad commands. The phrase comes from the New Testament.*

Blind spot (1) An area in the field of vision where nothing can be seen. (2) An area of knowledge of which a person is ignorant. The phrase is often used more specifically to imply a failure to recognize something that others can clearly understand (e.g. 'everyone else knows that Edmund is a liar, but Tony seems to have a blind spot about him and cannot see this').*

Blind test A situation in which people test the worth of something without knowing important aspects of its identity (e.g. testing the tastes of different types of cola without knowing the brand names of the colas they are tasting).*

---

denotes level of impoliteness

Blind with science Use superior knowledge of science or technology (especially through use of jargon) to confuse another person.*

Blink of an eye Something that happens in 'the blink of an eye' happens very quickly.*

Blinkered vision Having only a limited or even just a single opinion about something, and being unwilling to change. The term is derived from horse racing; some horses are fitted with blinkers (hoods that partly cover the eyes) that prevent them seeing much to either side of them.*

Block See *knock their block off, on the block, out of the blocks, put their head on the block, round the block* and *stumbling block.**

Blonde See entry below and: *don't be blonde.*

Blonde moment A moment of lack of intelligent thought. The phrase is potentially offensive and should be avoided.***

Blood See entries below and: *after their blood, bad blood, baying for blood, cold blooded, first blood, hot blooded, in cold blood, in their blood, like getting blood out of a stone, make their blood boil, make their blood curdle, make their blood freeze, make their blood run cold, new blood, out for blood, scent blood, sweat blood* and *young blood.*

Blood and iron Military power. The phrase is often used to indicate the use of force rather than persuasion.*

Blood and sand An exclamation of annoyance.**

Blood and thunder (1) Violent or very energetic physical activity. (2) Exaggerated claims or expressed feelings (e.g. 'the president's speech on the day war was declared was full of blood and thunder').*

Blood is thicker than water A saying that claims that loyalty to family members is greater than loyalty to anything else.*

Blood is up A person whose 'blood is up' is in an argumentative mood.*

Blood on the carpet Describes a serious argument in a company or other institution (e.g. 'there was blood on the carpet during the pay dispute'). The phrase is a deliberate exaggeration, and does not imply that blood has actually been spilt.*

Blood on their hands People who are responsible for the death of someone are said to have 'blood on their hands'. The phrase can refer to murder, or to causing a death by accident.*

Blood, sweat and tears A piece of work that requires blood, sweat and tears is one that requires a great deal of effort. The phrase is an exaggeration, and does not imply that the task will in reality require anyone to bleed, sweat or cry.*

Blood will out A phrase expressing the belief that, eventually, a person's genetically inherited characteristics (particularly those affecting personality) will display themselves, no matter how they have been raised.*

Blood's worth bottling If someone's 'blood's worth bottling', then they are seen as being a pleasant person and/or a good worker.*

Bloody but unbowed Still resolved on the same course of action in spite of receiving serious disappointments or pain.*

Bloody hell An exclamation of annoyance, either used by itself as a one-off piece of swearing, or in various grammatical permutations (e.g. 'what the bloody hell's going on here, then?', 'bloody hell, what do you think you're doing?', etc). The phrase was at one stage considered more offensive than it is these days, but the frequency of its use in the media has desensitized people to it, and it is now considered a relatively mild piece of swearing by many people. Nonetheless, avoid using the phrase if possible.**

Bloom is off the rose Something is no longer as novel or exciting as it was originally.*

Blot on the landscape An ugly building or other artificial feature that mars the appearance of area in which it is located. By extension, anything that mars an otherwise agreeable situation.*

Blot on their copybook A poor piece of work or misbehaviour that harms a person's reputation. A copybook was a school writing book used to practise penmanship. Obviously, a blot of ink would make a page of calligraphy look untidy.*

Blot on their escutcheon Something that harms their reputation. An escutcheon is a heraldic shield.*

Blouse and skirt An exclamation of surprise (West Indian).**

Blow a fuse Be angry.*

Blow a gasket Means the same as *blow a fuse*.

Blow a hole in Render useless.*

Blow away (1) Impress with a high level of skill. (2) Kill.*

Blow away the cobwebs Gain a new outlook on something or feel livelier after a period of being relatively listless. The phrase often implies this is because of the rejection of old methods of thinking and/or behaving.*

Blow-by-blow account An account of everything that happened (as opposed to a summary of what happened).*

Blow chunks Vomit.**

Blow high, blow low A phrase used to describe something that is inevitable.*

Blow hot and cold To alternate between enthusiasm and apathy. See *go hot and cold*.*

Blow off course Cause a serious disruption in plans.*

Blow off steam Release pent-up anger, energy or frustration.*

Blow out of the water Utterly refute an argument or claim.*

Blow sky-high (1) Completely refute an argument. (2) Utterly destroy something by an explosion.*

Blow the doors off Be considerably better than someone or something else.*

Blow the gaff Reveal a secret.*

Blow the lid off (1) Become uncontrollable. (2) Reveal a secret.*

Blow the whistle Means the same as *blow the gaff*.

Blow their cover Discover the true identity of someone who has been using a false identity.*

Blow their mind Do something that strongly affects another person (typically by doing something that they thought was impossible).*

Blow their own trumpet Be boastful.*

Blow their top Become angry.*

Blow them (1) In UK English, the phrase is an expression of annoyance. (2) In US English, the phrase means 'to engage in oral sex'.* (1) or *** (2)

Blow them off Sometimes used in the same way as *blow them*, but more commonly means 'annoy them'.*

Blow up in their face If something 'blows up in a person's face', then a plan a person has made has gone wrong and, in the process of going wrong, has caused serious problems for the person.*

Blow with the wind Change opinions or plans according to what others are doing or what circumstances dictate. The phrase is usually an accusation of failing to be resolute rather than praise for being accommodating and/or pragmatic.*

Blowing the money Spending large amounts of money. The implication is usually that this is all the money a person has or more money than they can afford to spend.*

Blown away Strongly impressed and/or pleased.*

Blue-arsed fly A busy person.**

Blue-eyed boy [or girl] An especially favoured person.*

---

* denotes level of impoliteness

Blue movie Movie that gives a graphic depiction of sexual activity.*

Blue pencil Censorship or censoring. So called because censors of wartime correspondence would often scribble out offending passages of writing using a blue pencil.*

Blue sky research Research directed at new areas of study without consideration of possible commercial benefits.*

Blue streak See *talk a blue streak*.

Blue touch-paper See *light the blue touch-paper*.

Blue yonder See *wide blue yonder*.

Bluff See *call their bluff*.

Blushes See *spare their blushes*.

Board See *above board, across the board, back to the drawing board, bring on board, come on board, go by the board, on board, on the drawing board, sweep the board* and *take on board*.

Boat See *float the boat, in the same boat, push the boat out* and *rock the boat*.

Bob and weave Make ducking and side-to-side movements (akin to those of a boxer in a fight).*

Bob's your uncle A phrase which basically means 'there you have it!' It is usually used after describing a process or plan, and carries the meaning that things will be easily achieved. Numerous theories of the origin of this phrase have been made, but there is no single plausible explanation.*

Body and soul The phrase means 'body and mind' and is used to emphasize that the speaker is working hard at something and is fully committed to the aims of the project he or she is working on (e.g. 'I'm giving body and soul to this piece of work'). *

Body beautiful A body shape considered to be attractive.*

Body blow A problem that causes serious difficulties.*

Bog off Impolite way away'.**

Bog standard Normal o quality.*

Boil See *boil down to, come to the boil* ana *off the boil*.

Boil down to Reduce to its basic components. Thus 'boiling down' a lengthy story means giving a summary of it.*

Bold as brass Outward-going and brave without apparent concern for what others might think of this behaviour. The phrase may be derived from a Mr Brass (one time Mayor of London) noted for behaviour of this type. Others have argued that it is because brass, like all metals, has no feelings and thus cannot comprehend the comments made about it. Because it looks like gold, it might be assumed to be more noticeable than other metals.*

Bollocks (1) Testicles. (2) An expression of disgust or denial (e.g. 'that's a load of bollocks!'). (3) A derivative – 'bollocking' – means a severe reprimand (e.g. 'he got a bollocking for making that mistake').***

Bolt See *bolt from the blue, make a bolt for* and *shot the bolt*.

Bolt from the blue Something completely unexpected.*

Bomb See *go like a bomb* and *put a bomb under it*.

Bondi See *give them bondi*.

Bone See entries below and: *bare bones, close to the bone, cut to the bone, feel in the bones, make no bones about it* and *work their fingers to the bone*.

Bone of contention The cause of an argument or a disagreement.*

Bone to pick Having a cause for an argument with someone.*

Bone up on Study.*

Book Used as a verb, the term can mean to reserve something (e.g. theatre tickets or an appointment) or to note somebody down for punishment (e.g. 'the referee booked the soccer player'). See *black books, bring to book, can't judge a book by its cover, close the book, closed book, cook the books, go by the book, in my book, in their bad books, in their good books, little black book, little red book, make a book, on the books, open book, read them like a book, suit their book* and *throw the book at them.*

Boom boom! Used after telling a joke to indicate that that is the end of the joke and that it is funny. The phrase was originally used by stand-up comedians, but these days is usually used in a more ironic fashion to indicate that the joke isn't all that funny (which of course *begs the question* – why tell the joke in the first place?). A variant is *I don't wish to know that, kindly leave the stage*, which was said by one of a pair of comedians on stage after the other had told a joke.*

Boot See entries below and: *died with their boots on, fill their boots, given the boot, hang up their…, heart sinks into the boots, lick their boots, pull themselves up by their bootstraps, put the boot in, quake in their boots, seven league boots, step into their boots, to boot, to their bootstraps, too big for their boots* and *tough as old boots.*

Boot is on the other foot The situation is reversed (e.g. if person A was dominant over person B but now person B is dominant over person A, then it could be said that 'the boot is on the other foot'.*

Boots and all Totally.*

Bootstraps See *pull themselves up by their bootstraps* and *to their bootstraps.*

Bore the arse off Be very boring.***

Bore the backside off Be very boring.**

Bore the pants off Be very boring.*

Bored rigid Means the same as *bored stiff.*

Bored stiff To be very bored (though parts of the anatomy do not have to become stiff).*

Bored to death To be very bored. The phrase is not literal.*

Bored to tears To be extremely bored (though crying is not necessary). The phrase may refer to crying out of frustration at being bored, or may refer to a state of such boredom that a person forgets to blink and thus tears well up in their eyes.*

Born See entries below and: *don't know they are born, not got the manners they were born with, there's one born every minute* and *to the manner born.*

Born and bred A person who is said to be a 'born and bred' something (e.g. 'a born and bred academic', 'a born and bread baker') is felt to be so utterly suited for something by background and upbringing that it is difficult to imagine them being anything else.*

Born in the purple Born to wealthy and influential parents.*

Born the wrong side of the bedclothes Means the same as *born the wrong side of the blanket.*

Born the wrong side of the blanket Born to unmarried parents.*

Born with a silver spoon in their mouth Describes a person born into a rich family. Typically there is the added implication that the family, as well as being rich, has considerable influence and is possibly aristocratic.*

Both feet on the ground Sensible and practical and thus unlikely to be prone to daydreaming or impractical thoughts.*

Bottle out Lose courage.*

Bottom See entries below and: *at the bottom of it* and *get to the bottom of it.*

Bottom drawer Collection of basic household items bought by an unattached person (usually woman) living in the parental home, in preparation for the day when they marry/cohabit and need the said items in a home of their own.*

Bottom falls out of it Typically describes how a once-prosperous industry suddenly becomes unprofitable because consumers suddenly buy another product

---

* denotes level of impoliteness

(e.g. 'after an initial period of prosperity, the bottom fell out of the dot.com market'). Can also describe a sudden decline in popularity in other things.*

Bottom line The most important facts in a situation (e.g. 'forget the details – what's the bottom line?'). The phrase is often used to indicate the things that must be done (rather than things that are desirable but not essential).*

Bottom of the heap At the least powerful and/or prestigious position.*

Bottom of the ladder Means the same as *bottom of the heap*.

Bottom of the pile Means the same as *bottom of the heap*.

Bottom out Reach the lowest point (e.g. of a line on a graph).*

Bottom rung Means the same as *bottom of the heap*.

Bottoms up A salutation before drinking an alcoholic drink. The request is to tip the bottom of the glass upwards in order to drink the contents – it does not refer to the drinkers' bottoms.*

Bought it Died.*

Bought the farm Means the same as *kick the bucket*.*

Bounce an idea off them Discuss an idea with someone.*

Bowing and scraping Being over-respectful to the extent that other people think a person looks ridiculous. The term comes from terms for polite gestures of obedience.*

Bowl of cherries An agreeable situation or experience.*

Box and cox Share accommodation with.*

Box clever Be skilful, but cautious.*

Box into a corner Force a person into a position where they have a restricted range of options. The phrase comes from boxing: a weaker opponent can be manoeuvred by the tactics of the stronger boxer into a corner of the boxing ring, where he (or she) is more vulnerable to attack.*

Boy next door See *girl next door*.

Boys will be boys An argument that apparently idiotic behaviour is to be expected from young males because it is 'in their nature'. The argument has little scientific merit and cannot be accepted as a valid reason for loutish behaviour.*

Brahms and Liszt Slang for 'drunk'. The phrase comes from Cockney rhyming slang.*

Brainstorming session A group meeting where ideas on how to solve a problem or attain a particular target are discussed. The implication is usually that discussion will not be restricted by having to follow a rigid agenda.*

Brass farthing Something of no worth. The phrase is usually used in a statement such as 'I wouldn't give a brass farthing', and thus is used to indicate that whatever is being discussed is of little or no value – e.g. 'I wouldn't give a brass farthing for their chances' (i.e. 'I feel their chances are poor') or 'I couldn't give a brass farthing' (i.e. 'I have no interest in the matter').*

Brass hats Senior officers in the armed services. Named after the brass ornamentation on the caps of their uniforms.*

Brass monkey weather Very cold weather. The term is derived from the phrase 'it's cold enough to freeze the balls off a brass monkey'. The origins of that rather colourful phrase are not known for certain, though interesting theories have been advanced.**

Brass neck Insolence.*

Brass ring A desirable prize (e.g. 'the competitors tried hard as they were all reaching for the brass ring').*

Brass tacks The most important parts of a discussion. The phrase *let's get down to brass tacks* means 'let's talk about the really important things we must discuss rather than talk about minor details'.*

Brassed off Means the same as *cheesed off.*

Brazen it out Survive criticism or interrogation by persisting in expressing an explanation that is false, or at least not completely truthful. The inference is that a person continues to express their story until the critics or interrogators give up trying to disprove the story.*

Bread and butter (1) The main or sole source of income (e.g. 'I earn my bread and butter in a rather dull job'). (2) The routine parts of a job (e.g. 'my bread and butter work is a matter of checking that forms are filled in correctly, but occasionally I get to do something rather more unusual and exciting'). (3) A description of a dull or unrewarding job (e.g. 'it's bread and butter work').*

Bread and butter letter A letter written as a matter of routine, especially a letter from a guest thanking the host or hostess for their hospitality during a visit.*

Bread and circuses A description of what keeps the majority of the population happy. The phrase comes from Ancient Rome, when it was said that most of the population could be kept content with a steady supply of basic foodstuffs and regular entertainments such as the Roman circuses (i.e. gladiatorial combats, criminals being fed to wild animals, etc.). The phrase is sometimes used in a derogatory sense to indicate either that a lot of people can be satisfied with very basic things and have few intellectually stimulating interests. It can also be used to imply that government or industry bosses are offering superficial forms of happiness to keep people happy rather than dealing with more serious problems.*

Bread is buttered See *know which side the bread is buttered.*

Bread upon the waters See *cast bread upon the waters.*

Breadline See *on the breadline.*

Break a butterfly on a wheel Use excessive force to achieve something.*

Break a leg The phrase actually means 'good luck'. The phrase was originally used amongst actors, where it is often considered unlucky to say things such as 'good luck' before a performance.*

Break bread with Eat with.*

Break cover Become noticeable after a period of being hidden from view. The phrase can refer to someone who literally was hidden and can now be seen, or to a person who appears in public after a period of being reclusive.*

Break fresh ground Means the same as *break new ground.*

Break new ground Do something innovative.*

Break rank A person who 'breaks rank' elects to do something that is not approved of by the group to which they belong.*

Break ship Fail to return to a job after a vacation.*

Break the back (1) To weaken something (e.g. 'I've broken the back of the structure, so it should easily fall'). (2) To deal with the hardest parts of a task, thereby making the rest of the task easier (e.g. 'he broke the back of the problem').*

Break the bank To spend more than is possessed in savings. The phrase 'it won't break the bank' means that a person can afford to buy it. It is sometimes used to suggest that a person is being mean with their money and that their complaints about how expensive something is are unreasonable because they can easily afford to buy it.*

Break the ice Use an *ice breaker.*

Break the mould Do something innovative.*

Break their back A phrase meaning to work very hard (e.g. 'I'm breaking my back on this task').*

Break their neck Means the same as *break their back.*

---

* *denotes level of impoliteness*

Breast beating Means the same as *chest beating.*

Breath See *breath of fresh air, breath of life, hold their breath, in the same breath, save their breath, take the breath away, waste their breath* and *with bated breath.*

Breath of fresh air (1) A welcome change from the usual activities. (2) A person is said to act like a breath of fresh air if their arrival creates an improvement on what was happening before they came.*

Breath of life (1) Something that is essential for continued survival. (2) A reviving force.*

Breathe down their neck Constantly harass or scrutinize with unnecessary thoroughness.*

Breathe fire Be extremely angry.*

Bred in the bone See *what's bred in the bone.*

Brewery See *couldn't organize a piss-up in a brewery.*

Brick short of a load Insane or intellectually ungifted.*

Brick wall See *like banging their head against a brick wall.*

Bricking it See *shit a brick.*

Bridge See *bridge the gap, build bridges* and *cross that bridge when we come to it.*

Bridge the gap Create a connection between two things or people previously thought to have nothing in common or even to be hostile to each other (e.g. 'realising that the merger would help both of them bridged the gap between the chairmen of the two companies').*

Brief See *hold a brief.*

Bright as a button Intelligent and/or cheerful and/or lively.*

Bright-eyed and bushy tailed Means the same as *bright as a button.*

Bright spark A clever person. The phrase is nearly always used sarcastically.*

Bright young thing An intelligent young adult. The phrase is nearly always used to describe someone who is not only intelligent but also attractive (and almost invariably a young woman) with a friendly outgoing personality.*

Bring a plate On a party invitation, it means 'bring food appropriate for a party with you'.*

Bring down a peg or two To lower in status, typically as punishment for arrogance.*

Bring down about their ears (1) Ruin an activity. (2) Create misfortune.*

Bring down the curtain Finish an activity.*

Bring down to earth Forcibly remind somebody with an unrealistic interpretation of a situation of the true state of affairs.*

Bring home Make the importance of something apparent.*

Bring home the bacon To be successful or, more generally, to earn money. The phrase probably derives from the ancient custom of giving sides of bacon or ham as prizes in competitions.*

Bring in from the cold Revive someone's or something's popularity after a period of unpopularity.*

Bring into play Introduce something new.*

Bring on board Integrate into a plan or include in a group.*

Bring the house down Be a great success with an audience.*

Bring them in on it Make someone part of a plan or scheme.*

Bring to bay Capture. The term is from hunting with packs of dogs – the 'bay' refers to the baying of hounds that have trapped the prey.*

Bring to book Punish in a court of law.*

Bring to heel Bring under close supervision or control.*

Bring to their knees Considerably weaken and/or defeat.*

Bring to their senses Make someone adopt a more logical opinion or behaviour.*

Bring up short Do something that forces someone to stop what they are doing.*

Bring up to code Renovate to make acceptable to new standards of regulations.*

Bring up to speed Bring up to date: inform someone of all the relevant information.*

Broad as it's long Describes the fact that two or more alternatives are equally desirable (e.g. 'it's as broad as it's long whether you do A or B first').*

Broad beamed Rather larger in the hips and buttocks than might be deemed aesthetically appealing.*

Broad church Any organisation or group that accepts people with a wide range of beliefs or methods of dealing with the same situation.*

Brown study Daydream.*

Brown tonguing Means the same as *ass licking*.

Browned off To be bored.*

Brownie points Credit or praise for doing a particular task.*

Bubble See entry below and: *on the bubble* and *prick the bubble*.

Bubble has burst A situation that was successful has suddenly and dramatically become a failure. The phrase often carries the implication that the situation was never truly successful in the first place, and that much of the supposed success was in fact illusory (e.g. 'the dot.com bubble has burst and shares have plummeted').*

Buck-passing Means the same as *passing the buck*.

Buck stops here See *passing the buck*.

Buck up Show increased effort and/or liveliness.*

Buck up their ideas Show increased effort and quality of work.*

Bucketing down Raining heavily.*

Buckley's chance Australian phrase denoting no or little chance of success.*

Bug Can mean an irritating person (e.g. 'he's an annoying little bug'), to annoy (e.g. 'stop bugging me!') or an illness (e.g. 'a lot of people have a nasty flu bug at the moment'). See also *bitten by the bug*.* or ** Note: a request to 'stop bugging me' is rather less polite than a general statement that, e.g., 'work is bugging me'.

Bugger all Ruder version of *damn all*.**

Buggin's turn A task which everyone in turn has to do, rather than one which someone is chosen to do because of their abilities. For example, in an office everyone may take turns to make the morning coffee.*

Bugs them Annoys them.*

Build a better mousetrap A phrase indicating that some inventions or innovations will have guaranteed success. It derives from the old saying that if a person invents a better mousetrap, then everyone will *beat a path* to that person's door (in other words, everyone will want to buy the new mousetrap). At a time when household vermin were more common than today, this may have been true, but these days the phrase is proverbial rather than a recipe for guaranteed commercial success.*

Build bridges Persuade people or groups previously hostile towards each other to become friends, or at least to be less hostile.*

Built like a brick shithouse Strong-looking.***

Built on sand Created on insecure foundations and thus likely to collapse. The phrase is used particularly of logically unsound arguments.*

Bulge See *battle of the bulge* and *have the bulge on*.

Bull at a gate See *charge like a bull at a gate*.

Bull in a china shop A person who is tactless or upsets people by not doing something with sufficient care and attention.*

Bullshit Bertie A person who talks a lot of nonsense but is under the delusion that they are an expert.***

Bully for... Followed by 'you' or 'them' or 'him' or 'her' etc. The phrase means 'well done' (e.g. 'bully for you – you did really well in your exams'). The phrase is often used sarcastically.*

Bum In UK English, the word is slang for a person's bottom, and is considered slightly rude. In US English, the word means 'of poor quality' or 'a hobo' or 'a vagrant' and is considered far less rude.* (USA) or ** (UK)

Bum bandit British abusive slang for a male homosexual. A very offensive term.***

Bum steer Misleading information.*

Bum's rush To be ignored or rejected.*

Bump along the bottom Perform at a consistently poor level.*

Bumper to bumper Close together.*

Bums on seats 'Bottoms on seats' – in other words, a theatre audience. The phrase usually refers to the need to attract a large enough audience to make a theatre commercially viable (e.g. 'the critics hate him, but he's good at getting bums on seats').*

Bundle of laughs Means the same as *barrel of laughs*.

Bunny See *bunny boiler* and *happy bunny*.

Bunny boiler A person with psychopathic or revengeful tendencies. The phrase is often used jokingly of an ex-boyfriend or girlfriend who was vindictive when the relationship finished. The phrase is derived from the film *Fatal Attraction*, in which a spurned woman revenges herself on the man who rejected her by boiling his daughter's pet rabbit.*

Buried under... Unless a literal physical burial is stated, then the term means 'overwhelmed by...' (e.g. 'buried under paperwork' means to have far too many administrative duties).*

Burn a hole in their pocket If a person feels that their money is 'burning a hole in their pocket', then they are anxious to spend money. The implication is usually that the person is being impulsive rather than prudent.*

Burn daylight Use artificial light when the daylight from a window is more than adequate for the task being done.*

Burn out Become exhausted. The phrase is often used of people who are in demanding and stressful jobs who reach a point where they are physically and/or psychologically incapable of continuing in their profession.*

Burn out of their system Become tired of doing something.*

Burn rubber (1) Drive at high speed and/or recklessly. (2) Leave with great urgency.*

Burn the candle at both ends Engage in an activity with too much energy, thereby tiring oneself out. Typically there is the added implication that the person concerned has been missing sleep, staying up too late, etc.*

Burn the floor Dance.*

Burn the midnight oil Work long hours on a project. Usually there is the implication that such work is well beyond the limits of normal working hours and that the work is difficult.*

Burn their boats Means the same as *burn their bridges*.

Burn their bridges Do something that prevents a return to an earlier stage and in effect commits to a particular plan or course of action (e.g. 'having resigned from his job, John had burnt his bridges – he had to move').*

Burn their fingers Fail badly in attempting to do something. The phrase often refers to a failed business or financial investment.*

Burning desire Strong desire.*

Burnt offerings Joking description of cooked food.*

Burst the bubble Destroy an illusion.*

Bursting at the seams At or exceeding maximum capacity.*

Burton See *gone for a burton.*

Bury the hatchet Make peace.*

Bury the tomahawk Means the same as *bury the hatchet.*

Bury their head in the sand The process of putting the *head in the sand.**

Bush telegraph Information received from gossip rather than an official source.*

Business Can mean 'general situation' rather than 'a commercial company'. Thus, *bad business*, for example, can mean that the general situation is bad. *Monkey business* means doing things ineptly or in a generally foolish way. See entries below and: *do the business, in business, like nobody's business* and *mean business.**

Business end The component of an apparatus that produces the finished product (e.g. the 'business end' of a rifle is the end of the barrel).*

Business is business A justification for doing unpleasant things to people (e.g. firing people who are friends) because a commercial enterprize must pay attention to profitability before emotional considerations.*

Busman's holiday A holiday that is spent doing an activity that is identical or very similar to that done at work (e.g. a literary critic who spends her vacation reading new books might be said to be taking a busman's holiday). The phrase is derived from bus drivers, who, in the days when buses were horse-drawn, were so attached to their horses that they would spend their holidays looking after their horses, or riding on the bus to ensure their horse was properly cared for by the substitute driver.*

Bust their ass (1) Can mean the same as *whip their ass.* (2) Can also mean the same as *bust their balls*, but slightly less rude.**

Bust their balls Work very hard. ***

Busted flush Something that has failed to reach expected standards of performance. The phrase comes from the card game of poker (a flush is a high-scoring sequence of cards of the same suit; a busted flush lacks a card necessary for a complete sequence and is very low- scoring).*

Busy bee A person who always appears to be busy, usually with the implication that they like being busy. Probably the phrase is derived from the observation that bees always appear to be busy, industrious animals.*

Butcher See *fit as a butcher's dog, have a butcher's* and *more meat on a butcher's pencil.*

Butler did it A joking attribution of responsibility for something. The phrase is derived from a spate of murder mystery stories in the 1920s and 1930s where the butler was the murderer.*

Butter-fingered Prone to dropping things.*

Butter up Flatter.*

Butter wouldn't melt in their mouth Meaning that they appear innocent. There is usually the implication that this appearance is deceptive and in fact they are guilty of something.*

Butterflies in the stomach Feeling nervous. The phrase comes from the 'fluttering' sensation sometimes felt in the stomach area when nervous (in fact caused by muscular contractions and excess stomach acid).*

---

* *denotes level of impoliteness*

Button See *all the right buttons, at the touch of a button, buttonhole, hot button, on the button, press the button* and *push their buttons.*

Buttonhole To insist on telling someone something, often against their will. The phrase is often used of people campaigning for a cause.*

Buy a pup Pay far more for something than it is worth. By a similar reasoning, *sell a pup* means to sell something for far more than it is worth. Both phrases usually indicate that the seller was acting fraudulently.*

Buy time Delay activities in order to gain more time for planning a response.*

Buzz off A request to go away.**
Note: the phrase only just gets a ** rather than * rating – it is very mild, and usually does not indicate a high level of anger.

By a canvas In a competition, if someone wins 'by a canvas' then they win by a small distance or difference in scores. The phrase is derived from rowing ('canvas' is the distance between the front of the boat and the first rower). There are similar phrases from other sports which also mean by a short distance or difference in scores – e.g. *by a nose* or *by a head.**

By a head See *by a canvas.*

By a long chalk See *not by a long chalk.*

By a long shot By a considerable distance, quantity or margin.*

By a nose See *by a canvas.*

By a whisker By a very small margin.*

By an eyelash Means the same as *by a whisker.**

By and large Generally.*

By hook or by crook By any means possible.*

By no stretch of the imagination An emphatic denial (e.g. 'by no stretch of the imagination would we support this proposal').*

By numbers In a mechanical fashion without any personal creative input. The phrase has numerous shades of meaning: e.g. (1) Following a set of instructions. (2) Performing a task that has become a simple matter of routine. (3) Performing a task without enthusiasm and simply doing things in a rote order fashion.*

By the book See *go by the book.*

By the dozen Means the same as *by the ton.*

By the gross Means the same as *by the ton.*

By the same token By the same reasoning process.*

By the score Means the same as *by the ton.*

By the seat of the pants Using intuition rather than training to accomplish something.*

By the sweat of their brow By their own hard work.*

By the ton In large quantities. Like similar phrases (*by the dozen/gross/score/yard*) the precise quantity is not indicated by the phrase – only a large quantity is implied. Generally, the dimension in which quantity is being measured is indicated by the last word in the phrase (e.g. 'by the ton' indicates as measured by weight, 'by the yard' as measured by length, etc.), but this is not universally applied.*

By the yard Means the same as *by the ton.*

By their fingertips Only just attainable.*

By word of mouth Spoken (rather than written) communication.*

C

Caboodle See *whole caboodle.*

Caesar's wife A person who must, because of the nature of their job or position, be morally beyond reproach.*

Cage See *who rattled its cage?*

Cain See *raise Cain.*

Cake See *cakes and ale* and *can't have your cake and eat it.*

Cakes and ale A time of trouble-free enjoyment.*

Call a spade a spade Speak in a direct manner.*

Call in a favour Suppose that person A did something for person B and at the time asked for nothing in return. If at a later date person A asked person B to do something for person A, then this would be described as 'calling in a favour'.*

Call in their chips Means the same as *call in a favour.*

Call it a day Stop doing something. The term can be used to describe either complete abandonment of something, or simply stopping work temporarily (e.g. at the end of the working day).*

Call it quits (1) Abandon an activity or plan. (2) Agree that a debt has been paid or a favour returned.*

Call of nature Need to excrete or urinate.*

Call on the carpet Means the same as *on the carpet.*

Call the shots Dictate how something should be done.*

Call the tune Means the same as *call the shots.*

Call their bluff If I call your bluff, then it means that I don't believe what you are claiming, and I am asking you to prove it (e.g. 'Harry didn't believe that Jessica owned five Rolls-Royces, so he called her bluff and asked her to show him the garage where she kept them').*

Call to arms Instructions to prepare for conflict or to join a campaign.*

Calling card An indication that someone has visited. The original calling card was literally a small card with the name of the person and their address that was left at the house if the owner was not in.*

Calm before the storm A period of unnatural calm before the onset of something unpleasant, such as an argument.*

Came up Was mentioned.*

Camp follower An unimportant person who declares allegiance to a group but plays no particularly important role in running or organising the group. The term originally described civilians who followed armies on the march, and who sold things to the soldiers.*

Can a duck swim? A sarcastic reply to a question to which the answer is obvious; for example, it might be the appropriate reply to the question 'would you like to be incredibly wealthy?'*

Can it A firm request for someone to be quiet.**

Can of worms See *open a can of worms.*

Candle See *burn the candle at both ends, can't hold a candle, not worth a candle* and *not worth the candle.*

Candy store See *like a child in a candy store.*

Cannon fodder (1) Originally, a very unpleasant term for soldiers considered unimportant for the success of an army in a battle; their only use was seen as to waste enemy shells in killing them (i.e. 'cannon fodder'). (2) The term is now sometimes used more generally for people considered unimportant and thus most easily dispensed with (e.g. the first to be made unemployed if a factory needs to lower the size of its workforce). (3) People assigned dangerous jobs or tasks.*

Can't get a word in edgeways Cannot get another person or people to listen to what others have to say because they will not let themselves be interrupted.*

Can't have it both ways See *have it both ways.*

Can't have your cake and eat it Meaning that if there are two mutually exclusive choices (i.e. you can have one or the other) you cannot have one and then the other. The phrase was originally 'you can't eat your cake and then have it', which makes a lot more sense than the modern version.*

---

* *denotes level of impoliteness*

Can't hear themselves think Be unable to concentrate because the surroundings are too noisy.*

Can't hold a candle A judgement of comparative worth (e.g. if A cannot hold a candle to B, then B is far better than A).*

Can't judge a book by its cover A saying meaning that the true nature of someone or something cannot be understood just from their appearance (i.e. what they have done, their opinions, etc. have to be assessed).*

Can't keep a good person down The belief that a person with skill and/or ambition will recover from misfortune.*

Can't make a silk purse out of a sow's ear It is impossible to make something graceful and refined out of poor-quality ingredients.*

Can't make head nor tail of it Cannot understand it.*

Can't rewrite history See *rewrite history.*

Can't see the wood for the trees Cannot see the general findings or implications because of an over-concentration on details.*

Canter See *at a canter.*

Cap See entries below and: *feather in their cap, if the cap fits, put on their thinking cap* and *set their cap at them.*

Cap in hand Someone who is 'cap in hand' is being obsequious and making a request for money or other assistance. The phrase comes from a time when practically everybody wore a cap or hat. A person asking for money would be talking to a social and/or financial superior, and thus out of politeness would have taken off his cap or hat and held it in their hands. The cap would not be held out for money as done by, e.g., some beggars.*

Cap it all Something that finishes a process or story. There is usually the implication that it is an event that is unexpected (e.g. 'to cap it all, whilst all this commotion was going on, Sarah arrived with news that she was pregnant').*

Capital See *with a capital...*

Carbon copy An exact duplicate. The phrase comes from the (now diminishing) use of carbon paper to produce a copy of a typed letter.*

Card-carrying member of... A very keen, almost fanatical supporter of... *

Cards close to the chest A person that keeps or plays their 'cards close to the chest' is a person who is unwilling to discuss his or her plans or thoughts.*

Cards on the table If someone puts their cards on the table, it means that they are expressing clearly what their feelings and intentions are.*

Cark it Die.**

Carpeting See *on the carpet.*

Carriage trade The richest customers.*

Carried by an acclamation A law or proposal that is accepted with great enthusiasm.*

Carried off by... Killed by... The phrase almost invariably refers to death from illness.*

Carrot See *carrot and stick* and *dangle a carrot.*

Carrot and stick A combination of bribe (carrot) and threat (stick) to persuade a person to do something. The phrase is derived from the fact that animals such as donkeys can be persuaded to follow a person holding an attractive piece of food, such as a carrot, or can be made to move by hitting a stick on to their flanks.*

Carry a torch Be in love with someone who does not love in return.*

Carry all before them Be completely victorious.*

Carry the can Take responsibility for something.*

Carry the day Win.*

Cart before the horse See *put the cart before the horse.*

Carved on tablets of stone Permanent and unalterable. There are various permutations of the phrase (e.g. 'carved in stone', 'set in tablets of stone', etc.).*

Cash cow A very profitable venture that requires little work to keep profitable over a long period of time. The phrase is meant to create an image of a cow that, when milked, produces money rather than milk.*

Cash in hand Payment in notes and coins (rather than cheque, credit card, or similar).*

Cash in their chips (1) Stop gambling. (2) Sell a share in a business. (3) Die.*

Cast adrift Isolate from a group or abandon.*

Cast bread upon the waters Do something (typically, something virtuous) without expecting anything in return. The phrase is from the Bible.*

Cast in bronze Means the same as *set in stone.*

Cast-iron case An argument that cannot be disproved.*

Cast-iron proof Irrefutable proof.*

Cast their mind back Attempt to remember something from the past.*

Castles in Spain Means the same as *castles in the air.*

Castles in the air An unrealistic set of plans or expectations.*

Casual pick up See *pick up.*

Cat among the pigeons See *put the cat among the pigeons.*

Cat and mouse See *play cat and mouse.*

Cat dragged in See *look like something the cat dragged in* and *look what the cat dragged in.*

Cat got their tongue Describes someone who is silent. The phrase is more often used in question form (e.g. 'has the cat got your tongue?' – i.e. 'why aren't you saying anything?').*

Cat in hell's chance No chance at all (e.g. 'with the present points deficit, they don't have a cat in hell's chance of winning the championship'). The phrase *don't have a cat in hell's chance* means 'have even less chance than a cat in hell' (i.e. the phrase emphasizes that there is no chance).*

Cat may look at a king A proverb expressing the argument that everyone, no matter what their social status, has the freedom and right to do certain things.*

Cat meat (1) Vulnerable to attack. (2) In trouble.*

Cat on a hot tin roof Means the same as *cat on hot bricks.*

Cat on hot bricks To be 'like a cat on hot bricks' is to be restless.*

Cat out of the bag See *let the cat out of the bag.*

Cat that ate the canary See *like a cat that ate the canary.*

Cat that got the cream See *like a cat that got the cream.*

Cat won't jump A phrase used to indicate that a plan is impractical.*

Cat's away See *when the cat's away.*

Cat's meow Means the same as *bee's knees.*

Cat's paw A person forced or tricked into doing something illegal or unpleasant for someone else.*

Cat's pyjamas Means the same as *bee's knees.*

Cat's whiskers Means the same as *bee's knees.*

Catbird seat See *in the catbird seat.*

Catch a cold (1) Become ill. (2) Encounter a problem.*

Catch a Tartar Become involved with an uncontrollable person who refuses to leave.*

---

* *denotes level of impoliteness*

Catch cold Find unprepared.*

Catch fire Become more exciting.*

Catch in the act Find doing something wrong. Is a shortened form of a longer phrase such as 'catch in the act of committing a crime', 'catch in the act of burglary', etc. The phrase may indicate a misdeed of any level of seriousness.*

Catch in the crossfire Become a victim of a dispute which one was not part of.*

Catch on the hop Find in an unprepared state.*

Catch red-handed Find in the act of doing something wrong. Supposedly derived from poachers found with the blood of the killed animal on their hands.*

Catch some zs Sleep ('zs' is pronounced 'zees').*

Catch the sun Be suntanned or sunburned.*

Catch their death Sometimes used in the longer form of 'catch their death of cold'. Contract a serious cold.*

Catch them flat-footed Surprise someone.*

Catch them napping Means the same as *catch them flat-footed*.

Catch them on their toes Fail to surprise someone.*

Catch 22 A situation in which whatever is done is doomed to fail and/or cause suffering.*

Catch with chaff Easily deceive.*

Catch with their hand in the cookie jar Find stealing or committing another misdeed.*

Catch with their pants down Discover doing something embarrassing and/or wrong, typically of a sexual nature.*

Caught short (1) Need to urinate. There is usually an implication that there is no lavatory conveniently near. (2) In a disadvantageous position.*

Caviar to the general Something that only a person with refined tastes will appreciate even and which is unappreciated or even disliked by the general population. The phrase is a quotation from *Hamlet*.*

Central casting See *straight from central casting*.

Centre court Means the same as *centre stage*. The phrase is derived from 'Centre Court' at Wimbledon, where some of the most important tennis matches are held.*

Centre stage The centre of attention. Thus a person who 'takes centre stage' is the one being attended to most of all. The phrase comes from the theatre, where the leading actors generally are placed in the area of the stage called 'centre stage' (i.e. the middle of the stage) for their most important moments in a play.*

Chain of command The hierarchical structure of the various levels of leadership in a group or organisation.*

Chair's action A decision-making process delegated to the Chair of a committee to make by him- or herself without the need to convene the committee to discuss the matter (i.e. basically the committee trusts the Chair to act on its behalf).*

Chalk and cheese Describing two totally dissimilar things or people (e.g. 'they are as alike as chalk and cheese').*

Champ at the bit Display impatience. The phrase is derived from a horse champing (i.e. biting down) on the bit (a piece of metal placed in the mouth and attached to the reins) when tired of standing and anxious to be moving.*

Chance in hell Means the same as *cat in hell's chance*.

Chance their arm Take a risk.*

Chance would be a fine thing A phrase nearly always used in reply to an over-optimistic statement by someone else. The phrase basically means 'yes, it would be nice if that happened, but the probability is low, so other, more realistic alternatives must be found'.*

Change gear Means the same as *shift gear.*

Change horses in midstream Change the way of doing something. The implication is that this is done after the first way of doing things was already established.*

Change of heart Change of feelings or attitude.*

Change of pace A change of lifestyle. The phrase can mean either a more hectic or more relaxed lifestyle – the context should indicate which meaning is intended.*

Change of scenery A change in jobs and/or home.*

Change the record A demand that someone finds something new to talk or write about, because they are being boring and/or annoying by only talking or writing about a very limited range of topics.*

Change their mind Alter their opinion.*

Change their tune Alter their opinions or professed beliefs.*

Chapter and verse The definitive information on a topic. The phrase comes from giving a precise reference to a passage in the Bible by citing the number of the chapter and verse.*

Charge like a bull at a gate Be reckless and/or impulsive.*

Charge the Earth Charge a lot of money. There is often an implication of making an excessive profit.*

Charity begins at home A saying that advises that a person should attend to the needs of their own family before considering being good to others. The phrase is less selfish than it may first appear. It is essentially arguing that people who profess an idealistic lifestyle but who are unkind to those who live with them are hardly being charitable. The saying is not intended to advocate selfishness.*

Charity fuck Having sex with someone because the person felt sorry for them (especially if they are considered physically unattractive).***

Charley horse A painful cramp in the arm or leg.*

Charm offensive A concerted effort to be nice to people with the aim of winning them over to an argument.*

Chase rainbows Have unrealistic aspirations.*

Chase the dragon Take heroin by heating it and inhaling the fumes.*

Chase their own tail (1) Engage in a pointless activity. (2) In a piece of research or an investigation, become very confused, to the point where the objectives are no longer clear. (3) A piece of research which examines the process of research rather than a genuine phenomenon.*

Chattering classes A derogatory term for a section of the middle classes, characterized by having more than enough leisure time to discuss politics, fashion, the arts, the news, etc., but not quite enough intelligence for the results of their discussions to be worth attending to.*

Cheap at half the price A deliberately nonsensical expression which means that whatever is being discussed is cheap.*

Cheap at the price A good bargain.*

Check out There are several common meanings: (1) to examine (e.g. 'check out the new Ford'); (2) to pay one's bill and leave a hotel or similar establishment; or (3) a place where items are paid for in a shop or supermarket.*

Cheek by jowl To be close together. 'Jowl' means the same as 'cheek'.*

Cheer to the echo Give great acclamation to.*

Cheesed off To be bored.*

Cherry See entry below and: *bite at the cherry, bowl of cherries, lose their cherry, pop their cherry* and *second bite at the cherry.*

Cherry on the cake Something that is a pleasing bonus, but not essential (e.g. 'the salary for the new job was sufficient incentive in itself to join the firm, but the cherry on the cake was the extra week of vacation'). The phrase is sometimes used sarcastically (typically indicated by context or tone of voice) to mean the *final straw.**

Cheshire cat See *grin like a Cheshire cat.*

Chest beating A public show of anger: the implication is that this is an insincere display intended to impress, rather than showing genuine feelings.*

Chestnut See *old chestnut* and *pull their chestnuts from the fire.*

Chew the carpet To be so annoyed about something as to become illogically angry.*

Chew the cud To think deeply about something.*

Chew the fat Means the same as *chew the rag.**

Chew the rag To discuss something thoroughly.*

Chew their ass Means the same as *chew their ear*, but ruder.***

Chew their balls Means the same as *chew their ear*, but far ruder.***

Chew their ear Tell someone off.*

Chick flick A movie that will be primarily enjoyed by women.*

Chick lit Literature that will be primarily enjoyed by women.*

Chicken and egg A chicken and egg situation occurs when it is impossible to determine which of two things happened first or which thing caused the other to happen. The phrase is derived from the riddle 'which came first – the chicken or the egg?' In other words, how can a chicken exist without hatching from an egg, but equally, how can an egg exist if it is not hatched from a chicken? (Being very pedantic, the correct answer is 'the egg', since animals capable of laying eggs existed a long time before chickens evolved.) *

Chicken feed (1) A small amount. (2) An insignificant person or group of people.*

Chicken out Fail to do something because of fear of the consequences.*

Chickens come home to roost Means the same as *come home to roost.*

Chief cook and bottle washer A joking term for someone placed in general charge of things.*

Child's play Describes any particularly easy task.*

Chill out Relax.*

Chinaman's chance See *not a Chinaman's chance.*

Chinese whispers The phenomenon that as a piece of news is told by a succession of people, the information becomes distorted. This has nothing to do with the Chinese people or language, but refers to a children's game of the same name that used the term 'Chinese whispers' for reasons now lost.*

Chink in their armour Means the same as *Achilles heel.*

Chip off the old block A child who is just like their parent in looks and/or behaviour.*

Chip on their shoulder Being persistently aggressive or argumentative.*

Chips are down The term is used to describe a serious turn of events when what happens next will almost certainly decide the outcome.*

Chop See *chop logic, chopping and changing* and *given the chop.*

Chop logic Be pedantic.*

Chopping and changing Constantly changing plans or ideas.*

Chuck a sickie Fake illness to take a day off work.**

Chuck it Usually used to advise someone to abandon a particular line of reasoning. It can also mean *get lost.***

Chuck it down Rain heavily.*

Chunks See *blow chunks.*

Circle the wagons Unite together to defend a common cause.*

Circling the airport Means the same as *out of it.*

Claim to fame The reason why someone is noteworthy. The phrase is often used jokingly of someone who is not particularly noteworthy (e.g. 'her claim to fame is that she was in the same class at school as Elton John').*

Clanger See *drop a clanger.*

Clap eyes on See.*

Clap hold of Grab.*

Class act Term of approval for somebody who is skilled at their job.*

Claws into them If person A has their claws into person B, it means that person A is controlling what person B does. There is usually an implication that this is a bad thing.*

Clean as a whistle (1) Physically clean. (2) Free from any guilt or suspicion of wrongdoing.*

Clean away If something is 'clean away' then it has totally disappeared, leaving no trace behind.*

Clean bill of health A declaration that a person is healthy or a machine or process is in a good state. The phrase is a maritime one, and refers to a ship being declared free of any crew or passengers with infectious diseases.*

Clean break A total severance. For example, a person making a 'clean break' in a relationship makes every effort not to meet the other person again.*

Clean breast See *make a clean breast of it.*

Clean hands Used in a statement such as 'have clean hands' the phrase means 'free of guilt'.*

Clean house Improve the running of an organisation, particularly by abolishing inefficient and corrupt practices.*

Clean out (1) Take a lot of money off someone else (typically it is implied this is by trickery or skill; e.g. 'Sally cleaned John out at a game of poker'). (2) Describes a lack of something (e.g. 'I'm clean out of fruit').*

Clean sweep See *make a clean sweep.*

Clean their clock Utterly defeat someone.*

Clean up Make a large profit.*

Clean up their act Make work or behaviour more acceptable and/or to a higher standard.*

Clear as a bell Totally clear or obvious.*

Clear as crystal Means the same as *clear as a bell.*

Clear as day Means the same as *clear as a bell.*

Clear as mud Very hard to understand. There is usually the implication that it is the description that is unclear rather than what the description is describing (e.g. 'what you're describing should be easy to understand, but your description has made it as clear as mud').*

Clear-cut Something that is clear-cut is easy to understand and is without doubt accurate.*

Clear off A command to 'go away'.***

Clear out (1) To leave, usually with the implication of taking all belongings as well. (2) Issued as a command, an order to leave.* (1) or ** (2)

Clear the air To discuss and settle an unsolved problem that had previously caused an emotionally uncomfortable state by being unresolved.*

denotes level of impoliteness

Clear the decks Prepare for an event by removing or dealing with anything that might interfere with the event. The phrase is derived from naval warfare, where the decks of a ship are cleared of anything not essential to battle before going into action.*

Clear up (1) Resolve or solve. (2) Make tidy.*

Cleft stick See *in a cleft stick.*

Click into place (1) Describes something or someone that is perfectly suited for the situation (e.g. 'the missing piece was found and it clicked into place in the space in the jigsaw'). (2) Describes the moment when something is finally fully comprehended (e.g. 'I had been working at the problem for several days when suddenly everything clicked into place').*

Climbing the walls Be agitated or annoyed.*

Clip their wings Restrict a person's freedom of movement or powers. Named after the practice of clipping the wings of prized pet birds to prevent them flying away.*

Cloak and dagger Refers to any secret activity involving danger and spying.*

Clock has beaten them The time allocated for an activity has elapsed, so the activity must stop.*

Clock is ticking A warning that there is a limited amount of time left in which to complete something and/or make a decision.*

Clock-watching Wanting an activity to finish. The phrase is usually applied to people who dislike their job and are constantly wondering when it will be time for a break or to go home, rather than attending to their work.*

Clocking off To finish work. The phrase comes from a once-common practice that workers upon arriving would insert a card into a 'clocking machine' that would mark when they started and finished

work on that day. It was used to check on people arriving late or leaving early.*

Clocking on To start work. See *clocking off.**

Close but no cigar Very close to the desired target but nonetheless a miss. The term comes from fairground stalls where the prize for hitting a target was a cigar. The stall holder would cry out 'close but no cigar' when someone nearly hit the target.*

Close call An event that was nearly a serious accident but in fact passed successfully.*

Close ranks (1) Unite in a common cause. (2) The phrase is often used more specifically when a group protects itself from scrutiny by all its members refusing to divulge information and/or generally being obstructive.*

Close-run thing Means the same as *close call.*

Close shave Means the same as *close call.*

Close the book Finish a task with no intention of returning to it.*

Close the case Means the same as *close the book.*

Close their eyes to Deliberately ignore.*

Close their mind to Create a *closed mind.**

Close thing Means the same thing as *close call.**

Close to home A remark that is 'close to home' is accurate and makes an argument that a person finds uncomfortable to think about.*

Close to the bone Describes something that makes people feel uncomfortable or embarrassed because it deals with something people would prefer was not discussed.*

Close to the knuckle Can mean the same as *close to the bone.* Can also be used to describe something that is barely within the limits of what people would consider socially acceptable or polite.*

Close to the mark Almost correct.*

Close up shop Means the same as *shut up shop*.

Close your eyes and think of England Supposedly advice given to English brides in the Victorian era about how to 'enjoy' sexual intercourse. The term is now used more humorously to refer to any event where one must endure something unpleasant for a higher cause.**

Closed book Someone (or something) about whom little is known and who discourages enquiries about their personal life.*

Closed mind A refusal to change opinion on, or discuss, something. The phrase is often used to indicate bigotry.*

Closed shop Workplace in which a person is compelled to belong to a specific trades union.*

Cloth ears Derogatory term for someone not very intelligent or someone who is not paying sufficient attention (e.g. 'hey, cloth ears, why aren't you listening to what I'm saying?').**

Cloud cuckoo land A place of impossible ideas; hence, someone said to be living there is a person with nonsensical notions. The term is derived from a play called *The Birds* by the Ancient Greek playwright Aristophenes.*

Cloud nine A state of extreme euphoria.*

Cloven hoof Something evil (the Devil is said to have cloven hoofs). The phrase is these days likely to be used jokingly.*

Clued up To be knowledgeable.*

Clutch at straws Means the same as *grasp at straws*.

Coach and horses See *drive a coach and horses through it*.

Coals of fire See *heap coals of fire on their head*.

Coals to Newcastle A pointless activity. The phrase was invented at a time when Newcastle was the centre of a thriving coal mining industry. Hence, taking 'coals to Newcastle' would be taking something to Newcastle that the area already had in abundance. *

Coast is clear A phrase used to indicate that nobody is watching and that something can be done without fear of anyone witnessing it. The phrase is derived from smuggling – smugglers would not attempt to land contraband unless they were certain that the 'coast was clear' (i.e. that there were no law officers waiting to arrest them).*

Coat tails See *on the coat tails of them*.

Cob on See *have a cob on*.

Cobwebs See *blow away the cobwebs*.

Cock a snook To make a derisive gesture at someone. The phrase is only ever used to describe what one person did to another person. It is never used directly as an insult (e.g. nobody ever says 'I cock a snook at you').*

Cock an ear Listen for something.*

Cock and bull story A lengthy rambling story which is usually utterly implausible. Many explanations for the origin of the phrase have been advanced.*

Cock of the walk The most important or dominant person in a group.*

Cocked hat See *knock into a cocked hat*.

Code See *bring up to code*.

Coffee table book A book that is primarily bought for its artistic appearance rather than intellectual content (it is often also rather large). The phrase derives from the habit of some pretentious middle-class people of having a collection of such books placed on a coffee table. The phrase is generally used in a derogatory manner to denote a book that is bought for display rather than serious reading.*

Coin a phrase To invent a phrase.*

Cold as charity Unpleasantly cold.*

* denotes level of impoliteness

Cold as ice In describing someone's mood, the phrase means 'unfriendly' and/or 'without pity'.*

Cold blooded (1) Describes someone with no moral sense or remorse (e.g. 'a cold-blooded killer'). (2) Describes someone who is unfriendly or seems to get little pleasure from a social life.*

Cold comfort A gesture or statement that is intended to be comforting in a time of distress, but which does not ease the distress and may even make it worse.*

Cold feet Reluctance to do something, or fear of doing something. The phrase usually implies that this follows an initial enthusiasm.*

Cold shoulder See *get the cold shoulder.*

Cold turkey See *go cold turkey.*

Collect dust Stay unused.*

Collision course (1) If someone sets out on a collision course, then they are intentionally planning to create a dispute. (2) A situation in which something unpleasant (e.g. an argument) is inevitably going to happen.*

Colour of their money The financial probity of what is being offered. If a person asks to see the colour of someone's money, they doubt their honesty or ability to pay.*

Colourful language Language containing an excessive proportion of swear words.*

Colours to the mast See *nail the colours to the mast.*

Columbo question A final question that is unexpected and makes a person uneasy and/or forces them to admit something they did not want to admit. Named after the eponymous detective hero of the TV series *Columbo,* who habitually used this technique to extract admissions of guilt.*

Come a cropper Have a bad accident or meet with serious misfortune.*

Come a gutser Means the same as *come a cropper.**

Come a purler Means the same as *come a cropper.*

Come across (1) Move from one group to another (e.g. 'he has come across from their group to ours'). (2) Discover (e.g. 'I was searching in the library yesterday when I came across this'). (3) Means the same as 'form a mental impression' (e.g. 'how does he come across to you?' means 'what does his appearance and behaviour make you think he is really like?').*

Come again? A request to repeat what has just been said.**

Come clean Confess to doing something.*

Come down (1) Become calmer. (2) Gain a more sensible, rather than idealistic or impractical, opinion of the situation.*

Come down like a ton of bricks Use considerable strength. The phrase is often used as a synonym for 'show extreme anger' (e.g. 'I'll come down on him like a ton of bricks if he disobeys me one more time').*

Come down off their high horse Become calmer or more relaxed after being angry or very moralistic.*

Come down to earth Become more rational and less emotional and/or unrealistic.*

Come down to earth with a bump Receive a *rude awakening.**

Come easy Be easily acquired.*

Come full circle Return, after temporary changes, to the way things were at the start.*

Come hell or high water In other words, come what may. The term is usually used as an assurance that the speaker will do what they have promised to do regardless of barriers in their way. The phrase basically means that even if the most awful calamities happen, the deed in question will be done.*

Come home to roost A problem that has 'come home to roost' is one that a person has created and hoped to avoid, but now must deal with.*

Come home to them Come to understand.*

Come in from the cold Be accepted by a group after a period of being unpopular.*

Come into line Conform to a set of standards, rules or regulations.*

Come into their own Begin working at what they are best suited.*

Come it strong Exaggerate.*

Come of age (1) Reach an age to be considered an adult in the laws of the country where a person is living (in the UK, 18 years). (2) In describing a process, institution or similar, reach a stage in development where it can be considered firmly established.*

Come off it An expression of doubt about what has just been said (e.g. 'come off it – that can't be true!').**

Come on (1) An expression meaning 'hurry up' (e.g. 'come on, we've got to leave soon or we'll be late'). (2) An expression indicating disbelief (e.g. 'come on, that can't be true!').**

Come on board Join a group or begin to support a cause or argument.*

Come on in Means 'come in'.*

Come on strong (1) Improve considerably. (2) Be very assertive or argumentative.*

Come on to Make amorous approaches to.*

Come out fighting In an argument or other confrontation, go immediately into attack rather than spend time in preliminary negotiations.*

Come out in the wash (1) Be solved. (2) Be explained or clarified.*

Come out of their shell Become less shy or cautious.*

Come out smelling of roses Emerge from a situation that was potentially damaging to the reputation with an unblemished record, or even an enhanced reputation.*

Come rain or shine A phrase used to describe something that is inevitable (e.g. 'we will have to do this, come rain or shine').*

Come the acid Be unpleasant (e.g. by making offensive or sarcastic comments).*

Come the old soldier Pretend to be ill in an attempt to avoid work.*

Come the raw prawn (1) Talk nonsense. (2) Lie.*

Come through for Succeed in doing something for someone. The phrase is usually applied to helping someone who has a problem.*

Come to a bad end Means the same as *come to a sticky end.*

Come to a boil Reach the point of greatest activity (a stage known as being *on the boil*); there is usually the implication that this is the climax of the activity, when most things will be resolved.*

Come to a grinding halt Slow down and stop.*

Come to a pretty pass Become unpleasant and/or worthy of criticism.*

Come to a sticky end Die in an unpleasant manner.*

Come to blows Become so angry in a dispute that people are close to becoming physically violent.*

Come to fruition (1) Reach a point where an activity produces the rewards that were planned and/or hoped for. (2) Reach maturity.*

Come to grief Suffer misfortune.*

Come to grips with Comprehend.*

Come to the boil Means the same as *come to a boil.*

Come to the crunch Reach a point where something must be done.*

Come to their senses Change to a more logical opinion or behaviour.*

Come to think of it A phrase that essentially means 'having thought more carefully' (e.g. 'although I dismissed your argument earlier, come to think of it you're probably correct').*

Come up against a brick wall Means the same as *hit a brick wall*.

Come up and see me sometime A light-hearted request that a person should call on the speaker in the future. The phrase was first used by a film actress called Mae West as a chat-up line in her films. However, today the phrase does not necessarily have that intention.*

Come up and see my etchings A light-hearted request that a person should call on the speaker in the future. The phrase was once used only as a euphemism for an invitation to have sexual intercourse, but it rarely has that implication these days (context should indicate which meaning is intended).*

Come up dry (1) Fail to find anything. (2) Fail.*

Come up roses Resolve in a fortuitous manner.*

Come up smelling of roses A person who 'comes up smelling of roses' emerges from a situation with no trace of scandal or wrongdoing being attributed to them. The phrase often indicates that it is strongly suspected that they are in reality guilty of something, but it has not been possible to find enough evidence to prove it.*

Come up smiling Be happy and content at the end of doing something. The phrase often implies that this happiness follows a period of unhappiness.*

Come up to scratch Meet an acceptable standard.*

Come up trumps Do something extremely well.*

Come up with the goods Means the same as *deliver the goods*.

Comes with the territory If something 'comes with the territory', then it is a disadvantageous or unappealing aspect of a situation. There is usually an implication that it is tolerated, because the benefits of the situation as a whole outweigh these concerns.*

Comfort food Food that creates a feeling of psychological comfort.*

Coming from Refers to the reason for a person's behaviour (e.g. 'where's he coming from?' means 'why is he behaving like that?').*

Coming out The process of coming *out of the closet*. The phrase is nearly always restricted to declarations of homosexuality.*

Coming out of their ears Possessing too much of something (e.g. a rich person might be said to have 'money coming out of their ears').*

Common as muck Derogatory phrase describing someone with very vulgar tastes and lacking in social etiquette or refinement, or the sort of items that such a person would consider acceptable or desirable. The phrase is often used by snobs to denote anyone who is working class, but the phrase can also be used about a nouveau riche person who has lots of money but very little aesthetic taste.**

Common or garden The most frequently encountered version of something, and by implication, uninteresting.*

Common touch The ability (particularly in someone who is a member of a 'higher' social class) to work or socialize with 'ordinary people'.*

Compare notes Exchange information and ideas on a particular topic. The phrase is often used when two or more people have been working independently on the same problem and are then brought together to discuss what they have found.*

Compliments of the house Free.*

Confucius says... The phrase is completed with a brief piece of advice, often enigmatic or humorous. The overt claim is that this is an example of the wisdom of the Eastern philosopher Confucius. On many occasions, the saying offered will not be by him, but instead is intended simply as a humorous observation (e.g. 'Confucius says no greater pleasure than seeing old friend fall off roof'). The sayings are often delivered in an imitation of some Chinese speakers who haven't quite mastered English constructions (e.g. 'Confucius he say...' etc.).*

Conjure up Create. The phrase is often used to describe creating something good from apparently meagre resources.*

Conjure with Contemplate.*

Conspicuous by their absence Absent from an event where they were expected. The phrase can refer to a person who has shirked their duties or someone who has deliberately stayed away from an event as a form of protest.*

Conspiracy of silence Refers to a group deliberately keeping something secret or refusing to comment on a particular matter.*

Control freak A person who has an obsessive or irrational need for everything to be done the way they want it, and who thus denies other people the opportunity to express themselves freely.*

Conversation piece A topic or item that is likely to generate a lot of discussion.*

Cook the books Engage in *creative accounting*.*

Cook their goose Make their life unpleasant, typically by punishing them or thwarting their plans.*

Cookie-cutter Describes something very predictable or composed of clichéd phrases and/or ideas.*

Cool as a cucumber Calm and without signs of panicking.*

Cool off Become calmer.*

Coon's age A long time ('coon' refers to a racoon).*

Cop a plea Try to negotiate.*

Cop hold of Grab.*

Cop it To receive punishment. See *fair cop*.*

Copybook See *blot on their copybook*.

Corn in Egypt Something that is plentiful.*

Corner See *box into a corner, cut corners, defend their corner, four corners of the earth, in a corner, in their corner, round the corner* and *turn the corner*.

Corridors of power Term describing the workings of government.*

Cost an arm and a leg Cost a great deal of money. Hence *give an arm and a leg* means to spend a great deal of money.*

Cost the Earth Be very expensive.*

Cotton on Learn.*

Cotton wool See *wrap in cotton wool*.

Couch potato A person who leads a lazy life and whose leisure hours are spent watching television, typically with the implication that they watch programmes of little intellectual merit whilst consuming beer and snack foods.*

Could care less A phrase that is being increasingly commonly used to mean 'couldn't care less'. The context should indicate if this is the intended meaning of the speaker.*

Could eat a horse If someone says that they 'could eat a horse', then they are very hungry. The phrase should not be taken literally.*

Could hear a pin drop It was very quiet.*

Couldn't...their way out of a paper bag The blank space is filled with a verb (common ones are 'box' and 'fight'). The phrase means that someone is too poor at

---

* denotes level of impoliteness

the skill described for them to be effective (e.g. if someone 'couldn't box their way out of a paper bag' then they are physically weak and/or a bad boxer).*

Couldn't care less Have no interest or concern.*

Couldn't give a... The phrase is followed by a single word or another phrase. The meaning is that the speaker has no interest in whatever is under discussion. The phrase varies enormously in politeness depending upon the precise words used. See *couldn't give a damn, couldn't give a fuck* and *couldn't give a toss* for examples.* or ** or ***

Couldn't give a damn In other words, to have no interest in whatever is being discussed. The term might originally be 'couldn't give a dam' (the 'dam' being an Indian coin of low value).**

Couldn't give a fig Means the same as *couldn't give a damn*, but slightly less rude.*

Couldn't give a fuck Means the same as *couldn't give a damn*, but much ruder.***

Couldn't give a monkey's Means the same as *couldn't give a damn*.**

Couldn't give a tinker's cuss Means the same as *couldn't give a damn*, but slightly less rude.*

Couldn't give a toss Means the same as *couldn't give a damn*.**

Couldn't organize a piss-up in a brewery The phrase essentially means 'too stupid to do even the simplest task'. A 'piss-up' is a drinking party (see *pissed*). Since a brewery is by definition full of alcoholic beverages, someone would have to be uncommonly stupid not to be able to organize a drinking party in such a location.***

Couldn't run a whelk stall An insult accusing someone of being too stupid to do a particular task. The implication is that running a whelk stall is a very easy task (whether it is or not has never, to the author's knowledge, been empirically examined), and if someone couldn't do that, then they certainly couldn't do whatever the task is under discussion.*

Counsel of despair Something attempted with little hope of it succeeding after everything else that could be attempted has failed.*

Counsel of perfection A solution that would work but is not pragmatic.*

Count on the fingers of one hand Describes something that is very rare (e.g. 'you can count on the fingers of one hand how often that has happened').*

Count sheep A method of inducing sleep (repetitively counting individual members of an imaginary flock is supposed to have a soothing effect).*

Count the cost Calculate the expense. Typically, this is the expense of repairing damage resulting from something going wrong or an unexpected accident.*

Count the pennies Be cautious in spending money.*

Count to ten Intentionally wait before saying something, so that what is said is considered rather than rash. The phrase is often given as advice when someone is in danger of losing their temper when about to make a reply.*

Count your chickens See *don't count your chickens.*

Courage in both hands See *take courage in both hands.*

Courage of their convictions See *have the courage of their convictions.*

Cover all the bases Means the same as *touch all the bases.*

Cover the costs Pay what is owed.*

Cover their back Protect against criticism.*

Cover their tracks To remove evidence of being responsible for something.*

Cover up Hide. The phrase generally refers to attempts to hide errors or misdoings.*

Cows come home See *until the cows come home.*

Crack a book Engage in study.*

Crack a bottle Open a bottle of an alcoholic drink (and by implication, have a drink).*

Crack heads together Means the same as *bang heads together.*

Crack of dawn Very early morning, when the sky is just becoming light.*

Crack of doom An ominous and/or loud noise. The phrase is derived from the noise which, according to the Bible, will be heard on the Day of Judgement.*

Crack of the whip See *fair crack of the whip.*

Crack up (1) Burst into laughter. (2) Suffer a nervous breakdown or experience severe mental distress.*

Cracked up to be See *not all it's cracked up to be.*

Cradle snatching Choosing a sexual or marital partner considerably younger. Note that there is no implication of paedophilia – the issue is the age difference, not the absolute age of the younger person.*

Cramp their style Make it difficult for another person to perform at their best.*

Crash and burn Fail.*

Crash course A rapid course of instruction that covers basic information and little else.*

Crash out (1) Sleep or fall asleep. (2) Become unconscious.*

Crawl out of the woodwork Someone who 'crawls out of the woodwork' is an unpleasant person who appears when there are opportunities for personal gain.*

Crawling with... If a place is crawling with ants, then there are a lot of ants; if a place is crawling with people, then there are a lot of people. The image presumably comes from the fact that insects crawl, and thus something infested with insects might be said to be crawling with them. From this the image has extended to talking about places crowded with people.*

Crazy like a fox Describing someone who appears to be doing something insane, but who in reality is acting with great cunning.*

Creative accounting Accountancy procedures designed to hide the true state of affairs. The term originally meant actions that were illegal, but can also mean producing a set of figures which, whilst not actually illegal, are not as forthright as they might be.*

Creature of habit Someone who has a set routine for doing things and thus how they will behave in certain situations is easily predicted. There is sometimes the implication that a person who is a creature of habit will be annoyed if their routine is altered. *

Credibility gap The difference between what is claimed to be true and what is actually true.*

Credit where credit is due Praise should be given where it is merited. The phrase is often used to describe a good deed by someone who is generally seen in a negative light (e.g. 'although Brian was usually incompetent, credit where credit is due – he did plan the party very well').*

Crest of a wave See *on the crest of a wave.*

Crimp See *put a crimp in.*

Crocodile tears An insincere display of sorrow or regret.*

Crook See *be crook on* and *go crook.*

Cross as two sticks Annoyed.*

Cross my heart and hope to die A phrase used to indicate the sincerity of a promise. The phrase is likely to be used in a joking manner these days, but when originally used, was a more serious oath.*

Cross purposes Two people or groups are 'at cross purposes' when either side mis-

---

* *denotes level of impoliteness*

understands what the other side is trying to say. The phrase is often used to describe two groups or people who, if they had communicated accurately with each other, would be in agreement. However, because they have misunderstood each other, they are arguing.*

Cross swords Argue.*

Cross that bridge when we come to it Recognize that there is a problem that will need to be solved in the future, but decide not to spend time either worrying about it or making plans on how to deal with it until the time when it has to be dealt with (e.g. 'at some point in the future we would have to deal with the problem of how to tell our parents; however, we decided that for the moment we would enjoy ourselves and cross that bridge when we came to it').*

Cross the floor Change allegiance to a group previously opposed.*

Cross the Rubicon Make a decision that commits to a particular course of action.*

Cross their fingers Hope that a plan is successful.*

Cross their palm with silver Pay money.*

Cross to bear A burden or difficulty that is a constant feature of a person's daily life. The phrase is derived from Christianity, and is heard in the longer phrase 'we all have our crosses to bear' (or similar). The phrase is often used as a mild rebuke to someone who has been complaining about their misfortunes, since there is an implication that everyone has problems that have to be dealt with without making a fuss.*

Crowning glory The supreme achievement or feature amongst a collection of impressive or praiseworthy things.*

Cruel to be kind Something that appears unpleasant in the immediate term, but in the long term will be beneficial.*

Cruising for a bruising Behaving in a manner likely to result in problems (e.g. being physically attacked).*

Crumbs from the table An inappropriately small share.*

Cry all the way to the bank To be rich in spite of being criticized for what one does. The origin of the phrase is in the idea that an artist who produces work which the public adores (and buys) but which the critics hate may cry at the critics' comments, but they will cry all the way to the bank where they will deposit lots and lots of money.*

Cry for the moon Be illogically upset because something unattainable cannot be had.*

Cry foul Protest that something is unjust.*

Cry from the heart A request or plea that expresses a deeply held emotion.*

Cry their eyes out Be extremely upset.*

Cry wolf Make a protest or warning that is ignored because previous protests or warnings have been false or inaccurate.*

Crying over spilt milk Protest or cry over something that has happened and cannot be repaired or rectified. The phrase is often heard in the form *no use crying over spilt milk*, which means that it is pointless crying or protesting about something bad that has happened, because this will not solve the problem.*

Crystal ball Any method of trying to anticipate what will happen in the future.*

Crystal ball gazing Speculating on what will happen in the future. Usually it is implied that this is a forlorn task.*

Cuckoo in the nest An unwelcome interloper.*

Cudgel their brains Work hard at solving a problem.*

Cultivate their garden Deal with personal matters.*

Cultural baggage A set of preconceptions created by being raised in a particular culture. These preconceptions may mar or distort understanding.*

Culture shock Feeling of stress or bewilderment caused by being unable to comprehend or react appropriately to a radical change in environment or culture.*

Culture vulture A person who is keen on the arts.*

Cunning plan See *I have a cunning plan.*

Cup runneth over A Biblical phrase meaning that someone is overwhelmed with happiness and riches.*

Cups See *in their cups.*

Curate's egg Something which is good in parts, bad in others. The phrase is derived from a cartoon in the (now defunct) magazine *Punch*, in which a sycophantic curate, rather than reject a bad egg (accidentally) given to him by a bishop at the breakfast table, declares that parts of it are quite excellent.*

Curious bed-fellows People who are on friendly terms with each other whom one would not predict would be such, because of different personalities, interests, etc. The term does not necessarily imply a sexual relationship.*

Curry favour Attempt to win favour. The phrase is often used disparagingly to describe someone who is being obsequious.*

Curtain twitcher A person who is obsessively interested in the activities of their neighbours.*

Cushion the blow Something that 'cushions the blow' reduces the pain or unpleasantness of unwelcome information (e.g. 'news that she had been accepted by Oxford cushioned the blow that she had been rejected by Harvard').*

Cut a dash Dress and/or behave in a very stylish manner likely to attract attention.*

Cut a deal Make an agreement.*

Cut a long story short Summarize a story or piece of information, or only provide the conclusion or other important information. The phrase is nearly always used when a speaker has spent too long describing something and now wants to hurry through the rest of it.*

Cut a rug Dance energetically.*

Cut a swathe through Comprehensively defeat or refute.*

Cut above Of higher quality.*

Cut and dried Completely settled.*

Cut and run Escape. The phrase is derived from nautical terminology – it has nothing to do with stabbing or similar.*

Cut and thrust Describes a situation which is highly competitive.*

Cut bait Means the same as *cut the cackle.*

Cut both ways Something that 'cuts both ways' has advantages and disadvantages and/or favours more than one side in a dispute.*

Cut corners Do a less thorough job than originally planned in order to save time, cost and/or energy.*

Cut dead Totally ignore a person in situations where they might have expected some attention to be paid to them.*

Cut down to size Make a person with an overly high opinion of themselves aware of their true status.*

Cut from a different cloth Very different in personality.*

Cut from the same cloth Very similar in personality.*

Cut it (1) Be of acceptable quality. (2) An abbreviated form of *cut it out.*

Cut it fine Do something with little allowance made for error or time. The phrase normally is used to indicate that something was done with very little time to spare.*

Cut it out A demand that someone stops doing something. The phrase is usually used to try to stop people doing something annoying or irritating.*

denotes level of impoliteness

Cut loose (1) Begin to think and/or act independently. (2) Exhibit unrestrained behaviour.*

Cut losses Abandon a project even though it will mean losing money and/or effort, because it is clear that the project will not succeed, even if more money and/or effort is put into it (i.e. losses are inevitable so stopping now will at least keep the losses as small as possible).*

Cut no ice Have no influence.*

Cut of his/her jib What someone appears to be like. The phrase nearly always is preceded with 'I don't like the...', meaning that the speaker doesn't like the appearance of the person in question. The term is a nautical one, referring to the surmised state of a vessel based on the appearance of the jib (one of the main sails).*

Cut off at the pass To intercept. The phrase is derived from western films, where a cliché command was to 'cut them off at the pass' (i.e. intercept them at the pass).*

Cut off in their prime Prevented from continuing working when exhibiting their greatest period of productivity.*

Cut off their nose to spite their face A person who would 'cut off their nose to spite their face' would damage themselves in their attempts to harm or disadvantage someone else.*

Cut out for Be ideally suited for a particular task or occupation.*

Cut some slack Be less demanding.*

Cut the... followed by a word or phrase (e.g. *cut the cackle*). Used by a listener interrupting a speaker, it means that the listener is bored with the speaker telling irrelevant or dull things, and wants the speaker to *cut to the chase.* ** or ***
Note: politeness varies according to the word used at the end of the phrase.

Cut the apron strings To become independent of one's parents.*

Cut the cackle A demand to *cut to the chase.* **

Cut the cord Means the same as *cut the umbilical cord.*

Cut the Gordian knot Solve a problem in a direct manner without getting sidetracked by niceties. The phrase is derived from the ancient legend that whoever could unravel the Gordian knot (a very intricate knotted rope) would conquer Asia. Alexander the Great took the simple expedient of severing the knot with his sword (and went on to conquer Asia Minor).*

Cut the ground from under their feet Conclusively demonstrate that the reasoning or justification for an opponent's arguments or actions is false or illogical.*

Cut the mustard Be of acceptable quality and/or vigour.*

Cut the umbilical cord Can mean the same as *cut the apron strings,* but is also used to denote becoming independent of anyone or anything that one has previously relied upon for help.*

Cut their teeth on Describes the first thing a person gains experience of in a particular area of work (e.g. 'I cut my teeth on lecturing to sociology students').*

Cut to ribbons Means the same as *cut to shreds.*

Cut to shreds (1) Comprehensively disprove an argument. (2) Humiliate.*

Cut to the bone Reduce to the bare minimum necessary. Often used of financial cutbacks when a company is in difficulties.*

Cut to the chase Move to the important part of the story, missing out unnecessary detail. The phrase can be used by a person impatient to hear the important part of the story (in which case, the phrase has a higher emotional level). Alternatively, the phrase can be used by a speaker to indicate that they are going to omit irrelevant details and just concentrate on the important bits of their story. The phrase is derived from movies, where the change from one scene to the next can be called a 'cut'. Hence, a 'cut to the chase' is a move to an exciting chase scene.* or **

Cut to the quick Make someone upset by a particularly unpleasant insult or tactless remark.*

Cut up nasty Means the same as *cut up rough*.

Cut up rough Be aggressive or awkward.*

Cut with a knife See *atmosphere that could be cut with a knife*.

Cut your cloth Means the same as *cut your coat according to your cloth*.

Cut your coat according to your cloth Make the best use of what has been given to you.*
Note: the phrase can be used in other forms (e.g. 'he must cut his coat according to his cloth'), but the 'your' form is the commonest.

Cuts both ways If something 'cuts both ways' then it applies to two people or groups, rather than just one person or group. The phrase is usually used to indicate that if person or group A has to do something to please person or group B, then person or group B has to do something to please person or group A as well.*

Cutting edge The most advanced form of something (typically technology or research). Thus, 'cutting edge stuff' is something that is technologically highly advanced.*

D

D-Day A day when an important decision will be made or an important project will be initiated. The term is a reference to the Allied invasion of Normandy in World War II, which was coded 'D-Day'.*

Dab hand Expert.*

Daft as a brush The term simply means being silly. The words are deliberately nonsensical.*

Daft on the right side Behave in an apparently eccentric or insane manner but which serves the self-interest of the person concerned.*

Daggers drawn Describes a situation in which two sides are bitter enemies.*

Damage control Activity designed to minimize the adverse reaction to a piece of scandal or unfavourable news.*

Damn all Nothing.**

Damn all to show for it Describes a situation where after a lengthy period of activity, nothing worthwhile has been produced.**

Damn straight Absolutely true.**

Damn with faint praise Describe something in such a lacklustre fashion that it implies criticism (e.g. describing something as 'alright, I suppose').*

Damned if you do, damned if you don't A description of a *no-win situation*.*

Damp squib Something that promises much, but fails to impress.*

Damsel in distress A woman in need of help. The phrase is derived from fairy stories and similar of a young, helpless (and attractive) woman in need of rescuing by a brave (and handsome) *knight in shining armour*. The phrase is used sarcastically and, given its connotations, might in some circumstances be seen as sexist.*

Dance attendance on Be extremely helpful.*

Dance on their grave Show disrespect for the memory of a dead person.*

Dance to their tune Obey someone else's wishes.*

Dangle a carrot Offer a person a reward to entice them into doing something or as an incentive to work harder. See *carrot and stick*.*

Dare See *I dare you.*

Dark horse Someone about whom too little is known for an accurate description to be made.*

Darken their door Visit someone. The phrase is these days often used jokingly. In early usage of the phrase, 'never darken my door again' was meant as a serious warning to someone not to visit again.*

Davy Jones's locker Underwater. Thus, someone who is 'in Davy Jones's locker' has drowned.*

Day in, day out Describes a regularly occurring event, often with the implication that a monotonous activity is being described.*

Day of reckoning (1) The day when a person is made to answer for an error or sinful act. (2) The day when a person discovers if they have succeeded (or failed) at something. *

Daylight robbery A rather exaggerated way of saying that something is expensive (e.g. 'five pounds for a bottle of lemonade? – that's daylight robbery').*

Daylights See *beat the daylights out* and *scare the daylights.*

Days are numbered A person or item whose 'days are numbered' has not long to last before death, destruction or being made obsolete.*

Dead and buried Absolutely finished with no prospect of being returned to.*

Dead as a dodo (1) Absolutely certainly dead. (2) Of no further interest. The dodo is an extinct species of bird.*

Dead as a doornail Absolutely certainly dead. A doornail is a component of a door knocker.*

Dead cat bounce Misleading signs of activity or promise in something that in reality is of no further use. The phrase is used in stocks and shares trading. Shares in a company heading for bankruptcy will show a dramatic fall followed by a slight rise. This may look like the start of a revival in fortunes, but more probably the rise will be small and temporary ('the dead cat bounce'). The analogy is that if a dead cat is dropped from a high building, it will bounce when it hits the pavement, but it's still a dead cat, and will not suddenly bounce back up to the top of the building. (Whether empirical proof of this has been attempted is uncertain.) *

Dead end Means the same as *blind alley.*

Dead from the neck down Intelligent, but with no discernible emotions.*

Dead from the neck up Stupid.*

Dead in the water Incapable of functioning effectively. Hence, an easy target for attack.*

Dead letter Something that is no longer done. The phrase is often used to describe defunct laws or outmoded practices.*

Dead man's shoes Describes an organisation where the only way to gain promotion is for someone more senior to die or leave, whereupon a more junior person will be promoted to *fill their shoes.* The implication is that being clever or innovative in such an organisation will not be rewarded with rapid promotion.*

Dead meat Vulnerable to attack.*

Dead of night In the early hours of the morning, when the majority of people are asleep. *

Dead of winter The coldest period of winter.*

Dead on their feet Exhausted.*

Dead ringer An exact copy or double of something. 'Dead' means in this sense 'absolute'. *

Dead to the world Very deeply asleep.*

Dead wrong Absolutely wrong. 'Dead' in this sense means 'absolutely'.*

Deadlier than the male A shortening of a quotation from a poem by Rudyard Kipling which argues that the female of the species is deadlier than the male. The phrase is generally used when a woman has done something particularly vicious. The phrase is potentially sexist, and caution should be applied in using it.*

Death on… An unpleasant or dangerous example of the category cited in the next word or phrase – e.g. 'death on two legs' is an unpleasant person.*

Death warmed up See *like death warmed up.*

Decisions, decisions Said by someone when overworked and having to make a difficult choice. The phrase can also be used ironically (e.g. when there are no difficult decisions to be made).*

Deep doo-doo Slightly ruder version of *deep trouble.* **

Deep pockets A person with 'deep pockets' is wealthy.*

Deep trouble Very serious trouble.*

Deep waters Something very complex and/or problematic.*

Deeply engrained Means the same as *dyed in the wool.*

Default option The choice that is taken if other options prove unsatisfactory.*

Defend their corner Vigorously defend an argument or point of view.*

Deliver the goods Do what is hoped for.*

Demon drink Alcoholic beverage.*

Deserts See *just deserts.*

Deuce of a… A very difficult… (e.g. 'a deuce of a problem' is 'a very difficult problem').*

Deuce to pay Trouble (e.g. 'there'll be deuce to pay about this mess').*

Developed into an art form Means the same as *got it down to a fine art.*

Devil See entries below and: *be a devil, between the Devil and the deep blue sea, play Devil's advocate, play silly devils, raise the Devil, sell soul to the Devil, sup with the Devil* and *talk of the Devil.*

Devil-may-care Describes the behaviour of a person apparently unconcerned with the consequences of their actions.*

Devil of a… Means the same as *deuce of a…*

Devil to pay Means the same as *deuce to pay.*

Devil's own Something that is an extreme version of something.*

Diamond in the rough Means the same as *rough diamond.*

Dice with death Do something dangerous.*

Did the Earth move for you? (1) The phrase originally meant 'did you have an orgasm?' after an unintentionally risible line in a novel by Hemingway. It is still sometimes used in a sexual context. (2) More recently, the phrase has been used in a wider context, to mean 'did you find something highly enjoyable?'**

Diddly squat See *got diddly squat.*

Die See entries below and: *cross my heart and hope to die, do or die, straight as a die* and *to die for.*

Die hard Be difficult to get rid of.*

Die in bed Die from disease or another 'natural' cause.*

Die in harness Die whilst still in paid employment.*

Die is cast Something is decided. The phrase refers to a die used in a game (often erroneously called 'a dice' which in fact is the plural of 'die') – once the die has been cast (i.e. thrown) the outcome is known.*

Die laughing To laugh a great deal (e.g. 'you'll die laughing at the new comedy show'). The phrase is an exaggeration. Although there are recorded cases of people dying after an extended bout of laughing, this is extremely rare.*

Die like flies Die in large numbers.*

Die of boredom The phrase is usually in the longer form of 'I could die of

---

* denotes level of impoliteness

boredom', and is used to express a state of extreme boredom. The phrase is a deliberate exaggeration; boredom is not noted as a major cause of death, otherwise the inhabitants of several English towns (e.g. Barrow-in-Furness) would have a very high mortality rate.*

Die on the vine Fail at an early stage.*

Died with their boots on Died whilst still employed. The phrase originally referred to soldiers who died in battle ('They Died With Their Boots On' was the title of a film about Custer's last stand).*

Different ball game Means the same as *new ball game.*

Different kettle of fish Radically different. See *pretty kettle of fish.**

Dig a hole for themselves Work ineffectively, making the situation worse than it was before.*

Dig a pit for Prepare a trap.*

Dig deep Use a large amount of (e.g. 'he dug deep into his reserves of strength and lifted the heavy weight').*

Dig in (1) Prepare to be attacked. (2) Eat. (3) In the phrase 'get a dig in' or similar, it means to criticize or insult someone or something.*

Dig in the ribs Poke another person in the ribs with an elbow. The action is done to either warn of danger or alert them to something funny.*

Dig in their heels Be obstinate.*

Dig their own grave A person who 'digs their own grave' does something that damages themselves. The phrase is generally used to describe something done unwittingly.*

Dig up dirt Through investigation, find damaging information that the people affected had hoped would not be discovered.*

Dim view See *take a dim view.*

Dime a dozen Commonplace.*

Diminishing returns (1) The principle that the more a person has of something, the less attractive each additional quantity becomes. For example, a starving man might rate a plate of cake very highly, but having eaten ten plates of cake, it is doubtful if the eleventh plate has the same appeal as the first. (2) Similarly, the principle that the reward gained from extra effort diminishes the more effort that is applied.*

Dingo's breakfast Nothing.*

Dip their toes in Make a tentative first attempt at something.*

Dirty linen See *wash dirty linen in public.*

Disappear down a crack in the floor Means the same as *let the earth swallow me up.*

Disappear up their own backside Slightly ruder version of *disappear up their own fundament.****

Disappear up their own fundament A contemptuous phrase describing the behaviour of someone who displays intelligence but lacks the ability to make any practical use of their skills.**

Disgusted of Tunbridge Wells A UK phrase that is intended to describe someone of very conservative opinions who finds any innovation (e.g. pop music) something to get cross about. The phrase comes from a habit of signing letters to newspapers and magazines with pseudonyms such as 'disgusted', 'angry taxpayer' etc. Tunbridge Wells is a small, inoffensive town, but is often used jokingly as a place where the sort of person who enjoys writing angry letters to newspapers might live.*

Dish it out Provide something. The phrase is often used to describe providing gossip or insults.*

Dish the dirt Gossip.*

Disturb a hornets' nest See *stir up a hornets' nest.*

Divide and rule Maintaining supremacy over opponents by encouraging them to fight amongst themselves rather than uniting in opposition.*

Do a disappearing act (1) Escape. (2) Make oneself hard to find when there is a difficult situation to be faced and/or hard work to be done.*

Do a number on Treat badly.*

Do a runner Escape (particularly from the police).*

Do bears crap in the woods? Means the same as *can a duck swim?****

Do bird Spend time in prison.*

Do for Work for. The phrase is particularly used of cleaning personnel. See *done for.**

Do it in their sleep Means the same as *do it standing on their head.*

Do it standing on their head Do something with little effort because the task is to them an easy one.*

Do it with a hand tied behind their back Means the same as *do it standing on their head.*

Do justice to Do something that is of suitable quality.*

Do or die (1) Describes a situation where something must be done or something very unpleasant will happen. (2) Describes an heroic attitude to being willing to do something dangerous even if it results in death.*

Do porridge Means the same as *do bird.*

Do the business (1) Do what is expected in the situation. (2) Have sexual intercourse.* (1) or *** (2)

Do the dirty (1) Behave badly towards someone. (2) Have sexual intercourse.* (1) or *** (2)

Do the honours Do a task for or on behalf of a group (e.g. carve the turkey at Christmas dinner, give a speech on behalf of a group, etc.).*

Do the rounds Be disseminated widely.*

Do the trick Achieve the desired outcome.*

Do their bit Contribute to something. There is usually the implication that a person who has 'done their bit' has already contributed or done as much as can be reasonably expected of them.*

Do their damnedest Try very hard.**

Do their head in (1) Become hopelessly confused (e.g. 'the problem's so hard it's enough to do your head in'). (2) Physically assault someone (e.g. 'if you don't watch it I'll do your head in'). (3) Become angry.* (1 and 3) or ** (2)

Do their lolly Means the same as *do their nut.*

Do their nut Become very angry.

Do their worst Enact their most extreme measures or something which shows their abilities to their full extent.*

Do them proud Do something that would make others proud of you. The phrase is often said to describe a well-run funeral (e.g. 'you did Aunt Gladys proud').*

Do themselves a mischief Cause injury to themselves.*

Do themselves justice If a person 'does themselves justice' then they do something that accurately exhibits their skills.*

Do to death Repeat a performance or act so many times that it loses all entertainment value and becomes boring.*

Dob them Inform on someone.*

Doctor ordered See *just what the doctor ordered.*

Doctors and nurses See *play doctors and nurses.*

Dodge the column Malinger or otherwise avoid work.*

Doesn't know Christmas from Bourke Street Australian phrase used to describe a not very intelligent person (Christmas traditionally has brightly lit trees, decorations, etc.; Bourke Street in Melbourne is noted for its lighting, displays, etc.). Names of other brightly lit streets may be used instead.*

Dog The term has two very different colloquial meanings. (1) When referring to a man, it is a term of joking approval for rather daring or risqué behaviour (e.g. 'you dog, sir'). (2) However, when applied to a woman, it is an insulting remark, meaning that she is ugly. See also *life in the old dog yet*.* (1) or *** (2)

Dog and bone Phone.*

Dog and pony show A visually attractive display.*

Dog days The hottest days of the year.*

Dog eat dog Vicious competition.*

Dog in the manger A person who doesn't need or want something, but makes sure that nobody else gets it (even though they may have a genuine need for it).*

Dog my cats An expression of astonishment.*

Dog tired Exhausted.*

Dog's age A long time.*

Dog's bollocks Curiously, given the normal use of the word 'bollocks' (see *bollocks*), this is an expression of praise (albeit not a very polite one). For example, 'this is the best computer available – it's the dog's bollocks'. The origins of the phrase are obscure, but it may come from a longer saying 'it's as clear as the bollocks on a dog that this is the best'.**

Dog's breakfast Means the same as *dog's* dinner.

Dog's dinner (1) An incoherent mixture of mismatching things. (2) A visually unappealing and over-ostentatious manner of dress (hence, *dressed like a dog's dinner*). Named after the assortment of leftovers from human meals that get fed to some dogs.*

Dog's life A life of hardship and unpleasantness.*

Dogs of war Mercenaries.*

Done and dusted Absolutely finished.*

Done deal Something already settled.*

Done for Destined for an unpleasant fate. The phrase nearly always means destined to die or become irreparably damaged. See *do for*.*

Done in (1) Murdered. (2) Very tired.*

Donkey See entries below and: *like giving a donkey strawberries*.

Donkey work Physically demanding and/or laborious work that is relatively uninteresting.*

Donkey's years A long period of time.*

Don't ask me The phrase is used as a reply to a question and indicates that the person does not know the answer. There is usually the implication that it was illogical to ask the question (e.g. 'don't ask me – you know that I wasn't there, so how could I possibly tell you what happened?').*

Don't be a stranger A phrase in general social use meaning that the person should stay in contact with the speaker.*

Don't be blonde Don't be stupid. The phrase is potentially offensive and care should be taken in using it.***

Don't bet on it Meaning 'it's not certain'.*

Don't come crying to me Means the same as *don't come running to me*.

Don't come running to me A warning that something is inevitably going to produce problems, and that the speaker will have no sympathy when this happens, because the problems could have been foreseen and thus avoided.*

Don't count your chickens The start of a longer saying – 'don't count your chickens until they're hatched'. The phrase advises a person not to anticipate something and make plans based on this anticipated outcome, but instead to wait to see what actually happens. Thus, *count your chickens* is to assume optimistically and perhaps mistakenly that something is going to happen the way it was planned.*

Don't get mad, get even Instead of just complaining about something, do something to resolve the problem.*

Don't get your knickers in a twist Means 'don't get over-excited' or 'don't get so annoyed'.**

Don't give a... See entries beginning *couldn't give a...*

Don't give a rat's ass Have no interest or concern.***

Don't give up the day job A negative comment about the quality of something a person produces in pursuing a hobby. In effect, the comment means 'don't give up your full-time job, because if you tried to earn money from what you produce as a hobby, you'd never get anyone to buy it'. The phrase is often used jokingly, rather than as a deeply felt insult.*

Don't go there (1) Don't enquire in too much detail. (2) Don't try to imagine the situation described.*

Don't have a cat in hell's chance See *cat in hell's chance.*

Don't have a hope in hell Means the same as *don't have a cat in hell's chance.*

Don't hide your light under a bushel See *hide their light under a bushel.*

Don't hold your breath See *hold their breath.*

Don't know from Adam To fail to recognize (e.g. 'Do you know this person?' – 'I've never seen him before; I don't know him from Adam').*

Don't know the half of it See *half of it.*

Don't know their arse from their elbow A phrase used to describe a person who is not intellectually gifted or lacks the knowledge required in a particular situation.***

Don't know they are born A rather contemptuous phrase indicating that some people do not realize how fortunate their lives have been and lack experience of hardship or difficulties.*

Don't lay a finger on... A warning not to physically harm someone.*

Don't look a gift horse in the mouth See *look a gift horse in the mouth.*

Don't mince words A demand that something is said clearly and directly.*

Don't pay the ferryman Don't pay someone until they have completed the task.*

Don't put all your eggs in one basket In other words, don't rely on just one thing or spend all your time on just one project or activity. The implication is that if a person relies on just one thing and it fails, then they have nothing else. For example, in investment, it's unwise to invest in just one company's shares. The phrase originates with the idea that if a person has a lot of eggs, what happens if he or she puts them all in one basket and that basket gets dropped? *

Don't shoot the messenger See *shoot the messenger.*

Don't take no for an answer See *no for an answer.*

Don't tell me The phrase is used before the speaker says something that is an obvious logical conclusion from what has just been said. For example, if someone says 'Harry came into the room balancing a box of eggs on top of a pile of papers he was carrying', another person might reply 'don't tell me – he dropped everything and broke the eggs'.*

Don't waste your breath See *waste their breath.*

Doom and gloom A pervading feeling of unavoidable misery.*

Door to door (1) Visiting all houses in a district. (2) The complete journey from one place to another.*

Dos and don'ts Rules.*

Dose of their own medicine Means the same as *taste of their own medicine.*

Dot the i's and cross the t's Make sure that everything is correct. The phrase is particularly used for checking documents.*

Double bind A difficult situation in which any solution is likely to create further problems.*

Double-edged sword Something that confers advantages but also carries disadvantages. *

Double or nothing Means the same as *double or quits.*

Double or quits A gamble in which a person who already owes money agrees to take a further gamble or engage in a competition. If the person wins, then they no longer owe any money. If they lose, then they owe double the money they previously owed. *

Doubting Thomas A person who refuses to accept something without very strong proof. Named after Jesus's disciple of the same name who refused to accept the Resurrection until he had seen Christ's wounds with his own eyes.*

Down and dirty (1) Sexually explicit. (2) Unappealing.**

Down and out (1) A homeless person, often by implication with an addiction problem as well. (2) Utterly defeated.*

Down at heel Looking unkempt. It is usually implied that this appearance is due to poverty rather than choice.*

Down in the dumps Miserable.*

Down in the mouth Depressed.*

Down in the world Lowered socio-economic status.*

Down on their luck In a state of misfortune.*

Down the drain Wasted. The phrase is often used of money that has been foolishly spent on something useless.*

Down the pan Failed.**

Down the river See *sell down the river.*

Down the road (1) In the future. (2) At a location nearby.*

Down to a fine art See *got it down to a fine art.*

Down to earth Realistic and unpretentious.*

Down to the ground Completely.*

Down to the line Describes a race or other competition where the competitors are evenly matched and the result cannot be predicted until the competitors cross the finishing line/the event is finished.*

Down to the wire Means the same as *down to the line.*

Downwardly mobile Declining in socio-economic status.*

Drag ass Move quickly.**

Drag on Be tedious.*

Drag their feet Be unwilling; typically, displaying this lack of enthusiasm by doing things slowly or constantly delaying starting something.*

Drag their heels Means the same as *drag their feet.*

Drag their name through the mud Means the same as *drag through the dirt.*

Drag through the dirt Publicly attack someone or something, typically publicising unpleasant or embarrassing information.*

Drama queen Someone who tends to be over-dramatic in their behaviour and exaggerates problems and successes.*

Draw a blank To fail to find or attain what was hoped for. For example, fail to recognize (e.g. 'I'd like to help you but I've drawn a blank; I've no recollection of the event at all'); fail to find (e.g. 'although they searched everywhere they drew a blank and the bracelet was not found'); fail to win (e.g. 'although they hoped to win what should have been an easy match, they drew a blank').*

Draw a line under If a line is drawn under something, it indicates that it is finished, and something new has begun.*

Draw first blood See *first blood*.

Draw in their horns Show more restrained behaviour.*

Draw stumps Stop doing something.*

Draw the line Establish what constitutes the limits of acceptable behaviour.*

Draw the short straw (1) Be selected to do something unpleasant that would not be done voluntarily. (2) Be unlucky.*

Draw their fire Cause a person to attack something other than their original intended target.*

Drawing board See *back to the drawing board*.

Dress rehearsal A practice of an event replicating, as far as possible, the actual conditions of the event itself.*

Dressed like a dog's dinner See *dog's dinner*.

Dressed to kill Being attractively dressed. There is typically an implication that what is being worn emphasizes the person's sexual attractiveness.*

Dressed to the nines In very glamorous and/or smart clothes.*

Dressed up to the nines Very smartly dressed.*

Drink like a fish Drink excessively.*

Drink under the table Drink more alcohol than another person or persons without passing out, being sick, or similar.*

Drink with the flies Drink alone.*

Drinking in the last chance saloon Making one final attempt to do something properly.*

Drinks are on them They will pay for the drinks.*

Drive a coach and horses through it Disprove an argument that is logically or factually weak (e.g. 'that's ridiculous – I could drive a coach and horses through that').*

Drive home Ensure that something is fully understood through the use of forceful argument.*

Drive up the wall Annoy.*

Driving at See *what are they driving at?*

Drop a bombshell Provide a piece of unexpected information. It is usually implied that the information is unpleasant.*

Drop a brick Means the same as *drop a clanger*.

Drop a clanger To make a mistake, usually with the implication that it is an embarrassing one. The phrase often is used to describe making an embarrassing remark.*

Drop a hint Make a hint or suggestion.*

Drop a line Write a letter or note to someone.*

Drop a word in their ear Informally tell someone. The phrase is generally used in situations where the person being told holds a position of power, and is being approached informally rather than via official procedures.*

Drop dead (1) Die suddenly. (2) An offensive remark indicating displeasure at someone. The phrase is often used as a vigorous denial or response to something.* (1) or ** (2)

Drop everything Abandon all ongoing activity. The phrase is usually used to describe appropriate behaviour in an emergency, when a very serious problem needs to be tackled immediately.*

Drop in Pay a visit.*

Drop in it Get someone into trouble. This can be deliberate (e.g. informing an

---

* *denotes level of impoliteness*

authority figure of someone's misdeeds) or accidental (e.g. a chance remark implicating someone in a misdeed). Sometimes the phrase indicates a situation where a person accidentally gets themselves into trouble by accident (more commonly the phrase in this circumstance will be *drop themselves in it*).*

Drop in the... Followed by a word of varying levels of politeness (e.g. 'soup', which is polite, or 'shit', which is not). The phrase means the same as *drop in it*.* or ** or ***
Note: politeness depends on word used at end of the phrase.

Drop in the ocean A tiny fraction of the total. In other words, a minute amount.*

Drop into their lap Obtain effortlessly.*

Drop it Cease discussing something. Used as a command ('drop it!') is a request that someone stops discussing something because the subject is annoying or unpleasant. *

Drop like a hot potato (1) Literally drop as if it were too painful to hold. (2) Rapidly and decisively sever social or working relations with someone.*

Drop like flies Die or collapse in large numbers.*

Drop names Engage in *name dropping*.*

Drop the ball Make a mistake and/or fail to complete a task.*

Drop the bundle If a person 'drops the bundle' they stop doing something they are not very good at.*

Drop the dime on Inform on someone.*

Drop the pilot Do something without the help usually employed (e.g. 'after a couple of successful attempts with Mary to assist, Sue decided to drop the pilot and try doing it by herself').*

Drop the sprog Give birth.**

Drop their aitches Fail to pronounce the letter aitch at the beginning of words beginning with 'h' (e.g. ''urry up with dinner, I'm 'ungry'). The phrase some-

times refers specifically to a failure to pronounce the initial letter aitch. However, more generally it is used by snobs as a general indicator that (from their viewpoint) a person has poor pronunciation and is ill-educated or working class.*

Drop their guard Become less defensive.*

Drown their sorrows Attempt to remedy a depressed feeling by drinking alcohol.*

Drop them (1) Terminate a relationship (the term usually implies that this is done in an unnecessarily brutal and callous manner). (2) Remove someone from a sports team.*

Drop themselves in it See *drop in it*.

Drowned rat Someone looking like a 'drowned rat' is soaking wet and dishevelled.*

Drug on the market (1) Of no value. (2) Impossible to sell.*

Drunk as a... The phrase almost inevitably means 'very drunk'. Words commonly used to finish the phrase include 'skunk', 'lord' and 'newt'.* or ** or ***
Note: politeness level depends on word at end of phrase.

Dry as dust (1) Lacking water. (2) Boring. (3) Very cerebral, with no obvious emotionality. *

Dry eye in the house See *not a dry eye in the house*.

Dry run A practice session.*

Duck See entry below and: *do ducks swim?, dying duck in a thunderstorm, have their ducks in a row, lame duck, like a duck to water, like water off a duck's back, play ducks and drakes with* and *weather for ducks*.

Duck and dive Avoid attack by being flexible and/or using mental agility.*

Due deserts Means the same as *just deserts*.

Duke it out Fight.*

Dukes up To raise fists at someone.*

Dull as dishwater Very uninteresting.*

Dull as ditchwater Means the same as *dull as dishwater.*

Dull the edge Make less. The phrase can refer to level of interest, sensation, pain or other things, depending upon context.*

Dump them (1) Terminate a relationship (the term usually implies that this is done in an unnecessarily brutal and callous manner). (2) Remove someone from a group.*

Dust away the cobwebs Means the same as *blow away the cobwebs.*

Dust settles See *when the dust settles.*

Dusty answer A response that is brief and uninformative.*

Dusty Miller Men with the surname 'Miller' often are nicknamed 'Dusty' (it is unlikely that this is their real first name). The nickname derives from the observation that millers generally get dusty from flour whilst working.*

Dutch courage Gaining courage by drinking alcohol. The phrase probably derives from earlier centuries when the Netherlands and Britain were at war, and the Dutch were seen in negative terms, including the (utterly false) idea that they had no real 'fighting spirit' and had to get drunk to fight.*

Dutch uncle Someone who acts as an adviser or counsellor on an informal basis.*

Dutchman See *I'm a Dutchman.*

Duty bound Compelled to behave in a particular way because of regulations or the duties associated with a particular job. For example, a police officer may personally feel that a person caught committing a crime should be let free but, because of the requirements of being a police officer, is 'duty bound' to arrest the person.*

Dyed in the wool If an attitude or behaviour is said to be 'dyed in the wool' then it is possessed very firmly, and it will be difficult to change through persuasion or training.*

Dying duck in a thunderstorm To have a forlorn or miserable expression.*

E

Eager beaver A keen, enthusiastic person.*

Ear See entry below and: *bend their ear, can't make a silk purse out of a sow's ear, cock an ear, chew their ear, drop a word in their ear, easy on the ear, flea in their ear, have the ear, in one ear and out the other, incline an ear, keep an ear out for, lend an ear, listen with half an ear, make a pig's ear, play by ear, prick up their ears, tin ear, turn a deaf ear to* and *word in their ear.*

Ear to the ground Having an especially good level of knowledge. The phrase is generally reserved for someone who has intensively studied a situation and can foresee future developments.*

Early bath See *take an early bath.*

Early bird A person who gets up and is active earlier in the morning than most people. There may also be an implication of being active and more likely to succeed. The saying 'the early bird catches the worm' argues that those who start early on a project and are generally lively (i.e. aren't lazy and sleep until late) are more likely to succeed.*

Early days The initial stages of something, when it is too soon to be certain of the outcome.*

Earn a crust Earn money. The phrase originally meant 'earn barely enough to survive', but these days is often used sarcastically to describe a very rich person.*

Earn a living Have paid employment. There is usually an implication that the salary is not excessively large.*

Earn an honest crust Means the same as *earn an honest penny.*

Earn an honest penny Earn money in a morally respectable way.*

Earn their corn Work hard and well enough to justify the salary.*

Earn their keep (1) Be a productive member of a household. (2) Be a useful household appliance. (3) Be a guest in a household who does household chores or similar in exchange for board and lodging.*

Earn their moccasins Prove worthy of something.*

Earn their spurs Means the same as *earn their moccasins.*

Earn their stripes Prove worthy of something. The phrase refers to gaining promotion in the police, armed forces, etc., where advancement through the lower ranks is marked by white chevron stripes on the sleeves of the uniform.*

Ears are burning A person's ears are said to be burning if someone has been talking about them when they were not there.*

Ears flapping Describes the state of a person who is eavesdropping on a conversation.*

Earth-shaking Something that is 'earth-shaking' is of great importance. The phrase is often used in the negative (e.g. 'nothing earth-shaking') meaning something that is unimportant or is used sarcastically.*

Earth-shattering Means the same as *earth-shaking.*

Earth swallow me up See *let the earth swallow me up.*

Earth to... A joking phrase imitating the radio calls of ground control to astronauts. The implication is that someone is not paying attention and might as well be on another planet because they are so unresponsive (e.g. 'Earth to Mark – have you heard anything I've said?').*

Earthly See *not have an Earthly.*

Easy as pie Easy.*

Easy come, easy go (1) The belief that something easily gained can be easily lost. (2) A relaxed view of a situation.*

Easy does it A command to do something gently and with care.*

Easy listening Rather bland music that requires no great intellectual analysis to appreciate and lacks a particularly forceful or aggressive rhythmic structure.*

Easy on the ear Agreeable to hear.*

Easy on the eye Agreeable to see.*

Easy on the pocket Affordable.*

Easy ride A trouble-free experience.*

Easy tiger A very mild rebuke to someone who is over-keen to do something.*

Easy touch Means the same as *soft touch.*

Easy virtue Promiscuity.*

Easy way See *hard way.*

Eat a horse See *could eat a horse.*

Eat alive This has several distinct meanings. (1) A person threatening to eat someone else alive is very annoyed with them (the threat is not of course literal). (2) A person repeatedly bitten by insects can claim to be being 'eaten alive'. (3) A person who is worried by something to the point that it preoccupies their thoughts and possibly makes them feel ill can be said to be 'eaten alive' with worry.*

Eat crow (1) To be made to do something unpleasant. (2) Be humiliated.*

Eat dirt Be humiliated.*

Eat humble pie To be made to do something humiliating or admit to being in the wrong. 'Humble pie' is made from the giblets of deer and was traditionally given to the 'lower orders'. Thus a nobleman made to eat humble pie rather than venison was being deliberately humiliated.*

Eat like a bird Eat very little. The exception to this is *eat like a gannet*.*

Eat like a gannet Eat large amounts (contrast with *eat like a bird*). Gannets are birds famed for their voracious appetites.*

Eat like a horse Eat large amounts.*

Eat like a pig Eat large amounts with bad table manners. There is often an implication that food is being eaten simply because it is edible, and the person is insensible to the quality of what they are eating. Pigs are famed for voracious appetites and their capacity to eat practically anything.*

Eat me Means the same as *bite me*.

Eat my shorts A rude reply, indicating rejection of what has just been said. The phrase was popularized by the TV show *The Simpsons*.**

Eat out of house and home Consume large amounts of a host's food, beyond the bounds of what would be considered polite behaviour.*

Eat their dust Be considerably behind another competitor in a race or other competition. *

Eat their heart out (1) Experience longing for someone or something. (2) Be envious. (3) Eat large quantities without restraint. See *eat your heart out...*

Eat this A verbal reply that precedes doing or saying something unpleasant (e.g. saying 'eat this' before hitting someone).**

Eat your heart out... The phrase is typically followed by the name of a famous person who is a noted exponent of whatever is under discussion, with the implication that what is being discussed is better than the named person is or was capable of. Thus, after a piano recital, a person might say 'eat your heart out Anton Rubinstein'. The phrase can be used with serious intent (i.e. the speaker really thinks that what is being discussed is good) or with ironic intent (i.e. the speaker thinks that what is being discussed is poor). See *eat their heart out*.*

Eaten all the pies Is fat. Offensive, and should not be used.***

Eating out of their hand See *have them eating out of their hand*.

Eclipsed by Made less important and/or high-ranking by (e.g. 'the Zog Model IV was considered very good until it was eclipsed by the arrival of the Zog Model V').*

Economical with the truth Lying.*

Edge out Defeat or replace by relatively unobtrusive methods.*

Effing and blinding Swearing.*

Egg See entries below and: *as sure as eggs is eggs, big butter and egg man, chicken and egg, curate's egg, don't put all your eggs in one basket, go suck an egg, kill the goose that lays the golden egg, lay an egg, over-egg the pudding, teach granny to suck eggs* and *walk on eggshells*.

Egg on Encourage.*

Egg on their face Be embarrassed or humiliated.*

Electric soup An alcoholic drink.*

Elementary, my dear Watson A joking phrase indicating that the speaker has solved a problem that others have found baffling with great ease. The phrase is a (supposed) quotation of Sherlock Holmes, the famous fictional detective (in reality, he never says this exact phrase in any of the books or short stories, but it is a good paraphrase of several very similar quotations).*

Elephant never forgets Said by a person when claiming that they have a good memory. Elephants proverbially have good memories and the speaker is comparing their memory skills to this. They are not otherwise claiming to be elephant-like.*

Eleventh hour The latest possible time that something could be done.*

Emerge from the ashes Means the same as *rise from the ashes.*

Emperor's new clothes Something that is ridiculous or of no worth that many people know is ridiculous or of no worth, but feel they cannot say this because (supposed) experts have said it is praiseworthy (e.g. the status of some modern art liked by art critics).*

Empty nest syndrome Feeling of loneliness in middle-aged parents created by their children having reached adulthood and moved out of the family home.*

Empty nester Person experiencing *empty nest syndrome.**

Empty of ideas (1) Having no ideas or imagination. (2) Question someone until they run out of anything new to say and/or suggest.*

End in tears See *it'll end in tears.*

End it all Commit suicide.*

End of civilisation as we know it (1) The literal end of a way of living that is characteristic of 'civilized life'. The term has been used to describe the state of a once civilized country after it has been taken over by a totalitarian, repressive regime (e.g. 'after the dictator took over, it was the end of civilisation as we know it for the people of that country'), and also in describing the threat to civilisation from enemy forces (e.g. 'if they invade, then it'll be the end of civilisation as we know it'). (2) Because the term has been overused in bad melodramas, and particularly bad science fiction movies (e.g. 'if the giant ants from Planet Zog take over, it'll be the end of civilisation as we know it'), it is now used jokingly as a response to any bad news, no matter how trivial (e.g. 'the photocopier is broken and won't be repaired until tomorrow – this could be the end of civilisation as we know it').*

End of story A phrase used at the end of a (usually spoken) description to indicate that that is all there is to relate.*

End of the line Means the same as *end of the road.*

End of the rainbow A non-existent place, signifying something that is desirable but highly unlikely.*

End of the road The limit beyond which something cannot continue.*

End of the world A serious (but not necessarily literally world-ending) problem or situation. See *it's not the end of the world.*

End of their tether The most annoyed someone can be without actually losing their temper.*

End up (1) Upside down. (2) Another way of saying the verb 'end' (e.g. 'how did we end up here?').*

Enemy See *how's the enemy?*

Engraved in stone Means the same as *set in stone.*

Enough is enough (1) A statement of warning to cease an activity (typically, an argument). (2) Similarly, a statement of exasperation that an activity has gone on too long.*

Enough said A statement indicating that enough information has been given. The phrase is used in several contrasting ways: e.g. (1) to compliment a speaker that they have efficiently summarized a situation in a few words; (2) to indicate that what the speaker is saying is distasteful and no more should be said; (3) to indicate that what is being said is irritating; or (4) to indicate that what is being said may provoke an argument and it would be politic to stop speaking.*

Enough to make a cat laugh Something that is very funny.*

Enough to sink a battleship A large quantity.*

Enter into the spirit Adopt the same attitude and emotional mood as others.*

Envelope See *push the envelope.*

Err on the right side Make a mistake that in fact is advantageous.*

Err on the side of… Behave in a manner that favours one thing over another. The commonest use of the phrase is probably 'err on the side of caution', meaning that the action taken is more careful than reckless.*

Etchings See *come up and see my etchings.*

Eternal triangle An emotional problem in which there are three people. The conflict is about which two of the three will become the permanent partners and, accordingly, who will be rejected. This is a staple plot for romantic stories.*

Even break A fair opportunity. See *never give a sucker an even break.*

Even keel See *keep on an even keel.*

Even stevens Evenly balanced.*

Ever and anon the way Always the same.*

Ever-decreasing circles To go round in 'ever-decreasing circles' is to work on problems that never seem to be solved and in which over time less and less worthwhile output is produced.*

Every avenue explored Means the same as *no stone unturned.*

Every last one Every member of a group or set.*

Every man for himself Every person is responsible for their own survival. The term is used in two common ways. (1) As a call to escape a dangerous situation (e.g. 'the building is on fire – every man for himself!') in which people are urged to escape rather than attempt to be heroic and rescue others. (2) As a description of a situation in which everybody was selfish (e.g. 'it was every man for himself in that office').*

Every man Jack Everybody.*

Every person for themselves A gender-neutral version of *every man for himself.*

Every picture tells a story In other words, something can be deduced from any visual scene. The term is sometimes used jokingly when someone enters a room wearing an unusual facial expression.*

Every trick in the book Every possible option.*

Every which way In all possible directions. The phrase often denotes a state of confusion or a difficult problem (e.g. 'I've tried every which way to solve it').*

Everyone has a price Expresses the belief that everyone can be bribed or coerced.*

Everyone's lips See *word on everyone's lips.*

Everything but the kitchen sink A joking expression meaning that everything that could be included has been. There is usually the implication that a lot of what has been included is unnecessary.*

Everything in the garden is… The phrase nearly always ends with a positive term such as 'blooming', 'rosy' or 'lovely'. The phrase simply denotes that the situation is agreeable. Occasionally the phrase is used for ironic effect and ends with a negative word such as 'rotten', in which case the phrase means that the situation is disagreeable.*

Everything's coming up roses Everything is well.*

Exception that proves the rule Something unusual that will test whether a generally held belief is correct. The word 'prove' is used in its older sense of 'test'. The phrase does not mean that exceptions must automatically support a generally held belief.*

Excuse my French Means the same as *pardon my French.*

Exhibit A The most important part of an argument or most important evidence. The term comes from the practice of labelling items of evidence used in law courts by the names 'Exhibit A', 'Exhibit B', etc.*

Extra mile See *go the extra mile.*

Eye See entries below and: *all eyes, apple of their eye, better than a poke in the eye with a* sharp stick, *bird's-eye view, blink of an eye, blue-eyed boy [or girl], bright-eyed and bushy tailed, by an eyelash, clap eyes on, close their eyes to, close your eyes and think of England, easy on the eye, feast their eyes on, flutter their eyelashes, get their eye in, give their eye teeth, give them the glad eye, green-eyed monster, half an eye, have an eye for, in a pig's eye, in the public eye, keep an eye on, keep an eye out for, keep half an eye on, keep their eye in, keep their eye on the ball, keep their eyes open, keep their eyes peeled, leap to the eye, make eyes at, mind's eye, mote in their eye, my eye, not a dry eye in the house, not bat an eyelid, one in the eye, open their eyes, pass their eye over, public eye, pull the wool over their eyes, raise their eyebrows, raised eyebrows, right between the eyes, scales fall from their eyes, see eye to eye, sheep's eyes, shut their eyes to, sight for sore eyes, smack in the eye, spit in the eye, square eyes, stars in their eyes, take their eye off the ball, turn a blind eye to, twinkle in their eye, up the boo-eye, up to the eyeballs, when Nelson gets his eye back, with eyes closed, with eyes open* and *worm's eye view.*

Eye candy Something or someone that looks attractive; there is usually the implication that the something or someone in question is also of low intellectual worth.*

Eye-catching Visually appealing and/or noticeable.*

Eye for an eye Part of a longer Biblical phrase that finishes with 'and a tooth for a tooth'. It expresses the view that wrongdoing should be met with retaliatory action. The phrase is often interpreted as justifying any sort of revenge, but this is a misreading of the original phrase, which argued that revenge should never go further than an act of equivalent severity.*

Eye of a needle A tiny opening.*

Eye of the hurricane Means the same as *eye of the storm.*

Eye of the storm (1) The essential part of an emotional argument. (2) The most emotionally upsetting part of an argument. (3) The phenomenon that during a complex situation (such as a serious and complex argument) there can be a period of time when everything seems unnaturally calm, which gives an uneasy and illusory sense that everything has been resolved (like a still pocket of air at the centre of some hurricanes).*

Eye on the main chance A person with an 'eye on the main chance' is constantly searching for methods of becoming rich, gaining promotion or otherwise gaining success. *

Eyeball to eyeball Very close to each other – the term is nearly always reserved for describing a hostile situation.*

Eyeballing (1) To look at something in a not very thorough manner to gain an initial idea of what it is about (e.g. 'from eyeballing the data I'd say things look promising, but I'll have to examine it more carefully before deciding firmly on anything'). (2) To try to out-stare someone (i.e. if two people stare at each other's eyes, see which one loses by looking away first).*

Eyeballs See *up to the eyeballs.*

Eyes are smiling If a person's 'eyes are smiling' then they have a happy or contented expression.*

Eyes bigger than their stomach Eating (or attempting to eat) more than can be comfortably digested.*

Eyes in the back of their head Being very observant and/or well-informed.*

Eyes out on stalks Expressing extreme surprise or interest.*

Eyes wide open Fully aware of the situation; showing a high level of attention.*

F

Face as long as a fiddle Means the same as *long face.*

Face fits If someone's 'face fits', then their attributes make them acceptable for a particular position or task.*

Face like a wet weekend Means the same as *long face*.

Face off Decide the outcome through confrontation.*

Face the music Accept punishment for a misdeed.*

Facts of life (1) Information about sexual intercourse and reproduction. (2) Basic information about the way in which people behave and what can be expected in the course of daily living.*

Faint hearted Timid.*

Fair The term can mean 'reasonable', but in some situations it may also mean 'large' (e.g. 'he inherited a fair-sized fortune' or 'the dog was a fair size').*

Fair and square (1) Honest. (2) Accurate.*

Fair cop Means the same as *bang to rights* and again derived from slang (as in 'it's a fair cop', supposedly said by criminals caught in the act of committing a crime). See *cop it*.*

Fair crack of the whip A reasonable opportunity to attempt to do something.*

Fair dinkum (1) Okay. (2) Real.*

Fair dos (1) Reasonable treatment or behaviour. The phrase is generally used as a request for reasonable treatment. (2) The phrase can also be used in the same way as *credit where credit is due*.*

Fair field and no favour A contest with no favouritism shown.*

Fair-haired boy [or girl] Means the same as *blue-eyed boy [or girl]*.

Fair suck of the pineapple An expression of disbelief or grievance that someone has done something unfair, such as taken more than their fair share of something.*

Fair suck of the sav Means the same as *fair suck of the pineapple*. A 'sav' is Australian slang for a saveloy sausage.

Fair weather friend (1) A person who is only friendly when the situation is trouble-free. (2) A person who cannot be relied upon in times of difficulty.*

Fair's fair A request for reasonable treatment.*

Fall apart at the seams (1) Fail comprehensively. (2) Have a nervous breakdown. (3) Collapse or disintegrate.*

Fall between two stools Fail to support or satisfy either of two alternative or opposing arguments or positions.*

Fall flat Fail. The phrase often specifically means 'anticlimax'.*

Fall flat on their face Fail, and because of the failure suffer loss of reputation.*

Fall for (1) Be deceived by. (2) Fall in love with.*

Fall from grace Be no longer liked or regarded as important.*

Fall into line Begin to follow orders and/or work as part of a team rather than following individual whims.*

Fall into place (1) Become understandable. (2) Means the same as *fall into line*.*

Fall into their lap Obtain effortlessly.*

Fall on deaf ears Be ignored or have no effect on emotions.*

Fall on stony ground Means the same as *fall on deaf ears*.

Fall on their feet Become involved in a rewarding and/or pleasant situation. There is often an implication that this was more by luck than intent.*

Fall prey to Be a victim of, or be brought into decline by.*

Fall short of Fail to meet the desired standard.*

Fall through the net Escape detection.*

Falling apart (1) When used to describe an emotional state (e.g. 'I'm so upset it feels like I'm falling apart') then it refers to a state in which a person feels as if they cannot cope. See *pull yourself together* for further discussion of this. (2) When describing a relationship, it means that the relationship has serious problems and may not last.*

False colours See *show their true colours.*

False dawn An apparently optimistic sign that is in fact illusory.*

Family jewels (1) Treasured possessions. (2) The male genitals.* (1) or ** (2)

Family silver See *sell the family silver.*

Family tree Record of a family's ancestors. The 'tree' refers to the tree-like pattern that a visual representation of a person's lineage can resemble.*

Famous for fifteen minutes A short-lived phenomenon or fashion. Like a *nine days' wonder*, the precise length of fame is not indicated by the phrase. A person who has been famous for a brief period of time is said to have had their *fifteen minutes of fame*.*

Famous last words The term can of course refer to notable phrases made by people when dying. However, it is usually used ironically to comment on somebody's over-optimistic or otherwise incautious remarks.*

Fan the flames Make an argument more intense by use of provocative language or behaviour. This may be done deliberately or accidentally.*

Fancy their chances Be hopeful of success.*

Far and away A method of emphasising 'far'. Thus 'far and away better' means better by a larger margin than 'far better'.*

Far be it from me to... Strictly speaking, the phrase means 'I am reluctant to...' (e.g. 'far be it from me to criticize you' means 'I am reluctant to criticize you'). The phrase is usually used when someone wants to say something unpleasant but wishes to make it sound less aggressive.*

Far cry from Utterly distinct from.*

Far-fetched Implausible.*

Far-flung A long distance away.*

Fashion victim A person who slavishly follows fashion trends and wears clothes that look ridiculous in the mistaken belief that they are fashionable and trend-setting (e.g. 'Michelle thought that her clothes were the last word in haute couture, but in reality she was a fashion victim').*

Fast girl A now rather dated expression indicating a woman who is considered sexually promiscuous. *

Fat cat A person who has too much wealth and/or privilege. The phrase is often used to describe senior managers in business who can award themselves outrageously large salaries and bonuses with apparent impunity.*

Fat chance Highly unlikely.*

Fat in the fire The cause of a problem.*

Fat lady sings See *it isn't over until the fat lady sings.*

Fat of the land See *live off the fat of the land.*

Fate in their hands An outcome that is dependent on others.*

Fate worse than death The term originally referred to a woman's loss of virginity before marriage (seen at the time as a great moral crime). Today it is generally used humorously to refer to something unpleasant a person would prefer to avoid.*

Fatted calf See *kill the fatted calf.*

Favourite daughter A famous woman especially liked in the country or region she was born in.*

Favourite son Male equivalent of *favourite daughter.*

Fear Greeks bearing gifts Means the same as *beware of Greeks bearing gifts.*

Feast of reason Erudite conversation.*

Feast or famine A situation in which there is either too much or too little, and never the correct amount.*

Feast their eyes on Admire.*

Feather in their cap A praiseworthy achievement.*

Feather their nest Accumulate riches, usually by illicit means, such as stealing from their employers.*

Fed up To be bored to the point of lethargy. The term derives from hawking – a bird of prey after eating will usually be unwilling to hunt and is said to be 'fed up'.*

Fed up to the back teeth (1) Very irritated by something; the phrase usually refers to annoyance at something that has been going on for some time. (2) Extremely *fed up*.*

Feel free An expression of permission to do something (e.g. 'feel free to look around the house').*

Feel in the bones Intuitively sense something without being able to give a logical explanation for it.*

Feel like death Feel very ill or tired.*

Feel like shit Feel ill.***

Feel the draught Experience problems. The phrase is especially used to describe a severe worsening in a person's finances.*

Feel the pinch Experience financial problems.*

Feel their age A person who says that they 'feel their age' means that they feel they are growing old because they are physically tired or otherwise enfeebled.*

Feel their collar Arrest them.*

Feeling oneself See *not feeling oneself.*

Feeling seedy Feeling unwell.*

Feet of clay A single defect in an otherwise praiseworthy personality. The phrase is used especially to someone who is made vulnerable by this defect.*

Feet under the table If a person has their 'feet under the table', then they have been accepted into a family in which they are not a relative by genes or marriage. The term often implies that the person has done this because the family has wealth or influence.*

Fell off the back of a lorry Stolen or otherwise improperly obtained.*

Fender bender An automobile accident.*

Fetch and carry Act as a menial servant carrying things at someone's orders.*

Few and far between Rare.*

Fiddling while Rome burns To do something trivial while more important things need to be done. The term originates with Emperor Nero, who reputedly played on the fiddle whilst a sizeable part of his capital burnt down.*

Fifteen minutes of fame See *famous for fifteen minutes.*

Fifth columnists Traitors working within a country or group with the purpose of weakening it and aiding the enemy.*

Fifth wheel Something superfluous.*

Fifty-fifty Describes something shared or apportioned equally ('fifty' refers to 50%).*

Fight a losing battle Be engaged in a task that is inevitably going to fail.*

Fight fire with fire Defend or counter-attack using the same methods as the original attack.*

Fight shy of Avoid.*

Fight the good fight Be engaged in an arduous task that is for a high moral cause. The phrase is often used jokingly to indicate a task that is tedious but necessary.*

Fight to the finish A contest that is fought with great vigour. The phrase often carries the meaning that the contest will continue until one side is utterly defeated.*

Fight tooth and nail Fight vigorously.*

Figure of fun A person who is predominantly regarded as somebody to ridicule or laugh at.*

Fill their boots (1) Take as much as possible. (2) Means the same as *fill their shoes.**

Fill their shoes Take over from someone else and succeed in this attempt (e.g. 'do you think you are experienced enough to fill the boss's shoes?'). More generally, the term can mean 'to be a replacement of adequate quality'.*

Final say The ultimate decision. For example, the person with the 'final say' is the person who will decide what will be done.*

Final straw The last in a series of annoyances that is the immediate cause of a person losing their temper. The implication is that the person has been patient but the 'final straw' was something that provided an irresistible impulse to become angry.*

Find God Acquire a religious faith.*

Find it in their heart Decide to do something. The phrase sometimes is used to describe a decision based upon compassion rather than logic.*

Find their feet Become capable of doing something. The phrase is often used to describe the process of learning how to work effectively in a new job.*

Finders keepers The start of a phrase that ends 'and losers weepers'. Expresses the principle that whoever finds something has the right to keep it. A dubious moral and legal principle, but the guiding philosophy of unpleasant children (and adults) the world over.*

Fine balance A problematic distinction between the membership criteria of two categories.*

Fine kettle of fish Means the same as *pretty kettle of fish.*

Fine line If there is a 'fine line' between two categories, then it only requires a minute change in the features of something for it to change from being classified as being in one category to being classified as belonging in another category.*

Fine points Details.*

Fine-tooth comb See *go through with a fine-tooth comb.*

Finest hour Greatest success.*

Finger in the pie Be involved in. The phrase usually implies that this involvement is for personal gain.*

Finger on the pulse Be fully aware of the situation.*

Fingers to the bone See *wear their fingers to the bone.*

Fingertips See *at their fingertips* and *by their fingertips.*

Fire and brimstone Describes a stern moralistic approach, often based upon a puritanical Christian doctrine.*

Fire and forget A process that once initiated needs no more attention in order for it to succeed.*

Fire away In a conversation, 'fire away' means 'proceed'. The phrase is often used to indicate that it is permissible to ask questions (e.g. 'may I ask you some questions?' may be met with a reply of 'fire away').*

Fire blanks Try to do something but fail. The phrase is sometimes used to describe a man who is sterile (e.g. 'Sue and Tom would like to have a baby, but Tom only fires blanks').*

Fire from the hip Respond rapidly without much thought.*

Fire in their belly Strongly determined.*

Fired up and ready to go To be in a high state of readiness to do something.*

Firing on all cylinders Working efficiently.*

Firing on all six Means the same as *firing on all cylinders*.

Firm hand Sometimes followed by either 'on the reins' or 'on the tiller'. Having good control over something or someone. The phrase often implies that this control involves the use of discipline.*

First among equals The best of a group and/or the leader.*

First base (1) The first stage in a plan or activity; unless this is reached, nothing else can be done. (2) The early stages of sexual activity ('second base', 'third base' and 'fourth base' describe increasing levels of intimacy). (3) The most basic state (e.g. 'before we discuss refinements of this plan, let's establish first base').* (1 and 3) or ** (2)

First blood The first success in a competition, contest or conflict (e.g. 'the home team drew first blood when they scored after twenty minutes').*

First come, first served The principle that the earliest people to apply for something in short supply will be given it, whilst latecomers will not get anything because supplies have run out.*

First light (1) Dawn or very early in the morning. (2) Initial appearance or initial impression.*

First magnitude Means the same as *first order*.

First off First.*

First order (1) A very good example of something. (2) Most important.*

First past the post A contest in which the winner is decided by whoever is first to finish or, alternatively, has the best points score. The phrase is sometimes used in discussions of elections, in contrast to the rather more complex proportional representation system.*

First thing At the start. The phrase usually indicates that something should have priority at the start of a forthcoming session/working day (e.g. 'I want this done first thing tomorrow morning').*

First things first The most important and/or urgent things should be given priority.*

First up The first thing in a list.*

First water Highest quality or the most extreme form of something. The term is derived from a method of grading diamonds.*

Fish for compliments Behave in a manner that invites others to pay compliments.*

Fish in the sea See *more fish in the sea*.

Fish in troubled waters Benefit from a troubled situation.*

Fish or cut bait A command to do something rather than just talk about it.*

Fish out of water A person who is in a situation for which their skills are totally unsuited and which may even place them at a disadvantage.*

Fish to fry Interests or commitments. Often heard in the phrase 'they have other fish to fry', indicating that they are not solely interested in one thing.*

Fishing expedition An enquiry that hopes to find information but has no preconceived, specific ideas about what that information will be.*

Fit a quart into a pint pot Means the same as *get a quart in a pint pot*.

Fit as a butcher's dog Very healthy. The phrase probably comes from the observation that a butcher's dog will be well-fed on meat.*

Fit as a fiddle Very healthy.*

Fit as a flea Healthy.*

Fit for the gods Of high quality.*

Fit like a glove Be a precise fit.*

Fit the bill Be what is required (e.g. in looking for a new lecturer, someone with a PhD and a list of research publications will 'fit the bill').*

---

* *denotes level of impoliteness*

Fit to a T To fit exactly.*

Fit to be tied Annoyed.*

Fit to bust With excessive force or energy.*

Fits and starts Sporadic.*

Fix their wagon (1) Cause their downfall. (2) Ruin their plans.*

Flagpole See *run it up the flagpole.*

Flash in the pan Transient. The phrase is often used to describe a person who does something successful or noteworthy on one occasion and then cannot repeat it. The phrase comes from the use of muskets: if they misfired, they would produce a bright flash (a 'flash in the pan') but not fire anything.*

Flat out (1) As fast as possible. (2) Without question.*

Flavour of the month (1) The current favourite. (2) The current fashion. The negative of this (*not flavour of the month*) means 'unpopular'.*

Flea in their ear A rebuke.*

Flesh and blood Relatives.*

Flesh creep See *make flesh creep.*

Flesh nor fish See *neither flesh nor fish nor fowl.*

Flex their muscles Do something that indicates power (and thus, level of potential threat).*

Flip the bird Make an offensive one-fingered gesture.**

Flip their lid Become angry or lose a normal sense of reason.*

Flip their wig Means the same as *flip their lid.*

Float the boat If something floats a person's boat, then they find it interesting and/or attractive.*

Flog a dead horse Waste time and energy on a hopeless activity.*

Flower of... The best examples of.*

Fluff See *bit of fluff.*

Fluffy bunny Derogatory term for someone who is naive or not intellectually gifted.*

Flushed with success In a euphoric mood following a success.*

Flutter the dovecotes Cause a disturbance.*

Flutter their eyelashes Show a sexual interest in. The phrase is nearly always used of women.*

Fly a kite Test something or gauge opinion.*

Fly high Prosper.*

Fly in the face of Behave in a manner opposed to.*

Fly in the ointment Something that mars an otherwise acceptable or pleasant situation.*

Fly off the handle Become angry. The phrase normally indicates that this temper loss is sudden and irrational.*

Fly on the wall A spy or unobtrusive observer.*

Fly on the wheel A person who is far less important than they think they are.*

Fly the coop Escape.*

Fly the flag (1) Represent a particular group or belief. (2) Be identified as belonging to a particular group or country.*

Fly the nest Leave. The phrase is often used to describe leaving the parental home to live independently.*

Flying blind Doing something without any guidance or assistance.*

Flying colours See *with flying colours.*

Foaming at the mouth In a state of excitement or anger.*

Fob them off Deter. There is usually an implication that this is done by using a weak excuse or failing to provide adequate reasons.*

Follow in their footsteps Choose a career or journey identical to someone else's.*

Follow suit Behave in a similar way.*

Follow their nose (1) Obey instinct rather than logic. (2) Move forwards. (3) Use a sense of smell to locate something.*

Food for thought Something that requires consideration.*

Fool around Behave in a foolish, unproductive manner.*

Fool's errand A pointless task which will yield nothing worthwhile. There is often the implication that the task is a demanding or boring one.*

Fool's gold Something that superficially appears valuable or useful, but is in fact worthless.*

Fool's paradise See *living in a fool's paradise.*

Foot in both camps Have allies and interests in more than one group. There is often the implication that the groups in question are opposed to each other.*

Foot in it See *put their foot in it.*

Foot in mouth The state of having said something highly inappropriate.*

Foot in the door Gained access. The implication is usually that access has been gained to something that is not easily entered, such as a prestigious organisation.*

Foot the bill Pay what is owed.*

Foot wrong See *never put a foot wrong.*

Footloose and fancy free Having no commitments.*

For a song Cheaply.*

For all that In spite of that.*

For all they know The phrase expresses the fact that someone's knowledge is limited (e.g. 'for all they know the solution might never be found').*

For auld lang syne Scottish Gaelic meaning 'for a long time ago', which is probably best expressed as *for old times' sake* (i.e. because it was done in the past, it should be respected now). The phrase is from a song by Robert Burns.*

For crying out loud An expression of exasperation.**

For dear life With determination.*

For good measure In addition. The phrase often implies that what is being added is superfluous or is there simply to reinforce the argument.*

For grim death Means the same as *for dear life.*

For it (1) In favour of something. (2) Be likely to be punished (e.g. 'you'll be for it when Mum catches you').*

For my money An expression of preference (e.g. 'for my money, Chopin was a better composer than Schumann').*

For old times' sake An argument that because something was done in the past, it should be respected now. The phrase is often used to persuade a reluctant person to do something because it would remind another person of happy times in the past.*

For real (1) True. (2) Telling the truth. (3) Used as a question, it means 'is that really true?' *

For the birds A matter of so little importance it is not worth attention or fuss. A phrase originally used to describe horse manure that contains seeds that small birds may pick at, but is otherwise of little use.*

For the hell of it For enjoyment or no very obvious reason.*

For the high jump Destined to receive punishment.*

For the life of them A phrase expressing that every effort has been made. It is usually said in conjunction with an admission of failure (e.g. 'for the life of me I can't remember where I put it').*

For the record The truth. The phrase is often used before issuing a denial of an

* *denotes level of impoliteness*

allegation (e.g. 'for the record, I did not do that').*

For the ride If someone is along 'for the ride' then they have no serious interest in the activity.*

For their sins As punishment. The phrase is often used in a self-deprecating manner to describe something actually gained through merit (e.g. 'I'm chief engineer, for my sins').*

For toffee Usually seen in the form 'can't...for toffee', meaning that the activity described is done badly (e.g. 'you're useless at soccer – you can't play for toffee').*

For two pins With very little encouragement.*

For what it's worth A remark intended to apologize that the information conveyed may not be of great interest or value, but should be mentioned. The phrase can indicate that something is genuinely of limited value, or it can be used disparagingly (e.g. 'for what it's worth, I won the Nobel Prize last week').*

For yonks For a long time.*

Forbidden fruit Something desirable that is not permitted. The phrase usually implies that the fact that something is forbidden is a large part of its attraction.*

Force down their throat Repeatedly present something (e.g. an argument).*

Force the issue Compel a decision to be taken and/or action to be taken.*

Force their hand Compel someone to do something.*

Fork out To pay.*

Forked tongue Someone with a 'forked tongue' is lying.*

Form See *bad form, good form* and *got form*.

Forty winks A brief sleep.*

Foul play Deliberate wrongdoing. The phrase is nearly always used as a synonym of 'murder'.*

Foul their own nest Inflict damage on themselves.*

Founding father The originator of something, or a member of a group that originated something. The phrase is often used of the original members of political or intellectual groups, or people who founded an institution.*

Four corners of the earth From all parts of the earth.*

Frankenstein's monster (1) Something that can no longer be controlled by the person who created it. (2) Something unappealing created from spare parts.*

Free and easy Lacking formality or pomposity.*

Free lunch See *no such thing as a free lunch*.

Freeze the blood Frighten.*

French leave (1) Unauthorized absence. (2) Departing without providing an explanation. (3) At a social gathering, leaving without saying goodbye to the host and/or hostess.*

Fresh blood Means the same as *new blood*.

Fresh out of... Recently used or sold the last of something (e.g. 'we're fresh out of milk' means 'we have no more milk').*

Friday afternoon job Something done in a slipshod manner. The phrase refers to the concept of workers on a Friday afternoon thinking too much about the weekend rather than the job they are supposed to be doing, and thus producing work of poorer quality.*

Friend at court A friend who has useful social contacts.*

Friend in need Part of a longer proverb – 'a friend in need is a friend indeed' – meaning that someone who is willing to help during times of difficulty is a true friend.*

Friend of Dorothy Slang name for a homosexual. The term is derived from the homosexual workers on the set of the movie *The Wizard of Oz* who befriended

Judy Garland, who played the part of Dorothy in the movie.**

Friends in high places A person with 'friends in high places' is on friendly terms with people who have powerful and/or influential jobs.*

Fries See *you want fries with that?*

Frighten the life out of Give a severe fright.*

Frighten to death Give a severe fright.*

Frog in the throat Hoarse voice.*

From day one From the very beginning.*

From hell Something 'from hell' is a very unpleasant or badly working example of something (e.g. 'the car from hell' is a car that breaks down a great deal). The phrase is usually used in a joking fashion. The term is sometimes used to denote an especially formidable opponent.*

From here to next week (1) For a long period of time. (2) In an extreme manner.*

From scratch From the beginning, starting with the most basic materials (i.e. nothing was pre-prepared).*

From the bottom of their heart Sincerely meant.*

From the dead (1) Returning to prominence after a period of not being noticed. (2) From a state of death or being very near to death.*

From the floor Describes something done by a member of an audience at a meeting. The phrase is often used to describe a speech by an attendee rather than a committee member at an important formal meeting such as a political rally or company annual general meeting.*

From the heart Means the same as *from the bottom of their heart.*

From the off From the beginning.*

From the same neck of the woods See *neck of the woods.*

From the shoulder Forthright.*

From the sidelines Means the same as *on the sidelines.*

From the sublime to the ridiculous (1) This phrase was originally somewhat longer, and finished with the words 'there is but one step'. The phrase in this context thus means that the difference between something sublime or wonderful and something of poor or ridiculous quality is often very small. (2) The phrase can also be used to describe moving from a serious topic to a less intellectual one (e.g. 'the TV news last night moved from the sublime to the ridiculous: it had a story about famine followed by one about a skateboarding duck').*

From the top From the start. Often refers to starting from the beginning of a piece of music.*

From the word go From the beginning.*

Frosting on the cake Means the same as *cherry on the cake.*

Fruits of labour The rewarding aspects of work.*

Fuck A swear word which can be used in just about every grammatical context. It has numerous meanings, only the main ones of which are listed here. (1) The term originally referred to sexual intercourse, and still has this meaning (e.g. 'I'd like to fuck him'). (2) It can be used to emphasize a point, to mean that the person feels strongly about something (e.g. 'of course I'm fucking angry'). (3) As a simple swear word (e.g. 'oh fuck!' – see the first few minutes of the movie *Four Weddings and a Funeral* for further illustration). (4) To mean that something is broken (e.g. talking about a broken machine – 'it's fucked'). (5) Used in the form 'fuck off' it means the same as 'piss off' (see *pissed*). (6) As a term of abuse (e.g. 'you fucker' or, alternatively, 'fuck you' or 'go fuck yourself'). (7) As an expression of exasperation (e.g. 'fucked if I know'). (8) As an expression of surprise (e.g. 'fuck me' – note this is not a literal request). Several different usages can be combined in one sentence. Hence, the phrase

oft-quoted by linguists about two car mechanics discussing a broken engine – 'the fucking fucker's fucked'. Which meaning is intended is heavily dependent upon context. None of them is considered polite, however.***
Note: the frequency with which this word is used varies enormously between people. Generally, if a person rarely uses the word, then its use indicates a strong emotion or surprise.

Fuck all Nothing. See *sweet Fanny Adams*.***

Fudge factor (1) A manipulation of data to give a desired, rather than truthful, result. (2) The degree to which such manipulation has taken place (e.g. 'a high fudge factor' would indicate considerable manipulation of the data).*

Full as a goog Drunk.*

Full circle See *wheel has come full circle*. The phrase is also used to mean that after a period of change, the situation is as it was before any change took place (e.g. 'we've come full circle but nothing has really changed').*

Full fig The ensemble of clothes appropriate for the occasion.*

Full marks Utterly correct or successful.*

Full Monty The complete thing.*

Full of beans To be lively and energetic.*

Full of it An insult. The phrase varies in precise meaning between contexts and speakers. However, it is generally implied that a person who is 'full of it' has an (inaccurately) inflated idea of their own worth and is largely inaccurate in their views. The 'it' is usually taken to mean 'bullshit'.**

Full of life Vigorous.*

Full of the joys of spring Cheerful to the point of being exuberant.*

Full of themselves Very self-satisfied.*

Full pelt As rapidly as possible.*

Full steam ahead Proceed with great energy.*

Full stretch Maximum effort.*

Full tilt Means the same as *full pelt*.

Fullness of time A period of time. The phrase does not specify how long this will be, but there is usually an implication that it will be a quite lengthy period. The phrase is often used in the form *in the fullness of time*, as a reply to a question about when something will happen. In this context, the phrase means 'at some point in the future' without being any more specific.*

Funny as hell Very funny. The phrase is, however, often used sarcastically (i.e. meaning 'not funny'). The only indications of which meaning is intended are context and (if spoken) the intonation of the voice.**

Funny old world Unusual things can happen in daily life. The phrase is often used as a comment upon hearing about something unusual.*

Funny thing Something unusual.*

Fur will fly There will be trouble.*

Future shock Feeling of stress or bewilderment caused by being unable to comprehend technological and cultural changes.*

G

Gaius publicus Means the same as *person in the street*.

Gallery See *play to the gallery*.

Game is up A secret is revealed or a plot exposed.*

Game over Something has ended or failed.*

Game's afoot In other words, let's get started on the task in question. The phrase was often used by Sherlock Holmes (who in turn was quoting Shakespeare's *Henry V*).*

Garbage in, garbage out The principle that something is only as good as its ingredients, and that if poor quality materials are used, the end product will likewise be of poor quality.*

Garden path See *lead up the garden path.*

Gather dust Stay unused.*

Gather steam Prepare.*

Gauntlet See *run the gauntlet, take up the gauntlet* and *throw down the gauntlet.*

Gave me the willies In other words, 'it made me frightened'. Note for American readers: 'willy' is one of the numerous UK slang words for the penis, so use of the word in anything but this (respectable) context can cause amusement to British listeners.*

Genie See *let the genie out of the bottle.*

Gentleman of leisure A man with no employment. The phrase is often used for someone who is retired or is so rich that they do not need to work.*

Gentleman's agreement An agreement bound by a code of honour rather than one with any legal standing. The phrase is arguably sexist and should be used with care.*

Genuine article An authentic example of something.*

Get a bang Gain enjoyment.*

Get a fix on (1) Physically locate. (2) Comprehend.*

Get a grip on yourself Often shortened to 'get a grip'. (1) The phrase can mean the same as *pull yourself together.* (2) It can also mean that a person should try harder to understand what's going on.*

Get a kick Enjoy.*

Get a life A demand to stop wasting time on something seen as frivolous, and do something more useful.**

Get a line on Learn about.*

Get a lot of stick Be criticized.*

Get a move on Hurry up. The phrase can be used as a command by itself ('get a move on!') where it generally means something more urgent than where the phrase is within a sentence (e.g. 'I really do think we should get a move on').*

Get a quart in a pint pot Attempt an impossible task. The phrase often refers specifically to attempting to fit an object into a space too small to accommodate it.*

Get a rise out of Annoy.*

Get a room A term of admonishment that a couple of people are being too sexually explicit in their behaviour in public and should go somewhere private. The phrase is usually meant kindly.*

Get a shift on Means the same as *get a move on.*

Get across Explain something.*

Get along (1) Have amicable relations. (2) A request to leave. (3) Move, especially in the sense of leaving (e.g. 'we'd better be moving along' means 'we had better be going'). (4) Cope.*

Get away The phrase generally means one of two things, depending upon the intonation of the voice of the speaker: (1) go away; (2) an expression of amazement at what has just been said. The context of the conversation should usually indicate which was intended.*

Get away from it all Leave a stressful or unpleasant situation. The phrase is often used to describe going on holiday.*

Get away with... The phrase is followed with a word indicating what the person 'got away with' (i.e. escaped punishment for). It usually is a deliberate exaggeration indicating that a person escaped punishment (e.g. the phrase 'get away with murder' rarely literally means this).*

Get away with it Do something deserving punishment, but avoid the punishment.*

Get bent A rude reply, indicating rejection of what has just been said.**

---

* *denotes level of impoliteness*

Get butterflies Get *butterflies in the stomach.*

Get by Exist in reasonably tolerable circumstances. The implication is that the situation could be better or worse than it is.*

Get cracking Start working on something energetically.*

Get down to it Begin work.*

Get down to the nitty gritty To get to the really important part of the discussion or to get to the important facts. For many years considered respectable, in recent times the term has been considered to be politically incorrect by some people since they argue its origins are in an old slave owners' term for the least valuable slaves. Other authorities have said that the term is derived from a term for an unwashed anus. Since neither origin of the term is very pleasant, caution over use is accordingly advised.* or **

Get even Achieve revenge.*

Get ideas (1) Have plans to do something that is utterly impractical. (2) Develop feelings of a sexual nature.*

Get in on the act See *in on the act.*

Get in on the ground floor Be involved with something from the earliest stages.*

Get into Become enthusiastic about something.*

Get into bed with them Enter into a business agreement or pact with someone. The phrase does not necessarily imply a sexual relationship.*

Get into shape Become physically fit.*

Get it (1) Understand (2) Have sexual intercourse on a regular basis.* (1) or ** (2)

Get it in the neck Receive punishment or verbal abuse.*

Get it off their chest If a person 'gets something off their chest', then they talk about something that has been worrying or angering them for some time.*

Get it together (1) Become organized. (2) Cease being confused.*

Get lines crossed Means the same as *get wires crossed.*

Get lost Usually means 'go away', with the implication that the person being told this is being a nuisance or is not wanted. It can also be a rather forceful rejection of an argument or an accusation.**

Get no change out of them Receive no help or fail to get a hoped-for response from someone.*

Get off (1) Have sexual relations with. (2) The same meanings as *get away.* See *tell them where to get off.* (2) or *** (1)

Get off my back A request that someone stops pestering or making unreasonable demands.**

Get off on the wrong foot Start a relationship in a manner that leads to misunderstandings or discord.*

Get off the dime Be decisive.*

Get off the ground Successfully start something (e.g. a project or plan).*

Get off the mark Begin.*

Get off their bike Become angry.*

Get off with Have sexual relations with.**

Get on the right side Become favourably regarded.*

Get on their nerves Be annoying or irritating.*

Get on with To live or work in harmony with. The implication is that the relationship is one of toleration rather than friendship.*

Get on with it (1) Do something. (2) A command to do something promptly rather than delaying.* (1) or ** (2)

Get out more See *they should get out more.*

Get out of bed on the wrong side To be angry or irritable for no obvious reason. The phrase probably derives from the superstition that putting the left foot on the floor first in the morning would bring bad luck.*

Get out of it (1) An aggressive way of saying 'go away'. (2) A way of expressing doubt about what has just been said (e.g. 'Camilla is having an affair with Edward? – Get out of it, that's impossible!').**

Get out of their face Cease pestering or irritating someone.*

Get out of town Expression of amazement or doubt about what has just been said.*

Get over it (1) Recover. (2) A command to stop fussing or worrying about something.*

Get physical (1) Become sexually active. (2) Become aggressive. (3) Become physically fit.* (2 and 3) or ** (1)

Get real An exhortation to think and act more sensibly and contemplate the real, rather than an imagined, situation.**

Get stiffed Be given unsatisfactory treatment.*

Get stuck into Become very interested in.*

Get stuffed A term of abuse meaning 'go away' or emphatically rejecting a suggestion.**

Get the... See entries below: the phrase being looked for may be under *given the ...*

Get the bird To be a failure. Usually describes a stage act that proves unpopular with an audience.*

Get the bit between the teeth Become excited about doing something. It is often implied that someone is so keen to do something that they are unlikely to be dissuaded from their chosen course of action. The term derives from horse riding – a horse with the bit (the metal section of the reins that should be in the back of the horse's mouth) between the teeth, is excitable and hard to control.*

Get the cold shoulder To be made to feel unwelcome. The phrase derives from the medieval habit of giving a guest cold shoulder of mutton (which is fairly unappetising and was normally reserved for the most junior of servants) when they had out-stayed their welcome.*

Get the fuck out Ruder version of *get the hell out*.***

Get the goods on Obtain information about.*

Get the green light Receive encouragement or permission to do something.*

Get the hand of Attain mastery and/or understanding of.*

Get the hang of Learn.*

Get the heck out Politer version of *get the hell out*.*

Get the hell out (1) Escape quickly. (2) Used as a command, an impolite way of telling someone to leave.**

Get the jump on Come into an advantageous position.*

Get the measure Understand.*

Get the message Means the same as *get the measure*.

Get the nod Be approved.*

Get the picture Comprehend.*

Get the show on the road Begin a project or journey.*

Get the wind up Annoy or unsettle.*

Get their act together Begin working properly.*

Get their back up Cause annoyance.*

Get their dander up Means the same as *get their back up*.

Get their end away Means the same as *have their end away*.

Get their eye in Acquire an ability.*

Get their fingers burnt Means the same as *burn their fingers*.

Get their goat Annoy.*

---

* *denotes level of impoliteness*

Get their hands dirty (1) Be directly involved in an illicit or immoral activity. (2) Be engaged in manual labour.*

Get their head down (1) Start work (the phrase generally refers to scholastic work). (2) Sleep.*

Get their head round... Comprehend something.*

Get their hooks into Gain control of.*

Get their...into gear A request to work or move faster. The two commonest uses of the phrase are probably 'get their asses into gear' and 'get their arses into gear'. Politeness varies according to the word used.* or ** or ***

Get their mitts on Gain access to, or possession of.*

Get their oats Have sexual intercourse.**

Get their own back Obtain revenge.*

Get their rocks off Have sexual intercourse.***

Get their sea legs Get used to something.*

Get their shit together Ruder version of *get their act together.****

Get their skates on Become more active and lively. The phrase is often used as a command (e.g. 'get your skates on! – we must be out of here in five minutes').*

Get their socks on Move faster.*

Get their zs Sleep. 'Zs' is pronounced 'zees'.*

Get them up (1) Wake someone (usually by waking them with a phone call or calling at their house). (2) In Australian slang, the term means to tell someone off.*

Get to an art form Become very skilled.*

Get to grips with Comprehend.*

Get to the bottom of it Discover the cause of something (e.g. 'Sarah declared that she would get to the bottom of the problem').*

Get to the point A demand that a speaker announces the *point of the story*. The term is usually used when people are irritated with a speaker who is taking too long to impart his or her message, giving unnecessary details, etc.**

Get up and go A high level of energy or enthusiasm.*

Get up steam Prepare to do something. There is usually an implication that at first progress will be slow, but will accelerate and/or get more efficient.*

Get up their nose Annoy.*

Get wind of Learn that. The phrase usually applies to a situation where someone learns about something they were not supposed to know about.*

Get wires crossed Be confused about something.*

Get you An exclamation of mild criticism, implying that what has been said is unfair or inaccurate.*

Get your act together Means the same as *pull yourself together.*

Ghost at the feast A person who spoils the enjoyment of what should be a happy occasion by being depressing.*

Ghost in the machine The mind (as distinct from the brain).*

Ghost of a chance A remote possibility. Most often heard in the form *not a ghost of a chance*, meaning no possibility at all.*

Ghost walks A theatrical expression meaning that people are about to be paid their salaries.*

Gift of the gab The skill of being a persuasive speaker. The phrase is sometimes used rather more loosely to mean 'talkative'.*

GIGO Abbreviation of *garbage in, garbage out.*

Gild the lily Spoil something attractive by adding supposed 'improvements'.*

Ginger group A group that motivates others into being more active or enthusiastic.*

Gird the loins Prepare to do something.*

Girl next door A woman of average attractiveness, from a similar social background, seen as a realistic prospect as a partner (as opposed to a fantasy figure of a very beautiful woman with a fabulously large income who in reality would be unattainable). The male version of the 'girl next door' is (not surprisingly) the *boy next door.*

Give a dog a bad name Proverbial expression, meaning that a bad reputation is hard to lose.*

Give a gobful Means the same as *give a mouthful.***

Give a mouthful Verbally abuse someone.*

Give an arm and a leg See *cost an arm and a leg.*

Give and take (1) Accepting each other's needs and wishes. (2) Peaceful co-existence in which nobody dominates a group and everyone is willing to make allowances for others' needs and wishes. Do not confuse with *give or take.**

Give as good as they get Respond to an attack with an equally effective level of force.*

Give both barrels To use a very strong verbal attack.*

Give colour to Means the same as *lend colour to.*

Give it a go Make an attempt at something.*

Give it a miss Forego.*

Give it a rest A relatively forceful request that an activity is stopped. For example, if someone has been nagging about something or talking about the same thing incessantly, the phrase 'give it a rest!' means 'please stop, you're being annoying'.*

Give it a whirl Means the same as *give it a go.*

Give it houseroom Be willing to use something or be associated with it.*

Give it some welly Do something energetically.*

Give it to (1) Punish or do something violent towards. (2) Have sexual intercourse with.* (1) or ** (2)

Give it up Cease.*

Give it up for... Applaud.*

Give me a break (1) A forceful request to stop something annoying (normally, criticising or nagging): e.g. 'give me a break – I'm doing the best I can'. (2) A statement of disbelief on hearing something that sounds improbable (e.g. 'give me a break – that's just too stupid to be believed').**

Give me strength An expression of exasperation.**

Give or take (1) Approximately. (2) Within a range of error of (e.g. 'the room is five metres long, give or take a couple of centimetres'). Do not confuse with *give and take.*

Give over A request to stop doing something (e.g. 'all that noise! – give over!').**

Give the big E Reject or dismiss a person with considerable insensitivity for their feelings.*

Give the elbow Reject or dismiss. The phrase is often used of dismissing someone from employment or ending a relationship.*

Give the finger Means the same as *give them the bird*, Definition 2. The phrase is (just about) polite, but the gesture it describes would be considered offensive.*

Give the game away (1) Tell a secret that explains how something works. The implication is usually that people have been baffled or entertained by something because they cannot understand how it was happening. When the game has been given away, the bafflement or entertainment goes with it. (2) Play so badly that the opposing side wins. The implication is that if play had been to the normal standard expected, then the opposing side would have been unlikely to win.*

Give the green light Encourage or permit something to be done.*

Give the lead Indicate to other people how they should behave.*

Give the nod Approve.*

Give their eye teeth Means the same as *give their right arm.*

Give their right arm Indicates that the person in question would be prepared to give up a lot in order to do something (e.g. 'I'd give my right arm to get tickets for the Final'). The offer to have their right arm amputated is not literal.*

Give them a bloody nose Inflict a serious defeat or setback on someone.*

Give them a break A request to someone to stop pestering or nagging another person (e.g. 'give her a break – can't you see she's finding things hard enough without you pestering her?').**

Give them a fit Annoy.*

Give them a mouthful Attack verbally.*

Give them a piece of their mind Verbally criticize someone (e.g. 'John gave Mary a piece of his mind').*

Give them a thick ear Physically punish.*

Give them a wide berth Avoid contact with.*

Give them an even break Provide someone with an opportunity to do something. The term often refers to an opportunity to work or to prove that someone can do a particular task.*

Give them an inch Part of a longer proverb that finishes with 'and they'll take a mile'. An argument that showing weakness or a concessionary nature will lead to people taking advantage and gaining far more than they are entitled to.*

Give them bondi Physically assault someone.*

Give them enough rope A saying that finishes with 'and they'll hang themselves'. The argument that some individuals given sufficient opportunity will bring harm on themselves.*

Give them grief (1) Annoy. (2) Strongly criticize.*

Give them gyp Annoy and/or be painful.*

Give them hell (1) Reprimand. (2) Make their lives unpleasant.*

Give them one To have sexual intercourse with someone (e.g. 'I'd like to give her one'). The phrase is nearly always used by a man about a woman. Use of the phrase is not recommended.***

Give them something to cry about A phrase used as a threat to someone who is making an unnecessarily vociferous protest about something trivial. The threat is that if they don't stop protesting, then a punishment that will give them a legitimate reason for protest will be administered.*

Give them the benefit of... If the phrase is finished with a phrase such as 'my wisdom', 'his experience' or similar, then it is usually intended as a sarcastic comment. For example, 'Helen gave Chris the benefit of her experience' may mean that Helen taught Chris something genuinely useful, but it probably means that Helen was telling Chris things he already knew, and that Helen was being patronising. Whether the phrase is intended to be sarcastic is dependent on the context. *Give them the benefit of the doubt* is unrelated to this phrase.*

Give them the benefit of the doubt Make a conclusion that favours someone when the evidence is ambiguous (e.g. 'the case against her was not absolutely conclusive, so the jury gave her the benefit of the doubt and decided she was not guilty').*

Give them the bird (1) To shout abuse at a performer or sports player. (2) To make an offensive hand gesture by raising the middle finger and keeping the other fingers in a clenched fist. The phrase in both senses is polite, but performing the gesture described in Definition 2 would be considered offensive.*

Give them the creeps Make someone feel nervous or revolted.*

Give them the flick Reject.*

Give them the glad eye Indicate a romantic or sexual interest in another person.*

Give them the pip Annoy them.*

Give them the shove Fire them from a job.*

Give them the slip (1) Avoid. (2) Escape.*

Give them their head Allow them to do something as they choose, without attempting to control them.*

Give them what for Punish. The phrase is often used in the form 'I'll give you what for'.*

Give themselves airs and graces See *airs and graces*.

Give up (1) Surrender. (2) Cease working on a problem or task because it has proved to be too difficult.*

Give up the ghost (1) Die or become beyond repair. (2) Lose all hope.*

Given away with... Followed by a name or phrase describing something commonplace (e.g. 'cornflakes'). Denotes something commonplace that can be easily attained.*

Given the axe Can mean the same as *given the sack*. Can also refer to the ending of a process (e.g. 'after ten years of broadcasts, the soap opera was given the axe').*

Given the boot Means the same as *given the sack*. The term may come from an image of a cross employer kicking a sacked worker off the premises. However, the term can simply mean to be made redun-

dant where the employee has not misbehaved.**

Given the bullet Means the same as *given the sack*.

Given the chop Can mean the same as *given the sack*. Can also refer to a product or similar on which production will be discontinued.*

Given the hook Means the same as *given the sack*.

Given the sack To be fired from a job. The term refers to an employee leaving a job being given a sack to carry away their personal belongings.*

Glad hand Insincere, over-exuberant greeting.*

Glad rags Best or most glamorous clothes, particularly the sort of clothing worn to a party.*

Glad to see the back of... Be glad that someone or something has gone.*

Glass ceiling An unacknowledged barrier preventing the promotion of women employees. The phrase is sometimes applied to members of minority groups.*

Glass houses See *people in glass houses*.

Gloves are off A contest or dispute is becoming increasingly vicious.*

Glutton for punishment A person who seems to become involved in difficult or dangerous situations to a perverse extent.*

Gnash their teeth Show angry behaviour.*

Gnomes of Zurich The people in charge of the Swiss banking system. The phrase derives from a period when it was felt that banks based in Switzerland were speculating on the money markets and adversely affecting economic conditions. The term is meant to be a joking one.*

Go a bundle Be very enthusiastic.*

Go ahead, make my day The phrase basically means 'do what you are intending and I will make you regret it'. The phrase was originally said by Clint Eastwood in a film in which he played a tough detective facing a criminal who was planning to shoot him – the implication was that if the criminal had tried to shoot, Eastwood would have shot him before he could reach his gun.*

Go ape Means the same as *go apeshit*, but more polite.*

Go apeshit (1) Become very angry. (2) Become very excited.***

Go as you please Unrestricted.*

Go at it like a rabbit Be sexually promiscuous.**

Go back a long way If people 'go back a long way', then they have known each other for a considerable period of time.*

Go ballistic To become very angry.*

Go bananas (1) Become very annoyed. (2) Go insane.*

Go behind their back To do something secretly. The phrase can imply that this is done in order to harm that person (see *behind their back*), but it can also imply that if one person refuses to do something, another person is approached in secret to see if they will do the same thing (e.g. 'Tom refused to do this for them, so they went behind his back and they secretly asked Harry if he would be willing to do it').*

Go belly-up (1) To fail catastrophically. (2) To die or fail past the point of recovery. The term is derived from the fact that a fish, when it dies, will float to the surface belly upwards.*

Go Buddha Become enigmatic and hard to understand.*

Go bung (1) Fail. (2) Die. (3) Become bankrupt.*

Go bush Reject formality and adopt a simpler way of life.*

Go by the board Describes an activity such as a project abandoned because it is no longer feasible.*

Go by the boards Means the same as *go by the board*.

Go by the book Perform a procedure exactly as described in official guidelines or rules.*

Go cold turkey Experience withdrawal symptoms after stopping taking addictive drugs. Can be used jokingly to describe a craving following giving up something pleasurable but non-addictive (e.g. a craving for watching soap operas having vowed to stop watching poor quality television programmes).*

Go crackers (1) Become insane. (2) Become very excited.*

Go crook (1) Fall ill. (2) Become annoyed.*

Go down A phrase with some surprisingly different meanings: (1) Be imprisoned for a crime. (2) Engage in oral sex. (3) Leave university at the end of a term or semester. (4) Be received (especially with reference to a talk or other presentation).* (1, 3 and 4) or ***(2)

Go down a bomb Be very popular.*

Go down badly Be badly received.*

Go down fighting Showing defiance even when faced with inevitable defeat.*

Go down like... Followed by a phrase indicating an unpopular thing, an unpopular activity or something that is bound to fail. The commonest form is *go down like a lead balloon*, but there are many others varying in politeness (e.g. 'go down like a bucket of cold sick', 'go down like a comedian in a funeral parlour', 'go down like Glasgow Empire on a wet Monday night', etc.). All mean 'to fail badly', usually with the added implication of becoming unpopular.* or ** or ***

Go down like a lead balloon Fail ignominiously.*

Go down well Be well received.*

Go down with all guns blazing Means the same as *go down fighting.*

Go down with all hands Suffer a serious defeat or loss.*

Go downhill Decline.*

Go Dutch Share the cost of something (usually a meal in a restaurant).*

Go easy on them (1) Give a less harsh punishment than might have logically been expected. (2) A request that a punishment be made less harsh (e.g. 'I think you should go easy on them, since they didn't fully realize what they were doing').*

Go fifty-fifty Means the same as *go halves.*

Go figure An expression of bemusement, typically said after someone has done something that does not seem logical or fair (e.g. 'nobody was cross with him and he said there was nothing troubling him, but he spent the day looking and acting depressed – go figure').*

Go for broke Risk everything on one action that will either bring spectacular rewards or produce ruination.*

Go for it A phrase exhorting people to work hard for a particular goal. During the 1980s it became synonymous with success-obsessed people who seemed to value money and power above friendship and trust. Accordingly, it is sometimes used ironically to parody such a person.*

Go for the jugular Make a very aggressive attack or criticism.*

Go forth and multiply The phrase (a quotation from the Bible) is sometimes used as a euphemism for *fuck off.***

Go gold Attain success.*

Go great guns Do something with great enthusiasm and/or energy.*

Go halves Divide or share equally (typically, share the cost of something).*

Go head to head Have a confrontation.*

Go hot and cold Feel embarrassed or shocked.*

Go in to bat for them To support someone's cause.*

Go it alone Work alone.*

Go it blind Behave carelessly without prior thought.*

Go like a bomb Move extremely quickly.*

Go like gangbusters Behave in an energetic manner.*

Go mad (1) Become insane. (2) Become angry. (3) Have (usually boisterous) fun. (4) Enjoy. (5) An instruction to enjoy something (e.g. a person giving another person a toy or something frivolous might say 'go mad', meaning 'enjoy it').*

Go native A contemptuous phrase used by Victorian colonialists to describe a white colonialist settler who rejected the values of white European society and instead adopted the lifestyle of the indigenous population. By extension, the phrase describes anyone who rejects officially sanctioned norms of behaviour in favour of the norms of another culture.*

Go nuclear Become very angry.*

Go nuts Means the same as *go mad.**

Go off the deep end React in an extreme way. There is often the implication that this reaction is illogically extreme.*

Go off with a bang Be a great success.*

Go on Depending upon the intonation of the speaker's voice and the context of the conversation, this may mean several things, but most commonly: (1) it is a request to carry on with what the person was talking about before an interruption or (2) it is an expression of amazement at what the speaker has just been told.*

Go on about Excessively talk about something.*

Go one better Do something better than someone else. The phrase is often used to imply that something has been done out of an obsessive urge to be better than everyone else (e.g. 'you just have to go one better than everyone else, don't you?').*

Go overboard Be overenthusiastic.*

Go pear-shaped Go seriously wrong.*

Go places Be successful.*

Go platinum Attain success.*

Go postal The phrase originally meant 'become homicidal', but more generally means 'become very angry'. The phrase originated in the USA after a spate of mass murders in which disgruntled postal workers killed their colleagues.*

Go public (1) Reveal a secret. The phrase usually describes revealing a secret by informing the news media. (2) Go from being a private to a public company.*

Go round in circles Perform a task that seems to accomplish nothing except increase the level of frustration. There is usually the implication that any attempt to find a solution leads back to the original problem.*

Go round the houses See *round the houses*.

Go spare (1) Become enraged. (2) Become superfluous to requirements.*

Go steady Have a long-term relationship with a sexual or romantic partner. The phrase is usually reserved for relationships that do not involve cohabitation.*

Go suck an egg A forceful request to stop interfering and/or to leave.**

Go the distance Last the full length of an arduous event.*

Go the extra mile Make an especially strenuous effort.*

Go the rounds Be disseminated widely.*

Go their own way Act independently.*

Go their separate ways (1) If people 'go their separate ways' then after a period of being united by belonging to the same group, they move away from the group (e.g. through changed ideologies, changed jobs, etc.). (2) Cease a friendship or relationship.*

Go through hell Endure great hardship and/or suffering.*

Go through the ceiling Means the same as *go through the roof*.

Go through the hoops Endure difficulties. The phrase is often used for having to undertake a difficult series of tests or a difficult training course.*

Go through the motions Perform a task with no real enthusiasm or thoroughness.*

Go through the roof (1) Become very angry (e.g. 'she went through the roof when she heard the news'). (2) Increase in value or size at a great rate (e.g. 'house prices have gone through the roof in the last two years').*

Go through with a fine-tooth comb To examine in minute detail.*

Go to blazes An expression of angry rejection or dismissal.*

Go to earth Hide.*

Go to glory Be destroyed.*

Go to ground Means the same as *go to earth*.

Go to hell An impolite way of telling someone to go away or vigorously rejecting what they have said.**

Go to hell and back Endure great hardship and/or suffering.*

Go to hell in a handbasket Means the same as *go to hell in a handcart*.

Go to hell in a handcart Deteriorate.**

Go to it (1) Do something briskly. (2) A command to do something without any further delay.*

Go to pieces Become upset and/or anxious to the extent of being incapable of functioning normally.*

Go to pot Means the same as *go to the dogs*.

Go to the country In politics, the phrase means 'call a general election'.*

Go to the dogs Show a severe decline.*

Go to the pack Means the same as *go to the dogs*.

Go to the wall Fail.*

Go to their head Something that 'goes to their head' predominates their thoughts. The phrase is generally used in two contexts: (1) if alcohol goes to a person's head, then they are drunk; and (2) if success goes to a person's head, then they become conceited and/or arrogant.*

Go to town (1) Do something very thoroughly. (2) Do something in an extravagant manner.*

Go too far Means the same as *overstep the mark*.

Go up in smoke Utterly fail.*

Go with a bang Means the same as *go off with a bang*.

Go with the flow Copy or accept the prevailing mood and/or behaviour.*

Go without saying It is expected.*

God's gift to... Strictly speaking, something that is very good for the named recipient. However, the phrase is nearly always used ironically (e.g. 'God's gift to women' describes someone whom women do not usually find desirable).*

Goes with the territory Something that is an inevitable feature of a situation.*

Going begging Something that is 'going begging' is available because nobody has so far claimed it. There is sometimes the implication that if nobody takes it, it will be thrown away.*

Going, going, gone The phrase traditionally marks the end of an auction item, meaning that the item can no longer be bid for. The phrase is sometimes used jokingly to indicate that an offer for something is about to be withdrawn unless there is a response.*

Going off (1) In British colloquial language, something that is either becoming rotten or going *off the boil*. (2) Beginning to dislike. (3) In Australian colloquial language, a term of praise for a social gathering that is enjoyable.*

Going places Becoming successful (but not necessarily yet successful).*

Going strong Doing well. The phrase is often used in the form 'still going strong', indicating that the original quality is still preserved.*

Going to the dogs Getting progressively worse.*

Golden calf Something admired for materialistic or greedy reasons.*

Golden egg See *kill the goose that lays the golden egg*.

Golden handcuffs A substantial payment given on starting a new job with the proviso that the new employee agrees to stay with the new employers for at least a fixed period of time.*

Golden handshake A payment given to a person on retiring or leaving an employer.*

Gone coon Something or someone whose fate (usually death) is a foregone conclusion ('coon' refers to a racoon).*

Gone for a burton The phrase when originally used in World War II meant 'to have died'. However, it is now used more generally about machinery and plans which are so faulty that they must be abandoned.*

Gone loco Gone insane.*

Gone to seed To have reached a stage where a person is considered too infirm to continue in their job or, less drastically, a stage where a person is doing a job as a matter of routine without being particularly energetic or innovative. The phrase comes from gardening – some plants, particularly vegetables, need to be picked before they have a chance to grow seed pods (i.e. 'go to seed') because after this point they are generally unusable.**

Gone to the great...in the sky To have died. The blank is filled in with a term associated with an activity of the deceased's (e.g. a dead teacher might be said to have 'gone to the great classroom in the sky').*

Gone west Broken.*

Good and... The phrase is intended to emphasize the meaning of the word or words that follow. For example, 'good and dead' means that something (or someone) is definitely dead. The emphasis is usually unnecessary.*

Good as new (1) Something old that is indistinguishable from something new. (2) Something that has been successfully restored to its original state.*

Good bet A wise choice that is unlikely to prove wrong.*

Good for a laugh Entertaining. The phrase is sometimes used to describe something that is of little value except to provide an amusing diversion.*

Good form (1) Correct etiquette. (2) A good physical condition. (3) Good prospects.*

Good innings Successful life and/or career.*

Good nick Good condition.*

Good offices Assistance.*

Good run for their money See *run for their money.*

Good Samaritan Someone who offers assistance without expectation of reward.*

Good screw (1) Large salary or profit. (2) An enjoyable sexual partner or sexual encounter.* (1) or *** (2)

Good spread A plentiful and varied supply of food provided for a meal. The phrase is generally used to describe a buffet-type meal at a party, wedding reception or similar.*

Goof around Behave in a foolish, unproductive manner.*

Goose See *goose is cooked, kill the goose that lays the golden egg* and *wouldn't say boo to a goose.*

Goose is cooked In trouble.*

Gory details Joking phrase that means the information that might be censored if someone prudish or sensitive was listening.*

Gospel truth The truth.*

Got another thing coming If someone has 'got another thing coming', then they are about to receive something unpleasant that they did not expect.*

Got diddly squat Means the same as *got squat.*

Got form Have a criminal record.*

Got it down to a fine art Be very skilful.*

Got it in for... Have a vindictive attitude towards.*

Got it in one Comprehended at once.*

Got it in them Have the ability.*

Got squat To have or to know nothing.*

Got their hallmark Means the same as *got their signature.*

Got their name written all over it Be absolutely characteristic of something a specific person would do or be capable of doing. The phrase is often used in one of two ways – either to denote something that a person is not admitting to doing but is almost certainly by them (e.g. 'deny it all you will, but it's got your name written all over it') or to describe something that is ideally suited to a person (e.g. 'the job that's been advertized has your name written all over it').*

Got their number Means the same as *have their number.*

Got their signature Be absolutely characteristic of something a specific person would do.*

Got what it takes Have the necessary abilities.*

Got you (1) An exclamation upon capturing or finding someone. (2) An exclamation indicating that a person finally understands what someone has been trying to explain.*

Grab the bull by the horns Means the same as *take the bull by the horns*.

Grab the headlines Be the most discussed piece of news.*

Grab the limelight Means the same as *grab the headlines*.

Grab with both hands Accept eagerly.*

Grand old man Revered older person who is a noted exponent in their field of expertise. *

Grandstand finish An exciting conclusion.*

Grasp at straws In a situation where a solution to a problem is being sought, and so far every possible solution has failed, a person might be said to 'grasp at straws' if they place hope in an implausible solution which an unbiased observer can see is hopelessly wrong.*

Grasp the nettle Deal directly with a difficult situation or problem.*

Grass is always greener The start of a longer phrase that ends 'on the other side'. The phrase ostensibly expresses the belief that conditions must be more favourable somewhere else. However, the phrase is usually used as a warning to people who are dissatisfied with their current situation and who want a change to consider the fact that practically everyone believes that another situation would be preferable, and merely thinking this does not mean that it is actually the case. Thus, the phrase means 'people always think that the grass is always greener on the other side'. For example, a person working for Company A might believe that someone working in Company B has a better job. However, by the same argument, someone working for Company B might believe that someone working in Company A has a better job.*

Grass grow under their feet See *not let the grass grow under their feet*.

Grass roots The 'ordinary' members of the public or a group (e.g. 'grass roots opinion' is what 'ordinary' people think about something).*

Grave See *turn in their grave*.

Graven image Something or someone that is the subject of misplaced over-reverence.*

Gravy train A system that offers high financial rewards in exchange for disproportionately easy work. The phrase is often used to describe jobs that seem unduly easy for the high salaries awarded, and that appear to be unfairly awarded.*

Gray area American spelling of *grey area*.

Grease the wheels Ensure that something works efficiently. There is sometimes an implication that bribes are used to ensure that something works efficiently.*

Grease their palm Bribe or persuade.*

Greased lightning Something very fast-moving.*

Greasy spoon A café with low standards of cleanliness, service and cuisine.*

Great and the good Rich and famous people.*

Great one for... A person who is noted for a particular activity or behaviour.*

Great outdoors A phrase usually intended sarcastically, denoting an enjoyment of activities that take place out of doors, such as hiking, camping and many sports.*

Great stuff Excellent.*

Great unwashed Ordinary people or, more specifically, working-class people. The phrase is usually used jokingly, but is considered unpleasant by some people and so should be avoided.**

Great white chief The person in charge. Care should be used in using this phrase since it is potentially racist on two counts: (a) the assumption that the most important person is white, and (b) the phrase is a supposed imitation of Native American use of English.**

Greatest thing since sliced bread A humorous way of saying that something is a useful invention. The phrase is also used ironically to indicate that what is under discussion is useless.*

Greeks bearing gifts See *beware of Greeks bearing gifts*.

Green around the gills Looking nauseous.*

Green-eyed monster Jealousy.*

Green fingers Ability to do gardening or horticulture.*

Green light An indication or command to begin.*

Green welly brigade Members of the British upper classes (named after the green wellington boots many of them a few years ago wore when in the country).*

Grey area Something about which there is uncertainty. This can refer to doubts about whether something belongs to one category or another (e.g. 'the issue of what is pornographic and what is not is a grey area') or, more generally, to an issue where a definitive answer has not been found (e.g. 'whether time travel will ever be possible is still something of a grey area for scientists').*

Grey matter The brain cells and hence, by association, the intellect. For example, if something 'exercises the grey matter' it is intellectually demanding.*

Grin and bear it Tolerate something unpleasant or unwelcome without complaint. The phrase is often used in the form 'you'd better grin and bear it' or 'you'll have to grin and bear it', meaning that not only must something be accepted as inevitable, but complaints will not be welcome.*

Grin like a Cheshire cat Have a very big grin. The phrase comes from the Cheshire cat, a character in *Alice in Wonderland*, who would slowly disappear – the last part of his image that disappeared was his grin.*

Grind to a halt Slow down and stop.*

Grindstone See *keep nose to the grindstone*.

Grip See *get a grip on yourself*.

Grist to the mill Experience. The phrase is often used to describe something that in itself is not very rewarding or interesting, but which cumulatively with other experiences will increase a person's knowledge and skills.*

Ground Zero (1) The epicentre of a bomb blast (particularly a nuclear bomb). (2) More generally, the most important target or aim.*

Grounds for... The phrase is usually followed by 'argument', 'discussion' or 'divorce', though many other words or phrases are possible. The phrase means 'basis for' or 'reasons for'. Thus if someone has 'grounds for an argument' they have reasons for being angry. 'Ground' can mean 'basis' or 'root'.*

Grow on trees See *it doesn't grow on trees*.

Grow up A demand that someone behaves sensibly.**

Grown grey [or gray] Become ill.*

Gun to their head Someone with a 'gun to their head' feels compelled to do something because of threats of punishment or something unpleasant.*

Gunning for Show hostility towards.*

Guns at dawn The phrase originally referred to fighting a duel with pistols (traditionally held at dawn). The phrase is now usually used jokingly to describe a dispute that has become too emotionally serious.*

Gut instinct Intuition.*

Gutful of piss Drunk.***

H

Hackles See *raise their hackles.*

Had a few In a state of intoxication or near-intoxication.*

Had it (1) Damaged, ill or worn out beyond hope of recovery. (2) Means the same as *had it up to here.* (3) In a situation where death, defeat or destruction is inevitable.*

Had it up to here To be tired to the point of anger of hearing about or dealing with a particular person or situation (e.g. 'I've had it up to here with answering questions about when the new photocopier will arrive'). The phrase can also be used in other forms (e.g. 'I've had it up to the eyeballs' – see *up to the eyeballs*).*

Had their chips Completely failed. The phrase is derived from gambling in casinos, where a gambler can only gamble for as long as they have gambling chips to play with. Once they have lost all their chips (i.e. had all their chips) then they must stop playing.*

Had their day (1) Be no longer of use. (2) Be no longer fashionable.*

Hail fellow well met An over-effusive greeting.*

Hair of the dog Sometimes followed by the words 'that bit you'. The phrase describes a (supposed) hangover cure in which a small quantity of alcohol is drunk.*

Hair-splitting Being pedantic.*

Half a chance A weak opportunity. The phrase is often used to describe how keen a person is to do something (e.g. 'given half a chance, she'll make an attempt to do it'). *

Half a loaf Something that is not all that is needed, but is nonetheless better than nothing at all.*

Half a minute Means the same as *half a moment.*

Half a mo Means the same as *half a moment.*

Half a moment (1) A brief period of time. (2) A request that someone briefly stops what they are doing (e.g. 'half a moment, I'd like a word with you').*

Half an eye Attend to something in a lacklustre fashion.*

Half-baked Not properly prepared.*

Half cut Inebriated.*

Half inch Steal. From Cockney rhyming slang for 'pinch'.*

Half measures (1) Little enthusiasm or commitment. (2) Poor quality and/or inadequate. *

Half of it The most important features. The phrase is most often used in the form *don't know the half of it*, meaning that the most important piece of information has not been revealed.*

Halfway house (1) The midpoint in a journey or activity. (2) A compromise. (3) A hostel for long-term patients and prisoners being rehabilitated into the community.*

Halt, who goes there? The traditional challenge of a military sentry. The phrase is sometimes used jokingly as a greeting.*

Halves See *not by halves.*

Ham actor A poor actor.*

Ham it up In acting, a bad performance characterized by ridiculously exaggerated emotions.*

Hamlet without the prince An event where the person who should have been the most important person there is missing.*

Hammer and tongs Vigorously.*

Hammer home Ensure that something is fully understood through the use of forceful argument.*

Hand in glove In close association. The phrase usually refers to an illicit activity.*

Hand in the dinner pail Die.*

Hand it to them Congratulate or praise them.*

* *denotes level of impoliteness*

Hand on the tiller The person with their 'hand on the tiller' is in control.*

Hand on the torch (1) Teach someone. (2) Pass the responsibility for something (particularly something with a long tradition) on to someone else.*

Hand over fist Recklessly and/or rapidly. The phrase is usually heard in the longer phrases of *spend money hand over fist* and *make money hand over fist.**

Hand them in (1) Return something. (2) Present someone to the police or similar organisation so that they can be arrested.*

Hand tied behind their back See *do it with a hand tied behind their back.*

Hand to mouth Only the basic necessities. For example, a 'hand to mouth existence' is one in which there is only money available for essential foodstuffs, shelter, etc., with no money available for luxuries or entertainment.*

Handbags at dawn A joking phrase describing a state of disagreement between two women.*

Handed on a plate Provided with something without exhibiting the effort or skill normally expected to attain it.*

Hands down Without doubt.*

Hands off (1) Do not touch. (2) Do not approach. (3) Do not interfere with.*

Hands-on (1) A 'hands-on' activity is one that requires a person to take part in the activity (i.e. it is not done automatically). (2) A 'hands-on' approach is one in which a person becomes involved in the activity, rather than delegating the work to someone else.*

Hands-on knowledge Knowledge acquired through practical experience rather than solely from theory.*

Handsome is as handsome does A proverb expressing the view that what a person does is more important than what they appear to be.*

Hang a left Go to the left.*

Hang a right Go to the right.*

Hang about This can mean the same as *hang around*, but in British slang it can also be used to indicate that a person has just realized that something is wrong (e.g. 'hang about! – there's something wrong about this').*

Hang an idea on Use something to examine the worth and/or substance of an argument or idea.*

Hang around To wait.*

Hang fire Wait.*

Hang loose Relax.*

Hang of a... A large quantity of.*

Hang on Has all the same meanings as *hang about*. It can also mean *hold it*. The precise meaning is conveyed by context.*

Hang on in there Encouragement to persevere at a difficult or unpleasant task.*

Hang on their lips Listen with great attention.*

Hang out with Spend time socially with.*

Hang them out to dry Leave them in a difficult situation.*

Hang tough Be resolute.*

Hang up (1) Terminate a telephone call. (2) A phobia or other irrational fear or dislike.*

Hang up their... Followed by the name of an item associated with an occupation (e.g. 'hang up their boots'). Retire from paid employment.*

Hanged, drawn and quartered The term originally referred to a particularly gruesome form of execution. It tends to be used today more jocularly to indicate being told off or punished.*

Hanging in the air Unresolved (e.g. 'the committee members failed to reach agreement and the issue was left hanging in the air').*

Hanging offence Originally a serious criminal offence that carried the death penalty. The phrase is often used in a joking manner to describe practically any type of transgression (the less serious the transgression, the greater the irony with which the phrase is being used). The phrase can also be used in the form 'I didn't realize it was a hanging offence', where the speaker is implying that the reaction to a transgression the speaker is accused of is far too extreme for the nature of the transgression.*

Hanging over them Threatening.*

Happy as a clam Extremely happy.*

Happy as a pig in muck Means the same as *happy as a clam*.

Happy as a pig in shit Means the same as *happy as a clam*.***

Happy as a sandboy Means the same as *happy as a clam*.

Happy as Larry Means the same as *happy as a clam*.

Happy bunny Means the same as *happy camper*.

Happy camper Joking term for someone who is happy or at least content with what they have received. The term is often used in the negative (e.g. 'following her announcement that there would be no Christmas bonus this year, the workers were not happy campers').*

Happy hunting ground Native American term for a paradise in the after-life.*

Hard act to follow Someone or something who has been very good and whom it will be difficult to match in ability. The phrase is often used of a good worker when they retire (e.g. 'Harry retires tomorrow – he was such a good worker, he'll be a hard act to follow').*

Hard as nails (1) A harsh personality with an absence of emotional warmth. (2) Physically hard.*

Hard at it Working energetically.*

Hard boiled Resilient and experienced.*

Hard case A resilient and aggressive person prone to violence.*

Hard cheese Bad luck.*

Hard nosed A harsh personality with an absence of emotional warmth.*

Hard put Finding it difficult.*

Hard way The difficult or painful way to do something. Often contrasted with the *easy way*, which is the relatively easier and/or less painful way of achieving the same ends. Having accomplished something the 'hard way' is often presented as being more fulfilling and praiseworthy than having reached the same ends using the 'easy way'. The exception is during an interrogation or an enquiry, when someone states 'this can be done the easy way or the hard way' (or similar). The phrase then means that the truth will inevitably be found, and this can be done by a quick confession (the easy way) or after prolonged questioning, possibly involving physical violence (the hard way).*

Hat See *at the drop of a hat*.

Hat in hand Means the same as *cap in hand*.

Hatches, matches and despatches Humorous description of the section of a newspaper listing births ('hatches'), engagements and weddings ('matches'), and obituaries ('despatches').*

Hate their guts Strongly dislike.*

Haul ass Move quickly.**

Haul over the coals Give a severe telling-off. The phrase comes from a medieval form of punishment.*

Have a ball Have a very enjoyable time.*

Have a bash (1) Make an attempt at doing something. (2) Host a party.*

Have a belly Have a tantrum.*

Have a bellyful Have so much of something that it feels unpleasant. The phrase can refer to over-eating or over-drinking,

* *denotes level of impoliteness*

or can mean that a person has heard more than they want about something (e.g. 'I've had a bellyful of your complaints').*

Have a bird Lose one's temper or otherwise lose a sense of calmness.*

Have a butcher's Have a look. The phrase is derived from Cockney rhyming slang ('butcher's hook – look').*

Have a cadenza Be agitated.*

Have a cob on Be angry.*

Have a cow Lose their temper. Not, as some people suppose, invented by the scriptwriters of the television show *The Simpsons*, but certainly popularized by that programme.*

Have a dig Insult or criticize.*

Have a down on Dislike.*

Have a go Attempt.*

Have a go at Criticize or nag.*

Have a good mind to... Be seriously intending to.*

Have a lend of Australian term meaning to take advantage of a person's gullible nature (e.g. 'can't you see that she's having a lend of you?').*

Have a lot on the ball Be very skilful.*

Have a mind of their own Be capable of making a decision independent of other people's advice or opinions.*

Have a mountain to climb Have something difficult to do.*

Have a naughty Australian slang for 'have sex'.**

Have a nice day Usually said on ending a conversation, the term is simply a polite way of terminating what is being said. It in effect means the same as 'farewell' ('fare well' – i.e. 'do well in what you are about to do'). However, for some reason the term annoys some individuals (particularly the British), who see the phrase as insincere, and some Britons may say it in a deliberately exaggerated American accent to denote an insincere business-person.*

Have a pop at Attack or criticize.*

Have a seat Sit down.*

Have a shot at Attempt.*

Have a thing about Have an unnatural preoccupation about.*

Have a tiger by the tail Be responsible for completing a task that, once started, cannot easily be abandoned or given to someone else, and which has proven to be unexpectedly problematic.*

Have an eye for Have an appreciation of. The phrase is often used to describe an ability to identify good works of art or talent.*

Have another thing coming Means the same as *have another think coming*.

Have another think coming A person who 'has another think coming' needs to reconsider their plans or expectations. The phrase is often used as a rebuke (e.g. 'if you think you're going out of this house dressed like that, then you've another think coming').*

Have bottle Possess courage and/or common sense.*

Have designs on Plan to do something to the person or item in question. There is usually an implication that this will be done either illegally or at least in a morally questionable manner.*

Have I got news for you A phrase indicating that the speaker is about to tell something very surprising.*

Have it away Have sexual intercourse.**

Have it both ways Manage to gain the benefits from two seemingly contradictory things. The phrase is often heard in the negative form *can't have it both ways*, meaning that a person can either have one thing or another, but not both.*

Have it coming to them Be likely to be punished for past misdeeds.*

Have it easy Have a less demanding experience than might normally be expected.*

Have it in for Have feelings of animosity towards.*

Have it off Have sexual intercourse.***

Have it your way A response that in effect means 'I don't believe your argument, but I can't be bothered to persuade you otherwise, so carry on believing it' (e.g. 'okay, have it your way – John and Sarah are having an affair. However, I don't believe it').*

Have its moments Be good or enjoyable in parts.*

Have kittens Be apprehensive.*

Have no truck with Have no dealings with.*

Have nothing on them (1) Have no incriminating evidence against someone. (2) Be less able than someone else (e.g. 'you may think you're good, but you have nothing on Brian'). (3) Possess no examples of a desired item. The desired item is usually money (e.g. 'I'd like to give you some money, but I've nothing on me').*

Have other fish to fry Have other matters to attend to. The phrase is often used to indicate that a person has more important things to do than deal with the problem being discussed (e.g. 'I can't be bothered with this – I've other fish to fry').*

Have the bulge on Have an advantage over someone else.*

Have the courage of their convictions Being prepared to put their beliefs to the test (e.g. 'if you really think your car is faster than mine, then you should have the courage of your convictions and race me at the local track').*

Have the drop on Be in an advantageous position over someone.*

Have the ear To be favoured by someone and to be able to gain access to them when others might find it difficult (e.g.

'the minister will get what he wants as he has the ear of the King').*

Have the guts Possess the courage.*

Have the heart Have the level of compassion necessary to do something. The phrase nearly always means 'have a low enough level of compassion'. Thus, 'he didn't have the heart to do it' means he had too much compassion and could not do something which required a sterner, less sentimental attitude.*

Have the history Be capable of doing something.*

Have the hots for Find sexually desirable.**

Have the jump on Means the same as *have the drop on.*

Have the last laugh Be proven correct after opposing arguments initially seemed more plausible.*

Have the last word Have the final judgement or pronouncement on something.*

Have their ass in a sling Means the same as *put their ass in a sling.*

Have their ducks in a row (1) Be organized. (2) Have a clear plan or memory of something.*

Have their end away Have sexual intercourse.**

Have their guts for garters An indication that someone is cross with someone else. The threat expressed is not literal.**

Have their number Understand them.*

Have their work cut out To have a difficult task to do.*

Have them cold Have the power to decide their fate.*

Have them down as... Have a firm opinion of.*

Have them eating out of their hand Have someone doing exactly what is wanted (e.g. 'I'll get her so well trained that she'll be eating out of my hand').*

---

* denotes level of impoliteness

Have them going Successfully deceive them.*

Have to their name Own.*

Have your cake and eat it See *can't have your cake and eat it.*

He who lives by the sword A proverb that finishes with 'dies by the sword'. In other words, someone who uses violent or unpleasant methods is likely to have them used against themselves.*

Head and shoulders above Considerably better than.*

Head around See *get their head round.*

Head hunting Recruiting a person for a job with a rival employer.*

Head in the clouds Absent-minded or daydreaming, rather than attending to the task that is supposed to be done.*

Head in the sand Behaving irrationally by ignoring problems that should be dealt with. Named after the ostrich's fabled habit of sticking its head in the sand when it senses danger.*

Head on the block See *put their head on the block.*

Head on the line See *put their head on the line.*

Head or tail of it See *can't make head nor tail of it.*

Head over heels Turned upside down. The phrase is generally used to describe the initial feeling of being in love.*

Head screwed on the right way Sensible.*

Head the bill Be the most important person. The phrase is typically used of the star of a show, but can be used jokingly to describe the most important member of an organisation.*

Head to head See *go head to head.*

Headless chicken See *like a headless chicken.*

Heads will roll There will be trouble. The phrase generally refers to situations where people are likely to be sacked for poor performance or mismanagement.*

Heap coals of fire on their head Make someone feel remorseful.*

Heaps of… A large quantity of… *

Hear them out Listen to what they have to say.*

Heart and soul If a person is described as putting 'heart and soul' into something, then they have worked very hard.*

Heart bleeds for them A phrase that originally sincerely meant sympathy for another person. The phrase is now often used ironically to indicate complete lack of sympathy.*

Heart in the mouth A very nervous or apprehensive state.*

Heart in the right place Have well-meaning intentions.*

Heart of gold Kindly and well-intentioned.*

Heart of hearts The beliefs and attitudes that a person truly believes (which may differ from the beliefs that they claim to have when talking to other people).*

Heart of ice Unaffected by emotional considerations.*

Heart of oak Brave.*

Heart of stone Cruel and/or unfeeling.*

Heart of the matter The fundamental cause or most important features of something.*

Heart on their sleeve See *wear their heart on their sleeve.*

Heart sinks into the boots Describes a sudden onset of feelings of depression (e.g. 'my heart sank into my boots on hearing the news').*

Heart to heart A discussion about emotional or personal issues between two people. The phrase generally implies that one person has an emotional problem that the other person is trying to help solve.*

Heart's content See *to the heart's content*.

Heart's desire The most wished-for thing or person.*

Heartbeat away (1) A short distance away. (2) A short period of time away.*

Heat of the moment Something done in the 'heat of the moment' is done without forethought during a busy activity when there is not time for contemplation before doing something. The implication is that something done in the heat of the moment is probably not what would be done if there were time for planning beforehand.*

Heave-ho Rejection. Thus, 'give the heave-ho to' means 'reject'.*

Heave into view Become visible.*

Heavens above An expression of surprise.*

Heavens opened It rained.*

Heavy on... A large quantity of ... *

Heavy on their feet Moving clumsily and/or slowly. This is contrasted with *light on their feet*, describing someone who is nimble (and also usually assumed to be fast-moving).*

Heavy weather See *make heavy weather of it*.

Heck of a... (1) A lot of a ... (2) An excellent example of... (3) A high magnitude of... *

Hedge their bets Avoid committing to just one thing (e.g. 'the man was uncertain who would win and hedged his bets, saying that the first candidate was most likely, but the second still had a chance'). The term can be used in a derogatory sense, implying that someone does not show dedication to a particular cause or cannot decide. It can also imply sensible caution. The term comes from betting – a person 'hedging a bet' would place a bet in the opposite direction to lessen the losses if the first bet failed. For example, suppose a woman bets 100,000 dollars at 10 to 1 on Team A to beat Team B. If she wins, she gets 1,000,000 dollars, but if she loses, she loses 100,000 dollars.

Suppose that she now puts a second bet of 20,000 dollars at 5 to 1 on Team B to beat Team A. If Team A wins, she wins 1,000,000 less the 20,000 lost bet, giving her a net gain of 980,000 dollars. If Team B wins, she wins 100,000 dollars from the second bet, and loses 100,000 dollars from the first bet – in other words, she comes out without loss (but without the second bet, remember she would have lost 100,000 dollars). Thus, the second, 'hedging' bet has a small effect if the big bet wins but makes the loss far less serious if the big bet loses.*

Heffalump trap A misfortune that a person brings upon themselves through their own foolishness. The phrase is derived from the stories of Winnie the Pooh.*

Heir and a spare Two children of the same parents (sometimes specifically two brothers). The phrase is derived from married couples in various royal families and the nobility who would carry on producing children until they had at least two sons – the eldest to inherit the title and another son who would inherit if anything untoward happened to the eldest son.*

Hell for leather Very quickly.*

Hell freezes over See *until hell freezes over*.

Hell hath no fury The start of a quotation that finishes with 'like a woman scorned'. The phrase is used when a woman exacts revenge for something done to her. The term is potentially sexist, and use of it is cautioned against.*

Hell of a... Means the same as *heck of a...*.**

Hell on... (1) An unpleasant example of the category cited in the next word or phrase (e.g. 'hell on two legs' is an unpleasant person). (2) Has a damaging or unpleasant effect (e.g. 'these shoes look nice but they're hell on my feet').*

Hell to pay Trouble (e.g. 'there'll be hell to pay' means 'there'll be trouble').*

Hell's half acre A long distance.*

---

* *denotes level of impoliteness*

Helping hand Assistance.*

Hen pecked Pestered and nagged by a woman. The phrase can cause offence, so caution is advised.**

Her indoors Joking term for 'wife' or female partner. Likewise, *him indoors* means husband or male partner.*

Her Majesty's Pleasure Prison.*

Here today, gone tomorrow Transitory.*

Here's looking at you A salutation before drinking an alcoholic drink. The phrase was used by Humphrey Bogart in the movie *Casablanca* (more accurately, he said 'here's looking at you, kid'). This explains why the phrase is often said in an execrable accent which is supposed to be Humphrey Bogart, but spoken by an Englishman is usually simply embarrassing.*

Hewers of wood and drawers of water Members of the general workforce considered unimportant and interchangeable.*

Hidden agenda The secretly intended outcome of an activity that is not the same as the aim that is publicly claimed. The term is often used to describe company managers who tell the workers they are working for one set of outcomes, but who are in secret really working for another set that will benefit them but be detrimental to the rest of the workforce.*

Hide their light under a bushel Describes someone who is modest about their skills or achievements. The phrase is often heard in the form *don't hide your light under a bushel*, which means 'don't be so modest'. The phrase is from the New Testament.*

Hiding to nothing If someone is on a hiding to nothing, then they are engaged on a task which will not yield anything useful.*

High and dry In a difficult situation.*

High and low Everywhere.*

High as a kite Intoxicated.*

High days and feast days Special occasions. The phrase is sometimes used in its original Christian sense of days in the Christian calendar that are marked by special religious services.*

High days and holidays Special occasions.*

High dudgeon Anger.*

High end Expensive and/or highest quality.*

High five A gesture involving two people slapping raised palms together. The gesture is used as a greeting/congratulation. Thus, someone calling for a 'high five' is asking for the listener to use this gesture.*

High flyer Successful person.*

High ground The person or group who possess the 'high ground' are at an advantage.*

High heaven See *smell to high heaven*.

High jump See *for the high jump*.

High maintenance Someone who is in many respects desirable, but who has expensive tastes and a demanding personality.*

High old... Especially noteworthy.*

High on the hog Luxurious living.*

High spots (1) Most noteworthy things. (2) Most enjoyable things. (3) Places of entertainment.*

High street (1) The principal district for everyday shopping needs in a town or city. (2) Used as an adjective, the typical features of something bought in shops in this area (e.g. 'if you shop on the Internet, things are cheaper than high street prices').*

High, wide and handsome Of impressive, aesthetically pleasing appearance.*

Highly strung Permanently anxious.*

Hilt See *up to the hilt*.

Him indoors See *her indoors*.

His Nibs Strictly speaking, a facetious term for someone who has a too high opinion of their own importance. However, the phrase seems to be mellowing to mean simply 'him'.*

Hit a brick wall Discover a difficulty with a plan that is either impossible or very difficult to solve.*

Hit and miss Imprecise. The phrase is often confused with *hit or miss*.*

Hit and run (1) A 'hit and run' accident is where a driver hits someone (usually a pedestrian) and drives off in an attempt to evade arrest. (2) The damage caused by an accident of this type.*

Hit for six (1) Have a profound effect on someone. (2) Be profoundly affected.*

Hit home (1) Be accurate. (2) Make a remark that is accurate and makes an argument that a person finds uncomfortable to think about. (3) Make the importance of something apparent.*

Hit it off Form a friendly relationship.*

Hit on Indicate a sexual interest in.**

Hit on an idea Have an idea.*

Hit or miss Of variable quality. The phrase is often confused with *hit and miss*.*

Hit paydirt Discover something very lucrative or informative.*

Hit the bottle Drink alcohol excessively. The term can describe a single bout of drinking or long-term alcohol abuse (e.g. 'he's been hitting the bottle for years').*

Hit the buffers Fail.*

Hit the ceiling Means the same as *go through the roof*.

Hit the deck Dive to the ground.*

Hit the ground running Be ready-prepared to start a job or, alternatively, to be suitably qualified for a job. The implication is that a person so equipped will get the job in question done quickly and efficiently.*

Hit the hay Go to bed.*

Hit the jackpot (1) Win a major prize. (2) Do something that has unexpectedly beneficial and/or successful results.*

Hit the mark (1) Make a correct judgement or answer. (2) Succeed.*

Hit the nail on the head Give an answer or judgement that is exactly right.*

Hit the road Begin a journey.*

Hit the roof Means the same as *go through the roof*.

Hit the sack Go to bed.*

Hit the skids Decline severely.*

Hit the town Enjoy an evening of socialising in a town or city. There is usually the implication that this involves consumption of alcohol and not very cerebral entertainment.*

Hit the trail Means the same as *hit the road*.

Hit the turps Means the same as *hit the bottle*. It does not mean that a person is literally drinking turps.*

Hitch horses together Work amicably.*

Hitch their wagon to a star Make use of contacts with a more powerful and/or successful person to advance one's career.*

Hobson's choice No option. Named after a seventeenth-century stable owner who hired horses and, instead of the usual practice of allowing customers to choose their horses, made them take whichever was the next available on the rota.*

Hog the limelight Means the same as *steal the limelight*.*

Hoist by their own petard To fall victim to their own plans. A petard was a primitive explosive device – thus, the phrase originally meant 'blown up by their own bomb'. *

Hold a brief Represent or support a particular argument or cause. Conversely, *hold no brief* means 'does not represent or support a particular argument or cause'.*

---

* *denotes level of impoliteness*

Hold a gun to their head Force a person to do something they would not have voluntarily done.*

Hold all the aces To have all the advantages available.*

Hold all the cards Means the same as *hold all the aces.*

Hold court Be the dominant person in a group. The phrase nearly always refers to a person who dominates a group of friends.*

Hold in contempt Have strong feelings of dislike towards someone or something.*

Hold it A demand to stop so that what has just been said or done can be thought about and/or discussed.*

Hold no brief See *hold a brief.*

Hold on Means the same as *hang on.*

Hold on to themselves Show self-reliance (i.e. rather than relying on others for help).*

Hold the field Remain undefeated.*

Hold the front page (1) A phrase used by newspaper editors instructing printers to stop printing because a new story has just been reported that will necessitate changing what goes on the front page (i.e. there is some exciting news). (2) The phrase is more often used jokingly to announce that something new or unexpected has happened.*

Hold the fort Can mean the same as *hold the shop* or may mean that a person should carry on for the moment with a difficult job and that help is going to be provided soon.*

Hold the line (1) Remain on the telephone whilst the person on the other end is temporarily absent. (2) Maintain an expressed belief or argument in spite of criticism.*

Hold the phone (1) Means the same as *hold it.* (2) An expression indicating that there is important information that needs to be attended to.*

Hold the purse strings Control the finances.*

Hold the shop To look after things for a while. The phrase was used by a senior shop or store assistant who would tell a junior member of staff that they were in charge of things whilst the senior assistant went out for a while. From this usage the phrase has spread to any situation in which someone is told that they are temporarily in charge. The 'hold' in the phrase is probably derived from the same idea as using 'grip' in *get a grip on yourself.*

Hold the stage Be the most dominant person in a situation.*

Hold their breath Wait anxiously for something to happen. Conversely, if someone says *don't hold your breath*, then they mean that it is unlikely that anything will happen.*

Hold their hand (1) Offer support when a person is feeling sad or insecure. (2) Instruct someone in a new skill at a slower rate than would normally be considered appropriate because the person is feeling insecure or uncertain of their abilities.*

Hold their horses A forceful method of asking someone to wait.*

Hold their own Successfully maintain their position in a competition or argument.*

Hold their tongue Say nothing.*

Hold them to it Make them fulfil a promise they have made.*

Hold themselves Means the same as *hold on to themselves.*

Hold to ransom Threaten to do something unpleasant unless demands are met.*

Hold up (1) A delay. (2) A demand for a pause.*

Hold water Be plausible.*

Holding the baby See *left holding the baby.*

Hole in the head Phrase denoting an undesirable state of affairs. The phrase 'I'd sooner have a hole in the head' denotes that the person thinks what is being offered is unattractive – it is doubtful if they honestly would prefer this.*

Holier than thou Unattractive, sanctimonious behaviour. The phrase often refers contemptuously to a person who uses outwardly pious behaviour to attempt to demonstrate that they are morally superior.*

Holy grail Something that is highly sought-after and elusive. This can be a physical object or something abstract (e.g. 'a true grand unifying theory is the holy grail of physics'). It does not have to have religious connotations.*

Holy of holies (1) The most sacred part of a place of worship. (2) A place of especial importance.*

Home and dry Successfully completed.*

Home and hosed Means the same as *home and dry*.

Home free Means the same as *home and dry*.

Home from home A place that is as comfortable or desirable as one's true home.*

Home, James The phrase is often followed with 'and don't spare the horses'. A jocular phrase told to a driver (whether or not they are called James or indeed male) on starting a journey home. The phrase is a reference to the instruction given by a rich person to their driver in the days when the horse and carriage was the preferred method of travel for rich people.*

Home run A decisive act that is unambiguously advantageous. Named after the most direct method of scoring a point in baseball.*

Homeward o'er the lea Travel in the direction of home. The phrase is a misquotation from Thomas Gray's *Elegy Written in a Country Churchyard* and is intended as an ironic or comical phrase. A journey that actually requires traversing a lea (i.e. pasture land) is not literally implied.*

Hone the idea Develop an idea into a logically more satisfying form.*

Honest broker An impartial mediator.*

Honest injun An expression of sincerity. Currently seen as somewhat old-fashioned, and potentially politically incorrect.**

Honest penny Money earned by honest means.*

Honour among thieves The concept that even amongst otherwise dishonest groups of people, there may be a code of basic conduct and decency. The phrase often specifically refers to thieves refusing to aid the police in capturing a fellow criminal.*

Honour bound Compelled to do something out of a sense of moral obligation.*

Honours are even No difference in performance.*

Hook, line and sinker The entire thing. The term is derived from fishing (the hook, line and sinker are in effect the bits of the fishing tackle which the fish could potentially swallow – usually only the hook is taken in).*

Hook up (1) Meet. (2) Provide.*

Hoops See *go through the hoops* and *put through the hoops*.

Hop in Get in.*

Hop it A request to go away (actually hopping away is not necessary).**

Hop the twig (1) Die. (2) Leave.*

Hope against hope Maintain faith in something in spite of strong evidence in favour of a contrary position.*

Hope chest Means the same as *bottom drawer*.

Hope in hell See *don't have a hope in hell*.

Hope springs eternal A phrase (actually an adaptation of a line of poetry by Alexander Pope) expressing the argument that people can be optimistic even in difficult situations.*

Hornets' nest A problematic situation that, like a real hornets' nest, is normally best left undisturbed. See *stir up a hornets' nest.**

Horse of another colour Something that is radically different.*

Horse sense Common sense.*

Horse's mouth The definitive source of information. Hence, *straight from the horse's mouth* means information that is completely reliable.*

Horses for courses People differ in their skills; thus, one person will have the best skills to tackle one sort of problem, whilst a different person would be best at dealing with another type of problem.*

Hostage to fortune (1) A foolish or incautious remark that incriminates or creates problems for the person who said or wrote it. (2) A promise that is impossible to fulfil.*

Hot air A derogatory term for a lot of talking without any practical results coming from it. The phrase is often used of political candidates at election time making plenty of promises about how they will improve the electorate's lives but then failing to change anything once elected.*

Hot and cold running... Readily available... *

Hot blooded Passionate. Contrast with *cold blooded.**

Hot button A controversial topic.*

Hot off the press The latest news or gossip.*

Hot on the heels Closely following. The phrase can literally mean that someone is physically close to a person ahead of them, or it can mean that there is little difference between two competitors or candidates.*

Hot potato A troublesome situation that it would be wise to avoid being involved with.*

Hot seat See *in the hot seat.*

Hot ticket A very popular theatrical performance or concert.*

Hot to trot Ready for action.*

Hot under the collar Angry about something.*

Hothouse flower A person who is overly sensitive and/or incapable of dealing with even slightly difficult or demanding situations.*

House divided against itself An organisation that fails to work effectively because of disputes between its members. The implication is that the organisation is likely to fail because of this.*

House of cards An over-ambitious plan that is almost certain to fail.*

Houseroom See *give it houseroom.*

How far can they go? What are the limitations on their activities? The phrase is sometimes used to describe the limits on the extent of sexual activity that a person is willing to allow.*

How long is a ball of string? Means the same as *how many beans make five?**

How many beans make five? The phrase is obviously nonsensical – when given as an answer to a question it means 'I don't know'. There is often an implication that the question itself is either pointless or silly. However, note that the phrase *know how many beans make five* means 'intelligent'.*

How the land lies The current situation.*

How the other half lives The lifestyles of another socio-economic group. The phrase nearly always refers to the extravagant lifestyles of some wealthy people.*

How's the enemy? Another way of asking 'what's the time?' Given that we live in a world in which so many things have to be done to deadlines, it's perhaps not surprising that some people see time as 'the enemy'.*

How's your father The phrase is not used as a question, but rather is used to describe something unseemly, liable to provoke embarrassment, or fraught with complications or trouble. For example, 'the whole affair was a right how's your father' might be taken to mean that the affair in question was complicated and unseemly. The phrase may also be used as a euphemism for 'sexual intercourse'.*

Howl at the moon Means the same as *bark at the moon.*

Hug a tree Derogatory term for a rather naive love of counter-culture.*

Hum and haw Be indecisive.*

Humble pie See *eat humble pie.*

Hundred and one reasons Lots of reasons.*

Hung, drawn and quartered A corruption of *hanged, drawn and quartered* (a person who is executed by hanging is 'hanged', not 'hung').*

Hung like a... Possessing a penis of a size commensurate with the animal named in the rest of the phrase (e.g. 'hung like a horse' indicates a large penis).***

Hurl chunks Vomit.*

Hustle their ass Means the same as *move their ass.*

Hustle their butt Means the same as *move their ass.*

I

I am not worthy A sarcastic or humorous response to an invitation, an offer, or a compliment. The phrase imitates the response of an overly obsequious servant given a reward by the head of the household (e.g. 'I am not worthy of such beneficence, oh great one').*

I ask you An expression of disgust. The phrase is usually intended to elicit sympathy or agreement from the listener (e.g. 'well, I ask you, what was I supposed to do?').*

I bet This has two principal meanings. (1) At the start of a phrase it means 'given the information I have, I predict the following will happen' (e.g. 'I bet they'll be married within twelve months'). (2) As a response to something, an expression of disbelief (e.g. 'it says in the paper that taxes will come down next year – huh! I bet!').*

I dare you The phrase has two very different meanings depending upon the context and the tone of voice. (1) The phrase can mean that the speaker is daring someone to do something. (2) It can also mean 'do not dare to do it'. Typically, the first is followed by a description of what the speaker wants to happen (e.g. 'I dare you to throw a snowball at the teacher'), whilst the second is said by itself or is repeated for emphasis (e.g. 'I dare you, I just dare you').*

I don't wish to know that, kindly leave the stage See *boom boom.*

I for one A phrase emphasising the strength of belief in the statement (e.g. 'I for one don't believe it').*

I have a cunning plan A joking phrase used as an introduction to a plan or proposal. It is a quotation from a popular British TV comedy series *Blackadder*, in which a well-meaning but intellectually ungifted dogsbody called Baldrick would regularly announce that he had 'a cunning plan' before expounding a comically impractical proposal.*

I tell a lie Phrase said immediately after someone has realized they have just said something that is incorrect (e.g. 'Brian is older than Sue. No wait, I tell a lie – it's the other way round').*

I want your babies Joking statement (often made by a man) indicating gratitude for something that someone has done for them.*

I'd sooner...than... The phrase sets an unattractive (and usually implausible) action against the action being discussed (e.g. 'I'd sooner mud wrestle my grandmother than see that film'). The phrase varies in politeness dependent upon how polite (or rude) the first action in the phrase is. The phrase should not be taken literally – what the speaker is indicating is that they find the action being discussed unattractive.* or ** or ***

Ice breaker (1) Something done deliberately to initiate conversation between people who do not know each other. This can vary from starting a simple discussion (e.g. 'isn't the weather nice at this time of year?') to a party (e.g. an 'ice breaker' party for new students). (2) Something that attempts to reconcile people who are not communicating with each other following a disagreement.*

Icing on the cake Means the same as *cherry on the cake.*

If it kills them If someone says that they will do something even 'if it kills them' it means that they will make a considerable effort.*

If it looks like a duck This is actually the start of a much longer phrase – 'if it looks like a duck, walks like a duck and quacks like a duck, it's a duck'. The phrase simply expresses the view that if something or someone looks and acts like it's supposed to, then it is what it appears to be.*

If looks could kill Describes a very hostile expression.*

If the cap fits The start of a longer saying – 'if the cap fits, wear it'. It means that a criticism that has been made is probably an accurate one. The implication is that either the person should accept the criticism or do something about making changes so the criticism no longer applies.*

If the mountain won't come to Mohammed The rest of the phrase is 'then Mohammed must go to the mountain'. The argument that, if problems arise, often the only way to solve them is to make an extra effort and/or compromise.*

If the shoe fits Means the same as *if the cap fits.*

If wishes were horses The start of a longer proverb, which ends 'then fools would ride'. The proverb argues that merely hoping for something will not make it happen.*

If you can't beat them join them A piece of advice that argues that if an enemy cannot be defeated, then it might be pragmatically sensible to join with the enemy. The phrase is usually used in a humorous way.*

If you can't lick them join them Means the same as *if you can't beat them join them.*

I'll be a monkey's uncle An expression of surprise.*

I'll get you A threat of punishment or revenge.*

I'll go to the foot of our stairs An expression from the North West of England indicating total amazement.*

I'll kill you Almost invariably a threat of punishment or revenge rather than actual murder.*

Ill wind See *it's an ill wind.*

I'm a Dutchman A phrase added on to the end of a statement the speaker does not believe (e.g. 'if he's a graduate of Harvard then I'm a Dutchman'). The phrase can also be used in the form 'or I'm a Dutchman', where it follows a statement of what the speaker does believe (e.g. 'it's a fake or I'm a Dutchman').*

I'm all right, Jack An accusation that someone is being selfish; because their interests are protected, they have no interest in helping others. The phrase is often used of someone who has a well-

(or over-) paid job who can cause misery to others through either inaction (e.g. a worker not fulfilling a contract on time) or action (e.g. a government minister issuing ludicrous policies) but whose own position is seemingly utterly impregnable and unaffected by the consequences of their actions.*

Impression management Attempting to create a favourable impression.*

Improve the shining hour Make optimal use of the situation and/or time allocated.*

In a bad place Feeling depressed, burdened with problems and vulnerable.*

In a cleft stick In a difficult situation where any possible solution is far from satisfactory.*

In a corner In a difficult position or situation. Thus, *out of a corner* (or *out of a tight corner*) refers to an escape from a difficult situation.*

In a fog Baffled.*

In a hole In a difficult situation.*

In a huff In a bad mood.*

In a jiffy In a short period of time.*

In a nutshell In summary.*

In a pig's eye An expression of disbelief.*

In a pinch Means the same as *in a tight spot*. See *at a pinch*.

In a rut In a boring, uninspiring, depressing situation that is difficult to escape. The phrase usually describes an unappealing job or lifestyle.*

In a tight corner Means the same as *in a corner*.

In a tight spot In a difficult situation.*

In Abraham's bosom Dead; in Heaven.*

In all but name Functioning exactly like something or someone with an official title or label, but without the title or label. For example, at various times in history weak monarchs have been told everything they should do and say by advisers, who might thus be said to rule the country 'in all but name'.*

In at the kill Be present at the conclusion. There is often an implication that this proves rewarding or profitable.*

In bad odour Not favoured.*

In bed with (1) Formed a close alliance with. (2) Having sexual relations with.*

In business Means 'everything is prepared, so we can start work'. It is used in conversation more than writing (e.g. 'we've got everything we need, so now we're in business').*

In by the back door To gain admission or acceptance by unconventional means. The phrase is frequently used to mean gaining admission or acceptance by illegal methods.*

In cahoots In conspiracy.*

In clover In a state of great contentment. The phrase comes from the fact that cows prefer pasture with a high content of clover.*

In cold blood Something done in cold blood is done deliberately and without the excuse of being angry and temporarily incapable of controlling one's actions. A murder in cold blood is one that was carefully planned rather than, for example, the unfortunate result of an argument that became violent.*

In deep Involved in a situation to a great extent. If the situation is an illegal one, then a person 'in deep' is in serious danger of criminal prosecution if caught.*

In deep do-do Slightly ruder version of *in deep water*.**

In deep shit Ruder version of *in deep water*.***

In deep water In serious trouble.*

In dock Being repaired. Do not confuse with *in the dock*.*

In Dutch Encountering problems.*

* denotes level of impoliteness

In evidence Something 'in evidence' is something that can be noticed. The phrase usually implies that what can be noticed is important or unusual.*

In fine feather In a good mood.*

In fine fettle In good condition.*

In first flush In the early stages, when showing the greatest promise and energy.*

In fits In a state of great amusement.*

In for a penny, in for a pound Describes a situation in which *any* commitment or interest makes someone irredeemably part of something.*

In for it Expecting to receive punishment.*

In for the chase Ready for action.*

In force In large quantities.*

In full cry Describes a forceful protest.*

In full flight Escaping as quickly as possible.*

In full flood Displaying a high level of energy.*

In full flow Can mean the same as *in full flood*, but also can mean talking without hesitation.*

In full swing At the maximum level of activity.*

In funds (1) Financially solvent. (2) Possessing money.*

In germ At a preparatory stage.*

In good nick To be in good condition.*

In good odour Favoured.*

In good time (1) Eventually. (2) On time or ahead of schedule. Context should indicate which meaning is intended.*

In harness (1) At work. (2) Working together.*

In hock In debt.*

In hot water In trouble.*

In kilter Balanced or harmonious.*

In like Flynn The term means to perform a quick and successful seduction. It originated from tales of the supposed success of the film star Errol Flynn in such matters.**

In midstream In the middle of a process.*

In mothballs Not being used. There is usually an implication that, although not being used, it may be used on future occasions.*

In my book A phrase that means 'in my personal opinion' (e.g. 'in my book it's okay to do that').*

In on it Means the same as *in on the act*.

In on the act To have knowledge of what's going on. Hence, *get in on the act* means to gain knowledge of what's going on. There is often an added implication that to be 'in on the act' is to be aware of something being kept secret from most people.*

In one ear and out the other If a person is told something and it's said that it's 'in one ear and out the other', then it is implied that either (1) the person was not paying attention or (2) the person lacked the intellectual ability to understand what they were told.*

In one piece Unharmed.*

In over their head Means the same as *out of their depth*.

In parentheses (1) Pertinent to what is being discussed, but not essential. (2) An additional piece of information.*

In passing Describes something done without any importance or emphasis being attached to it. The phrase is usually used to describe something that is said.*

In perspective Considered objectively.*

In pocket Having made a profit or at least not made a loss.*

In pod Pregnant.**

In pop At the pawnbroker's.*

In purdah Barred from contact with others. The phrase originally referred to Indian women kept hidden from strangers.*

In shirtsleeves A shirt or blouse is the outermost garment on the upper half of the body (i.e. other things are being worn as well). The phrase denotes that the weather is warm or hot.*

In stitches In a state of great amusement.*

In the air The phrase can mean *hanging in the air*, but it may also mean 'promised' or 'likely to happen soon'.*

In the altogether Naked.*

In the bag (1) If something is 'in the bag' then it is almost certain that it will be achieved (e.g. 'are you sure you can do this job?' – 'don't worry, it's in the bag'). (2) In a state of drunkenness.*

In the balance In other words, undecided. For example, if it is unsure if a very sick person is likely to live or die, it is said that their life is 'in the balance'.*

In the ballpark To be approximately correct.*

In the black To have a bank account in credit.*

In the buff Naked.*

In the can Already completed. The phrase comes from movie-making – developed film is kept in circular cans.*

In the cards Means the same as *on the cards*.

In the catbird seat In a position of importance or power.*

In the clear (1) No longer in danger. (2) Free from blame. (3) In a sports competition, a long way ahead of opponents in points or distance.*

In the club Pregnant.**

In the dock (1) Being accused of wrongdoing. (2) Being a defendant in a trial. Do not confuse with *in dock*.*

In the doghouse In disgrace.*

In the driving seat In control.*

In the family way Pregnant.*

In the first place Initially.*

In the flesh Physically present. The phrase is often used in describing meeting a famous person who has previously only been seen on television, at the movies, etc., or, alternatively, meeting a person with whom one has corresponded, talked to on the telephone, etc., but never physically met.*

In the frame (1) Suspected of having done something. (2) The centre of attention.*

In the fullness of time See *fullness of time*.

In the Gazette Have a bankruptcy publicized.*

In the gift of… Something that the person named in the phrase has the power to grant (e.g. 'the prize is in the gift of Simon' means that Simon will decide to whom the prize will be given).*

In the hole Owe money.*

In the hot seat Be responsible for a crucial decision. The phrase is often used for the person in charge of something.*

In the know Means the same as *in on the act*.

In the lap of the gods If something is 'in the lap of the gods' then its outcome can no longer be influenced, and things must be allowed to take their course.*

In the limelight To be the centre of attention. The phrase is derived from the days when theatre spotlights were called 'limelights', and the star of the show would be lit especially strongly by them.*

In the long run In other words, in the future. The phrase nearly always is applied in situations where the immediate value of something is compared with its long-term usefulness (e.g. 'in the long run buying a more expensive hi-fi will be worth it, because it will need repairing less often').*

In the loop (1) Part of a group or process. (2) Privy to information known only to a limited few people. The opposite is *out of the loop.**

In the lurch In a problematic situation.*

In the money Rich.*

In the nick of time Just in time.*

In the open (1) Not secret. (2) Outdoors.*

In the palm of their hand In their control.*

In the picture Comprehending.*

In the pink Healthy.*

In the pipeline In preparation.*

In the public eye A person 'in the public eye' is well known and their activities are reported with considerable frequency by the news media.*

In the pudding club Pregnant.**

In the raw (1) Naked. (2) In very cold weather. (3) In its most basic form.*

In the red Have a bank account in debit, or more generally be in debt.*

In the road Being an obstruction.*

In the round A play or concert in which the audience surrounds the whole of the stage.*

In the running A plausible candidate for something. The phrase is usually used in describing applicants for a job or potential prize-winners. Someone who has little or no chance of being chosen is said to be *out of the running.**

In the saddle In control.*

In the same ballpark Means the same as *in the same league.*

In the same boat Have the same problems and advantages as another person (e.g. 'we're in the same boat – you and I both need to find a solution to this problem or we're both in equal trouble').*

In the same breath Refers to a situation where someone says one thing and then follows it with another statement that apparently contradicts the first (e.g. 'in the same breath he promised greater spending power and higher taxation').*

In the same league To be of approximately equivalent quality or ability.*

In the shit Less polite version of *in the soup.****

In the soup Experiencing a serious problem.*

In the sticks In a remote rural location. The phrase is a relative one, and generally denotes somewhere that the speaker thinks is obscure, rather than being obscure by a more objective measure.*

In the tent pissing out There are various versions of this phrase, which in its longest form is something like 'I'd sooner have them in the tent pissing out than outside the tent and pissing in'. The phrase expresses the view that it is better to have an unpleasant person as an ally than as an enemy.***

In the thick of it In the most demanding and/or busiest part of something.*

In the twinkling of an eye Something that happens 'in the twinkling of an eye' happens very quickly.*

In the wrong box (1) In a difficult situation. (2) Misclassified.*

In the zone In a position to finish something successfully.*

In their bad books In disgrace.*

In their bad graces Not liked.*

In their blood Genetically inherited.*

In their corner Offering support and encouragement.*

In their cups Drunk.*

In their dreams A response indicating that what has just been said is hopelessly beyond what the speaker is capable of accomplishing (e.g. 'when I'm a millionaire' leading to the reply 'in your dreams!').*

In their element In a situation for which they are ideally suited.*

In their face Very direct and confrontational. See *in your face.**

In their good books In favour.*

In their good graces Liked.*

In their grip In their control or capable of coming under their control.*

In their hair Being irritating.*

In their hip pocket Means the same as *in their pocket.*

In their pocket Under another person's control.*

In their range Means the same as *in their reach.*

In their reach Capable of being attained.*

In their shell-like The full phrase is 'in their shell-like ear', an overly poetic phrase said for comic effect. The phrase essentially means that the speaker wants a private chat or needs to convey a piece of information in a more private setting.*

In their sights Describes something that is wanted or desired and is likely to be attained. *

In their veins If someone has something *in their veins,* then they are very gifted at it.*

In tow If someone is 'in tow' then they are accompanying someone else, usually in a position of inferiority.*

In trim In good condition.*

In two minds Undecided.*

In with Friendly with.*

In with a shout Has a reasonable chance.*

In your face (1) Describes a person who is too strident or unsubtle. (2) A term of abuse indicating that something has been achieved that an opponent did not expect.* (1) or ** (2)

Incline an ear Be favourable towards.*

Indian file A group of people following each other in a single line (i.e. rather than walking side-by-side).*

Indian summer (1) A period of warm weather towards the end of the summer season when normally the first signs of autumn would be expected. (2) A period of unusually high productivity and/or success in later life.*

Industrial action A strike by a labour force – in other words, industrial *in*action.*

Industrial strength Very powerful.*

Ins and outs The full details of something.*

Inside information Information that is supposed to be kept secret. The phrase nearly always refers to confidential plans dealing with strategy or similar.*

Inside out If someone knows something 'inside out' then they know everything there is to know about it.*

Into orbit To a greater level of magnitude.*

Into the dumper Into an even worse situation.*

Into the groove In a state of happiness and/or enjoyment.*

Into thin air The state into which something goes if it disappears (e.g. 'it vanished into thin air').*

Invent themselves Permanently alter personality and/or behaviour to convey a particular impression.*

Iron entering the soul (1) Becoming sterner about something, having previously been more prepared to attend to emotional considerations. (2) Becoming less emotionally accommodating due to ill-treatment.*

Iron fist in a velvet glove Describes a regime that is outwardly pleasant and polite, but is in reality run by fear and repression.*

Iron out the wrinkles Deal with minor irritations or problems. The phrase is generally used to describe the resolution of minor problems before a large-scale project or piece of work is finished.*

Iron rations Basic provisions.*

* denotes level of impoliteness

Irons in the fire The range of options or ongoing activities a person has.*

Is the Pope Catholic? Means the same as *can a duck swim?*.*

It doesn't grow on trees It is not plentiful. The phrase is often used as a gentle rebuke if someone is naively supposing that a particular item or commodity can be used liberally. See *money doesn't grow on trees.*

It figures It appears logically plausible.*

It isn't over until the fat lady sings A warning that a situation might still change (i.e. don't presume too soon). The phrase refers to the observation that several famous operas reach their climax with an aria from the lead female character. Since in popular imagination (but not all that frequently in reality) female opera singers are rather buxom and overweight, the phrase expresses the belief that until the fat lady sings, the opera isn't finished.*

It never rains but it pours A phrase expressing the belief that some things never occur in small quantities.*

It takes two to tango A phrase expressing the belief that in a dispute the fault is never all on one side.*

It'll come out in the wash In other words, over time something that feels unpleasant now will stop feeling quite as bad. Alternatively, over time something will sort itself out without needing to take much action now.*

It'll end in tears A prediction that something will not end happily.*

It'll mean changing the light bulb A phrase that means 'it will be considerable work for little effect'. The phrase comes from the British television series *Red Dwarf*, a science fiction comedy series. In one episode, one of the characters demands that the space ship goes from yellow to red alert, prompting the reply from another crew member that this will mean changing the light bulb.*

It'll play in Peoria Meaning that it will be acceptable to people with unsophisticated tastes. The phrase is American theatrical slang (and a rather unfair judgement on the citizens of Peoria). The name of another place is sometimes used.*

It's a free country An argument that something is permissible. The phrase is used in several ways, among the commonest of which are the following. (1) As a reply to an attempt to prevent an intended action (e.g. 'it's a free country, I can do what I like'). The argument being made is that certain human freedoms are protected by law, including the right to behave in a wide variety of ways. Thus, 'it's a free country' in this instance is claiming that something is perfectly legal. (2) As a humorous granting of permission (e.g. 'do you mind if I smoke?' might get the reply 'it's a free country'). In this context, the phrase sometimes indicates that the person saying 'it's a free country' is not very keen to give permission but feels they must because there are no sound grounds for objecting other than personal preference. (3) As a protest against an attempted infringement of personal freedoms (e.g. 'it's a free country, they can't do that').*

It's an ill wind A proverb that finishes with 'that blows no good'. In other words, it is very unusual for a situation to be so bad that nobody benefits from it.*

It's beyond me It is something that cannot be understood.*

It's not rocket science See *rocket science.*

It's not the end of the world Words of consolation indicating that although something seems bad, it is not as bad as it might be (in other words, it's not the end of the world, which is about the most catastrophic thing people might imagine).*

It's only rock 'n' roll In other words, it's not meant to be taken too seriously.*

It's their funeral The phrase can be paraphrased as 'they are about to do something foolish and it will result in something unpleasant, but it is their own decision to do this, and only they will experience anything unpleasant as a result of their actions, so let them get on with it'.*

It's their lookout Means the same as *it's their funeral.*

It's their show It is their responsibility.*

Itching palm A strong desire for money. The phrase usually indicates that there are few scruples about how the money is obtained.*

Itching to Having a strong urge to.*

Itchy feet A restless desire for change.*

Ivory tower A person said to be living or working in an ivory tower is one who is sheltered from the unpleasantness of everyday life. The phrase is often used by non-academics of university lecturers under the (erroneous) assumption that doing research and teaching are easy activities.*

J

Jack of all trades Someone who is adept at a wide range of tasks. The phrase is sometimes completed with 'and master of none', indicating that although a person is adept at many things, he or she is ultimately not an expert in anything.*

Jam tomorrow The promise of something pleasant or rewarding that never in fact arrives. A fuller version of the phrase is 'jam tomorrow and jam yesterday but never jam today'. Thus, the phrase describes a promise that is never going to be fulfilled.*

Jeeze Louise An expression given in response to something unreasonable or unfair.**

Jekyll and Hyde A person who alternates between two radically different personalities (typically, one is pleasant, the other not). The phrase derives from the book

by Robert Louis Stevenson which described a 'mad scientist' who radically changed personalities after taking a potion.*

Jesus wept The phrase is in fact the shortest verse in the the Bible, but has become used (and generally is interpreted) as an expletive.***

Jewel in the crown The most attractive feature and/or biggest accomplishment.*

Jiffy See *in a jiffy.*

Job for the Marines A difficult task. The phrase is often used sarcastically.*

Job's comforter A person who tries to comfort someone else but actually makes things worse, either deliberately or accidentally.*

Job's worth A person who would rather obey the letter rather than the spirit of the regulations governing their employment. It thus describes every miserable curmudgeon of a shop assistant or security guard who will do nothing to help customers because it's not in their job description. The phrase is derived from the phrase 'it's more than my job's worth to do that', frequently uttered by such individuals.*

Jobs for the boys Sinecures from nepotism. In other words, lucrative (and comparatively undemanding) jobs which are provided for friends of influential people such as politicians and senior civil servants and which the general public never gain the opportunity to apply for.*

Joe [or Jo] Public Means the same as *person in the street.*

Joe Six-Pack Means the same as *person in the street,* or sometimes more specifically a person of limited aesthetic sensibilities and a rather crass attitude to intellectual accomplishments.*

Join the choirs invisible Die. The phrase is nearly always used jokingly. If a person pronounces 'invisible' as 'invisibyool' they are imitating the pronunciation of the phrase by a character in the *Monty Python* 'dead parrot sketch'.*

Join the club If person A describes something that happened to them, and person B replies 'join the club', then person B is indicating that the same thing has happened to them.*

Join the great majority Die.*

Joke is on them If the joke is on a person, then they have been made to look foolish or have failed in their plans. The phrase is often used to denote someone who planned to make someone else look foolish, but has ended up being the victim themselves.*

Joker in the pack (1) An unpredictable member of a group. (2) A term of mild disapproval for the member of a group most likely to do or say something foolish.*

Judas kiss Betrayal.*

Juggle balls in the air Means the same as *keep balls in the air*.

Jump down their throat Respond with unnecessary aggression. The phrase is often used to describe someone who responds with irrational bad temper to an innocuous statement.*

Jump in (1) Interrupt. (2) Get in.*

Jump in line Means the same as *jump the queue*.

Jump in with both feet Show a wholehearted commitment.*

Jump on the bandwagon Join a popular cause or activity. The phrase usually implies that someone joins because it is popular and other people are doing it, rather than because they have a genuine interest.*

Jump out of their skin Be very frightened and/or surprised.*

Jump ship (1) Describes a sailor deserting a ship (when in port). (2) Resign from a job.*

Jump the gun Begin to do something before the correct time. The phrase is derived from athletics races – a runner who 'jumps the gun' sets off before the starting pistol has been fired.*

Jump the queue (1) Join a queue other than at the end of the queue (i.e. act unfairly). (2) Get the opportunity to do something before others who were seemingly more entitled. The phrase often implies that this is done through unfair means.*

Jump the rails Fail to follow the expected plan.*

Jump the shark Move from being entertaining to being of indifferent or poor quality. The phrase is often used of long-running television shows at the point where they begin to lose audience interest. The phrase comes from the 1970s situation comedy *Happy Days* – in one episode (considered by many critics to mark the start of the decline) one of the characters water skis over a shark.*

Jump the track Means the same as *jump the rails*.

Jump their bones Have sexual intercourse with.**

Jump through hoops Be required to do unnecessarily irksome tasks in order to attain a desired outcome.*

Jump to conclusions Means the same as *leap to conclusions*.

Jumping up and down Very angry.*

Jury is out The issue is undecided.*

Jury rig (1) Bribe or threaten members of a jury to return a particular verdict. (2) Adjust or alter components to perform a task for which they were not specifically designed.*

Just about Approximately.*

Just deserts A punishment that matches the severity of the misdeed.*

Just kill me Means the same as *just shoot me*.

Just shoot me A joking expression of apology after making a mistake.*

Just shout A request to ask for help in the future (e.g. 'if you need help in the future, just shout'). There is no literal implication that the request has to be shouted.*

Just what the doctor ordered Something that gives the optimal benefit. The phrase is usually used jokingly to describe something the speaker finds pleasurable, such as an alcoholic drink.*

K

Kangaroo court Self-appointed group of people who decide if a person is guilty of something. The phrase is usually used as a condemnatory phrase of groups of workers who decide they are the fit judges of other workers and what is an appropriate reward or punishment for other people's actions.*

Kangaroos loose in the top paddock Insane, eccentric or intellectually ungifted.*

Keen as mustard Eager.*

Keep a dog and bark yourself See *you don't keep a dog and bark yourself.*

Keep a lid on (1) Keep under control. (2) Keep secret.*

Keep a straight face Maintain a facial expression and demeanour of calmness although having a strong need to laugh or smile.*

Keep an ear out for Listen for a specified event to happen (e.g. 'keep an ear out for the doorbell ringing').*

Keep an eye on Watch and/or attend to.*

Keep an eye out for Watch for a specified event to happen (e.g. 'keep an eye out for their car arriving').*

Keep at arm's length See *arm's length.*

Keep at bay Prevent someone or something having an effect by preventing them from doing something. The origin of the phrase is probably similar to that for *bring to bay.* *

Keep balls in the air To run several tasks at the same time.*

Keep cave Keep lookout.*

Keep half an eye on Watch and/or attend to whilst concurrently doing something else. The phrase is often used to indicate that something is not being done with sufficient attention.*

Keep in shoe leather Have a subsistence wage.*

Keep in the dark Withhold information from.*

Keep it at bay Prevent something from attacking or otherwise having an effect or influence.*

Keep mum To remain silent, or to keep a secret. See *mum's the word.* *

Keep nose to the grindstone Keep working hard. The phrase may imply working hard at a difficult or boring job, or may be used jokingly to describe work that is either undemanding or only of average difficulty.*

Keep on an even keel Keep things relatively safe and secure.*

Keep open house Be hospitable.*

Keep options open Means the same as *leave options open.*

Keep out of their hair (1) Avoid. (2) Not annoy.*

Keep passing the open windows Don't do anything foolish. The phrase originated as advice to dissuade people contemplating suicide by jumping from a high window.*

Keep regular hours Be predictable in their behaviour.*

Keep tabs on Follow or keep informed about.*

---

* *denotes level of impoliteness*

Keep taking the tablets Joking comment implying that someone is behaving in an eccentric or illogical manner (i.e. that they are acting as if insane and should be on medication).*

Keep the ball rolling Keep an activity going; the phrase is often used to describe keeping a conversation going by introducing new things to talk about when people are tired of the topic being discussed.*

Keep the flag flying Maintain support for, or representation of, something or someone in spite of difficulties.*

Keep the pot boiling Maintain interest in something.*

Keep the wolf from the door Have enough money and possessions to avoid being homeless, suffer effects of poverty, hunger, etc. The phrase is often used facetiously.*

Keep their cool Remain calm.*

Keep their end up Manage to do an allotted task under difficult circumstances.*

Keep their eye in Maintain an ability.*

Keep their eye on the ball (1) Keep watching the movement of a ball in a sports match. (2) Monitor events carefully. If people *take their eye off the ball*, then they fail to watch the movement of the ball or fail to monitor events with sufficient care.*

Keep their eyes open Means the same as *keep their eyes peeled*.

Keep their eyes peeled Remain observant.*

Keep their eyes skinned Means the same as *keep their eyes peeled*.

Keep their feet (1) Physically retain their balance. (2) Fail to be deterred.*

Keep their feet on the ground Have *both feet on the ground*.*

Keep their hair Have not gone bald.*

Keep their hair on Remain calm. The phrase is often used in the form 'keep your hair on!' which is given in reply to someone expressing anxiety or agitation.*

Keep their hand in Practise a skill.*

Keep their head Remain calm and logical.*

Keep their head above water Survive. The phrase is often used to denote remaining solvent in times of financial problems.*

Keep their head down Remain inconspicuous.*

Keep their nose clean Avoid punishment.*

Keep their nose out (1) When describing another person (e.g. 'they kept their nose out') it means refraining from being nosey. (2) When issued as a command (e.g. 'keep your nose out of my business!') it is more aggressive and is a command for someone to stop interfering and/or being nosey.* (1) or ** (2)

Keep their pecker up (1) In UK English, the phrase means 'remain resolved and/or optimistic'. (2) In US English, the phrase means 'maintain a penile erection'. Caution in use is thus advised.* (1) or *** (2)

Keep their powder dry Be prepared.*

Keep their shirt on Do not lose their temper. The phrase is nearly always used as a command or a response to someone who looks as if they are about to lose their temper.*

Keep them dangling Keep someone feeling uncertain.*

Keep them posted Keep them informed.*

Keep them sweet Keep them contented.

Keep themselves to themselves Be secretive or avoid providing much personal information.*

Keep under their hat Keep secret.*

Keep up with the Joneses Strive for social respectability by copying the behaviour of typical members of the desired social class. The phrase is often used to describe rather pathetic individuals who strive to have the same lifestyles as richer neighbours.*

Keep your chin up Advice to maintain a cheerful, positive attitude, even though the situation may be a difficult one to deal with.*

Kettle of fish See *different kettle of fish* and *pretty kettle of fish*.

Key moment A *turning point* or, more generally, a time in development where something of great importance happens (e.g. a key moment in a married person's life might be the first time they met their future spouse).*

Kibosh on... To put the kibosh on something is to either spoil it or to stop it.*

Kick around (1) Discuss. (2) Abuse. The context should indicate which meaning is intended.*

Kick ass (1) Be commanding and authoritative and get things done. (2) Powerful and appealing (e.g. 'the track has a kick ass rhythm').* (2) or ** (1)

Kick at the cat An opportunity.*

Kick butt Means the same as *kick ass* (though generally restricted to definition 1).

Kick down the ladder (1) A person who 'kicks down the ladder' prevents others from using the same methods to attain success that he or she used. (2) Disowning former friends and/or colleagues.*

Kick in the pants A stimulant to induce greater effort.*

Kick in the teeth Severe disappointment. The phrase usually implies that this is the result of betrayal or a failure to honour a promise.*

Kick into touch Reject or declare unimportant.*

Kick off Begin.*

Kick out of bed See *wouldn't kick out of bed*.

Kick over the traces Reject or refuse to acknowledge rules and regulations.*

Kick the bucket Die.*

Kick the habit Stop doing something that until now has been done regularly. The word 'habit' does not in this case necessarily indicate an addiction.*

Kick their ass Dominate or punish someone.**

Kick their butt Means the same as *kick their ass*.

Kick their heels Wait to be told what to do. The implication is that people 'kicking their heels' could and should be gainfully employed but instead are wasting their time. Compare with *kick up their heels*.*

Kick them when they're down Do something unpleasant to a person when they are already in a weakened and/or vulnerable position.*

Kick up a fuss Means the same as *kick up a stink*.

Kick up a stink Make a strong complaint.*

Kick up dust Make a fuss.*

Kick up the arse Means the same as *kick in the pants*, but less polite.**

Kick up the backside Means the same as *kick in the pants*, but less polite.**

Kick up their heels Enjoy. Compare with *kick their heels*.*

Kick upstairs Remove someone from a position in which they are incompetent and/or causing harm by apparently giving them a promotion. The promotion is almost invariably to a job that carries little real influence.*

Kid gloves Gentle treatment.*

Kid's stuff Means the same as *child's play*.

Kill me See *just kill me*.

* denotes level of impoliteness

Kill or cure A method that will either completely succeed or completely fail.*

Kill the fatted calf Have a lavish celebration to celebrate meeting someone not seen in a long time. The phrase is from the New Testament and refers to the parable of the *prodigal son*. These days it is often used sarcastically to indicate that someone seen frequently will be given a modest form of refreshment.*

Kill the golden goose Means the same as *kill the goose that lays the golden egg*.

Kill the goose that lays the golden egg Destroy a successful and/or lucrative scheme.*

Kill the messenger Means the same as *shoot the messenger*.

Kill them A joking remark made when there are a group of people and someone has just said something ridiculous or impractical. *

Kill themselves laughing Be greatly amused.*

Kill two birds with one stone Fulfil two aims with a single act (e.g. 'by taking his daughter to the movies, Charles gave his wife a few hours' rest and also pleased his daughter, thereby killing two birds with one stone').*

Kill with kindness Harm or destroy by being over-indulgent (e.g. giving an obese person a present of a large box of chocolates).*

Kill you See *I'll kill you*.

Killing See *make a killing*.

King is dead, long live the king The phrase is used upon announcing the death of a British monarch and the immediate succession of the next monarch (there are of course variants, e.g. 'the King is dead, long live the Queen', etc., depending upon the genders of the people involved). The phrase is used more generally to indicate that although a person in a particular position of power may go, another will immediately take their place.*

King's ransom A large amount of money.*

Kingdom come Eternally.*

Kiss and make up Make amends after a disagreement. There is not necessarily a requirement to kiss.*

Kiss and tell Provide details of a sexual or amorous encounter. The phrase is often used to describe stories sold to tabloid newspapers in which a sexual encounter with a famous person is recounted (and in which kissing seems usually to be the least of it). *

Kiss ass Engage in *ass licking*.***

Kiss it goodbye Admit that something is irretrievably lost.*

Kiss of death The modern use of the phrase is derived from the Mafia's supposed habit of kissing an intended victim, indicating that they are to be killed (in turn derived from Judas betraying Jesus by kissing him). The phrase usually means that a particular individual act is the final and sure sign that something will fail. It is thus nearly synonymous with some meanings of the *straw that broke the camel's back*.*

Kiss the rod Accept punishment.*

Kissed the Blarney stone A person who has 'kissed the Blarney stone' is very talkative and persuasive. The phrase comes from the legend that kissing a particular stone on the ramparts of Blarney Castle (near Cork in Eire) gives a person the powers of verbal persuasion.*

Knee high to a grasshopper Very small. The phrase is nearly always used to describe someone very young.*

Knee-jerk reaction A rapid response that is made automatically without any appreciable contemplation of its appropriateness.*

Knickers in a twist A state of agitation.**

Knight in shining armour A person who solves a problem, gets others out of difficulty, or commits a similar praiseworthy action. The phrase is derived from fairy stories and similar tales where a brave and handsome knight rescues the *damsel in distress*, kills the terrifying monster, etc.*

Knight of the road A person who travels on roads a great deal as part of their employment.*

Knock for a loop Astonish.*

Knock for six (1) Utterly defeat. (2) Strongly affect.*

Knock heads together Means the same as *bang heads together*.

Knock into a cocked hat Be far better than (e.g. 'the new model knocks the old one into a cocked hat').*

Knock into shape Improve performance. The phrase often implies that this will be done using harsh methods.*

Knock into the middle of next week Hit very hard.*

Knock it off A demand to stop doing something.*

Knock me down with a feather An expression of total amazement (e.g. 'I was so surprised you could have knocked me down with a feather').*

Knock off (1) Sell. (2) Kill.*

Knock off their perch (1) Supplant. (2) Surprise.*

Knock on the door Apply to join.*

Knock on the head Find the definitive answer.*

Knock out (1) Render unconscious. (2) Produce (e.g. 'this is a small piece of work that I knocked out in a couple of hours').*

Knock spots off Be considerably better than.*

Knock the crap out Ruder version of *knock the stuffing out*.***

Knock the shit out Ruder version of *knock the stuffing out*.***

Knock the stuffing out Weaken.*

Knock their block off A slang expression meaning 'knock their head off'. A threat to do physical harm to someone (e.g. 'I'll knock your block off!'). The phrase is not a literal threat of decapitation.**

Knock their socks off Means the same as *knock them dead*.

Knock them dead Greatly impress with a high quality performance.*

Knock them in the aisles Means the same as *knock them dead*.

Knock them sideways Shock or surprise someone.*

Knock themselves out Work very hard. See *knock yourself out*.*

Knock yourself out Means the same as *go mad*, definition 5.

Knock up (1) To awaken by knocking on a person's door. (2) To make pregnant. The first meaning is almost exclusively British. British readers are accordingly advised to use the phrase with caution (e.g. 'I called round early and knocked her up' may create an unfortunate impression in an American listener).*

Know how many beans make five See *how many beans make five?*

Know in the biblical sense Having sexual relations with. The phrase derives from the Bible's use of 'know' to mean 'having sex with'.*

Know it backwards To know something very well.*

Know the ropes Be familiar with, and competent in, what is required.*

Know the score Have a competent knowledge of the situation.*

Know the way the wind blows Be fully aware of the situation and be able to predict what will happen next.*

Know their onions Be knowledgeable.*

* *denotes level of impoliteness*

Know what to charge Describes a retailer or other commercial enterprise that charges high prices.*

Know what's what Possess an adequate level of information.*

Know where the bodies are buried Know some important information that other people are anxious should be kept secret.*

Know which side the bread is buttered Be loyal to those who pay the most or offer other kinds of reward.*

Know who's who Know the identity and importance of people involved in a particular situation.*

Knuckle down Begin to behave sensibly after a period of lax behaviour and/or laziness. *

Knuckle under Means the same as *knuckle down*.

L

Labour of Hercules A demanding task.*

Labour of love Something done for the simple pleasure of doing the task or to please someone else.*

Ladies who lunch Women with sufficient income who can afford not to work, and spend their time socialising, shopping and having lengthy lunches at expensive restaurants (i.e. whilst others have to work). The term is often used disparagingly.*

Lady of leisure A woman with no employment. The phrase is often used for someone who is retired or is so rich that they do not need to work.*

Lair it up Be vulgar or ostentatious.*

Lamb to the slaughter A person almost certain to fail or have unpleasant experiences. The phrase is often used of people who are too unskilled or inexperienced for a situation in which they will face far more skilful and dangerous opponents.*

Lame duck A person handicapped in some manner. More generally, a person who is not particularly good at something.*

Land of Nod Sleep.*

Land of the living Wakefulness.*

Land on their feet Means the same as *fall on their feet*.

Landslide victory Overwhelming victory.*

Large as life Undeniably there. The phrase is often used to emphasize that a person really was present at an event.*

Larger than life Describes a person or thing that is very conspicuous and thus attracts a disproportionate amount of attention.*

Last chance saloon See *drinking in the last chance saloon*.

Last ditch effort A final attempt to do something. Usually the implication is that more orthodox methods have failed and the final attempt is something done in desperation.*

Last resort An option to be used only if all else has failed.*

Last straw Means the same as *final straw*.

Last thing (1) Literally, the last thing that is done in a sequence. (2) Late at night.*

Last word (1) The final judgement or pronouncement on something. (2) The most fashionable.*

Late in the day Towards the end of an activity. The phrase often indicates that something is of no value because it has appeared too late (e.g. 'it's a bit late in the day to be proposing changes, isn't it?').*

Late in the game Means the same as *late in the day*.

Lathered up (1) Excited. (2) Overexcited.*

Laugh a minute Very funny. The phrase is nearly always used sarcastically to describe something that is very depressing.*

Laugh all the way to the bank Become rich easily.*

Laugh in their face Mock or show scorn.*

Laugh is on them The side that had appeared victorious is now defeated.*

Laugh like a drain Laugh loudly.*

Laugh out of court Reject as ridiculous. The phrase is often used to describe an illogical argument.*

Laugh the other side of their face Experience the emotional feelings of being punished after experiencing pleasure from committing a misdeed.*

Laugh themselves sick Laugh for a long time.*

Laugh themselves silly Means the same as *laugh themselves sick*.

Laugh up their sleeve Hide their amusement.*

Law of the jungle The belief that those who are strongest and most aggressive are predestined (and indeed deserve) to win.*

Law unto themselves Capable of doing what they please with little regard for other opinions, conventions or even the law of the land.*

Lay a finger on… See *don't lay a finger on…*

Lay a ghost to rest Settle a troublesome or worrying issue.*

Lay an egg Fail spectacularly.*

Lay at their door Identify the person or group responsible.*

Lay down the law Issue commands about how things should be done.*

Lay it on the line Give straightforward, unambiguous information.*

Lay it on thick Exaggerate and/or be very voluble.*

Lay it on with a trowel Exaggerate.*

Lay it straight Means the same as *lay on the table* (definition 1).

Lay low (1) Reduce to a state of misfortune. (2) Hide.*

Lay off (1) An expression indicating that a person has been pestered too much about something (e.g. 'lay off! – I want a change of subject'). (2) To make a person unemployed (e.g. 'because of the worsening economic situation, Amalgamated Widgets had to lay off half its workforce today').* (2) or ** (1)

Lay on the table (1) In UK English, the phrase means to present a piece of honest, straightforward information. (2) In US English, the phrase means to postpone something. See *table a motion*.*

Lay on their oars Means the same as *rest on their oars*.

Lay to rest Resolve something.*

Lead a merry dance Create trouble.*

Lead by the nose Have complete control over someone.*

Lead down the garden path Means the same as *lead up the garden path*.

Lead in their pencil Energy and/or enthusiasm. The phrase often refers to sexual drive.*

Lead up the garden path Deceive. There have been several theories of the origin of the phrase, including: (a) the argument that it refers to leading an animal to slaughter and, (b) in notable contrast, the argument that it refers to taking someone into the garden with the aim of seduction.*

Lead with the chin Be aggressive. The phrase refers to a stance in boxing.*

Leap down their throat Means the same as *jump down their throat*.

Leap in the dark A speculative or risky action.*

Leap to conclusions Make a decision before all the evidence has been heard, usually based on emotions and prejudice rather than logical reasoning.*

Leap to the eye Be very noticeable.*

Learn the ropes Acquire the skills necessary to fulfil the requirements of a particular job or task.*

Leave no stone unturned Do something thoroughly. The phrase usually refers to a search or an investigation.*

Leave options open Not commit to a particular course of action that would exclude other courses of action being taken.*

Leave the door open Provide an opportunity. The phrase is often used to describe a plan that allows for amendments.*

Leave the nest Means the same as *fly the nest*.

Leave their mark Have a long-lasting effect.*

Leave them cold Leave people feeling unimpressed.*

Leave them standing Be far better than.*

Leave under a cloud Depart in disgrace or with a suspicion of wrongdoing.*

Left at the post Failed to compete or provided very poor competition.*

Left field Unexpected.*

Left footer Roman Catholic.*

Left holding the baby To be given a difficult situation to deal with, usually with little prospect of help. In other words, like a woman left to look after a baby after the father of the child has deserted them.*

Left holding the bag Means the same as *left holding the baby*.

Leg over Sexual intercourse.*

Leg up Assistance in starting something.*

Lend a hand Assist.*

Lend an ear Listen.*

Lend colour to Make a tale more plausible by adding details to it.*

Less is more Originally the phrase was used in architecture, to mean that an environment with less detail is more aesthetically satisfying. The term is now used more generally to mean that if something is used sparingly, it may have a more pleasing effect than if its presence is overwhelming (e.g. garlic in cookery).*

Less than no time Rapidly.*

Let bygones be bygones Forget past grievances and attempt to be more friendly.*

Let down Disappoint.*

Let down gently Inform someone of bad or upsetting news in a sensitive manner.*

Let down their guard Be less defensive.*

Let it all hang out Means the same as *let their hair down*.*

Let it drop (1) Reveal a piece of information in a casual manner. The phrase is nearly always used for a piece of information that is scandalous or of great importance that might not normally be expected to be announced simply in a passing remark. (2) Cease discussing something.*

Let it lie Avoid drawing attention to something (typically, something that is likely to cause arguments if attention is drawn to it).*

Let it ride Do not act upon something, at least for the moment. Note that there is no implication that the matter will not be returned to later.*

Let off steam Release pent-up anger, energy or frustration.*

Let rip Proceed without restraint. The phrase often refers to verbally attacking someone.*

Let sleeping dogs lie Leave something alone, because to do anything may cause a disproportionate amount of trouble.*

Let slip Reveal something in conversation.*

Let the cat out of the bag To reveal a secret. There are several theories about the origin of this phrase.*

Let the dog see the rabbit Permit the person delegated to do a task to get on with it.*

Let the earth swallow me up An expression of embarrassment – the person is feeling emotionally uncomfortable and is expressing a strong need to escape the situation they find themselves in.*

Let the genie out of the bottle Initiate something that is hard to control. Thus, *put the genie back in the bottle* refers to managing to control something that is difficult to control.*

Let the side down A person who 'lets the side down' disappoints the group to which he or she belongs through his or her actions. The implication is usually that, as a result, other members of the group will have more problems than before.*

Let their hair down Relax and/or act in an unrestrained manner.*

Let themselves go Become unconcerned about appearance, health or normal standards of decorum.*

Let up Relief or cessation (e.g. 'they questioned us for two hours without let up').*

Let's be having you (1) A demand to work or move faster. (2) A request to start something (e.g. 'I'd like to see the first group – let's be having you').*

Let's get down to brass tacks See *brass tacks*.

Level best The highest standards that can be attained when making a genuine effort.*

Level playing field Showing no favouritism.*

Level with them Be truthful with them.*

Licence to print money A lucrative process.*

Lick and a promise Hastily and poorly done job.*

Lick into shape Improve performance.*

Lick their boots Means the same as *ass licking* (only politer).*

Lick their lips Hopefully expect.*

Lick their shoes Means the same as *lick their boots*.

Lick their wounds Brood upon, and repair damage resulting from, defeat.*

Licking ass Means the same as *ass licking*.

Lie back and think of England Means the same as *close your eyes and think of England*.**

Lie doggo Remain very still.*

Lie low Hide.*

Lie of the land What something is like. The phrase is generally used to describe the current state of a problem or project.*

Lie through their teeth Lie with no justifiable moral reason for doing so.*

Lie to their face Tell a lie with no discernible sign of guilt.*

Life after… The phrase is followed by a word or another phrase indicating the event in question (e.g. 'retirement', 'being made redundant', 'colostomy', etc.). The phrase refers to the lifestyle of a person rather than simply the issue of whether they are living or dead.*

Life and soul of the party A person who is especially lively and agreeable at parties and thus helps others enjoy parties. The phrase is sometimes used as a euphemism for someone who got embarrassingly drunk or sarcastically to describe a person who is miserable and makes parties less enjoyable.*

Life in the fast lane The lifestyle of rich, famous and fashionable people.*

Life in the old dog yet Phrase expressing surprise or approval that, in spite of appearances to the contrary, an older

---

* *denotes level of impoliteness*

adult is capable of performing well at the activity under discussion.*

Life of Riley To have an easy, stress-free life with either no work or an easy job to do.*

Life under... The typical living and/or working conditions when a particular person or group was in power. The phrase can be used to describe an historical epoch (e.g. 'life under the Romans') or a contemporary setting (e.g. 'life under the current President').*

Life with a capital L The realities of a normal lifestyle, rather than a sheltered lifestyle where one may be protected from learning too many unpleasant things.*

Lift a finger Do the bare minimum of activity. The phrase is often used in the negative form (e.g. 'you won't lift a finger to help') indicating that someone is lazy or unwilling to help others.*

Lift the elbow Drink alcohol.*

Light a fire under Make more active and/or motivated.*

Light bulb See *it'll mean changing the light bulb*.

Light of their life The person most loved.*

Light on... Followed by a word or phrase indicating what a person is 'light on'. The phrase means 'lacking' (e.g. 'light on experience' means 'lacking experience'). An exception to this is *light on their feet*.*

Light on their feet See *heavy on their feet*.

Light the blue touch-paper To annoy someone. The phrase is generally used for specific occasions when someone says a single phrase that is sufficient to start a fierce argument. The phrase comes from the instructions on a firework to 'light the blue touchpaper and stand back'.*

Light the fuse Initiate a problem or situation.*

Light the touchpaper Means the same as *light the fuse*.

Lightning never strikes twice The (statistically dubious) belief that having experienced one rare event, there is no possibility of another rare event occurring.*

Lights are on Start of a longer phrase, that usually ends 'but there's nobody home' (or similar). A description of a person who appears alert but in reality is slow to respond and/or lacking in intellectual giftedness.*

Lights their candle See *whatever lights their candle*.

Like The word can be used to mean the same as 'as if' (e.g. 'like you'll really do that'). Used in this sense, the word generally expresses doubts that what is described will occur (e.g. 'like that's really going to happen') or that what has just been said is true (e.g. 'like you care').*

Like a cat that ate the canary Means the same as *like a cat that got the cream*.

Like a cat that got the cream A phrase used to describe someone who is looking very pleased or smug.*

Like a child in a candy store Means the same as *like a child in a sweet shop*.

Like a child in a sweet shop Being free to do something personally enjoyable without restraint.*

Like a dog with two dicks Ruder version of *like a dog with two tails*.***

Like a dog with two tails Describing a very happy person.*

Like a dose of salts Rapidly.*

Like a dream Successfully.*

Like a duck to water A person who learns a new skill 'like a duck to water' learns very quickly, as if they are naturally suited to the task.*

Like a headless chicken A person behaving 'like a headless chicken' is behaving illogically. There is usually the implication that they are panicking about something that could be easily solved if they dealt with the problem in a logical way.*

Like a scalded cat Something that is moving 'like a scalded cat' is moving very quickly.*

Like a Trojan (1) Hard-working. (2) Honourable.*

Like banging their head against a brick wall The phrase sometimes continues with ' – it's nice when it stops'. The phrase describes the frustration of engaging in an effortful task that seems destined to fail.*

Like billy-o The phrase means 'at an extreme' (e.g. a person running quickly might be described as 'running like billy-o').*

Like blazes Means the same as *like billy-o*.

Like death warmed up Describing the state of feeling ill. It is usually meant to sound humorous.*

Like father like son The principle that someone is likely to resemble their parent in behaviour.*

Like fury Vigorously.*

Like getting blood out of a stone If something is 'like getting blood out of a stone', then it is very difficult or even impossible.*

Like getting blood out of a turnip Means the same as *like getting blood out of a stone*.

Like giving a donkey strawberries A never-ending task.*

Like grim death With determination.*

Like lightning Rapidly.*

Like mother like daughter Means the same as *like father like son*.

Like nobody's business Means 'very well' or 'very expertly' (e.g. 'he's going through this work like nobody's business').*

Like nothing on Earth Unusual. The phrase does not literally mean 'extraterrestrial', however.*

Like sardines Packed closely together.*

Like shit off a shovel Very quickly.***

Like shooting fish in a barrel Means the same as *like taking candy from a baby*.

Like someone possessed With a high level of agitation and activity.*

Like stink With great vigour.*

Like taking candy from a baby Something done with ease.*

Like talking to a brick wall Describes the frustration of talking or writing to someone who is unresponsive. The phrase is often used to describe attempting to give a person instructions that they then ignore.*

Like the back of their hand If someone says that they know something 'like the back of their hand', it means they know it very well.*

Like the clappers Very quickly.*

Like water off a duck's back (1) Having no effect. (2) Failing to adhere.*

Likely story A sarcastic phrase expressing disbelief in something.*

Limb of Beelzebub The phrase was originally a very serious accusation that someone was acting in an evil or sinful manner. These days the phrase is more likely to be used rather less seriously to indicate that someone or something is displeasing (e.g. 'this photocopier is always going wrong – I swear it's a limb of Beelzebub').*

Limelight See *in the limelight* and *steal the limelight*.

Line in the sand A firm limit to what a person is prepared to do and/or approve.*

Line of country Area of specialist knowledge.*

Line of least resistance The method likely to prove least difficult.*

Lion's share The largest proportion.*

Lips are sealed A promise to keep a secret (e.g. 'my lips are sealed – I won't tell anyone else what you told me').*

Listen with half an ear Listen for something whilst concurrently doing another task. The phrase is often used to indicate not listening for something with sufficient attention.*

Lit up (1) A facial expression of great pleasure or hope. (2) Drunk. (3) Lit a cigarette, cigar or pipe.*

Little bird told them A joking explanation of how someone learnt about something. The intention is to avoid revealing the name of the person who provided the information.*

Little black book A list (often in a small address book) kept by a sexually active person with a list of addresses of sexual partners.*

Little black dress A dress of simple design and black in colour suitable for most social occasions (for women, obviously; it is difficult to think of any conventional social occasion where a man wearing a little black dress would be considered suitably attired). The term is sometimes used to indicate an item that is suitable for a wide range of occasions.*

Little escapes them They are very observant and/or well-informed.*

Little ray of sunshine A person who can make others cheerful. Nearly always used sarcastically.*

Little red book A collection of phrases by Chairman Mao in Communist China, which was used as a propaganda tool. The term is sometimes used to denote any publication which is felt to contain propaganda rather than facts or reasoned argument.*

Little tin god Someone undeserving of veneration. The phrase is often used of people who have too high an opinion of themselves.*

Live a lie A person 'living a lie' is consistently behaving in a manner that requires them to repress their true nature (e.g. a married man who is homosexual).*

Live a little Do something frivolous or daring.*

Live and breathe... Followed by the name of an activity. Someone who 'lives and breathes' something has an almost fanatical interest in it.*

Live high on the hog Enjoy a luxurious lifestyle.*

Live in the past Be excessively preoccupied with reviving old memories or of using outmoded methods and values.*

Live it up Have a hedonistic lifestyle.*

Live life to the full See *to the full.*

Live off the fat of the land Have the best or most desirable things.*

Live off the land Exist on what can be found.*

Live on borrowed time Literally, a person who is living on borrowed time is alive after a date when they were expected to die. By extension, the phrase is used to describe anyone or anything that continues to function after a point when it was expected they would be made to stop.*

Live on their hump (1) Be self-sufficient. (2) Survive on reserve supplies, usual supplies having been severed or exhausted.*

Live on their nerves Be in a neurotic state.*

Live one A person acting in an eccentric manner (e.g. 'we've got a live one here').*

Live out of a suitcase Lack a permanent home and live at a succession of temporary addresses.*

Live their own life Have a lifestyle that matches their own wishes rather than attempting to please others.*

Live to fight another day Survive an unpleasant experience (the term is often used in an exaggerated fashion, and does not necessarily mean that there was a threat of death). *

Live under (1) Live somewhere governed by a particular person or regime (e.g. 'she lived under the rule of Mussolini'). (2) Possess a particular attitude or belief (e.g. 'she lived under the impression that everyone was basically good'). (3) Possess a particular identity (e.g. 'He lived under the name of Mr Saunders').*

Living daylights See *beat the living daylights out* and *scare the living daylights*.

Living in a fool's paradise Having unrealistically optimistic opinions.*

Living large Living well and enjoyably.*

Living memory If something occurred within 'living memory' then some people who are alive today were alive when the event happened.*

Living off the backs of people Earning money by taking money off others and not giving anything in return.*

Living rough Being in a state of extreme poverty and homeless.*

Load of balls See *balls*.

Load the dice against Make something harder than it would normally be.*

Loaded for bear To be prepared for any sort of challenge. The phrase comes from hunting: the ammunition for hunting a small animal such as a rabbit will not be very effective against a bear, but the ammunition for hunting a bear will also be effective against a rabbit (rather too effective, perhaps). Therefore, a hunter going 'loaded for bear' is using bear-shooting ammunition that will also suffice for killing other animals he or she might encounter.*

Lock and load Prepare for a conflict or argument.*

Lock horns Enter into an argument or other form of confrontation.*

Lock, stock and barrel The entire thing. The term is derived from gunmaking (lock, stock and barrel are the principal components of a gun).*

London to a brick Australian phrase meaning 'absolutely certain' (e.g. 'it's London to a brick he'll be here').*

Lone voice A single person or group expressing an opinion that is different from that of the majority.*

Long and the short of it All that ultimately matters.*

Long arm of coincidence The phrase refers to the fact that sometimes coincidence can link very different and seemingly unrelated things, events or people.*

Long arm of the law The phrase is an observation that the power of the police to detect criminal activity and arrest people can be strong.*

Long chalk See *not by a long chalk*.

Long face A miserable facial expression.*

Long game The long-term perspective.*

Long in the tooth To be old (can refer to humans, machines or indeed any sort of process or activity). The term probably derives from the phenomenon that some mammals have receding gums as they get older, which makes their teeth look longer. The term is not very polite if referring to a human.* or **

Long run See *in the long run*.

Long story The phrase is used in several ways in a description of a series of events. However, in all instances the intention is to indicate that there is a logical justification for something, but in order to save time the full reasons will not be given (e.g. 'long story, but may I have extra time to complete this task?' or 'long story, but the archbishop and I were stuck in the lift with an amorous gorilla').*

Long-winded Using too many words to describe something. Usually an implication of pomposity as well.*

denotes level of impoliteness

Look a fright Have an unattractive appearance.*

Look a gift horse in the mouth Show ingratitude or an illogical level of suspicion of a gift or offer of help. The phrase is often heard in the negative form of *don't look a gift horse in the mouth,* which advises that gifts or offers of help should be accepted gracefully without quibbling.*

Look after number one Be selfish and put personal interests before those of others.*

Look as if seen a ghost Have a frightened expression.*

Look down on Be snobbish about and/or regard as inferior.*

Look down their noses at Means the same as *look down on.*

Look high and low Search thoroughly.*

Look like a million dollars Appear to be in excellent and/or praiseworthy condition.*

Look like a tornado hit it Have a very untidy appearance.*

Look like it Appear to be so.*

Look like something the cat dragged in Look very untidy.*

Look lively Means the same as *look sharp.*

Look over their shoulder In a state of anxiety or apprehension.*

Look sharp Be alert and/or quick.*

Look smart Means the same as *look sharp.*

Look the other way Means the same as *turn a blind eye to.*

Look to their laurels Be aware of the need to keep working to preserve their pre-eminence at something.*

Look up (1) Find some information from a book, the Internet or similar. (2) Visit someone. *

Look up to Admire.*

Look what the cat dragged in Depending upon the context and tone of voice, this can be an insult or a sarcastic but friendly greeting.* (greeting) or ** (insult)

Loose cannon A person whose behaviour is unpredictable and uncontrollable, and is likely to be as much a danger to the group to which he or she belongs as an asset.*

Lose caste Move from a higher to a lower social status.*

Lose face Lose some authority or social standing as a result of being discovered to have made a mistake or to have behaved badly.*

Lose it (1) Become incapable of continuing something. (2) Become angry. (3) As a command, 'lose it' means to take something off or to hide it.*

Lose sleep Worry excessively.*

Lose the plot (1) Become incapable of continuing something. (2) No longer able to comprehend something.*

Lose the thread No longer able to comprehend something.*

Lose the will to live Sometimes used jovially to indicate feeling extreme boredom.*

Lose their cherry Do something for the first time. The phrase originally referred to loss of virginity and is still mainly used in this way.***

Lose their cool Means the same as *lose their rag,* but slightly politer.*

Lose their head Lose a sense of calm and become illogical.*

Lose their marbles Become insane.*

Lose their rag Lose their temper.*

Lose their shirt Lose a large amount of money. The phrase usually implies that the loss reduces a person to extreme poverty.*

Losing battle A task doomed to failure.*

Lost cause Doomed to fail.*

Lost for words Utterly amazed to the point of being incapable of producing a coherent statement.*

Lost on them If something is lost on a person, then they fail to appreciate and/or understand it.*

Lost soul A person who appears rather pathetic and incapable of looking after themselves. *

Lounge lizard A person who seems to serve no purpose other than permanently attending parties and socialising.**

Love a duck A general expression indicating surprise or sympathy.*

Love me, love my dog This may refer to the speaker's canine companion, but more usually simply means 'tolerate my ways and lifestyle or don't try to be friends with me'.*

Lower their guard Be less defensive.*

Lower their sights Become less ambitious.*

Lowest of the low The most immoral or unworthy.*

Luck of the draw The result of chance, rather than deliberate planning.*

Lull before the storm A period of unnatural calm before the onset of something unpleasant, such as an argument.*

Lump in the throat A feeling of extreme emotion. The phrase nearly always refers to a feeling of great sorrow.*

Luxury! In my day... The phrase is used as an ironic response to a description of deprivation and/or hardship. The phrase comes from a comedy sketch called 'the Four Yorkshiremen' performed by the *Monty Python* cast during a stage show and subsequently released as an audio recording. It involves four Yorkshiremen telling increasingly improbable tales about hardships during childhood. Several of these tales are met with a contemptuous response of 'luxury! In my day...' before commencing upon an even more improbable and surreal story of hardship.*

M

Mad The term can mean 'insane', but in certain contexts it can mean 'very angry'. Common examples of the latter include 'mad as hell', 'mad as anything', 'mad beyond belief' and 'mad at you'. See *mad about (or on) something*.*

Mad about (or on) something (1) Very keen or interested about something. (2) Very annoyed about something (see *mad*).*

Mad as a hatter Insane or eccentric.*

Made of marble Able to resist temptation and/or emotional considerations.*

Made of money Rich. Often heard in the reverse form – *not made of money*, meaning 'not rich'.*

Made their bed See *they've made their bed they'd better lie in it.*

Magic carpet Joking term for any method of fast travel.*

Magic circle The term can refer to the (entirely respectable) Magic Circle, an organisation for stage conjurors. The term is also sometimes used to describe sarcastically a (real or imagined) secretive group believed to be the 'real power' in an organisation.*

Make a bad fist of... Do it badly.*

Make a beeline Strictly speaking, to travel in a straight line. In practice, the phrase means 'to travel by the shortest possible route'.*

Make a bolt for Attempt to escape by running towards something (e.g. 'she made a bolt for the door').*

Make a boob Make a mistake.*

Make a book Accept wagers or bets on something.*

Make a break Attempt to escape.*

Make a clean breast of it Make a full confession to a wrongdoing.*

Make a clean sweep (1) Win everything. (2) Remove unnecessary or unproductive people, items and/or practices in an attempt to revitalize something.*

Make a day of it Spend a whole day doing something. The phrase is typically used to describe choosing to spend time doing something enjoyable rather than doing it in a rushed manner.*

Make a drama out of... Exaggerate a minor problem so that it appears practically insurmountable.*

Make a fast buck Earn money quickly. The job done is by implication temporary rather than permanent employment.*

Make a go of Succeed.*

Make a good fist of... Do it well.*

Make a hash of Fail badly at doing something.*

Make a killing Make a large profit.*

Make a long story short See *cut a long story short.*

Make a mark Do something noteworthy.*

Make a meal of (1) Exaggerate. (2) Be too fussy about, and/or expend too much energy on, something. (3) Eat.*

Make a mint Earn a large amount of money.*

Make a mockery of Reduce to a farcical and/or weakened state. This can be done deliberately or through ineptitude.*

Make a monkey of Make appear foolish.*

Make a mountain out of a molehill Exaggerate. The phrase is typically used to describe exaggerating a tiny problem into a catastrophe.*

Make a move Begin to do something.*

Make a move on Indicate sexual interest in someone.*

Make a name for themselves Become famous and/or respected in their field of work.*

Make a night of it Spend a whole evening or night doing something.*

Make a noise Do something in a manner likely to attract attention.*

Make a packet Become wealthy.*

Make a pass at Express a sexual or romantic interest in.*

Make a pig of themselves Behave in a gluttonous manner.*

Make a pig's ear Make a mess of something.*

Make a pile Means the same as *make a packet.*

Make a pitch for Attempt to gain.*

Make a play for Attempt to gain, persuade or impress.*

Make a quid Have paid employment.*

Make a rod for their own back Create difficulties for themselves.*

Make a thing of (1) Be unreasonably fussy about. (2) Regard as vital.*

Make an effort Try.*

Make an honest man of him Marry him. The phrase is derived from *make an honest woman of her.*

Make an honest woman of her Marry her. The phrase originally referred to marrying a pregnant woman (at a time when a baby born out of wedlock was regarded far less favourably). However, it is now generally used without this connotation.*

Make both ends meet Means the same as *make ends meet.*

Make bricks without straw Try to do a job without all the necessary equipment.*

Make do Cope with inadequate resources.*

Make ends meet Earn enough money to provide enough for at least the basic necessities of living.*

Make eyes at Look at someone with obvious sexual intent.*

Make faces Make ridiculous or grotesque facial expressions.*

Make flesh creep Create a feeling of disgust.*

Make free of Treat without an appropriate level of respect.*

Make good (1) Succeed. (2) Restore. (3) Make financial reparations.*

Make good their escape Escape.*

Make great play Elaborate upon, or draw attention to.*

Make hair curl Create a feeling of fright. Usually the phrase is used jokingly.*

Make hair stand on end Create a feeling of fright.*

Make hay Do something whilst an advantageous situation lasts.*

Make head or tail of it Understand. The phrase is often used in the form *can't make head nor tail of it*, meaning a failure to understand.*

Make heavy weather of it Behave as if something is far more difficult and/or laborious than it actually is.*

Make it big Be successful. The phrase is often used in a derogatory fashion to denote someone who has become financially successful but has little cultural sophistication. *

Make it hot for them Make something difficult and/or unpleasant for them.*

Make it snappy Do it quickly.*

Make light of (1) Do easily. (2) Dismiss as trivial.*

Make like Imitate.*

Make mincemeat of Decisively defeat.*

Make money hand over fist Earn money at a fast rate.*

Make music together Be romantically compatible.*

Make nice Be sociable.*

Make no bones about it (1) To say something directly without attempting to hide anything. (2) In a derivation of the first meaning, the phrase may be used to tell someone that the speaker is very serious about something (e.g. 'make no bones about it, you'll be in trouble if you follow this plan').*

Make or break Something that is 'make or break' will either completely succeed or completely fail.*

Make the best of Make the optimal use of what is provided.*

Make the cut Reach an acceptable standard. The phrase is often used in sporting events to describe the best players who are the only ones allowed to compete in the latter stages of a competition.*

Make the grade Reach the required standard.*

Make their blood boil Make very angry.*

Make their blood curdle Create a feeling of terror or extreme fright.*

Make their blood freeze Means the same as *make their blood run cold.*

Make their blood run cold Shock or frighten.*

Make their bow Make their first appearance in a new job.*

Make their day Please someone. The phrase usually implies that this pleasure will be the best emotion felt on that day.*

Make their mark Have a long-lasting effect.*

Make their mind up To make a decision. The phrase often implies that making the decision has not been easy.*

Make their mouth water Induce feelings of hunger or interest.*

denotes level of impoliteness

Make their own luck Succeed through effort and taking advantage of the situation rather than assistance from others.*

Make their toes curl (1) Create a feeling of embarrassment. (2) Create a strong reaction.*

Make tracks Leave.*

Make up for lost time (1) Over-indulge in an activity because of not having the opportunity to do it earlier. (2) After a period of being behind schedule, work harder or move faster so that now things are on schedule.*

Make up leeway Recover from a poor position (e.g. from being behind schedule).*

Make waves (1) Complain and/or make difficulties. (2) Create excitement or interest.*

Making of them If something is 'the making of someone' then it is the factor which is crucial in producing a personality or skill seen as advantageous.*

Man about town A now rather dated phrase describing a man who has an active social life, is well-liked, has good fashion sense, and knows the fashionable places to go.*

Man for all seasons A person who can adapt to any situation.*

Man in the street See *person in the street*.

Man of leisure A man with no employment. The phrase is often used for someone who is retired or is so rich that they do not need to work.*

Man of letters An educated man.*

Man of straw Means the same as *straw man*.

Man on the Clapham omnibus Term first used in the 1900s that means the same as *person in the street*. The sort of person who would regularly travel on the bus service to and from Clapham (a district of London) was believed to be representative of an average British inhabitant. Since then, people have begun to realize that (a) using 'man' in phrases excludes half the human race and (b) districts of London are not particularly representative of the rest of the UK. Accordingly, the phrase should be avoided.*

Man's best friend A dog.*

Manner born See *to the manner born*.

Manners they were born with See *not got the manners they were born with*.

Many a good tune played on an old fiddle Proverb expressing the view that an older person may be just as accomplished and skilful as a younger person.*

Many a slip The start of a proverb that finishes 'between the cup and the lip' (there are variants). The phrase expresses the view that a lot of things can go unexpectedly wrong in any undertaking, and accordingly, vigilance is required.*

Many moons ago A long time ago.*

Map See entry below and: *put on the map*.

Map on to (1) Concur or match with. (2) Integrate with.*

March to a different beat Do things differently. The phrase often denotes someone who consciously does things in a manner opposed to, or radically different from, the prevailing system of beliefs and practices.*

March to a different tune Means the same as *march to a different beat*.

Mare's nest Something that appears of great interest but is illusory.*

Mark my words Attend carefully to what I say. The phrase is often used before a person makes a prediction that they feel is important.*

Mark of Cain A sign of disgrace. The phrase originally meant the sign of having committed murder, after the Biblical character Cain.*

Mark their card Provide information.*

Mark time Engage in a boring or unexciting activity whilst waiting for the opportunity to do something more interesting and/or rewarding.*

Marriage of convenience A marriage or alliance in which the people or groups involved have no real affection for each other, but who benefit in other ways from the arrangement.*

Marry money Marry someone wealthy.*

Massaging the figures Means the same as *creative accounting.*

Matter of form (1) Correct etiquette. (2) Commonplace or routine.*

Matter of life and death A very important matter.*

Matter of record Something that is undeniably true and for which documentary or other proof can be produced.*

Matter of report Means the same as *matter of record.*

Matter of time If something is a 'matter of time', then it is believed that it will certainly happen at some point in the future.*

Mean business Be serious about something.*

Meanwhile back at the ranch The phrase is sometimes used to indicate a change in who or what is being talked about in a lengthy story. The term is meant as a joke. The phrase was originally used as a caption in early silent movies when the action moved back to a scene at the ranch.*

Meet half way Be conciliatory and agreeable to a compromise.*

Meet the case Be of the required standard.*

Meet the costs Pay what is owed.*

Meet their maker Die.*

Meet their match Strictly speaking, meeting someone of equal ability. The phrase is usually used inaccurately, to mean meeting someone of superior ability.*

Men from the boys See *sort out the men from the boys.*

Men in suits Business managers. The phrase is often used disparagingly to refer to people who put profitability before morals or who fail to think of the effects their policies have on workers' welfare.*

Men in white coats Medical personnel. The phrase is often used more specifically to refer to psychiatrists.*

Mend fences Reconcile after an argument.*

Mentioned in dispatches Praised.*

Merry Christmas See *and a merry Christmas to you too.*

Mess around Engage in frivolous, unproductive activity.*

Mess them around Annoy them by creating confusion or failing to fulfil a promise.*

Mess with their head Annoy or confuse.*

Meter is running A fast response is needed, because time and/or energy and/or resources are being wasted.*

Methinks the lady doth protest too much A misquotation of a line from Shakespeare's *Hamlet*, used to indicate that a person seems suspiciously keen on denying something (which suggests that they in fact are guilty of what they are denying).*

Method in their madness Behaviour that appears insane or eccentric, but in fact has a cunning purpose.*

Mickey Finn A covertly drugged drink.*

Mickey Mouse When used as an adjective and without obvious reference to the Disney organisation (e.g. 'a Mickey Mouse operation') it describes something done in a shambolic, unskilled manner (presumably after the rather chaotic behaviour of Mickey Mouse in some of his cartoons).*

* *denotes level of impoliteness*

Midas touch The ability to be financially successful.*

Middle course A procedure that is less extreme than some other options.*

Middle of nowhere Remote.*

Middle way Means the same as *middle course*.

Mile a minute Rapidly.*

Mile off See *see it a mile off*.

Mileage may vary See *your mileage may vary*.

Miles away Daydreaming or absent-minded.*

Milk and honey Comfort and riches.*

Milk and water Feeble.*

Milk in the coconut Something that is difficult to explain.*

Milk of human kindness Kindness to others.*

Milking the system Taking unfair and/or unethical advantage of a set of regulations.*

Million and one reasons Lots of reasons.*

Million to one shot A remote possibility.*

Millstone round their neck A severe annoyance that hampers progress.*

Mince matters (1) Means the same as *mince words*. (2) Make something unnecessarily confusing.*

Mince words Use language that fails to state something clearly.*

Mind over matter A mental process triumphing over an opposing physical one. The phrase is used in a wide variety of permutations (e.g. a clever but physically weak person defeating a stronger but less intelligent opponent; a person committing a physically demanding feat through strong willpower when by physical measures alone they should have failed).*

Mind the shop Means the same as *hold the shop*.

Mind their p's and q's See *p's and q's*.

Mind your back A warning that something capable of inflicting injury is approaching from behind.*

Mind's eye The internal mental state. The phrase is often used as a synonym of imagination.*

Minor key Unless specifically referring to music, the phrase means 'subdued'.*

Mint condition Unspoilt; the phrase is usually used to describe an old item that appears brand new.*

Miss a beat Hesitate.*

Miss the boat Fail to do something. The phrase generally refers to a failure to take advantage of an opportunity.*

Miss the bus Means the same as *miss the boat*.

Miss the cut Fail to reach an acceptable standard. See *make the cut*.*

Miss the point Fail to understand.*

Missing link (1) A person or thing that is required for a procedure to work. (2) In evolutionary theory, the species that links humans to apes. Thus, someone who appears uncouth and ill-mannered may be referred to as 'the missing link'.*

Mixed bag Something that is a 'mixed bag' is varied. This can refer to, for example, different physical features (e.g. 'are they all the same colour?' – 'no, they're a mixed bag') or quality (e.g. 'is the CD any good?' – 'it's a mixed bag: some tracks are excellent, others are quite poor').*

Mixed blessing Something that is partly beneficial but also has disadvantages.*

Mohammed must go to the mountain See *if the mountain won't come to Mohammed*.

Moment of truth The time when the success or failure of a plan is revealed, or, more broadly, an important *turning point*.*

Monday morning quarterback A person full of opinions about how something should have been done better after the event has taken place.*

Money burning a hole in their pocket Having an irresistible urge to spend money.*

Money doesn't grow on trees A (usually gentle) rebuke if someone is asking for something too expensive. The phrase basically means that money is not easily obtained and that, accordingly, some things cannot be afforded. See *it doesn't grow on trees*.*

Money for jam Means the same as *money for old rope*.

Money for old rope Something lucrative and easy to do.*

Money no object See *no object*.

Money to burn Sufficient finances to be able to afford lavish spending.*

Monkey business See *business*.

Monkey on a stick A restless and/or agitated person.*

Monkey on their back An annoyance.*

Monkey suit Evening dress for a man (i.e. black dinner jacket and trousers, black bow tie, etc.).*

Month of Sundays A long time. Often heard in the phrase 'never in a month of Sundays', indicating that something is highly improbable.*

Moonlight flit (1) Escape creditors by leaving secretly at night. (2) Escape the family house at night to run away with a lover.*

More bang for the buck Better value.*

More fish in the sea Words of consolation offered when a person has lost a boy-friend or girlfriend (e.g. 'never mind – there are plenty more fish in the sea'). The phrase means that there are plenty more potential partners in the world.*

More fool... A rebuke meaning that greater thought or care should have been

taken, and then a problem would not have been created.*

More haste, less speed Advice to slow down the rate at which a task is being performed, because going too quickly is likely to result in errors. The proverb makes far more sense if one remembers that 'speed' can also mean 'success' (e.g. if the proverb is rewritten as 'more haste, less success' it is rather easier to under-stand).*

More meat on a butcher's pencil A joking way of saying that someone is thin.*

More power to their elbow More strength and/or health. The phrase is often used as a term of praise, expressing the hope that someone will enjoy better strength and/or health.*

More than one way to skin a cat There is more than one way to do something. The phrase is often used when a conventional method is being rejected (e.g. 'the usual method of doing this seems unwise in this case, but don't worry, because there's more than one way to skin a cat').*

More than one way to skin a rabbit Means the same as *more than one way to skin a cat*.

More the merrier The opinion that the more people are involved, the better it is.*

More's the pity An expression of regret.*

Morning, noon and night Constantly.*

Morton's fork A situation in which any choice that is made will lead to unattrac-tive consequences.*

Mote in their eye A trivial fault. The implication is usually that a person finding faults in others usually has much bigger faults of their own.*

Moth to a flame A person who is like a 'moth to a flame' has a strong urge to do something. There is sometimes the impli-cation that this urge will harm them.*

---

* denotes level of impoliteness

Motor mouth A very talkative person who has little concept of when it would be appropriate to keep quiet.**

Mould-breaking Innovative.*

Mountain to climb See *have a mountain to climb.*

Mousetrap See *build a better mousetrap.*

Movable feast Something that does not have to be done on a particular date or time. The phrase is derived from Easter and other Christian festivals which are held on different dates each year according to a complex formula (in contrast to, say, Christmas Day, which is always fixed on 25 December).*

Move Heaven and Earth Work extremely hard.*

Move in for the kill Prepare to conclude something.*

Move it A strong command to do something (the implication is that someone is currently too inactive).**

Move mountains Make considerable effort.*

Move the goalposts To change the rules or desired outcomes after a piece of work has begun. The phrase is an analogy – if during a soccer game someone moved the goalposts every time someone kicked a ball at the goal area, the game would be very frustrating. Similarly, telling people to work to attain a particular set of outcomes, and then changing the set of outcomes, creates frustration and annoyance. The term is often used of (UK) government education policy.*

Move their arse Means the same as *move their backside.****

Move their ass Means the same as *move their backside.***

Move their backside (1) Show some effort. (2) The phrase is often used as an impolite way to mean 'move' (e.g. 'I wish they would move their backside').**

Move with the times Have a modern, rather than old-fashioned, set of attitudes.*

Mover and shaker A person who is instrumental in getting things done.*

Much of a muchness Describes two or more things that are of approximately equal quality.*

Muck in Give assistance.*

Mud in your eye A traditional informal toast upon having a drink.*

Mud slinging Spreading rumours or making scandalous accusations. See *name is mud.**

Muddy the waters Make more complicated.*

Mug's game An activity that is dangerous and/or foolish.*

Mum's the word To keep a secret about something. The word 'mum' means 'no speech' rather than 'mother'.*

Murphy's law The fatalistic argument that in any activity something is bound to go wrong.*

Music to their ears Received with pleasure.*

Mutton dressed as lamb Something (or someone) made to appear younger than it actually is. The phrase is often used in a derogatory fashion of an older woman dressed in clothes felt more suitable for a younger age group.*

My ball If a person says 'my ball' he or she is indicating that they will deal with what is being discussed (e.g. if a question is asked to a panel of people, the person saying 'my ball' is declaring that they will answer it). The phrase comes from tennis doubles, where if a ball looks as if it will be within reach of both players on one side, a player might call out 'my ball' to make sure that he or she will have clear access to it and that the partner player will get out of the way.*

My eye An expression of disbelief (e.g. 'my eye! – I've never heard such nonsense').*

My foot Means the same as *my eye.*

My pigeon Means the same as *my ball.*

N

Naff off An impolite way of saying 'go away'.**

Nail a lie Uncover a lie.*

Nail-biting Describes something that creates a feeling of nervousness or apprehension.*

Nail in the coffin Something that adds to the decline of someone or something.*

Nail the colours to the mast Make a firm declaration of opinions or belief. There is often the implication that such a declaration will not be totally popular and may attract criticism. The phrase is derived from naval battles in sailing ships. Since a sign of surrender was to lower the identifying flags (or colours), nailing the colours to the mast meant they couldn't be lowered, and hence declared the intent to win or die in the attempt.*

Naked truth The truth. The phrase implies that the truth may be simpler and less appealing than a complex set of lies and half-truths that are commonly believed to be accurate.*

Name dropping Deliberately and boastfully making mention of famous or influential people who are personal acquaintances.*

Name is mud If someone's name is mud, then they are in disgrace.*

Name of the game The features of the situation that are the most important, and in particular the desired outcome of the situation.*

Name to conjure with (1) The name of an important person. (2) A name that is unusual or unintentionally humorous.*

Name written all over it See *got their name written all over it.*

Nasty piece of goods An unpleasant person.*

Nasty piece of work Means the same as *nasty piece of goods.*

Nature of the beast The basic characteristics of a problem or situation.*

Near the knuckle Means the same as *close to the knuckle.*

Near the mark Almost correct.*

Necessary evil Something that in itself is unpleasant but unavoidable if something that is desired is to be gained (e.g. unpleasant in-laws).*

Neck and neck In a competition or race, a situation in which competitors are very similar in performance.*

Neck of the woods A small geographical region. The phrase is often heard in the form *from the same neck of the woods,* meaning that things or people originate from homes that are very close to each other.*

Need a hand? If a person asks 'need a hand?' they are asking if assistance is required.*

Needle in a haystack Something extremely difficult to find.*

Needs must A justification for doing something normally considered unpleasant or undesirable because the pragmatic nature of the situation demanded it.*

Neither flesh nor fish nor fowl Something that cannot be categorized.*

Neither flesh nor fish nor good red herring Means the same as *neither flesh nor fish nor fowl.*

Neither hair nor hide No sign or indication at all.*

Neither here nor there An expression indicating that something is not very important or is uninteresting (e.g. 'it's neither here nor there whether we watch the rest of this play, since neither of us are enjoying it').*

Neither hide nor hair Means the same as *neither hair nor hide.*

Nerves of steel Impervious to shock or anxiety.*

Nest of vipers (1) An unpleasant situation. (2) A group of people who are noted for being unpleasant by being scheming and 'bitchy'.*

Never give a sucker an even break Never give someone who is poor or otherwise unfortunate the opportunity to improve their position. The phrase is often meant ironically.*

Never hear the end of it Means the same as *never hear the last of it.*

Never hear the last of it Be nagged or constantly reminded about something.*

Never-never A credit scheme. Thus, something bought on 'the never-never' has been bought on credit.*

Never-never land An imaginary place. The phrase is often used in describing an impractical or impossible proposition.*

Never put a foot wrong Never make a mistake.*

Never rains but it pours A proverb expressing the view that problems never occur in isolation but in groups.*

Never see daylight again Never again be released or revealed.*

Never the twain shall meet Two groups of people who are so radically different in personalities or opinions that there is no possibility that they would ever happily or peacefully co-exist with each other.*

New ball game Something completely different.*

New black If something is 'the new black', then it is a new fashion that is likely to become ubiquitous. The phrase is derived from the fashion industry, where black is often regarded as the 'standard' colour

for dresses (see *little black dress*). See *new rock and roll.* *

New blood New people introduced into an organisation with the intention of introducing some new approaches and ideas.*

New broom A newly appointed person expected to make radical changes to working practices.*

New kid on the block A new arrival. The phrase comes from the US term 'block', meaning a set of buildings between the intersections created by two streets joining the street on which the buildings are situated. Hence, the term means 'new kid in the neighbourhood'.*

New money See *old money.*

New one on them Something previously unknown to them.*

New rock and roll A new form of entertainment that is currently very popular or is predicted will become very popular. The phrase is derived from the immense popularity rock and roll music enjoyed in the 1950s. See *new black.* *

Nice little earner Used to describe a business venture that produces acceptable profits, usually with the implication that it is easy to run.*

Nice touch A pleasing detail.*

Nigger in the woodpile Something unexpected and unpleasant. The phrase is now considered offensive and should not be used.***

Night of the long knives A revenge attack (often by devious means) on a collection of people. The phrase originally referred to assassinations, but now often refers to relatively milder (though still unpleasant) actions such as widespread dismissals from jobs.*

NIMBY See *not in my back yard.*

Nine days' wonder A short-lived phenomenon or fashion. It does not necessarily have to last precisely nine days.*

Nine to five Dull routine. The phrase is derived from the typical working hours for most workers.*

Nineteen to the dozen Continuously and rapidly.*

Nip in the bud Stop something before it can develop (typically, the phrase refers to preventing something mildly unpleasant from developing into something extremely unpleasant). The phrase is derived from gardening – by controlling the buds that develop on a plant, a gardener can control the plant's development.*

Nit pick Find fault by finding trivial errors in details that have no real importance.*

Nitty gritty See *get down to the nitty gritty.*

No better than they should be A person who is 'no better than they should be' has a poor sense of sexual propriety or morality. The phrase is nearly always applied to a woman.*

No big deal See *big deal.*

No-brainer A very obvious decision.*

No can do It cannot be done.*

No cigar See *close but no cigar.*

No comment A phrase indicating that the speaker will not discuss something. It is habitually used by people when asked to speak about something where they are accused of an illegal or at least morally dubious activity. The phrase can also be used jokingly as an admission of responsibility for a minor misdemeanour (e.g. 'did you eat the last cup cake?' – 'no comment'). See *plead the fifth.*

No contest (1) A competition in which the opponents are unevenly matched to the extent that the result is a foregone conclusion. (2) In US law, a plea by the defence to accept punishment without formally admitting guilt.*

No dice Means the same as *no way.*

No end of... A large quantity of.*

No flies on... Indicates that someone cannot be easily deceived, and is intelligent.*

No for an answer The phrase has two principal forms. (1) *Won't take no for an answer* describes a person who refuses to accept that someone is refusing their suggestion or offer. This can be used to describe another person (e.g. 'she is stubborn – she won't take no for an answer') or to describe oneself (e.g. 'I insist on paying for this, and I won't take no for an answer). (2) *Don't take no for an answer* is advice to someone to be resolute and get what they are sent for (e.g. 'you must get an interview with Mr Smith – don't let anybody put you off and don't take no for an answer').*

No-go area Means the same as *no-go zone.*

No-go zone A place or an activity that it would be unwise to enter into because it is dangerous.*

No great shakes Of no especial worth.*

No holding them If there is 'no holding' a person, then they are very keen to do something.*

No holds barred No restriction on the methods that may be used. The phrase generally refers to particularly vicious fighting or arguing.*

No kidding (1) A statement that what is being said is true, implausible as it may sound (e.g. 'no kidding, that's what really happened'). (2) Used as a response, it means 'I believe you, even though it sounds implausible' (e.g. 'have you heard that Eric is dating Jane?' – 'no kidding').*

No law against it An argument that what is being done is not illegal. However, there is usually an implication that although strictly speaking what is being done is not illegal, it is also not very pleasant or polite.*

No love lost between them There is a feeling of animosity between them.*

No man's land An area of uncertainty. *

---

* denotes level of impoliteness

No mean... Followed by a word (usually 'feat' but others are possible). The phrase means 'good' or 'praiseworthy'.*

No more Mr Nice Guy An indication that the speaker has had enough of trying to be pleasant and reasonable and will now have to be more unpleasant with people in order to get the results he or she needs.*

No names, no pack drill A phrase derived from army life, meaning that if the names of the perpetrators of a breach of regulations aren't known, then individuals cannot be punished.*

No object Does not matter. The phrase is most often used in the longer phrase *money no object*, meaning that financial considerations will be of no relevance.*

No oil painting Ugly.*

No picnic Difficult and/or dangerous.*

No pot to piss in Be very poor.*

No problem Not difficult. The phrase can be used as a descriptive phrase (e.g. 'there is no problem with this') or as a reply to a question indicating that something will be done, or has been done, without difficulty.*

No room to swing a cat Describing a room or other place that is very small. The phrase is probably derived from the cat o' nine tails (a type of whip) rather than a live cat.*

No saying It is impossible to judge.*

No shit (1) A phrase emphasizing the truth of something (e.g. 'no shit, that's really what happened'). (2) A response to a statement indicating surprise at what was said but also indicating acceptance of the truth of the statement (e.g. 'Jack told me that he and Mary are getting divorced' – 'No shit').***

No shit Sherlock A sarcastic comment meaning that what has just been said is very obvious.***

No side Lack of pretensions or snobbishness.*

No skin off their nose It has no appreciable effect on them.*

No smoke without fire The belief that ambiguous evidence or rumours amount to tangible proof of something.*

No stone unturned Nothing has been ignored, everything has been explored. The phrase is often used of a piece of research or an investigation.*

No strings attached See *strings attached*.

No such animal It does not exist. The phrase can be applied to a non-human animal, a human or to a concept.*

No such luck Regrettably not (e.g. 'did your team win today?' might get a reply of 'no such luck' from a disappointed fan).*

No such thing as a free lunch Meaning that, for everything, something is always expected in return; or alternatively, that everything that is received has to be worked for.*

No sweat Easy.*

No time like the present If something is to be done, it is best done at once.*

No two ways about it It is unambiguous.*

No use crying over spilt milk See *crying over spilt milk*.

No use to man or beast In other words, completely useless.*

No way A strong expression of denial (e.g. 'no way will I do that').*

No way, Jose ('Jose' is pronounced 'Ho-say') Means the same as *no way*. The word 'Jose' makes a rhyming sound – the phrase can be directed at anyone of either gender (i.e. not just people called Jose).*

No-win situation A situation in which whatever a person does they cannot win, and most probably will end up worse off than when they started.*

No worries Australian phrase meaning approximately the same as 'that's alright' or 'it's okay'.*

Nobby Clark Men with the surname 'Clark' (or the alternative spellings) often are nicknamed 'Nobby' (it is unlikely that this is their real first name). The nickname derives from the nineteenth century, when clerks were seen as being more 'genteel' than manual workers, and nicknamed 'nobby' (loosely, meaning 'upper class').*

Nobody's fool Intelligent.*

Nod's as good as a wink No more explanation is necessary and the implication of what was said is understood.*

Nodding acquaintance Someone who is known slightly, but not well.*

Nodding terms In a state of knowing slightly, but not well.*

Noes have it See *ayes have it.*

Non-linear Angry.*

Non-U Not within the code of etiquette adopted by the upper classes. The phrase is sometimes used snobbishly to refer to working-class taste or customs.*

Nose in the air Having a snobbish attitude.*

Nose to derrière Means the same as *nose to tail.*

Nose to tail Closely packed together.*

Not a chance in hell No chance at all.*

Not a Chinaman's chance No hope whatsoever of a happy outcome. The phrase derives from late nineteenth/early twentieth century USA, when Chinese immigrant workers were frequent victims of violence and murder, with seemingly no protection from the (supposed) law enforcement agencies.*

Not a clue (1) An admission of ignorance (e.g. a person not knowing the answer to a question might say 'not a clue'). (2) Lack of knowledge (e.g. 'you've not a clue how to do this, have you?').*

Not a dicky bird Nothing.*

Not a dog's chance No chance.*

Not a dry eye in the house Describes a movie or stage performance that has a strong emotional effect on the audience. The phrase can be used seriously or humorously.*

Not a full... A phrase usually followed by either 'quid' or 'shilling'. The phrase indicates insanity or lack of intelligence.*

Not a ghost of a chance See *ghost of a chance.*

Not a hope in hell No hope at all.*

Not a patch on Of poorer quality than.*

Not a penny No money at all. The phrase can be used to indicate lack of payment that someone thinks is rightfully theirs (see *not one red cent*). It can also be used to indicate extreme poverty (e.g. 'I've not a penny in the world').*

Not a sausage Absolutely nothing.*

Not all beer and skittles A phrase used to express the fact that things are not always pleasant or easy.*

Not all it's cracked up to be *Cracked up to be* means 'what it is claimed to be'. Thus, 'not all it's cracked up to be' indicates that something is not what it is claimed. The phrase is usually used to indicate that something is disappointing.*

Not all there See *all there.*

Not as black as they are painted In other words, not as unpleasant or nasty as they are usually supposed to be. The term is considered offensive by some people (who think the phrase is linking skin colour with offensiveness). Accordingly, caution should be used.**

Not bat an eyelid Show no emotion or surprise.*

Not by a long chalk The expression in effect means 'not very accurate' or 'not by any means'. The term is generally used when a speaker wants to indicate that the gap between a desired and an actual state of something is very big. For example, 'did you finish first in the race?' might get the reply 'not by a long chalk' if the person finished in a very poor position.*

Not by halves If something is done 'not by halves' then it is done thoroughly.*

Not care a hoot Have no interest or concern.*

Not care two hoots Means the same as *not care a hoot.*

Not cricket Unfair. Derives from the belief of some English people that cricket is the epitome of sportsmanship.*

Not feeling oneself Feeling ill. Thus, *feeling oneself* is feeling well. However, given the possible double entendre in the term ('feeling oneself' could, in the sort of mind alert to double meanings, be construed as meaning 'masturbation') a little caution should be taken over its use.*

Not flavour of the month See *flavour of the month.*

Not for all the tea in China An emphatic refusal.*

Not give a... See entries beginning *couldn't give a...*

Not give a hoot Have no interest or concern.*

Not give two hoots Means the same as *not give a hoot.*

Not got the manners they were born with Very rude and/or uncouth.*

Not half (1) Of much lower magnitude (e.g. 'Sue is not half as good as Jane at sprinting'). (2) Absolutely (usually heard as an exclamation – e.g. 'was Hitler a bad person?' might get the response 'not half!').*

Not have a bean To be very poor.*

Not have a clue Have no knowledge of something.*

Not have a leg to stand on Have no reasonable justification.*

Not have a pot to piss in Be very poor.***

Not have a prayer Means the same as *not have an Earthly.*

Not have an Earthly Not have even the remotest chance.*

Not have any of it Refuse to cooperate.*

Not have the faintest Have no understanding or memory of something.*

Not have the foggiest Means the same as *not have the faintest.*

Not have two pennies to rub together Be poor.*

Not in my back yard An attitude of opposition to anything bad happening in the local neighbourhood. There is usually an additional attitude that although something cannot be allowed to happen in the local neighbourhood, it is perfectly acceptable if it happens elsewhere. The phrase is often used to describe middle-class protestors objecting to, for example, a new road being built near their (expensive) houses, but who will happily drive on new roads built near other people's houses. The phrase thus more generally means 'selfishness disguised as righteous indignation'. The phrase is sometimes shortened to *NIMBY*, and people with a 'not in my back yard' attitude are often described as 'NIMBYs'.*

Not just a pretty face Not only physically attractive, but clever as well. The phrase is often used jokingly.*

Not know if coming or going In a state of confusion.*

Not know the meaning of the word Appear to have no understanding of the concept being described.*

Not know what hit them Be utterly surprised.*

Not know what to do with themselves Be bored because of lack of potential activities or amusements.*

Not know where to put themselves Feel embarrassed.*

Not let the grass grow under their feet (1) Be active. (2) Respond quickly.*

Not long for this world Limited life expectancy. The phrase is sometimes used seriously, and sometimes jokingly. The tone of voice and/or context should indicate which meaning is intended.*

Not made of money See *made of money*.

Not miss a beat A person who does not miss a beat is someone who does not allow anything to interfere with what they are doing. The phrase is most often used to describe a person who does not pause after receiving an unexpected reply, but continues to speak fluently and maintains his or her argument.*

Not miss a trick Make optimum use of everything.*

Not much cop Of poor quality.*

Not my bag In other words, 'not something I feel competent to do or discuss'.*

Not my pigeon Means the same as *not my bag*.

Not on Unacceptable.*

Not on my watch An emphatic rejection, meaning 'not whilst I am in charge'.*

Not on your life An emphatic rejection of a suggestion.*

Not on your Nellie An emphatic rejection of a suggestion (e.g. 'will you come to the dance with me?' – 'not on your Nellie').**

Not one red cent No money at all. The phrase is usually used to describe lack of payment when a person feels they deserve to have been paid.*

Not playing with a full deck Stupid.*

Not put it past them Believe that they are capable of doing it.*

Not see for dust Leave with speed and determination.*

Not the be-all and end-all See *be-all and end-all*.

Not the full quid Not particularly intellectually gifted.*

Not the full shilling Means the same as *not the full quid*.

Not the only fish in the sea Expresses the same sentiment as *more fish in the sea*.*

Not the only pebble on the beach Can mean the same as *not the only fish in the sea*, or more generally expresses the opinion that someone is not irreplaceable.*

Not their cup of tea Describes something that a person does not like.*

Not their day A day which seems to bring nothing but misfortune.*

Not their scene Means the same as *not their cup of tea*.

Not to be sneezed at Not to be discounted.*

Not to put too fine a point on it To speak candidly.*

Not turn a hair Show no emotion or surprise.*

Not waving but drowning Appearing to be alright, but in fact in difficulty.*

Not within coo-ee Australian version of *not within striking distance*.

Not within striking distance To be a long distance away. The phrase often refers to not being close to achieving something rather than physical distance (e.g. 'they were not within striking distance of winning').*

Not worth a candle Of little or no value.*

Not worth a hill of beans In other words, worthless.*

Not worth the candle Not worth the expense and/or effort involved.*

Not worthy See *I am not worthy*.

Nothing by halves A person who does 'nothing by halves' does a thorough piece of work.*

Nothing daunted Unafraid.*

Nothing doing (1) An expression of refusal (e.g. a request to do something unpleasant might be met with a response

---

* *denotes level of impoliteness*

of 'nothing doing'). (2) Nothing happening.*

Nothing further from their mind Not being considered. The phrase is often used as a protestation of innocence that something is not being thought of and is not a motivation behind a questionable action (e.g. the accusation that 'you only want to go because Justine will be there' may be met with the reply 'nothing could be further from my mind'). The phrase may be used in a humorous or sarcastic manner, usually revealed either by context or the tone of voice.*

Nothing new under the sun The opinion that nothing 'new' is truly new, since it is made of elements that pre-existed. The phrase is generally used in a more cynical or jaded form to indicate that a fashion that its practitioners think is original is simply an amended version of something that has been done before.*

Nothing on them (1) Be of lesser quality than them. (2) Have no incriminatory evidence against them.*

Nothing to write home about Of little interest or worth.*

Now, now A mild admonishment.*

Nowt as queer as folk There is nothing that offers as many surprises and variety as human behaviour. The word 'queer' denotes 'unusual' and the phrase predates the use of the word as slang for 'homosexual'.*

Nuclear See *go nuclear*.

Nudge nudge, wink wink Said after a statement with a sexual double-meaning, meant to signal that a double entendre should be looked for in the statement, rather than accepting it literally.*

Number is up Something is inevitably going to happen. The phrase often implies that this will be either death or something very unpleasant.*

Nuts Insane.*

Nuts about [or on] something Very keen or interested about something.*

Nuts and bolts The basic and/or most important details.*

Nutty as a fruitcake (1) Insane. (2) Eccentric.*

O

Oar See *poke their oar in* and *rest on their oars*.

Occam's razor The principle that if there is more than one explanation for something, always choose the simplest one.*

Odour of sanctity Unattractive level of piety.*

Of the blood Genetically related.*

Of the essence Essential.*

Of two minds Undecided.*

Off and on (1) Alternate between two states (e.g. a relationship in which a couple vary between being friendly and argumentative can be said to be 'off and on'). (2) Occasionally.*

Off base Means 'incorrect' (e.g. 'your judgement is hopelessly off base on this issue').*

Off beam Means the same as *off base*.

Off colour To feel unwell or to perform below the expected standard. The phrase probably comes from the fact that (white) people's skin colour may change noticeably if they are ill with some medical conditions, such as jaundice.*

Off form Doing less well than would be normally expected.*

Off pat Perfectly.*

Off target Unsuccessful.*

Off the air See *on the air*.

Off the back of a lorry Something 'off the back of a lorry' is stolen, and thus buying it is in itself a crime.*

Off the beaten track Remote; usually used to describe a pleasant place or area that is not visited by many tourists.*

Off the blocks Means the same as *out of the blocks*.

Off the boat Originally described a recent immigrant to a country, and was often used offensively. The phrase is sometimes used to describe someone who has recently joined a group.**

Off the boil Less successful or interesting than previously.*

Off the case No longer working on a particular project or activity.*

Off the cuff Describes something done without any prior preparation.*

Off the cuff remark A remark made *in passing*, and which the speaker did not intend to be taken seriously.*

Off the hook (1) Escape punishment. (2) A telephone handset not properly replaced on its base unit (so that calls cannot be received) is 'off the hook'.*

Off the mark Inaccurate.*

Off the pace (1) Behind the leading group. (2) Of a lower standard than the best examples.*

Off the peg Ready prepared and ready to use. The phrase is particularly applied to clothing.*

Off the rack Means the same as *off the peg*.

Off the rail Means the same as *off the peg*.

Off the rails Insane.*

Off the record A person who says that they want to say something 'off the record' means that they cannot be formally attributed as having said it.*

Off the shelf Ready prepared and ready to use. The phrase implies that it was not custom-designed for the job, and therefore if it proves satisfactory it may be fortuitous. Note that *off the peg* (or one of its synonyms) is usually used when the item in question is clothing.*

Off the top of their head A guess or initial thoughts.*

Off the wall Eccentric or unusual.*

Off their chump Insane or severely lacking in sensible judgement.*

Off their face Drunk.*

Off their feed Not interested in food in a manner that suggests illness as the cause.*

Off their game Doing badly.*

Off their hands Something that is no longer their responsibility.*

Off their head (1) Insane. (2) Intoxicated.*

Off their oats Feeling unwell or devoid of energy or appetite.*

Off their own bat Do something by themselves without being prompted or told.*

Off their rocker Insane.*

Off their trolley Insane.**

Offer they can't refuse The phrase can literally mean an offer that is so good that a person would be foolish to refuse it. It also may mean a threat that a person cannot refuse for fear of (often violent) punishment. The latter form was popularized by the movie *The Godfather*.*

Office telegraph Information received from gossip amongst members of an office or company rather than from official sources.*

Oil and water Describes two people or viewpoints that cannot be easily reconciled.*

Oil the wheels Make something operate more efficiently.*

Old Adam 'Primitive' behaviour without moral sense.*

Old as the hills Very old.*

Old boy network A group of men united in identity by coming from a similar social and educational background, and who will tend to favour each other rather than use unbiased judgement. The phrase is most often used as an explanation of

denotes level of impoliteness

why someone with low abilities gets a good job when there were much better alternative candidates (because the employer comes from the same social group), but it can be applied to other examples of unfair preferment. Generally, an 'old boy network' is understood to refer to rich white males, but the term can be applied to other social groups where there is similar unfair preferment.*

Old chestnut A story or piece of information that has been heard repeated so often that it is uninteresting or even boring. There is sometimes the implication that the story or piece of information is false or at least inaccurate, but by being regularly repeated it has been accepted as fact.*

Old days The past. The temporal distance this indicates varies enormously. Most commonly, it refers to a time before an old person was born. However, much longer or shorter temporal distances may be meant, and these can only be gained from context.*

Old flame A previous girlfriend or boyfriend.*

Old girl network Female version of the *old boy network.*

Old hat Already known and thus no longer capable of raising interest or excitement.*

Old money Wealth accumulated through several generations of inheritance. In some class systems, there is a snobbish implication that people with such wealth are 'superior' to people from *new money* backgrounds, where the wealth has been accumulated by them personally or within one or two generations. There is often the added implication that people from old money backgrounds have greater command of social etiquette than people from new money backgrounds.*

Old school tie A symbol of belonging to the *old boy network.**

Old soldier See *come the old soldier.*

Old trout An old person (particularly an old woman) of unattractive appearance and hostile attitudes. The phrase should be avoided.***

Old wives' tale A fanciful or inaccurate story or piece of information that is widely (but erroneously) believed to be true.*

Oldest profession Prostitution.*

Oldest trick in the book A well-known method. The phrase usually means a method of deception that should be well known. Thus, if someone 'falls for the oldest trick in the book', then they have been surprisingly lacking in judgement.*

Olive branch An offer of peace or reconciliation.*

On a dime Means the same as *on a sixpence.*

On a hiding to nothing Engaged in an activity almost certain to fail.*

On a high In a very good mood.*

On a knife edge Describes a situation in which the outcome is highly uncertain and accordingly has generated a feeling of tension.*

On a mission Have something to do and be resolutely determined to do it.*

On a plate Something given 'on a plate' is something easily obtained. See *on their plate.**

On a promise Very confident of receiving something. The phrase is nearly always used to describe the secure expectation of sexual intercourse.*

On a razor's edge Means the same as *on a knife edge.*

On a roll Enjoying a period of especially good luck or good performance.*

On a short fuse Easily annoyed.*

On a silver platter Means the same as *on a plate.*

On a sixpence Something that can be done 'on a sixpence' can be done easily in a confined space. The phrase is often used of the turning circle of cars.*

On a string If someone is 'on a string' then they are controlled or influenced by someone else.*

On about If someone is 'on about' something, then they are talking about it.*

On all fours On hands and knees.*

On at them Pestering.*

On bended knee The phrase describes a kneeling position. The phrase is often used to describe a very emotional plea for help (e.g. 'on bended knee I beg you to help me'). A person does not literally have to adopt a kneeling position.*

On board A person who is 'on board' is a member of a team and/or is willing to support a particular cause or argument.*

On cue At the right time and place.*

On deck Already prepared for the task to be done.*

On different wavelengths See *on the same wavelength.*

On fire Excited or aroused.*

On firm ground Describes a piece of reasoning that cannot be faulted.*

On form Doing well.*

On paper Two rather contrasting meanings: (1) Potentially feasible (e.g. 'on paper, it should work, but it's yet to be tried out'). (2) Available in a tangible written or printed form, and thus providing more definite proof than a spoken report.*

On side (1) Concurring. (2) Legitimate and/or cannot be discounted.*

On stream Currently available or operational.*

On tap Readily available.*

On target Successful.*

On tenterhooks In a state of anxiety or anticipation.*

On the air Describes a programme that is currently being broadcast on television or radio, or is in the schedules (i.e. is regularly broadcast). A programme that is not currently being broadcast or that is not in the schedules is *off the air.**

On the back of a fag packet Means the same as *on the back of an envelope.*

On the back of a postage stamp Usually part of a longer phrase such as 'you could write all they know on the subject on the back of a postage stamp'. Since postage stamps are quite small, what is meant is that the person knows very little about the subject in question.*

On the back of an envelope Refers to something roughly planned or estimated, that needs refinement before it will be reliable. The phrase comes from the image of a person making a preliminary plan by writing on anything available, such as the back of an envelope.*

On the ball Alert and aware of what is going on, and able to respond promptly and sensibly to things.*

On the barrel To pay for it at the point of purchase (i.e. not to use credit).*

On the barrelhead Means the same as *on the barrel.*

On the blink Describes a piece of machinery that is faulty.*

On the block If something is 'on the block' then it is being sold at auction.*

On the blower On the phone.*

On the boil See *come to a boil.*

On the books (1) Describes a person who is formally registered as a member of a workforce, club, etc. (2) Describes a job that is scheduled to be done.*

On the bottle Drinking alcohol to excess.*

On the brain A person who has something 'on the brain' is obsessed with it. The exception to this is 'water on the brain', which usually indicates a disease (specifically, an inflammation of the brain).*

★ denotes level of impoliteness

On the breadline To be very poor. The phrase is derived from 'the breadlines', i.e. queues for bread and basic foodstuffs offered by various government and charitable organisations in areas of extreme economic deprivation.*

On the broo Claiming social welfare benefits.*

On the bubble To be in a difficult and/or dangerous situation.*

On the button Means 'exactly correct'.*

On the cards Very likely to happen.*

On the carpet In serious trouble. Hence, to receive a *carpeting* is to receive a severe telling-off.*

On the case To be working on a particular problem or piece of work. Contrast with *on their case.**

On the coat tails of them Gain success or wealth through being associated with another, more important person, rather than through any personal skills.*

On the crest of a wave (1) Very successful. (2) More generally, in good spirits.*

On the cusp About to happen.*

On the doorstep Within a short distance.*

On the dot Utterly punctual.*

On the downgraded Worsening.*

On the drawing board At a preparatory stage. See *back to the drawing board.**

On the edge of their seat Excited. The phrase is often used to describe an audience excited by a movie or stage performance, particularly one where the ending is uncertain.*

On the fiddle Engaged in a fraudulent activity.*

On the fly Something done 'on the fly' is performed whilst doing another activity simultaneously.*

On the fritz Means the same as *on the blink.*

On the game Being a prostitute.*

On the go Energetic.*

On the grapevine Rumour.*

On the ground Reality, as opposed to fanciful ideas.*

On the hoof (1) Without lengthy prior planning. The phrase is often used to describe how well a person can deal with problems and/or questions which they have not anticipated. (2) Still alive.*

On the hook Having responsibility.*

On the hop Surprised or unprepared.*

On the horizon Describes something that is strongly anticipated will happen in the future.*

On the horns of a dilemma In a difficult situation in which all options appear unattractive.*

On the house Free.*

On the job (1) Currently engaged in a task. (2) Having sexual intercourse.* (1) or ** (2)

On the knocker Selling products or canvassing for political parties from door to door (i.e. making unsolicited calls to houses).*

On the lam Attempting to avoid being captured (typically by the police).*

On the level Honest.*

On the lookout (1) Alert to signs of danger. (2) Constantly searching for something.*

On the make Looking for opportunities for advancement and/or profit. The phrase usually implies that a person who is 'on the make' is also unscrupulous.*

On the mat Severely reprimanded.*

On the mend Recovering.*

On the money Correct.*

On the nail (1) Means the same as *on the barrel*. (2) Accurate.*

On the nod Agreed without debate.*

On the nose Accurate.*

On the off chance In the unlikely event.*

On the Q.T. Means the same as *on the quiet*. 'Q.T.' is meant to represent the pronunciation of 'quiet'.

On the quiet Something done 'on the quiet' is done secretly.*

On the rag Having a period.***

On the razzle Having an enjoyable time.*

On the rebound In a period after ceasing a relationship with a sexual or romantic partner. The phrase is often used to describe meeting a new partner during this phase (e.g. 'I met Emma on the rebound from Charlotte').*

On the receiving end Being the recipient of something unpleasant.*

On the record (1) True, since there is undeniable proof that the matter in question occurred. (2) Something that can be attributed to the person saying it (as opposed to *off the record*).*

On the rocks (1) In difficulties. (2) A drink with ice.*

On the ropes In a difficult situation, facing almost certain misfortune.*

On the safe side Being cautious rather than daring.*

On the same page (1) On the same side. (2) Having similar ideas/knowledge.*

On the same wavelength If people are 'on the same wavelength', then they understand each other. If people do not understand each other, then they are *on different wavelengths*.*

On the scent Have a realistic prospect of finding something or someone.*

On the shelf (1) No longer wanted. (2) Without a partner.*

On the side of the angels To do what is morally correct. Although of religious origin, the phrase is not restricted to religious matters.*

On the sidelines A person observing 'on the sidelines' cannot take part in what they are observing.*

On the skids In a pronounced state of decline.*

On the slate On credit.*

On the sly Surreptitiously.*

On the spot (1) In a difficult situation. (2) Present at the event (e.g. 'the reporter on the spot where the event is taking place'). (3) At the location where something happened.*

On the take Obtaining money illegally. The phrase usually describes taking bribes or committing petty thefts from an employer.*

On the town Socialising, particularly visiting attractions in a city, such as restaurants, nightclubs and similar.*

On the up and up Improving in status.*

On the wagon To be teetotal.*

On the warpath In a bad mood, looking for a confrontation with someone.*

On their back (1) A person who is 'on their back' is ill. (2) A person who is 'on the back' of another person is being a nuisance.*

On their case Be very annoying to someone. Contrast with *on the case*.*

On their game Doing well.*

On their hands Something that must be dealt with.*

On their head Their responsibility.*

On their hind legs Standing. The phrase nearly always also means 'speaking'.*

On their last legs Near death or obsolescence.*

On their mind If something is 'on a person's mind' then it is preoccupying them.*

On their nerves Annoying or irritating them.*

On their own ground (1) Physically in their own neighbourhood. (2) In their own area of expertise.*

---

* denotes level of impoliteness

On their plate Their workload. See *on a plate.**

On their tod On their own.*

On their toes Alert.*

On their uppers Have little or no money or resources.*

On tick On credit.*

On to something Have a high probability of discovering something of importance.*

On toast In a vulnerable position.*

On top do In a state of great excitement.*

On top of the world In a very good mood.*

On your bike (1) Slang expression meaning 'go away'. (2) Slang expression meaning 'do something'.**

On your marks An instruction to race competitors that the race is about to begin. Accordingly, in a wider sense, a warning that something important is about to happen.*

Once bitten The start of a saying – 'once bitten, twice shy'. This means that if doing something results in being emotionally or physically hurt or otherwise ends in failure, a person will be less willing to try to do the same thing again.*

Once every... If the phrase is followed by the name of an obscure event (e.g. 'once every Preston guild') then it means the same as *once in a blue moon.**

Once in a blue moon Indicating a very rare event (under very exceptional circumstances, the moon can appear blue).*

One and the same The identical thing or person. The phrase is nearly always used to confirm an identity (e.g. 'is it really you?' might get the reply 'the one and the same').*

One big... Emphasizes the magnitude of whatever is described in the following phrase (e.g. 'it's been one big waste of time').*

One born every minute See *there's one born every minute.*

One door closes The start of a proverb that finishes 'another opens'. In other words, if something has come to an end, there are other new things that can be done instead.*

One fell swoop A single action that completely accomplishes its aim.*

One fine day At some time in the future.*

One foot in the grave Have a life-threatening illness. The phrase is often used jokingly to describe later life.*

One for the road A final drink before parting.*

One good turn The start of a proverb that finishes with 'deserves another'. In other words, if person A does something for person B, then person B should feel obliged to do something for person A.*

One in the eye An annoyance, or something that at least temporarily thwarts a plan.*

One jump ahead Further ahead than someone else in the planning or execution of something and thus holding an advantage.*

One man [or woman] band An organisation or business that is either literally just one person, or that would fail but for the work of a particular person.*

One man [or woman] show Means the same as *one man [or woman] band.*

One night stand (1) A person with whom one has sexual relations on only one occasion. (2) A concert or theatrical performance given in a particular place only once. The implication is that the performer is either of poor quality or relatively unknown, and thus only gets to work sporadically.*

One of the boys Means the same as *one of the lads.*

One of the lads Belonging and accepted by a group of men who have a common interest in stereotypical masculine pursuits such as drinking, sport and never talking about anything requiring emotional considerations. This is either the acme of success or a damning indictment, depending upon one's point of view.*

One of those days A day when everything seems to be going wrong.*

One of those nights A night when everything seems to be going wrong. Generally specifically describes an evening out that goes wrong.*

One over the eight To be drunk.*

One step forward, two steps back A derogatory description of any policy or way of working in which nothing seems to be accomplished in spite of a lot of activity. Alternatively, a description of an action that makes things worse than before.*

One swallow doesn't make a summer A minor symptom of something does not guarantee that something exists. For example, seeing one swallow flying around does not mean that hot summer weather is guaranteed.*

One that got away Something that could not be attained and which has grown more desirable in memory and/or telling to others.*

One too many Excess alcoholic drink to the point where inebriation has been induced. The phrase is often used as a euphemism for very, rather than just mildly, excessive drinking.*

One way ticket A situation with only one possible outcome.*

Only game in town The most important thing.*

Only obeying orders The phrase is used in a derogatory sense to mean that someone did what they were told to do without questioning whether their actions were moral. The implication is that if they had followed their conscience rather than orders, then they would never have done what they did. The phrase

came to have its current implication after the statement 'I was only obeying orders' was used by many senior Nazis as a defence argument in the Nuremberg war crimes trials.*

Open a can of worms Discover or create a serious and complex problem.*

Open and shut case Something in which the conclusion is so obvious right from the start that the end result is no surprise.*

Open arms See *with open arms.*

Open book Someone (or something) about whom everything is known, with no attempt to hide any secrets.*

Open door See *push at an open door.*

Open door policy (1) Be always available to receive visitors or listen to complaints or enquiries. (2) Have allocated times when a person is available to see visitors (i.e. no other events are scheduled to overlap with this time).*

Open sesame A means of gaining access to something normally difficult to enter.*

Open the door to Permit something to be done.*

Open their eyes Make a person aware of something they previously did not know or adequately appreciate.*

Open their mind Typically means the same as *open their eyes,* but can also mean more generally making someone more receptive to new ideas.*

Open with them Honest with them.*

Opportunity knocks A chance for success.*

Opposite sides of the same coin Means the same as *two sides of the same coin.*

Orders See *only obeying orders* and *orders is orders.*

Orders is orders Meaning 'if an order has been given, it must be obeyed, no matter how strange or ridiculous you may personally feel it is'.*

Other half Means the same as *better half.*

Other side of the coin An argument presenting an opposite point of view.*

Other things being equal Means the same as *all things being equal.*

Out and about Having an unexceptional normal lifestyle.*

Out at the elbows Ragged or worn out.*

Out cold Unconscious.*

Out for blood Describes people who are determined to make someone suffer.*

Out for the count (1) Unconscious. (2) Utterly defeated. The phrase comes from boxing – a boxer who is 'out for the count' is one who, having been knocked down, fails to stand up by the time the referee has counted to ten, and thus loses the contest.*

Out in the cold A person left 'out in the cold' is being excluded from a group or activity.*

Out in the open No longer secret.*

Out like a light Quickly asleep or unconscious.*

Out of a corner See *in a corner.*

Out of a tight corner See *in a corner.*

Out of bounds Something that must not be visited and/or discussed.*

Out of harm's way Safe.*

Out of it To be insensible. The phrase is often used of someone who is too tired or inebriated to think logically. It can also be used jokingly of someone who seems intellectually incapable of understanding an argument.*

Out of joint Disorientated or not correctly integrated.*

Out of keeping Uncharacteristic.*

Out of kilter Out of balance or lacking harmony.*

Out of line A state of disobedience.*

Out of order (1) Against regulations or expected standards. (2) Broken.*

Out of pocket Made a financial loss.

Out of pocket expenses Expenses incurred that were paid with a person's own money and which can be subsequently claimed back from a fund, because they were a necessary expense during a business trip or similar.*

Out of sight (1) Hidden from scrutiny. (2) In 1960s hippy slang, a term of high praise (e.g. 'Hendrix's guitar playing was out of sight').*

Out of sight, out of mind A proverb expressing the opinion that something or someone not encountered regularly is likely to be forgotten or appreciated less.*

Out of sorts Feel unwell or to be in a bad mood.*

Out of the ark Joking term meaning that something is very old and accordingly is unlikely to function as well as something more recent (e.g. 'he drove an old car that was like something out of the ark').**

Out of the blocks Describes how quickly someone starts to do something (e.g. 'first out of the blocks' means they were the fastest to start, 'last out of the blocks' means they were slowest, etc.). The phrase is derived from athletics sprint races, where runners use starting blocks.*

Out of the blue Unexpectedly (e.g. 'the news of the promotion was completely unexpected and came like a bolt out of the blue').*

Out of the box (1) Something that can be used 'out of the box' is ready to use without further assembly being required. (2) In a phrase including an indication of order (e.g. 'first out of the box', 'third out of the box' etc.) the phrase simply means the same as the stated order (e.g. 'first out of the box' simply means 'first'). (3) The phrase describes how a person will behave on first meeting them (e.g. 'he will come out of the box bad-tempered'). (4) In Australian slang, the phrase can mean 'good'. Do not confuse with *out of their box*.*

Out of the closet A person *coming out* of the closet is admitting to something that they have previously hidden. The phrase was originally used to describe gay men and women declaring publicly that they were homosexual. However, the phrase is now used more generally for any type of admission of a previously kept secret.*

Out of the frame (1) Not suspected of having done something. (2) Not attended to.*

Out of the frying pan Often followed by the rest of the phrase – 'and into the fire'. To escape from one unattractive situation only to immediately be placed in another unattractive situation.*

Out of the loop See *in the loop*.

Out of the picture No longer relevant.*

Out of the road A demand to stop causing an obstruction.**

Out of the running See *in the running*.

Out of the window Rejected.*

Out of the woods No longer in danger.*

Out of their box Drunk or affected by drugs. Do not confuse with *out of the box*.*

Out of their depth In a situation which they lack the ability to deal with.*

Out of their gourd Behaving in an irrational manner. The phrase often implies that this is due to intoxication.*

Out of their head To be intoxicated or insane.*

Out of their mind (1) Insane. (2) Severely mistaken.*

Out of their skull Means the same as *out of their head*.

Out of their tree Means the same as *out of their head*.

Out of thin air Used to describe something or someone that appears unexpectedly (e.g. 'he suddenly appeared out of thin air').*

Out of this world Extremely good. The phrase does not literally mean 'extraterrestrial', however.*

Out of touch (1) No longer in communication. (2) No longer conversant with current trends.*

Out on a limb Isolated and/or without aid.*

Out to get them Wanting to inflict punishment.*

Out to lunch Insane.*

Out with it Means the same as *spit it out*.

Outside the box Innovative, unconventional or eccentric.*

Over a barrel A person who is 'over a barrel' cannot win or escape punishment no matter what they do.*

Over-egg the pudding Spoil the effect of something by including too much.*

Over my dead body An expression of opposition to something (e.g. 'you'll do that over my dead body').*

Over the counter (1) Legitimately purchased without subterfuge. In contrast, *under the counter* refers to something purchased illegally. (2) Describes a medicine that can be bought without a doctor's prescription.*

Over the fence (1) Australian term meaning 'unacceptable'. (2) From the neighbours.*

Over the hill To have reached a stage where a person is considered to be incompetent at a particular task. More generally, to be considered 'too old'.**

Over the hump Finished with the most unpleasant and/or difficult parts of something.*

Over the limit Drunk.*

Over the moon A state of great happiness.*

Over the odds Too expensive or otherwise beyond expectations of what is reasonable.*

---

* *denotes level of impoliteness*

Over the road The phrase can mean 'across the other side of the road' but can also mean 'over there' (e.g. which could be across a room, the other side of the corridor). The context should indicate which meaning is intended.*

Over the top An exaggeration to the point of being ridiculous. Used to describe anything that is too extreme to be plausible, such as melodramatic plays and films, or reactions to events that are too extreme (e.g. having a temper tantrum over a lost paper clip).*

Over the top of their head Means the same as *over their head.*

Over their head (1) Too difficult to be understood. (2) Something done without consulting a person who should have been consulted (and by implication, would probably have objected).*

Over yonder Over there.*

Overplay their hand Try to achieve too much with the resources available.*

Overshoot the mark Means the same as *overstep the mark*, though sometimes with an implication that what has been done has been accidental.*

Overstep the mark Do something that is beyond the limits of what is considered permissible and/or acceptable. There is often the implication that this was done knowingly. See *overshoot the mark.**

Overturn the applecart Means the same as *upset the applecart.*

Owe them a living A person who feels that someone or something 'owes them a living' feels that they are automatically entitled to a job or financial and/or material support. The phrase is often used in the negative form 'the *world doesn't owe them a living*', expressing the belief that people are not automatically entitled to anything and should work for what they receive.*

Owe them one Feel obliged to repay a debt or favour.*

Own goal In soccer, an own goal is scored when a person accidentally strikes a ball into their own goal (i.e. they score a goal for their opponents). More generally, the phrase describes a mistake that creates extra problems for the person who made it.*

Own up Confess.*

Own worst enemy See *their own worst enemy.*

P

Pack a punch Have a strong effect.*

Pack it in Stop doing something. Used as a description (e.g. 'they packed it in') it is fairly mild, but used as a command (e.g. 'pack it in') it is more forceful and less polite.* or ** (if used as a command)

Pack their bags Prepare to leave. If used as a command, it is rather more emotionally forceful (and is similar to *sling their hook*). For example, 'have you packed your bags yet?' is a polite question. However, 'pack your bags!' is a command to go and indicates that the speaker is not pleased.* or ** (if used as a command)

Packing heat Carrying a gun.*

Paddle their own canoe Work without any assistance.*

Page Three girl A female model who appears topless. The phrase derives from the UK tabloid newspaper *The Sun*, which introduced a picture of such a model on a daily basis, always on page three. The models are generally stereotyped as large-chested with few intellectual accomplishments.*

Pain in the arse Ruder version of *pain in the neck.****

Pain in the ass Means the same as *pain in the arse.****

Pain in the backside Means the same as *pain in the neck*, but ruder.**

Pain in the elbow Means the same as *pain in the neck.*

Pain in the neck An annoyance; there is often the implication that this is a long-standing rather than short-lived annoyance.*

Pain in the nether regions Means the same as *pain in the neck,* but slightly ruder.**

Pain in the proverbial Means the same as *pain in the neck.*

Pain in the rear end Means the same as *pain in the neck,* but slightly ruder.**

Paint into a corner Means the same as *box into a corner.* The image comes from a person foolish enough to paint a floor in such a way that they end in the corner of the room, incapable of getting out of the room without walking on wet paint, and thus doomed to stay in the corner of the room until the paint dries.*

Paint the Forth bridge A never-ending task. The Forth road and rail bridges in Scotland are large structures and demand continuous repairs (including repainting).*

Paint the town red To have a good night out, usually with the implication of drinking too much and generally not being on best behaviour.*

Pale See *beyond the pale.*

Pandora's box Something that is harmless if left alone, but once disturbed creates havoc and/or considerable problems.*

Panic button See *push the panic button.*

Pants down See *catch with their pants down.*

Paper bag See *couldn't...their way out of a paper bag.*

Paper over the cracks Attempt to deal with a problem by disguising its effects, rather than deal with the causes of the problem.*

Paper tiger An apparently threatening person or thing who in fact is harmless.*

Par See entry below and: *above par, below par, under par* and *up to par.*

Par for the course What would normally be expected.*

Pardon my French Please excuse my swearing.*

Pare to the bone Means the same as *cut to the bone.*

Part and parcel An integral component.*

Part of the furniture A person who has become accepted into a group of people so that his or her presence is not remarked upon.*

Parting of the ways A separation. The phrase can be used in several ways: e.g. (a) a disagreement after a period of agreement; (b) people following different careers after shared time together (e.g. after working on a common project).*

Party's over The phrase can be used to indicate that a period of enjoyment has come to an end and that now some serious work must be done, but it is also used more generally simply to indicate that something has finished.*

Pass by on the other side Avoid.*

Pass current Be accepted as true.*

Pass muster Be of an acceptable standard.*

Pass the baton Give someone else the responsibility for a particular task.*

Pass the buck See *passing the buck.*

Pass the hat round Request voluntary payments for something.*

Pass the sick bucket A joking or facetious remark indicating displeasure in something just witnessed. The phrase is often used as a comment on something that is over-sentimental or insincere.*

Pass their eye over Examine not very thoroughly.*

Passing acquaintance Means the same as *nodding acquaintance.*

Passing the buck (1) Giving the responsibility for something unpleasant to someone else. (2) More generally, refusing to accept responsibility. The phrase is said to originate from card games in the American 'wild west' where the 'buck' (originally a type of knife, subsequently a silver dollar or counter) was placed in front of the person whose responsibility was to deal the cards. Since the dealer was nearly always the person blamed if anything went wrong, this was not the most pleasant of tasks. Hence, passing the buck (i.e. getting someone else to deal the cards) was giving someone else the responsibility for a disagreeable task. If someone declares that the *buck stops here*, he or she is saying that they will take responsibility.*

Past it A derogatory term for someone assumed to be too old to be capable of doing anything useful or important.**

Past its sell-by date Outmoded.*

Pat on the back Expression of approval.*

Patter of tiny feet The presence of a child or children.*

Pave the way Make something possible by doing the initial work necessary for it to occur. *

Pay for itself If an item 'pays for itself', then the amount of money it earns or saves is equal to or greater than its purchase and maintenance costs.*

Pay its way Be useful and worth the cost of buying and maintaining.*

Pay lip service Do something without any sincerity or particular effort.*

Pay the Earth Pay a lot of money.*

Pay the piper Pay the bill for something.*

Pay their dues Do what is expected and appropriate.*

Pay their respects Visit someone.*

Pay their way Be useful and worth the cost of employing.*

Pay through the nose To pay an excessive amount for something. Probably derived from a Viking form of extortion, in which people were threatened with mutilation of their nose unless they paid money.*

Pays to… It is worthwhile to… *

Peach of a… A very good and/or desirable example of a… *

Peaches and cream A pale, unblemished skin with pale, pink cheeks.*

Pear-shaped See *go pear-shaped.*

Pearls before swine Something of high quality presented to people incapable of appreciating it.*

Peas in a pod Items very similar in appearance.*

Pedal to the metal Accelerating hard in a car.*

Peed off Has the same meanings as *pissed off.* Is very slightly less rude, but use is still cautioned against.***

Peel me a grape The phrase is used sarcastically to denote somebody who is so wealthy, lazy and/or decadent that it could be imagined that they would, given the chance, have a servant peel grapes for them rather than eat the skin of the grapes like anyone else. By extension, the phrase is used sarcastically as a retort when somebody asks for something that they are apparently too lazy to do for themselves.*

Peel out Leave or quit.*

Peg See *bring down a peg or two.*

Penis on wheels An expensive fast car owned by a (typically middle-aged or older) man. The phrase derives from the argument that such a car is being used (consciously or subconsciously) as an expression of virility, and may be compensating for a lack of, or decline in, virility in the owner.***

Pennies from Heaven Unexpected advantages or pleasures.*

Penny drops Realisation is attained.*

Penny for them Means the same as *penny for your thoughts.*

Penny for your thoughts A joking remark to a person who appears to be daydreaming.*

Penny wise, pound foolish Being obsessive about minor savings of money, thereby incurring bigger expenses as a result. For example, refusing to spend money on repairing a broken garden gate, then getting sued when a visitor gashes their hand on it.*

People in glass houses The start of a proverb, the rest of which is 'shouldn't throw stones'. In other words, people who themselves can be criticized should not vociferously criticize others.*

Perish the thought An expression of rejection of support for an idea or prospect. The phrase can be used in several ways, such as an expression of disapproval of an idea (e.g. 'do you think Brian might be made Chairman?' might be met with 'perish the thought!' if Brian is an unpopular or implausible candidate) or as a qualifying statement before raising an unwelcome prognosis (e.g. 'perish the thought, but what would we do if Brian became Chairman?').*

Person in the street A recent (and non-sexist) form of *man in the street*. The term refers to the average person and is generally used when discussing public opinion (e.g. 'what does the person in the street think about the new government policy?').*

Person of the cloth A Christian minister.*

Person of the moment A person who is currently considered important or who is temporarily famous.*

Pick holes Criticize.*

Pick nits Means the same as *nit pick*.

Pick of the crop The best.*

Pick out of a hat Choose randomly.*

Pick their brains Ask for advice or information (e.g. 'I'd like to pick your brains about this problem because I know you have some expertise in these matters').*

Pick to pieces Heavily criticize.*

Pick up (1) Understand. (2) Adopt (as in *pick up the ball and run with it*). (3) Offer a lift in a car or taxi, or someone who is given a lift in a car or taxi. (4) A person encountered on a social occasion with whom one has sexual relations with no emotional commitment, usually only on one occasion (often described as a *casual pick up*).*

Pick up on Learn about. The phrase often refers to learning something by chance.*

Pick up some slack Means the same as *take up the slack*.

Pick up the ball and run with it Means the same as *take the ball and run with it*.

Pick up the baton Accept the responsibility for something previously the responsibility of someone else.*

Pick up the bill Pay a debt.*

Pick up the pieces Attempt to return a situation to a state of relative normality after an argument or disturbance.*

Pick up the tab Means the same as *pick up the bill*.

Pick up the thread Come to a state of comprehension.*

Pick you up A medicine or other substance designed to make a sick or depressed person feel less sick or depressed.*

Pie eyed Inebriated.*

Pie in the sky Something unrealistically optimistic.*

Piece of ass A sexually desirable person. The phrase can be used of either gender, but tends to be used of women. It is offensive to many people and use of the term should be avoided.***

Piece of cake Something very easy.*

Piece of piss Less polite form of *piece of cake*.***

Piece of the action A person wanting a 'piece of the action' wishes to share in an activity that he or she thinks is going to be rewarding by being financially rewarding and/or exciting. The term was used by American gangsters to describe their share in profits from illegal activities.*

Piece of the pie Means the same as *piece of the action.*

Pierce their heart Cause a feeling of strong emotion.*

Pig in a poke Something bought or acquired whose identity and/or value is unknown until after purchase or acquisition.*

Pig in the middle A person who finds themselves involved in a disagreement where they belong to neither side but find themselves affected adversely by the situation.*

Piggy in the middle Means the same as *pig in the middle.*

Pigs might fly An expression of disbelief. Usually used in reply to an improbable statement (e.g. 'I might win the lottery' might get a reply of 'yes, and pigs might fly').*

Pile it on Over-elaborate.*

Pile on the agony Make things increasingly unpleasant.*

Pillar of society A person highly respected in their community.*

Pillar of strength A person who can be relied upon to offer assistance and support.*

Pillar to post The whole length.*

Pin back their ears Listen attentively.*

Pin it on Attribute responsibility to.*

Pinch See *at a pinch* and *that's the pinch.*

Pins and needles (1) The tingling sensation as a numb part of the body regains feeling. (2) A person on 'pins and needles' is very anxious or in a state of expectation that something is going to happen.*

Pip to the post (1) Win by a narrow margin. (2) Win at the last moment.*

Piping hot Extremely hot.*

Pipped at the post Defeated at the last moment.*

Piss in the same pot If two or more people are said to 'piss in the same pot' it means they have interests in common and/or work together.***

Piss in the wind Engage in something futile.***

Piss on their parade Ruder version of *rain on their parade.****

Piss or get off the pot A strong demand to either do something or leave – the implication being that something should have already been done.***

Pissed The term has several meanings depending upon context and culture. In all meanings, however, the term is slang and considered offensive. (1) The term literally refers to urination. Thus, 'I have had a piss' means 'I have urinated'. (2) In UK slang, the term usually refers to being drunk (e.g. 'he went to the pub and got pissed'). (3) In US slang, the phrase means 'angry'(e.g. 'damaging his video made him really pissed at you'). (4) In UK slang, the term can also mean 'angry' if in the phrase *pissed off* (e.g. 'damaging his video made him really pissed off at you'). However, note that the phrase 'pissed off' can also mean 'ran away' (e.g. 'as soon as he saw there was trouble he pissed off out of here'). (5) The phrase 'piss off' commonly either means 'go away' or is a strong refutation of an accusation (e.g. 'did you steal it?' – 'piss off'). (6) *Take the piss* is a less polite version of *take the mickey*. See *couldn't organize a piss-up in a brewery, no pot to piss in, piece of piss, piss in the wind, pissed as a newt* and *piss or get off the pot.****

Pissed as a newt To be very drunk. The origins of the phrase are unknown; certainly, newts are not noted inebriates. See *pissed.****

Pissed off See *pissed.*

Piss-up in a brewery See *couldn't organize a piss-up in a brewery.*

Pit of the stomach If an emotion is felt 'in the pit of the stomach' then it is felt strongly.*

Pity fuck Means the same as *charity fuck.*

Place in the sun An advantageous position.*

Plain as a pikestaff (1) Obvious. (2) Unattractive.*

Plain Jane (1) An unattractive woman. (2) A woman who is habitually soberly dressed, avoids make-up, etc.*

Plain sailing Easy.*

Plan B An alternative plan. The phrase is usually applied to a plan that is used when the first plan fails.*

Plant dragon's teeth Means the same as *sow dragon's teeth.*

Plates of meat Feet. The phrase comes from Cockney rhyming slang.*

Play a blinder Do something extremely well.*

Play a hunch Guess.*

Play ball To 'play ball' is to cooperate.*

Play both ends against the middle Support all the opposing sides in an argument.*

Play by ear (1) Do something unrehearsed. (2) Adjust behaviour and actions in response to the situation (rather than rigidly following a pre-arranged plan).*

Play by the rules Behave in a legal and morally correct manner.*

Play cat and mouse Instead of immediately defeating an opponent, repeatedly trick and then disillusion them that they have a chance to win or escape. The phrase is derived from the way in which a cat will play with a captured mouse before finally killing it.*

Play catch-up Attempt to draw level with someone currently in a better position.*

Play Devil with Damage.*

Play Devil's advocate Present the argument for the opposite case without necessarily believing it. The term is derived from the title of 'Devil's Advocate' given to a cardinal in the Vatican who, in the process of deciding if a person is suitable for canonisation, is assigned the task of finding evidence against a person being made into a saint.*

Play dirty Act in an unfair manner.*

Play doctors and nurses Engage in sexual activity.*

Play ducks and drakes with Fail to behave seriously.*

Play fast and loose (1) Be irresponsible. (2) Be sexually promiscuous.*

Play footsie (1) Engage in flirtatious behaviour by gently rubbing a foot against a partner's foot in a formal setting, such as when seated at a restaurant table. (2) Be engaged in a covert business deal.*

Play for keeps Have long-term plans.*

Play for time Deliberately delay proceedings in the hope that this will be advantageous.*

Play games (1) Behave in an inappropriately frivolous manner. (2) Do something that shows lack of respect or even malice.*

Play God (1) Behave in an arrogant manner. (2) Make decisions about the fates of people. There is usually an implication that this is done through an improper use of power. (3) As a medical practitioner, decide who should be given a life-saving treatment and who should not, and thus who should live and who should die.*

Play hard to get Feign lack of interest in the approach of a potential suitor or new employer to encourage them to make a more attractive offer.*

Play hardball Be very firm and decisive, and generally be uncompromising.*

Play hell Complain.*

Play hell with (1) Disrupt. (2) Complain.*

Play hookey Be absent without permission. The phrase especially applies to pupils avoiding school.*

Play into their hands Unwittingly do something that is advantageous to an opponent.*

Play it cool Be nonchalant.*

Play it safe Be cautious.*

Play it straight Behave honestly.*

Play kissy-kissy Be overly friendly in the hope of gaining favour.*

Play merry hell Complain.*

Play politics Do something to attain an advantage, rather than out of genuine belief.*

Play possum (1) When under attack, pretending to be unconscious or dead. (2) Pretending to know nothing about the matter being discussed.*

Play second fiddle Have a less important role or status. The phrase is often used in the form 'play second fiddle to...', followed by the name of a person who is of higher status.*

Play silly buggers Means the same as *play silly devils*, but less polite.**

Play silly devils Behave in a stupid, irritating manner.*

Play the ace To do something that demonstrates great skill. There is often the implication that what was done was unexpected.*

Play the can Means the same as *play the fool*.

Play the field Engage in casual relationships without making a serious attempt to commit to a longer-lasting relationship. The phrase often implies that a person enjoys sex with their partners but is too selfish or immature to offer a deeper emotional bond.*

Play the fool To behave stupidly and/or playfully.*

Play the game Obey the rules and behave in a courteous manner.*

Play the goat Means the same as *act the fool*.

Play the market Engage in financial speculation.*

Play the old soldier Means the same as *come the old soldier*.

Play the percentages Use a cautious approach in a plan that involves probable rather than certain outcomes, carefully calculating the odds of something happening, contingencies if something unwelcome happens, etc.*

Play the person, not the ball Attempt to defeat an opponent by finding weaknesses in their personality and exploiting them.*

Play the white man A demand that someone behaves fairly. The phrase can be interpreted as racist (i.e. that white people are seen as fair and, by extrapolation, that people of other skin colours are unfair) and thus should be avoided.***

Play their cards right Perform skilfully (can be at anything, not just cards). The phrase is often used in the form 'if you play your cards right, then...', indicating that an attractive reward is available to a person if they perform well (e.g. 'if you play your cards right and work hard, then one day you will be promoted').*

Play their game Do what someone else expects or hopes will be done.*

Play them at their own game Use the same tactics and methods as an opponent.*

Play them false Deceive and/or betray.*

Play themselves in Become used to the prevailing conditions.*

Play things by the book Means the same as *go by the book*.

Play to the gallery Seek popular acclaim without regard for other considerations.

The phrase derives from actors who would (depending on the play) either try for quick laughs or produce an over-emotional performance which appealed to the (supposedly) less sophisticated members of the audience seated in the gallery part of the theatre (i.e. in the cheaper seats), but which left the connoisseurs in the more expensive seats feeling that they were seeing a poor performance.*

Play up To be awkward and/or refuse to cooperate.*

Play with a straight bat Do something fairly and honestly without attempting to trick or intimidate.*

Play with fire Engage in a dangerous activity.*

Plead the fifth The 'fifth' is the Fifth Amendment to the Constitution of the USA. The phrase means that someone reserves the right to remain silent to particular questions, because answering them might be incriminating (e.g. 'Did you rob the store?' – 'I plead the fifth'). The comment can be used jokingly to avoid answering an embarrassing or awkward question. It thus can have a role similar to that of *no comment.**

Pleased as Punch In other words, very pleased. The phrase probably derives from the Punch puppet, which has a permanent smile on its face.*

Plot thickens The situation has become more complicated.*

Plough a lonely furrow Work at a task without assistance.*

Ploughing away Working hard at something.*

Plum in their mouth Having an upper-class British accent.*

Plumb the depths (1) Reach a low level of quality. (2) Be especially depressed. (3) Enquire deeply.*

Poach on their territory Do something that is more properly another person's right and privilege to do.*

Poacher turned gamekeeper A person who changes from being against something to representing its interests.*

Poetic justice Punishment for misdeeds that is particularly appropriate (e.g. a poisoner who dies from food poisoning).*

Poetic licence Describing something inaccurately because it is artistically preferable.*

Point a gun at their head Force a person to do something they would not have voluntarily done.*

Point blank Directly, with no attempt to disguise.*

Point of no return (1) The moment when any further action makes an irrevocable commitment to something. (2) The stage in a journey or activity where it becomes less wasteful of time and energy to continue to the end rather than turn back.*

Point of the story The message that a story is intended to convey. For example, the point of the story of the three little pigs can be argued to be to make adequate preparations against possible threats. See *get to the point.**

Point of view Can mean the view that someone sees, but more usually refers to what someone thinks and feels about a particular issue. Thus, if a person has a 'different point of view' then they think and feel differently about something.*

Point out To indicate or show.*

Point scoring Attempting to prove superiority by winning arguments over trivial matters.*

Point the finger Accuse.*

Point up Make note of (usually refers to the identification of a problem).*

Points scoring Debating in a petty way where minor arguments are won whilst ignoring the more substantial issues.*

Poisoned chalice Something that appears attractive but in reality is far less appealing or even is dangerous. The phrase probably comes from the various folk tales where a person is tricked into drinking a poison or evil magical potion from an attractive-looking chalice (a type of drinking vessel).*

Poke borak at Make fun of.*

Poke fun at Make fun of or insult.*

Poke in the ribs Means the same as *dig in the ribs.*

Poke their bib in Interfere.*

Poke their nose in Interfere or be over-inquisitive.*

Poke their oar in Interfere.*

Poker faced Expressionless.*

Pole position The top-ranking position.*

Poles apart Very different from each other.*

Politically correct Satisfying current moral standards. The phrase is generally used in the context of something that is now considered offensive when in earlier times it was not (e.g. 'that's not politically correct these days').*

Poor little rich boy A wealthy man who gets no satisfaction from his wealth and lifestyle. The phrase is often used contemptuously, to indicate someone who has the resources to agonize over how unhappy they are whilst living in great luxury.*

Poor little rich girl Female version of *poor little rich boy.*

Poor relation An inferior version.*

Pop out (1) To appear suddenly. (2) To go out, generally with the implication of it being a brief journey (e.g. 'I'll just pop out to the store for some milk').*

Pop the question Propose marriage.*

Pop their cherry Have sexual intercourse with a person who was until that time a virgin. The phrase is sometimes used to refer to introducing a person to a new non-sexual activity.***

Pop their clogs Die.*

Pork pies Lies. The phrase is Cockney rhyming slang.*

Porridge See *do porridge.*

Port of call A place to visit.*

Postage stamp See *on the back of a postage stamp.*

Pot calling the kettle black Someone who makes a criticism that just as much applies to themselves (e.g. like Pol Pot calling Hitler a vicious dictator).*

Pot luck (1) Chance. (2) A situation where what is offered is all that is available (frequently used in this meaning of the phrase with regard to the range of food available to an unexpected guest).*

Pot to piss in See *not have a pot to piss in.*

Pots of... A large quantity of... *

Pound of flesh Something that can be demanded by a strict interpretation of the law or other regulations, but which is, by a more universal moral code, an unreasonable or even abhorrent thing to demand.*

Pound the pavement Means the same as *pound the streets.*

Pound the streets Walk the streets.*

Pour cold water on Be disparaging about.*

Pour petrol on the flames Means the same as *fan the flames.*

Powder their nose A euphemism for going to the lavatory. Chiefly used by women.*

Powers that be People in charge.*

Practise what they preach Behave in their own lives as they exhort others to do in theirs. The phrase is nearly always used to indicate a person who does not 'practise what they preach' (i.e. is a hypocrite).*

Praise the Lord and pass the ammunition A pragmatic acceptance that at times unpleasant things must be done for a morally just reason.*

Prawn See *come the raw prawn.*

Preach to the converted Make an unnecessary effort by trying to persuade people to adopt a cause or set of beliefs that they already follow.*

Precious little Very little.*

Pregnant pause A period of silence that is meaningful, simply because it is silent. The phrase is often used to describe a silence following a surprising revelation as people ponder its implications.*

Prepare the ground Make subsequent work in the same area easier.*

Presence of mind The ability to behave rationally.*

Present company excepted With the exception of the people present at the time of speaking.*

Press home Ensure that something is fully understood through the use of forceful argument.*

Press home the advantage Make use of an advantage to ensure that victory is gained.*

Press the button Start something.*

Press the flesh Shake hands. The phrase is nearly always used of politicians and famous people greeting other people at a reception or other social or publicity-raising event.*

Press the tit Can mean the same as *press the button* or, more simply, mean to press a button.*

Pretty kettle of fish A muddle. See *different kettle of fish.*

Pretty penny A large amount of money.*

Pretty please (1) A joking way of saying 'please'. (2) A 'pretty please' can be a request for something that will require more work or effort than usual (e.g. 'this is a pretty please – could you work half an hour later tomorrow night?'). The phrase is an imitation of a child asking for an especially big favour.*

Previous incarnation Means the same as *previous life.*

Previous life Unless the speaker is talking about a belief in reincarnation, then 'previous life' refers to a previous career or lifestyle.*

Price on their head (1) The value of a reward for the capture of a criminal. (2) More generally, someone with a 'price on their head' is sought for punishment. This latter use can be used jokingly.*

Prick the bubble Destroy an illusion (e.g. be the cause of a situation in which the *bubble has burst*).*

Prick up their ears Listen carefully.*

Pricking of their thumbs A sense of something about to happen.*

Pride comes before a fall Meaning that if someone is proud then eventually they will experience a worsening of their fortunes. The phrase has the implication that being too proud about personal accomplishments is to *tempt fate.*

Pride of place The highest status.*

Prime the pump Engage in *pump priming.*

Primrose path A course of action that appears attractive but will ultimately be ruinous.*

Proclaim from the rooftops Make known. The phrase is often used to describe someone who is keen for as many people as possible to know something.*

Prodigal son A person who squanders money left or given to them by parents on a dissolute lifestyle. The phrase is derived from the parable by Jesus about one such individual who, having spent all his money, was welcomed back by his father.*

---

* *denotes level of impoliteness*

Prolong the agony Make an unpleasant situation last longer than necessary.*

Promise the Earth Make an extravagant promise that is unrealistic.*

Promise the Moon Means the same as *promise the Earth*.

Promises, promises A retort indicating that although something is promised, it is unlikely ever to be done.*

Proof of the pudding Shortened form of the longer saying 'the proof of the pudding is in the eating'. 'Proof' in this instance means 'test' (from the same origin as, for example, 'proving grounds').*

Prop up the bar Be a regular drinker in a bar.*

P's and q's Refers to etiquette. Hence, *mind their p's and q's* is advice to behave well and, more generally, to be careful. There are many suggestions for the phrase's origins, none unanimously convincing.*

Public enemy number one (1) A notorious criminal wanted by the police. (2) A person who is deeply unpopular with the general public.*

Public eye The popular media (TV, newspapers, etc.).*

Publish or perish A guiding principle of many universities is that unless an academic consistently publishes in learned journals, then he or she will be fired or (possibly worse) be forced to attend numerous administrative committees.*

Pull a fast one (1) Behave dishonestly. (2) Deceive.*

Pull faces Means the same as *make faces*.

Pull in their horns Show more restrained behaviour.*

Pull out all the stops Make a considerable effort.*

Pull rank Use the authority of having a higher rank or status to ensure that something is done. The phrase is often used to denote an unfair situation where a subordinate's better ideas are ignored because someone in a higher position of authority wants things to be done differently.*

Pull strings Unfairly affect events by using influence by means other than those officially sanctioned. See *pull the strings*.*

Pull the other one The start of a saying – 'pull the other one, it's got bells on'. An expression of disbelief in what has just been said.*

Pull the plug Abandon or stop a project or course of action.*

Pull the rug The phrase nearly always finishes with 'from under them'. Do something surprising that places someone else at a disadvantage.*

Pull the strings Influence what others think and do. See *pull strings*.*

Pull the wool over their eyes Deceive. The phrase refers to the fact that when wig-wearing was a gentleman's fashion, pulling the wig (nicknamed a 'wool') over someone's eyes stopped them seeing anything.*

Pull their chestnuts from the fire Solve a person's problems for them.*

Pull their finger out Do something rather than debate what should be done without actually doing anything.*

Pull their leg Tease someone.*

Pull their socks up A demand to try harder. The phrase comes from the image of a schoolchild looking untidy because their knee-length socks have sagged down and need to be pulled up.*

Pull their weight Work at the level expected of them.*

Pull themselves up by their bootstraps Improve through personal efforts rather than relying on other people's help.*

Pull themselves up by their shoelaces Means the same as *pull themselves up by their bootstraps*.

Pull to pieces Means the same as *pick to pieces*.

Pull up stakes Move somewhere else.*

Pull up stumps Cease doing something.*

Pull yourself together A demand to be more rational and less emotional. It is usually used about a person who is making a fuss when a bit of calm thought would solve the problem. People sometimes imagine that personalities are made up of a set of components such as kindness, sense of humour, etc., and that these are joined together in a stable package. If someone becomes too emotional or distressed about something, then it is thought that it is as if part of their personality has moved away from this package (i.e. they are *falling apart*), and so they need to 'pull themselves together'.*

Pulling it in To make money *hand over fist*.*

Pulling power Skill at attracting potential sexual partners.*

Pulling teeth Describes work that requires a great deal of effort to achieve even the smallest effect.*

Pulling the chain Means the same as *yanking the chain*.

Pump iron Do weight training.*

Pump priming Enable something to work by doing initial preparations that make it possible (e.g. 'pump priming' grants to universities that enable the establishment of infrastructure so that research can then take place).*

Punch the clock Have paid employment. Generally the phrase refers to employment in a job with a set routine.*

Punt at Attempt.*

Pup See *buy a pup*.

Pure and simple In its most basic form.*

Pure as... The phrase is generally followed by a word or phrase denoting purity (e.g. 'the driven snow') and thus the phrase means 'pure'. However, sometimes the phrase is followed by a word or phrase that is palpably impure (e.g. 'slush'), in which case it is being used jokingly to indicate something (or someone) impure.*

Purple prose Language that is too elaborate and uses over-dramatic phrases.*

Push at an open door Exert far more effort than should be necessary to get a simple task done.*

Push-button response A very predictable and rapid response.*

Push the boat out Spend far more than usual on entertaining yourself or others.*

Push the envelope Test the limits of what can be done.*

Push the panic button A panicking response.*

Push their buttons Stimulate or arouse someone.*

Push their luck Risk punishment or something else unpleasant by more extreme behaviour and/or activity than usual.*

Push their oar in Make uninvited comments.*

Push under their nose Show someone something for approval.*

Pushing up daisies Dead.*

Put a bomb under it Utterly destroy something in the hope that when rebuilt it will be more efficient. The phrase is often used to describe wanting to do something with an inefficient institution or practice (e.g. 'I'd like to put a bomb under it and start again').*

Put a cork in it Means the same as *put a sock in it*.

Put a crimp in Spoil or lessen the enjoyment of something.*

Put a damper on Make less exciting.*

Put a finger in the dyke Prevent a serious problem by acting promptly. The phrase is derived from a Dutch story of a boy

---

* denotes level of impoliteness

who put his finger in a hole in a dyke, thus preventing the hole getting bigger and a serious flood starting.*

Put a finger on it Identify it.*

Put a name to Recall the name of something or someone.*

Put a rocket under it Can mean the same as *put a bomb under it*. Can also mean to speed a process up, often with the implication that this is done by telling workers to be more efficient and less lazy.*

Put a seal on Make something definite.*

Put a seal to Indicate approval or acceptance.*

Put a sock in it A forceful request to be quiet. Probably derived from a method of making early gramophone record players quieter by stuffing a piece of cloth (such as a sock) in the horn of the player.**

Put a spoke in a wheel To sabotage or otherwise spoil a plan. The phrase probably refers to a type of brake used on some types of cart.*

Put a stopper in Curtail activity.*

Put across (1) Explain something. (2) Be very willing to have sexual intercourse.* (1) or ** (2)

Put back the clock Means the same as *turn the clock back*.

Put backbone into them Make someone behave in a more decisive, firm manner.*

Put down roots Become an established part of the local community.*

Put flesh on Provide details.*

Put hair on their chest A joking claim that a strong-tasting food or drink (typically an alcoholic drink) will have restorative powers. The claim is not meant to be taken seriously.*

Put heads together Work on a problem together.*

Put into their head Create an idea in another person.*

Put it about (1) Spread a rumour. (2) Be sexually promiscuous.* (1) or ** (2)

Put it behind them Forget or discount a past unpleasant event.*

Put it like this Present in a particular way. The phrase is often used before presenting a more easily comprehended version of an argument.*

Put it to Present an argument or allegation to someone.*

Put it to bed Finish a project or piece of work.*

Put money on (1) Place a bet. (2) Make a firm prediction.*

Put off the evil day Avoid doing something unpleasant.*

Put off the scent Prevent from finding.*

Put off their stroke Worsen the quality of someone's work.*

Put on a shorter leash Place greater restraints on activities and/or behaviour.*

Put on airs and graces See *airs and graces*.

Put on hold Means the same as *put on the back burner*.

Put on ice Means the same as *put on the back burner*.

Put on notice Warn of something about to happen. This is usually something unpleasant (e.g. dismissal if a further infringement of contract).*

Put on the back burner To temporarily stop work on something, typically with the intention of returning to it at a later date.*

Put on the front burner To restart work on something, or to give something a higher priority.*

Put on the map Make famous.*

Put on the Ritz Behave in an ostentatious manner.*

Put on their thinking cap Think with a great deal of effort about something.*

Put one over on Deceive.*

Put out (1) Extinguish or stop. (2) Be very willing to have sexual intercourse. The phrase is relatively old-fashioned, and was primarily used of women.* (1) or ** (2)

Put out of its misery End suffering. The phrase is often used of killing a wounded animal that is beyond curing. See *put out of their misery.**

Put out of their misery End suffering. The phrase can refer to killing an injured animal, but may also refer to telling someone information that they are longing to know (obviously the relevant use will be provided by the context in which the phrase is used). See *put out of its misery.**

Put out to grass Retire from employment or make redundant.*

Put out to pasture Means the same as *put out to grass*.

Put right Amend an error.*

Put stock in Trust in.*

Put that in their pipe and smoke it A phrase added at the end of a reply intended to express the strength of feeling on the matter, and indicate that what has been said should be accepted.*

Put the acid on Attempt to persuade someone to lend money.*

Put the arm on Attempt to force someone to do something through force or the threat of force.*

Put the bite on Attempt to persuade someone to lend money. There is usually the implication of applying threats (e.g. violence or blackmail).*

Put the blocks on Prevent something happening.*

Put the boot in (1) Physically attack someone with considerable violence. (2) Verbally attack someone with great ferocity.*

Put the cart before the horse Do things in the wrong sequence. The phrase can also sometimes mean having a wrong set of priorities (i.e. that things that are trivial are treated as very important and vice versa).*

Put the cat among the pigeons Create a disturbance or consternation by announcing some unexpected information.*

Put the clock back Can mean the same as *turn the clock back*. Can also mean to adjust the clock by putting the hour hand back one hour to allow for seasonal time adjustments.*

Put the fear of God into Frighten; the phrase often implies that this is done by threats or arguments rather than shocks.*

Put the finger on Inform against.*

Put the flags out Celebrate.*

Put the frighteners on Threaten.*

Put the genie back in the bottle See *let the genie out of the bottle.*

Put the lid on Stop, or bring something under control.*

Put the mockers on Prevent or damage.*

Put the moves on Means the same as *make a move on*.

Put the record straight Correct the errors and/or misconceptions in a description of an event.*

Put the screws on Force someone to do something. The phrase refers to the use of thumbscrews (torture instruments used to extract confessions).*

Put the skids under Worsen.*

Put the squeeze on Threaten.*

Put their ass in a sling Get someone into trouble.**

Put their back into it A demand to work harder.*

Put their feet up Take a rest.*

Put their foot down (1) Impose authority. (2) Make a car accelerate.*

Put their foot in it Make an embarrassing mistake.*

Put their hand to the plough Begin work.*

Put their hands in their pocket Pay.*

Put their hands together Applaud.*

Put their hands up (1) Surrender. (2) Admit to something.*

Put their head in a noose Means the same as *put their head on the block.*

Put their head on the block (1) Risk their reputation by supporting a particular argument. The phrase is often used to describe experts who risk losing their reputation as experts by making a prediction about the outcome of an event (e.g. 'Professor Smith put her head on the block and predicted that the pottery was late Etruscan'). The phrase comes from execution by beheading, where the victim placed their head on a special chopping block. (2) Do something likely to attract punishment, annoy someone, or provoke something else unpleasant.*

Put their head on the line Means the same as *put their head on the block.*

Put their heart into it Worked with great enthusiasm and determination.*

Put their house in order (1) Restore to normality after disorder. (2) Amend an undesirable state of affairs through reforms.*

Put their mind to Think about.*

Put their money where their mouth is Do something, rather than just talk about doing it.*

Put their nose out of joint Annoy or make to appear foolish.*

Put their shirt on Bet a large amount of money on. The phrase literally implies betting all possessions and money on.*

Put through the hoops Make someone endure difficulties. The phrase often describes administering a difficult series of tests or a difficult training course.*

Put through the wringer Subject to a gruelling and/or emotionally upsetting experience.*

Put through their paces Give them a demanding task to assess their abilities.*

Put to bed (1) Completely finish. (2) Solve a troublesome problem.*

Put to sleep Kill an animal that is too badly injured to be nursed back to health.*

Put to the sword Kill.*

Put two and two together Draw the correct inference from the available evidence. The phrase sometimes ends with 'and make four'. See *put two and two together and make five.*

Put two and two together and make five Draw conclusions from the available evidence that are speculative rather than based solely on the available evidence. The phrase in itself does not indicate whether the speculations are correct or wrong, but usually the context in which the phrase is placed will indicate this. See *put two and two together.*

Put up This has three rather distinct meanings. (1) The literal meaning of physically installing or raising something. (2) As a prefix in *put up job*, it means that something was rigged or fixed to have a particular outcome. (3) It can mean to tolerate something (e.g. 'I don't know how you put up with his rudeness').*

Put up job A fraudulent situation.*

Put up or shut up A demand to not just talk about something, but actually do it.**

Put years on Feel and/or look far older than the actual age.*

Put yourself in my shoes A request that someone tries to understand how the speaker thinks and feels about something. There is usually an added implication that a person has been unreasonable in expecting the speaker to do something, and if they properly understood what the speaker thought, felt and was capable of doing, they wouldn't have asked the question.*

Put words into their mouth (1) Induce someone to say something. (2) Make a false account of what someone else said or wrote.*

Putty in their hands Easily persuaded or controlled.*

Pyramid selling (1) A business practice in which profit is made by selling to people who then sell the goods on to other people at a higher price, who in turn sell to others at an even higher price (e.g. A sells to B at 1 dollar per unit, B sells to C at 1.50 dollars per unit, C sells to D at 2 dollars per unit, and so forth). Each level of transaction is to more people (thus, a diagram of the transactions can look like a pyramid, as the transactions spread out from the original source). Done in an honest manner, this is the basis of most capitalist economies. (2) A fraudulent practice in which people are tricked into buying goods to sell on to other people on the promise that a large profit can be made. However, the goods are usually not worth the money paid for them, and thus can only be sold at a loss (whilst the people who originally sold the goods have made a dishonest profit). It is usually this latter definition which most people understand, and 'pyramid selling' is used as a synonym for dishonest commercial practices.*

Q

Quake in their boots Be very afraid.*

Quart in a pint pot See *get a quart in a pint pot.*

Queensberry Rules The original 'Queensberry Rules' governed boxing (they were created by a group headed by the Marquess of Queensberry in the nineteenth century), and were felt by many people to codify fair play and honour in competition. By extension, 'Queensberry Rules' can be used to describe any standard of 'respectable' or polite behaviour. Thus, someone who 'doesn't play by Queensberry Rules' is dishonourable or lacks a sense of fairness.*

Queer as folk See *nowt as queer as folk.*

Queer Street Being in debt or, more generally, to be in serious trouble. The phrase is unrelated to the use of 'queer' as an offensive term for 'homosexual'.*

Queering the pitch Altering things so that conditions become appreciably worse. The phrase is unrelated to the use of 'queer' as an offensive term for 'homosexual'.*

Question of time Means the same as *matter of time.*

Quick and dirty Something that is rapidly completed, provides an appropriate solution to a problem, but could not be judged intellectually or aesthetically satisfying.*

Quick as a flash Quick.*

Quick off the mark Means the same as *quick on the draw.*

Quick on the draw Having fast reactions.*

Quick on the uptake Capable of understanding something quickly.*

Quids in Considerable profit from a transaction.*

Quiet as a tomb Means the same as *quiet as the grave.*

Quiet as the grave Silent.*

Quite a handful Difficult to control.*

Quite the little... Followed by a word or phrase describing a person. The phrase is usually used in a sarcastic manner (e.g. 'quite the little chatterbox' used sarcastically means that someone should be quiet).*

Quote – unquote Indicates that something said is a quotation of what someone else said.*

---

* denotes level of impoliteness

R

Rabbit boiler Means the same as *bunny boiler*.

Race against time An activity in which there is a limited amount of time in which to complete it. The phrase often denotes that something calamitous will happen if the activity is not completed by then.*

Rack off Forceful way of saying 'go away.'**

Rack their brains Think very hard about something. The phrase is usually used as part of an admission of failure (e.g. 'I've racked my brains on this matter, but I cannot think of a solution').*

Raft of... A large quantity of... *

Raging bull (1) A powerful and aggressive person. (2) A person who talks a lot of nonsense but is under the delusion that they are an expert. The phrase is a pun – 'Raging Bull' is a movie title, but 'bull' can also mean 'bullshit' (meaning 'non-sense').* (1) or ** (2)

Rags to riches Move from poverty to wealth.*

Rain cats and dogs Rain heavily (note that some people use the term to describe more specifically heavy rain with a strong wind). There are numerous explanations of the phrase, but in no instance is it implied that either cats or dogs are actually falling from the sky.*

Rain cheque [or check] See *take a rain check*.

Rain on their parade To spoil enjoyment of something (typically, something they have spent a long time planning). This is akin to planning a big parade or carnival and then having torrential rain ruin the event.*

Rain or shine Inveitably.*

Rainbow See *end of the rainbow*.

Rainy day A problematic time. The phrase usually implies that the problems are caused by the need for money. Hence phrases such as 'rainy day fund' or *saving for a rainy day* indicating prudent saving as an insurance against such an eventuality.*

Raise Cain To make trouble or to cause a disturbance. Cain was the first murderer mentioned in the Bible, and thus someone 'raising Cain' is imagined to be raising the spirit or ghost of Cain.*

Raise hell (1) Complain. (2) Create a disturbance.*

Raise the ante Means the same as *up the ante*.

Raise the bar (1) Raise standards. (2) Make the task harder.*

Raise the Devil Means the same as *raise Cain*.

Raise the roof Make a loud noise.*

Raise the stakes This can mean the same as *up the ante*. However, it usually means that something has become more dangerous or that more now depends on a particular outcome (e.g. 'by quitting her old job before going to the interview, Sally had raised the stakes; if she didn't get a new job, she would be in serious financial trouble').*

Raise their eyebrows Express disapproval or surprise.*

Raise their hackles Annoy.*

Raise their hat Indicate approval.*

Raise their sights Become more ambitious.*

Raised eyebrows Disapproval or surprise.*

Rake over the coals Examine or talk about something that happened in the past and which should now have been forgotten.*

Rake them over the coals Means the same as *haul over the coals*.

Rake's progress A life that becomes increasingly morally degenerate and ends in destitution.*

Raking it in To make money *hand over fist.**

Ram home Ensure that something is fully understood through the use of forceful argument.*

Ram it in Means the same as *ram home.*

Ramping up Increasing.*

Rap over the knuckles Rebuke.*

Rara avis Latin phrase meaning the same as *rare bird.*

Rare as hens' teeth Extremely rare.*

Rare as rocking horse droppings Means the same as *rare as hens' teeth.***

Rare as rocking horse shit Means the same as *rare as hens' teeth.****

Rare bird An unusual person; the term can indicate someone with desirable qualities (e.g. 'a very gifted musician is a rare bird') or undesirable qualities (e.g. 'thankfully people as evil as Hitler are rare birds').*

Rat run A faster route between two points that is circuitous but avoids traffic hold-ups.*

Rat's ass See *don't give a rat's ass.*

Rats deserting a sinking ship The full phrase is 'like rats deserting a sinking ship'. A nautical superstition is that rats living in an old ship would leave it before it left port if they sensed that it was due to sink on the voyage ahead. The phrase might thus logically be taken to mean 'to have forewarning of disaster'. However, it is usually used to describe people of questionable loyalty who desert a company or other group when it gets into difficulties.*

Rattle sabres Threaten aggression.*

Rattle their cage See *who rattled its cage?*

Rattle their dags Make haste.**

Raw See *come the raw prawn, in the raw, touch a raw nerve* and *touch on the raw.*

Raw deal Unfair treatment.*

Reach for the stars Be ambitious.*

Read between the lines Discover through analysis what something really means rather than accepting its superficial appearance. The implication is typically that the surface appearance presents a rather less sinister meaning.*

Read like a book Easily interpret.*

Read my lips A speaker saying this is emphasising that what follows should be attended to because he or she is adamant about it (e.g. 'read my lips – you are not going to the party dressed like that').*

Read the entrails Means the same as *read the signs.*

Read the Riot Act To command that an undesirable activity is stopped. Or more generally, to tell off. The phrase comes from the Riot Act, a British law now repealed, but widely used in the eighteenth and nineteenth centuries. Crowds of protestors who appeared to be planning to riot would be confronted by an officer of the law or other official who would read out the contents of the Riot Act. In essence, this informed the crowd that any misbehaviour would be breaking the law.*

Read the signs Interpret the situation.*

Read them like a book If someone can be 'read like a book' then it is very easy to understand from their behaviour what they are planning to do and their thinking.*

Read up Study.*

Ready for the off Prepared to begin something (almost always the phrase is used with reference to starting a journey).*

Ready to roll Means the same as *ready for the off.*

Real McCoy The genuine thing or person (as opposed to a fake or an impostor). There are numerous explanations of the phrase, most involving an historical figure called McCoy who did something to prove he was 'the real McCoy'.*

Reality bites (1) The truth can sometimes be unpleasant. (2) Describing the moment when a person realizes that the true situation is much worse than they had thought.*

Reap the harvest Be affected by the products of a project or piece of work.*

Reap what they sow Be affected by the results of their own actions.*

Rear its head Appear.*

Rebel without a cause A person (usually in their teens or early twenties) who is disaffected with their life but who does not subscribe to a particular belief system, and does not belong to a protest group concerned with a specific moral, religious or political issue.*

Receiving end See *on the receiving end.*

Recharge the batteries Recuperate.*

Recipe for disaster A situation that has a high probability of producing misfortune.*

Red carpet Special treatment reserved for a very important guest. Hence to *roll out the red carpet* is to offer such treatment. The phrase comes from the custom of putting down a strip of red carpet for important guests to walk on as they enter a building.*

Red cent See *not one red cent.*

Red flag before a bull Means the same thing as *red rag to a bull*.

Red-handed See *catch red-handed.*

Red herring A misleading argument or piece of evidence in an investigation.*

Red in tooth and claw The phrase originally referred to the more hostile aspects of the natural world, but is now more generally applied to any aggressive situation where little pity is likely to be shown.*

Red letter day A day on which something noteworthy occurs.*

Red light A signal or command to stop.*

Red light district An area with a high level of prostitution.*

Red rag to a bull Something that can be guaranteed to annoy a particular person. The phrase comes from the belief that the colour red annoys bulls.*

Red tape Unnecessary bureaucracy; the term is often used for laws and regulations which prevent an ordinary person getting justice or getting something done, and which seem to protect civil servants, local government officers and similar from ever facing the consequences of their mistakes (e.g. 'trying to get planning permission involves a person in so much red tape it's a wonder that anything ever gets built in this country'). The term is derived from the red tape and ribbons traditionally used to bind legal documents.*

Redress the balance Restore to equilibrium.*

Reds under the bed A paranoid fear of secret communist incursion into a country's infrastructure as a prelude to a communist take-over.*

Reduced circumstances Financially poorer than before.*

Reinvent the wheel (1) Waste time and energy preparing something that is already easily available. (2) Waste time and energy contemplating basic theoretical issues when there are more immediate practical concerns.*

Relieve their feelings Swear or otherwise behave in an aggressive manner as a means of expressing anger.*

Remains to be seen Yet to be decided.*

Report from the front line The latest news on something; usually an implication that the news is an accurate report of what's going on, rather than an interpretation.*

Rest is history What follows after this point is already well known and does not need to be repeated.*

Rest on their laurels Be complacent after a period of work has attained success.*

Rest on their oars Relax after a period of activity.*

Rest their case (1) Finish presenting an argument. (2) A comment indicating that what has just been presented is an irrefutable argument. This can also be used when a person unwittingly says or writes something that supports their opponent's argument; in which case their opponent might retort 'I rest my case'.*

Return the compliment (1) Reply to a compliment with a similar pleasantry. (2) Respond to an insult or attack with another insult or attack.*

Reverse of the coin Means the same as *other side of the coin.*

Revolve around Be wholly or principally dependent upon.*

Rewrite history Attempt to alter the interpretation of events that have already happened. The phrase *can't rewrite history* indicates that although interpretations of an event can alter, the fundamental facts cannot change.*

Rewrite the record books A hyperbolic phrase beloved of sports commentators that means that a sportsperson has beaten a sporting record (e.g. reduced a record race time by a couple of hundredths of a second).*

Rhyme or reason See *without rhyme or reason.*

Rich and famous The words 'rich' and 'famous' by themselves are adjectives, but the phrase 'rich and famous' is often used as a noun, denoting people who are (logically enough) rich and famous.*

Ride bodkin Travel in a railway carriage, aeroplane or similar, in a squashed position between other people.*

Ride for a fall Behave in a manner that is likely to result in something unpleasant happening.*

Ride off into the sunset End happily. The term, usually used ironically, refers to a clichéd ending in Westerns, where the hero and his girl would ride off out of town in a landscape lit golden by a glorious sunset.*

Ride roughshod over Disregard other people's arguments or emotional needs.*

Ride shotgun Be in the front passenger seat of a car.*

Riding on Depending on.*

Right arm See *give their right arm.*

Right as rain In good condition.*

Right between the eyes Describes something that makes a very strong impact (either a literal physical strike or a strong mental impression).*

Right hand doesn't know what the left hand is doing Describes an organisation or group in which the activities of one section are in contradiction to the activities of another section.*

Right off the bat Describes something that happens at or close to the beginning (e.g. 'right off the bat he was asking awkward questions and didn't stop until the end').*

Right one A person behaving irrationally or misguidedly.*

Right up their alley Means the same as *right up their street.*

Right up their street Something which appeals to their tastes and/or is something they know a lot about or are skilful in.*

Ring a bell Stimulate a faint memory. If something 'rings a bell', a person thinks they've heard about it before, but cannot be absolutely certain.*

Ring off the hook Describes a phone that rings constantly.*

Ring the changes Make alterations. The phrase comes from bell-ringing, where 'ringing the changes' means to ring a set of bells in every possible sequence.*

* *denotes level of impoliteness*

Ring the knell Proclaim the end or imminent end of something.*

Ring their bell Arouse someone's interest (usually, but not necessarily, sexual).*

Rip-off (1) A deception or fraudulent practice. (2) Something that whilst legal is very over-priced.*

Rip off (1) Deceive or commit a fraud. (2) Over-charge for goods or services.*

Rip to shreds Means the same as *cut to shreds*.

Rise and shine A demand to get out of bed and be cheerful about it.*

Rise from the ashes Recover from a serious setback or loss. The phrase comes from the legend of the phoenix, a mythical bird that burst into flames when it died, and then regenerated from the ashes of the fire.*

Rise through the ranks Attain promotion to a high level of status, having started at a very lowly position.*

Rise to the bait Become annoyed by a provocative remark or action.*

Rising star A person who is in the process of becoming famous or well respected for their work.*

Rite of passage An occasion held to mark a transition between one status and another (e.g. marriage, first job, etc.).*

Road to nowhere Something that has no prospect of producing anything of use or value. *

Roaring trade A large number of customers.*

Rob Peter to pay Paul Take from one person and give to another.*

Rob them blind Steal, extort or cheat a person out of a large quantity of money.*

Rock back on their heels Surprise.*

Rock solid Secure, safe and/or reliable.*

Rock the boat Make a situation more difficult by creating new problems. There is often the implication that the situation was initially peaceful and that the creation of new problems was done because either a person wanted to create trouble or did not have the wisdom to see that they would create problems.*

Rocket science Joking term for any topic considered to be too intellectually difficult. The phrase *it's not rocket science* means 'it's actually not as difficult as it appears'.*

Rocky road to... A difficult method of attaining something.*

Rod of iron A harsh system of rule.*

Roll in the hay Have sexual intercourse.**

Roll in the sack Means the same as *roll in the hay*.

Roll out the red carpet See *red carpet*.

Roll over and have their tummies tickled If people want to 'roll over and have their tummies tickled' then they are totally in agreement with a proposal or plan.*

Roll their own Do something for themselves.*

Roll up their sleeves Prepare to do some work.*

Roll with the punches Avoid or get used to the unpleasant aspects of a situation.*

Rolled into one All part of one integral unit.*

Rolling drunk Very inebriated.*

Rolling in it Rich.*

Rolling in money Means the same as *rolling in it*.

Rolling in the aisles Finding something extremely funny. The image is drawn from the idea of audience members at a theatre finding what is on stage so funny that they are helpless with laughter to the point that some of them fall out of their seats and roll around in the aisles.*

Rolling stone A person incapable of commitment who feels a continuous need to explore new places and experiences.*

Roman holiday An 'entertainment' derived from watching other people suffer.*

Rome See entry below and: *all roads lead to Rome, Roman holiday* and *when in Rome*.

Rome wasn't built in a day A proverb expressing the view that notable achievements can take considerable time and effort to achieve.*

Roof falls in A very unpleasant event occurs.*

Room at the top The opportunity for promotion to the top levels of an organisation.*

Room for doubt Meaning that something is not absolutely certain and that the evidence leaves the possibility that there is more than one plausible explanation (e.g. 'the evidence leaves room for doubt that Oswald was the only assassin').*

Room to swing a cat See *no room to swing a cat*.

Root and branch (1) At all levels. (2) Thorough.*

Root cause The most important and/or original cause of something.*

Rooting for Supporting.*

Roses See *come up roses, come up smelling of roses* and *everything's coming up roses*.

Rot sets in Problems start.*

Rotten apple Means the same as *bad apple*.

Rotten to the core Bad, with few or no redeeming qualities.*

Rough and ready Not very elegant or aesthetically pleasing, but sufficient for the task.*

Rough around the edges Not totally completed or trained. The phrase usually indicates that, although imperfect, something or someone 'rough around the edges' will nonetheless be suitable.*

Rough diamond A pleasant person, though lacking in 'refined' manners.*

Rough edge of their tongue A verbal attack.*

Rough end of the pineapple Harsh or unpleasant.*

Rough end of the stick Means the same as *rough end of the pineapple*.

Rough ride An unpleasant experience.*

Rough trade The phrase means the same as *bit of rough*, sometimes with the added implication that the person is a prostitute who cultivates an appearance of coarseness in order to appeal to a particular type of client who finds this sexually stimulating.***

Roughing it Means the same as *slumming it*.

Round figure An approximation (e.g. 1,230,786.11762 in a round figure is 1.2 million).*

Round the bend To be insane. The phrase is often used jokingly to describe unusual rather than truly insane behaviour (e.g. 'you like liver and onions and Brussels sprouts? You must be round the bend').**

Round the block Around the immediate neighbourhood (e.g. 'I'll go for a walk round the block'). The phrase is sometimes used in the same sense as *round the houses*.*

Round the clock Continuously (e.g. 'they kept watch on him round the clock').*

Round the corner (1) If something is 'round the corner' it can be found by going round the corner (i.e. not by making the angular edge of a corner rounded). (2) If talking about time, then if something is 'round the corner' it is due to happen soon.*

Round the houses If someone goes 'round the houses', they use excessive detail in describing something.*

Round the twist Means the same as *round the bend*.

Rounds of the kitchen Someone who gets the rounds of the kitchen is given a severe telling-off. The phrase is usually used about arguments within a family.*

Rub it in Make something unpleasant even more unpleasant.*

Rub noses Greet. A literal rubbing of noses (i.e. one person rubs their nose against another's) is only expected in some aboriginal cultures.*

Rub salt in the wound Can mean the same as *twist the knife*. It can also refer to a person who, in trying to be pleasant to someone who is upset, actually makes things worse. The term refers to an old remedy for treating cuts or abrasions by rubbing salt into the wound. This supposedly helped the healing process, but at the time made the wound far more painful.*

Rub shoulders Be in regular close proximity.*

Rub their hands Express excitement or hopeful anticipation.*

Rub their nose in it Humiliate by making something unpleasant or embarrassing even more unpleasant or embarrassing.*

Rub up against Meet.*

Rub up the wrong way Annoy. The implication is that a different choice of actions or words would not have caused annoyance. There are several variants of the phrase (e.g. 'rub them up the wrong way', 'rub their fur the wrong way', etc.).*

Rubber neck Stare intrusively at something. The phrase is generally used to describe the behaviour of people who stop to look at a crime scene or accident.*

Rude awakening A sudden shock. The term usually describes a person's discovery that in reality things are not as pleasant as they thought, and that until now they have been too complacent (e.g. 'Tom had enjoyed using his credit card for shopping, but had a rude awakening when the bill arrived in the mail').*

Ruffle feathers Annoy.*

Rule of thumb A method that will give an approximate answer that will nearly always be acceptably accurate for the purpose intended.*

Rule the roost Be leader of a group. There is often the implication that this is a small group. The term probably derives from one cockrel being the dominant bird in a group of chickens.*

Rumour has it It is rumoured.*

Run a mile An expression of panic (e.g. 'if I saw a rat in the bath I'd run a mile'). The expression is hyperbole.*

Run a tight ship Be in charge of something that is run with strong discipline and a rigid obedience of regulations.*

Run-around If someone is being given the 'run-around' then they are being deliberately delayed and/or deceived.*

Run before they can walk Over-ambitious.*

Run down (1) Cease operations in a gradual manner (e.g. 'work at the factory is gradually being run down prior to closure next year'). (2) Tired (e.g. 'all this extra work is making him look run down'). (3) A summary (e.g. 'thank you for giving me a run down of the report and saving me the bother of reading all of it').*

Run dry Use up all resources.*

Run for it Escape.*

Run for their money (1) If someone or something 'gives a run for their money' then they are of a good standard. (2) If someone has had 'a run for their money' then they feel they have had a worthwhile experience. The phrase is sometimes used in the form *good run for their money*.*

Run high Strongly.*

Run interference Protect someone from attack by providing a distraction.*

Run into (1) Meet by chance. (2) Collide with.*

Run it past Present something for assessment.*

Run it up the flagpole Part of a longer phrase – 'let's run it up the flagpole and see who salutes it'. It essentially means that a description of a plan should be given to a group of people to see if anyone likes the plan. The image is derived from flag-raising ceremonies where dignitaries salute a flag as it is raised up the flagpole.*

Run of the mill Ordinary; usually the implication is that if something or someone is 'run of the mill' then it does not deserve much discussion.*

Run off their feet A person who is 'run off their feet' is working hard at something and is finding it difficult to cope with the workload. The phrase usually implies that the workload is excessive.*

Run out of steam (1) Become exhausted. (2) Lose enthusiasm or drive.*

Run out of town (1) Eject or remove. (2) Comprehensively defeat.*

Run past Present for inspection and/or approval.*

Run ragged Make exhausted.*

Run rings round them If person A 'runs rings round' person B, then it means that person A is far more gifted or intelligent than person B.*

Run round in circles Can mean *go round in circles*. Can also mean to work hard but achieve little because the hard work has not been directed into sensibly planned activity.*

Run the gamut Consider or experience everything.*

Run the gauntlet Endure a punishment. The term is derived from a Swedish military punishment called a 'gatlopp' rather than anything to do with gauntlets or gloves.*

Run them close Be almost as good at something as someone else.*

Run to earth Find someone or something that has been hunted for.*

Run to ground Means the same as *run to earth*.

Run with the hare and hunt with the hounds Maintain cordial links with both sides in a dispute.*

Runners and riders The entrants in a horse race. Also, a joking way of describing a set of candidates for a job or other position.*

Running battle A conflict which goes on for a long time with neither side willing to concede.*

Running on empty Exhausted of energy and/or other resources.*

Running sore A long-standing grievance or cause of annoyance.*

Rush of blood A sudden, irrational change in mood or thought.*

Rush their fences Be unnecessarily hasty.*

S

S-H-ONE-T An attempt to say the word 'shit' politely. Spoken out loud it sounds quite inoffensive, but written down ('SH1T') it looks like the word 'shit'.**

Sack See *given the sack*.

Sackcloth and ashes Extreme repentence.*

Sacred cow Something or someone so venerated that nobody dares contemplate criticism.*

Sacrifice on the altar of... Cause suffering (or even death) because it suits the purposes of a particular cause or belief (e.g. 'the manager was sacked because his team had lost five games and gate receipts were falling: another person sacrificed on the altar of commercial interests').*

Sad The term can of course mean 'unhappy'. However, it may also be used to indicate that someone is behaving in a way that is considered a waste of time or rather pathetic. Whether someone is really 'sad' is often a matter of opinion, rather than an absolute judgement.*

Saddled with a problem To be given a problem that cannot be passed on to someone else. This is likened to a horse with a saddle strapped on to it which no amount of kicking or wriggling will remove.*

Safe as houses Very safe and/or reliable.*

Safe bet A wise choice. The implication is that the choice is the one most likely to succeed, but may not give as high a reward as other, riskier choices (e.g. 'investments in foreign markets may bring higher returns but also higher risks; for those who are more cautious, a safe bet is Treasury stock').*

Safe pair of hands A person who can be trusted to do something efficiently.*

Sail close to the wind Take risks in the hope that this will bring a more favourable outcome than a more cautious approach.*

Sail under false colours See *show their true colours.*

Salt of the earth A phrase derived from the New Testament, usually interpreted as praise. It generally means 'the best type of people', and is often used to refer to unpretentious people.*

Salt the books Means the same as *cook the books.*

Salt the mine Fraudulently make something appear more appealing than it actually is. The phrase comes from the confidence trick of scattering particles of precious metal around a worthless mine, making the prospective buyer think the mine contains a rich, untapped seam.*

Same but different Means the same as *two sides of the same coin.*

Same difference A phrase indicating that two or more things have the same basic meaning, even though they may appear different.*

Sandwich short of a picnic Insane or intellectually ungifted.*

Sauce for the goose Often finished with the rest of the proverb, which is 'is sauce for the gander'. In other words, what is suitable for one person or situation is suitable for another as well.*

Save face Retain dignity and/or reputation.*

Save the bacon To solve a problem or to rescue someone from a problem they are having. *

Save the day Successfully resolve a problem.*

Save their ass Means the same as *save their skin,* only ruder.***

Save their bacon Means the same as *save their skin.*

Save their blushes Means the same as *spare their blushes.*

Save their breath Stop arguing because it will have no effect.*

Save their hide Means the same as *save their skin.*

Save their neck Means the same as *save their skin.*

Save their skin Rescue someone from a problem they are having.*

Save time Reduce the time taken to complete a task.*

Saved by the bell Rescued from defeat or something unpleasant by intervention (intentional or otherwise) at the last moment. The phrase is derived from boxing – a boxer doing badly might be saved from being knocked out by the sound of the bell signalling the end of the round.*

Saving for a rainy day See *rainy day.*

Say a mouthful Say something noteworthy.*

Say the word Issue a command.*

Say their piece Present a pre-prepared statement or complaint.*

Say when In serving drinks, a request by someone pouring an alcoholic drink or cocktail that the recipient indicates when an acceptable quantity of alcoholic drink or mixer has been poured out.*

Scales fall from their eyes Become aware.*

Scare the bejesus Means the same as *scare the daylights*.

Scare the daylights Give a severe shock.*

Scare the living daylights Means the same as *scare the daylights*.

Scared shitless Very frightened.***

Scent blood Detect a weakness in someone. The phrase usually describes detecting a weakness in an opponent.*

School of hard knocks A phrase used by someone to indicate that they think they have had an unfortunate life (e.g. 'I was brought up without privileges – I was brought up in the school of hard knocks'). The phrase is considered rather self-pitying and should be avoided.*

School of thought A method of thinking about something. The phrase may refer to an academic theory or more generally to an accepted opinion.*

Schoolchild See *as every schoolchild knows*.

Score an own goal Produce an *own goal*.*

Score points Make cleverer or more forceful arguments than another person. The phrase is often used to describe someone who is deliberately trying to make another person appear intellectually inferior in a rather petty manner.*

Scotch mist Usually heard in a phrase such as 'what do you think that is – Scotch mist?' It means that someone has failed to notice something that is very obviously there in front of them.*

Scout's honour Truthfully.*

Scrape an acquaintance Get to know someone.*

Scrape the barrel Means the same as *scrape the bottom of the barrel*.

Scrape the bottom of the barrel Take the worst possible from the range of choices. It is usually implied that this is not through choice, and that the better choices have already been taken. The phrase is often used to describe a mediocre team or group (e.g. 'she was scraping the bottom of the barrel when she selected this team').*

Scratch the surface Attain only a rudimentary level of achievement.*

Scratch their head Be baffled.*

Scream bloody murder Means the same as *scream blue murder*.

Scream blue murder Loudly protest.*

Screw loose Insane or eccentric.*

Sea See *at sea, get their sea legs* and *worse things happen at sea*.

Seal of approval An indication that something has been approved by someone. The indication can be spoken or written – it does not necessarily have to be a seal. The phrase comes from the fact that documents used to have a wax seal, imprinted with an official symbol, placed upon them to indicate legality. More recently, the wax seal was replaced by a postage stamp. Hence *stamp of approval*, which means the same as 'seal of approval'.*

Seal their fate Ensure that they will experience something unpleasant.*

Seams See *bursting at the seams* and *fall apart at the seams*.

Search high and low Search thoroughly.*

Search me An expression of personal ignorance or mystification.*

Second banana Second-in-command.*

Second bite at the cherry A second opportunity to attempt to do something.

---

* *denotes level of impoliteness*

The implication is that the first attempt failed or was not perfect.*

Second childhood (1) Dementia. (2) A feeling of rejuvenation and a renewed interest in simple, enjoyable pleasures experienced by some people in middle or old age.*

Second hand Pre-owned.*

Second string to their bow An additional skill or resource.*

Second to none The best.*

See a man about a dog (1) Keep an appointment. The phrase is used to indicate that the precise nature of the appointment is not going to be disclosed. (2) Euphemism for going to the lavatory. Chiefly used by men.*

See daylight Acquire insight.*

See eye to eye Agree.*

See in (1) Experience something (e.g. 'will you see in the New Year with me?'). (2) Enjoy something (e.g. 'I don't know what you see in modern art').*

See it a mile off Identify something very easily. The phrase is often used of a very predictable plot in a play or similar (e.g. 'you could see the ending a mile off').*

See it coming Means the same as *see it a mile off.*

See life Experience a range of things rather than stick to a dull, rather repetitive lifestyle.*

See reason Come to understand a logical argument. The phrase usually implies that this understanding is reached after previously behaving illogically or supporting an untenable argument.*

See stars Hallucinate seeing brief flashes of light. The phenomenon (usually temporary) is a neurological condition arising from being hit on the head or (sometimes) fainting. *

See the back of... See *glad to see the back of...*

See the elephant Gain experience. The phrase is often used of travelling to different lands and seeing a wide variety of sights that cannot be seen in one's country of origin.*

See the funny side Recognize a humorous aspect to an otherwise serious situation.*

See their way clear Agree to do something.*

See them anon See them later.*

See them coming Able to predict what they will do.*

See them right Ensure that they are well treated and/or recompensed.*

See which way the cat jumps Means the same as *see which way the wind blows.*

See which way the wind blows Assess the situation before committing to a decision.*

Seeing things Having hallucinations.*

Seen better days Describes something that has become damaged or looks shabby through repeated use or simple ageing.*

Seen it, bought the T-shirt The phrase is a shortened version of a longer phrase – 'I've read the book, seen the film, and bought the T-shirt'. It refers to the habit of popular works of fiction being made into movies and the movies producing a range of souvenirs (such as T-shirts). The phrase thus means 'I know everything about this topic', usually with the implication that the speaker is bored by it.*

Seize the day Use whatever opportunities arise.*

Self-made man/woman A person who has become successful by their own efforts rather than by relying on others (e.g. through inherited wealth, patronage, etc.). The term is sometimes used snobbishly of someone who has wealth but does not come from an aristocratic family and is apparently ignorant of etiquette.*

Sell a bill of goods Cheat a person by selling them something worthless or unpleasant.*

Sell a pup See *buy a pup*.

Sell-by date See *past its sell-by date*.

Sell down the river Betray.*

Sell for a mess of pottage Stupidly sell something for far less than it is worth.*

Sell it short Fail to recognize its value.*

Sell like hot cakes If something 'sells like hot cakes' then it is in great demand.*

Sell soul to the Devil Literally, offer one's immortal soul to Satan in exchange for earthly pleasures. The phrase is often used to denote that someone is strongly motivated to do something (e.g. 'she'd sell her soul to the Devil to win the championship').*

Sell the family silver Dispose of items that once sold cannot be retrieved. The phrase is most often used of a policy that may bring short-term gains but whose long-term benefit is questionable.*

Sell their soul to the Devil Have no moral scruples. There is no accusation that someone has undergone a Satanic ritual.*

Sell them a dummy Deceive.*

Sell them a lemon Deceive (particularly in commerce – a 'lemon' is a poor quality product).*

Sell them short Fail to recognize their value.*

Send in the clowns To do something to distract attention from a mishap. The term is derived from the traditional call by a circus ringmaster to put the clowns into the ring when an accident occurred and the audience needed to be distracted.*

Send the right message Present an argument or statement that is well received. The phrase is often used to describe a situation such as an interview or presentation where what will please the audience is unknown.*

Send the right signals Means the same as *send the right message*.

Send the wrong message Present an argument or statement that is badly received and/or misunderstood.*

Send the wrong signals Means the same as *send the wrong message*.

Send them flying Cause them to fall over.*

Send them packing Dismiss someone in a fairly brusque manner.*

Send to Coventry Deliberately to ignore a person, even to the point of refusing to speak to them. The origins of the phrase are uncertain.*

Separate the men from the boys Decide who is truly capable of doing a task. The phrase is gender-specific and caution is thus advised.*

Separate the wheat from the chaff Decide what is wanted or good and what is not wanted or of little value.*

Serious money Large amounts of money.*

Serve out their time Means the same as *serve their time*.

Serve their time (1) Finish a jail sentence. (2) Finish doing a job or other position which had a contractually fixed period of appointment. (3) Complete an apprentice's training.*

Serve two masters (1) Have two managers, both of whom must be obeyed, and who have conflicting demands. (2) Attempt to follow two irreconcilable sets of principles.*

Set alarm bells ringing Begin to feel apprehensive about something (e.g. 'the news that our beloved head of department was leaving to be replaced by someone new was enough to set alarm bells ringing').*

Set back on their heels Surprise.*

Set in concrete Means the same as *set in stone*.

Set in motion Initiate an activity.*

---

* denotes level of impoliteness

Set in stone Already firmly fixed and unalterable. The phrase is often used in the negative to indicate that something can be changed (e.g. 'it's not set in stone – we can still make alterations').*

Set out their stall Present their argument.*

Set right Amend an error.*

Set the ball rolling To start off an activity, such as a conversation (e.g. 'to set the ball rolling, I asked him to tell me about his childhood').*

Set the cat among the pigeons Means the same as *put the cat among the pigeons*.

Set the heather on fire Means the same as *set the town on fire*.

Set the place on fire Means the same as *set the town on fire*.

Set the scene Provide preparatory information.*

Set the Thames on fire Means the same as *set the town on fire*.

Set the town on fire To do something notable that is talked about. The reverse (e.g. 'it didn't exactly set the town on fire') indicates that something was dull or disappointing.*

Set the world on fire Means the same as *set the town on fire*.

Set their cap at them Express a romantic interest in someone.*

Set their face against Show opposition towards.*

Set their hand to the plough Begin work.*

Set their heart on Have a strong desire for.*

Set their sights Intend to attain or achieve.*

Set their teeth on edge Irritate.*

Set to (1) About to (e.g. 'the Government is set to announce new policies next week'). (2) An argument (e.g. 'there was a set to last night about where to go on holiday').*

Settle the score Have revenge.*

Seven league boots To have 'seven league boots' is to have the ability to walk or run quickly.*

Seventh heaven Means the same as *cloud nine*.

Sex it up Make more appealing.*

Shag on a rock Feel isolated or lonely. The image is of a solitary shag (a sea bird) sitting on a rock. Note to non-British readers: 'shag' also means 'sexual intercourse' in British slang. Accordingly, the phrase 'I feel like a shag on a rock' should be used very carefully when speaking to a Brit.*

Shaggy dog story A joke notable for the length of its telling. Often the final punchline is disappointingly weak.*

Shake a leg To dance.*

Shake their booty Dance (generally refers to the curious movements seen at nightclubs).*

Shaken up Disturbed or frightened.*

Shanks's pony Walking.*

Sharp as a needle Intelligent.*

Sharp end (1) The most unpleasant of possible punishments or injuries. (2) The most advanced form of something (usually technology or academic research). (3) The most important.*

Sharp end of the tongue To receive the sharp end of someone's tongue is to be told off or to receive a particularly offensive insult.*

Sharpen their ideas Become more alert and intellectually active.*

Sharpen up Become more alert and intellectually active.*

She'll be apples Australian phrase, means the same as *she'll be right*.

She'll be right Australian phrase meaning that things will be okay and, by implication, that worrying about something is unnecessary.*

She's apples Means that something is alright. Although an Australian phrase, the phrase probably has its origin in Cockney rhyming slang ('apples and spice – nice').*

Shed-load of… A large quantity of… *

Sheep from the goats See *sort out the sheep from the goats.*

Sheep's eyes A look of amorous intent that the person making the expression thinks looks alluring but to an impartial observer looks ridiculous.*

Sheets to the wind See *three sheets to the wind.*

Shell-like See *in their shell-like.*

Shell out Means the same as *fork out.*

Shift gear Change the level of activity. The phrase nearly always indicates an increase in activity.*

Shift the goalposts Means the same as *move the goalposts.*

Shift their arse Means the same as *move their arse.*

Shift their ass Means the same as *move their ass.*

Shift their backside Means the same as *move their backside.*

Shift their ground Change their opinions.*

Ships that pass in the night People who know each other for only a brief period of time. *

Shipshape and Bristol fashion Everything is correct and clean and tidy.*

Shirt See *in shirtsleeves.*

Shirt lifter Male homosexual. A very offensive term.***

Shirt off their back Every possession possible. The phrase is often used to indicate that someone is being rapacious (e.g. 'they'd have the shirt off my back if they could') or extremely generous (e.g. 'I'd give him the shirt off my back if I thought it'd help').*

Shirtsleeves weather Warm enough not to need coats, jackets, sweaters, etc.*

Shit a brick An exclamation of annoyance.***

Shit bricks Be very frightened.***

Shit happens In other words, sometimes unpleasant things happen for no very obvious reason.***

Shit hits the fan See *when the shit hits the fan.*

Shit hot Very exciting and/or innovative.***

Shit off a shovel Something moving 'like shit off a shovel' is moving very quickly.***

Shit or get off the pot Means the same as *piss or get off the pot.*

Shoe is on the other foot Means the same as *boot is on the other foot.*

Shoes See *dead man's shoes, fill their shoes, if the shoe fits, lick their shoes, put yourself in my shoes, shoe is on the other foot* and *walk a mile in another person's shoes.*

Shoo-in An absolute certainty.*

Shoot a line Tell an exaggerated or implausible story or argument.*

Shoot down in flames Defeat an argument completely.*

Shoot from the hip Respond rapidly without much thought.*

Shoot it out Engage in the final, decisive stages of an argument.*

Shoot me See *just shoot me.*

Shoot the breeze Have a chat.*

Shoot the messenger Blame the person conveying bad news as if they were the cause of the bad news. Thus, *don't shoot the messenger* is advice not to do this.*

Shoot the moon To escape (typically, to escape creditors) by leaving secretly at night.*

Shoot their mouth off Talk in a manner lacking in decorum. For example, (a) talk in a boastful or offensive manner likely to

---

* *denotes level of impoliteness*

offend others; (b) talk about things that were supposed to be kept secret.*

Shoot themselves in the foot Harm or bring misfortune on themselves. The phrase usually implies that this is done through incompetence rather than simple misfortune.*

Short and curlies Pubic hair. If someone has someone else 'by the short and curlies' then they have a powerful control over them.***

Short change (1) In a financial transaction, fail to give all the money that is owed. (2) Provide less of a service than was originally promised.*

Short end of the stick If someone has the 'short end of the stick', then they are at a disadvantage.*

Short fuse See *on a short fuse.*

Short hairs Means the same as *short and curlies.*

Short of Means 'lacking' or 'have too little of' (e.g. 'I'd like to buy it, but I'm short of cash').*

Short work An easy or quickly accomplished task.*

Shorter leash See *put on a shorter leash.*

Shot across the bow A 'shot across the bow' is a warning that a particular action is disapproved of and that a change must take place, otherwise punishment will follow. The phrase comes from the practice of a naval vessel firing a warning shot in front of a ship to make it stop or change course.*

Shot at... To have the opportunity to 'have a shot at' something is to be given the opportunity to do something. Likewise, if someone says that they will 'have a shot at' doing something, it means they will try to do it.*

Shot by both sides To be in disagreement with more than one group in an argument. There is usually the implication that the person in question has no allies and that everybody disagrees with him or her.*

Shot in the arm A boost or encouragement.*

Shot in the dark A guess, or an attempt to do something which is the product of guesswork.*

Shot the bolt Tried everything possible and failed.*

Shot to pieces Damaged to the point of being irreparable.*

Should get out more A joking phrase implying that someone is lacking in knowledge about everyday life.*

Shoulder the burden Accept all or most of the responsibility for dealing with a problem. *

Shoulder to cry on A sympathetic person willing to listen to another person talking about their problems.*

Shoulder to shoulder United in a common cause.*

Shoulder to the wheel A person who puts their 'shoulder to the wheel' engages in demanding and/or difficult work.*

Shout See entry below and: *all over bar the shouting, in with a shout, just shout* and *their shout.*

Shout from the rooftops Make known. The phrase is often used to describe someone who is keen for as many people as possible to know something.*

Show a clean pair of heels Run away.*

Show a leg Get out of bed.*

Show must go on (1) The belief in the theatrical profession that, no matter what misfortunes may befall a theatrical company, a show must be presented for the paying customers. (2) By extension, the belief that, no matter what adversities happen, life still goes on and things and people must be dealt with in spite of sorrow and/or depression.*

Show of hands (1) A vote in which people raise their hands to indicate support for a range of proposals, and the proposal that gets the largest number of hands raised wins. (2) A quick (and not necessarily accurate) measure of strength of support for something.*

Show-stopping Something outstandingly good or praiseworthy. The phrase is usually applied to a theatrical or concert performance.*

Show the flag Demonstrate allegiance to a group, country or cause.*

Show their cards Means the same as *show their hand*.

Show their hand Reveal their plans or beliefs.*

Show their roots Reveal their social, country or regional origins through manner of speech or behaviour. The phrase is often used of someone who for reasons of social advancement has tried to disguise their origins that are unintentionally revealed.*

Show their teeth Reveal their strength and/or animosity.*

Show their true colours Show true, rather than false, behaviour. The phrase is often used when an unpleasant person has been deceiving people into thinking he or she is a pleasant person. When he or she finally shows what they are really like, then they are said to be 'showing their true colours'. The phrase comes from when sailing ships were the normal seagoing transport. At times of war or piracy, a ship intending to capture or destroy another ship might *sail under false colours* (i.e. fly the flag of a nation friendly to other ships) until it was close enough to be a threat and only then would it take down the false flags and put up its own – i.e. show its true colours. Thus *sail under false colours* means 'to deceive'.*

Show them the door (1) Eject from the room or house. (2) Firmly express lack of interest or support.*

Show up (1) Appear (e.g. 'guess what showed up in the mail this morning'). (2) To embarrass (e.g. 'Harold's mother showed him up in front of his friends by talking about his bed-wetting problem').*

Shrug off Quickly and easily overcome.*

Shuffle off this mortal coil Die. The phrase is a quotation from *Hamlet*, and is nearly always used jokingly.*

Shuffle the deck Change a way of doing things.*

Shut the door on Deny further discussion and/or activity.*

Shut the stable door after the horse has bolted Do something too late.*

Shut their eyes to Means the same as *turn a blind eye to*.

Shut up A forceful request to be quiet. The phrase may refer to 'shutting up' the lips.**

Shut up shop Cease work or another activity. The phrase can mean a temporary cessation (e.g. at the end of the working day) or a permanent cessation.*

Shut your face Means the same as *shut up*. The term may be derived from days when soldiers wore helmets: a request to 'shut your face' to a person wearing a helmet – i.e. to close the visor of their helmet – would mean that they would be difficult to hear.***

Shy of Almost but not quite.*

Sick as a dog To be ill; generally used to describe someone who is very ill.*

Sick as a parrot A phrase meaning 'to be miserable'. It became popular during the 1970s in the UK, largely because soccer players who'd lost a match would say they felt 'as sick as a parrot' when interviewed after the game. The exact origins of the phrase are unknown, but it has been used, with varying degrees of popularity, for several centuries.*

---

* denotes level of impoliteness

Sick to death So bored with something that the mere mention of it creates feelings of anger.*

Sick to the stomach Annoyed or deeply offended.*

Sight See *in their sights, lower their sights, raise their sights* and *set their sights.*

Sight for sore eyes Something or someone whose arrival is welcome.*

Sign of the times Something that is very indicative of contemporary culture.*

Sign on the dotted line Formally agree to do something by signing a contract.*

Sign the pledge Promise to be teetotal.*

Significant other A person who is emotionally important to another person. The phrase nearly always refers more specifically to a marital or cohabiting partner.*

Silence is golden Silence (or at least peacefulness) is a desirable thing. The phrase is sometimes offered as a rebuke to someone who has been noisy or over-talkative.*

Silent as a tomb Silent.*

Silent majority The majority of people (particularly voters) who are not vociferous in their opinions.*

Silk purse See *can't make a silk purse out of a sow's ear.*

Silly buggers See *play silly buggers.*

Silly season (1) A period in the year (August in the UK) when there tends to be relatively little political or other news (because most people are on holiday) and, in order to fill up newspapers and news bulletins, more bizarre stories (which at other times of the year would be dismissed as too trivial) are given prominence. (2) A period in the year when employees, students or similar tend to act in a bizarre manner within a particular organisation.*

Silver lining The optimistic or positive aspect of something that initially appears to be nothing but problematic or disappointing.*

Silver tongue Eloquence.*

Sing a different tune Adopt a new opinion or argument.*

Sing for their supper Perform a task as a requirement of receiving something (e.g. food and lodging).*

Sing their praises Praise.*

Singing from the same hymn sheet All relating the same story or argument.*

Sink a battleship See *enough to sink a battleship.*

Sink in Be understood.*

Sink or swim A situation which ends in total success or total failure. It is also usually implied that no assistance is available to people who encounter difficulties.*

Sinking ship See *rats deserting a sinking ship.*

Siren song Something that proves an irresistible lure, but creates problems.*

Sit at their feet Be their pupil or student.*

Sit on a powder keg Be in a potentially dangerous situation.*

Sit on the... Remain a long time in... *

Sit on the fence Be neutral or undecided. The term is often used in a derogatory sense to denote a failure to commit to something.*

Sit on their hands Deliberately not doing something.*

Sit tight (1) Remain in the same place. (2) Remain resolute. (3) Take no action.*

Sit up Show sudden interest in something. The phrase sometimes finishes with 'and take notice'.*

Sitting comfortably? See *are you sitting comfortably?*

Sitting duck Something or someone in a vulnerable position.*

Six feet under Dead.*

Six of one and half a dozen of the other Used to describe a situation in which both sides are evenly balanced in strength. It is often used to describe a situation in which two groups of people are equally to blame for a mishap.*

Six of the best The phrase originally meant six hits with a cane on the hand or buttocks (a traditional punishment in British schools until the 1980s). However, the phrase now can be applied (usually jokingly) to any punishment.*

Sixes and sevens A state of confusion.*

Sixty-four thousand dollar question The principal problem whose solution would bring the greatest benefit.*

Size of it The nature of the situation or problem.*

Skate on thin ice Do something that is dangerous, likely to fail and/or be susceptible to attack or criticism.*

Skeleton at the feast Means the same as *ghost at the feast.*

Skeleton in the closet An embarrassing piece of information about a family, group or person that the family, group or person would prefer to keep secret.*

Skeleton in the cupboard Means the same as *skeleton in the closet.*

Skid Row (1) An area of a town or city that is inhabited by very poor people, has high crime levels, is in a poor state of repair, etc. (2) A state of extreme poverty.*

Skin alive A threat to 'skin you alive' indicates that the speaker is angry with the person being addressed. The threat is not literal.*

Skin of one's teeth Used to indicate a very narrow margin – typically, how close something came to an accident (e.g. 'we escaped serious injury by the skin of our teeth'). The phrase comes from the Old Testament.*

Skirt See *bit of skirt.* The term can also be used as an offensive term for 'women' and should be avoided.***

Skive off Be absent from work or school without permission.*

Sky's the limit There is no limit.*

Slack See *cut some slack* and *take up the slack.*

Slam dunk Something unambiguous. The phrase is derived from a spectacular method of scoring in basketball, in which the player jumps so that their hand goes over the top of the net and the ball is dropped or thrown into the hoop.*

Slap on the back Praise.*

Slap on the face (1) An unexpected and unpleasant piece of information. (2) A rebuke.*

Slap on the wrist A mild rebuke.*

Slave over a hot stove Work hard at preparing a meal. The phrase is often used as a joking exaggeration.*

Sledgehammer See *use a sledgehammer to crack a nut.*

Sleep See entries below and: *do it in their sleep, let sleeping dogs lie* and *put to sleep.*

Sleep like a log Sleep very deeply.*

Sleep of the just Sleep undisturbed by feelings of guilt or worry.*

Sleep with Have sex with.*

Sleeping partner A person who plays no managerial role in a business, but provides financial support for it.*

Slice of the action Means the same as *piece of the action.*

Slice of the pie Means the same as *piece of the action.*

Sliced bread See *greatest thing since sliced bread.*

Sling their hook (1) Slang expression meaning 'go away'. (2) Depart.**

Slip See entries below and: *many a slip.*

Slip of a... Someone small and slim (e.g. 'slip of a thing', 'slip of a girl' etc.).*

Slip of the pen Written form of *slip of the tongue.*

Slip of the tongue An error in speaking. The phrase often refers to a mistake that is unintentionally humorous or revealing about the speaker's personality.*

Slip on a banana skin Make a mistake. The phrase usually indicates that the mistake was avoidable if someone had been more sensible or cautious.*

Slip through the fingers Escape capture or acquisition. The phrase usually indicates that capture or acquisition was attainable but was not done through incompetence.*

Slip through the net Escape detection.*

Slip under the radar Means the same as *slip through the net*.

Slip up Make an error.*

Slippery customer A person who is difficult to deal with. There is usually an implication that they are evasive or untruthful.*

Slippery slope Something that will almost inevitably lead to problems.*

Slow day A day with little activity.*

Slow off the mark Means the same as *slow on the draw*.

Slow on the draw Slow to respond.*

Slow on the uptake Slow to learn.*

Slumming it Living in a state of extreme poverty. The phrase can also be used sarcastically to describe someone living in great affluence.*

Smack in the eye Means the same as *slap on the face*.

Small beer Of little importance.*

Small hours Late at night and very early in the morning.*

Small potatoes Means the same as *small beer*.

Smart Alec Someone who is *too clever by half*.**

Smart cookie A clever person.*

Smashed Intoxicated.*

Smashing Highly enjoyable (e.g. 'we had a smashing time at the zoo').*

Smell a rat Detect or suspect deception.*

Smell blood Means the same as *smell fear* or, more generally, means to detect a weakness.*

Smell fear Detect that someone is nervous or frightened. The term is often used in descriptions of people who will take sadistic pleasure in using this information (e.g. 'don't let them smell your fear, or they will be even worse').*

Smell of... The overwhelming implication or appearance (e.g. 'there is a smell of deception about the situation' means that the deception can be inferred or is apparent).*

Smell right Appear to be plausible and/or trustworthy.*

Smell something fishy Have suspicions that something is not what it appears to be.*

Smell to high heaven Have a strong smell.*

Smell wrong Appear to be implausible and/or untrustworthy.*

Smelling of roses See *come out smelling of roses* and *come up smelling of roses*.

Smoke See *go up in smoke* and *no smoke without fire*.

Smoke-filled room Bargaining conducted in private between a small group of individuals that determines the outcome of events to a large number of people (e.g. political bargaining).*

Smoking gun Conclusive evidence of guilt. The term comes from detective stories – if someone is found by the body of a person who has been shot, holding a gun still smoking from being fired, then it seems reasonable to assume who did the shooting.*

Smooth ruffled feathers Make someone less agitated.*

Snake in the grass (1) An unanticipated problem or danger. (2) The term is sometimes used (not entirely correctly) to describe a traitor or disloyal associate.*

Snap their fingers at Show contempt towards.*

Snap their hand off Eagerly accept an offer.*

Snap their head off Respond in an unpleasant or aggressive manner. The phrase often implies an irrationally severe response.*

Sneezes See *when…sneezes…catches a cold.*

Snob value Something with 'snob value' has a high level of social desirability within middle- and upper-class culture.*

Snook See *cock a snook.*

Snookered Means the same as *behind the eight ball.*

Snowball in hell's chance Means the same as *cat in hell's chance.*

Snug as a bug Warm and comfortable.*

So and so A relatively mild term of rebuke for an annoying person (e.g. 'he has been such a so and so over the past few days').*

So far as it goes Its limitations.*

So far round they're coming back again Insane or eccentric.*

So far so good Everything is as anticipated. The phrase refers to an interim stage in a plan. It is often used to describe the situation up to the point where something went wrong.*

So help me Sometimes the phrase finishes with the word 'God'. The phrase is used to emphasize that the speaker is sincere in what they are saying (e.g. 'so help me, I promise I will get this done').*

So sue me A retort to a complaint. The implication is that the complaint is unreasonable or excessive.**

So there A term of abuse or rebuke indicating that something has been achieved that an opponent did not expect.*

So there you have it That is the totality of the information.*

Soccer mom A middle-class woman with school-aged children who is especially active in assisting in school and other community activities (such as school soccer matches). There are often negative implications of parochial values and living vicariously for her children's success.*

Sock it to them (1) Create a very favourable impression. (2) Create a memorable impression through aggressive or forceful behaviour.*

Sod Shortened form of the word 'sodomite', though this is not usually explicitly meant in the uses of the word. It is a moderately rude word in the UK at least, and use is therefore strongly cautioned. There are several uses of the word in everyday language. (1) It can be used as a rebuke to a person (e.g. 'you rotten sod'). (2) In the phrases *sod it* and *sod off* it can be used as an expression of annoyance. (3) It can be used as an adjective to express greater feeling (e.g. 'it's sodding useless' means something worse than 'it's useless').**

Sod it An expression of exasperation.**

Sod off An impolite way of saying 'go away'.**

Sod's law The fatalistic argument that, in any activity, something is bound to go wrong.**

Soft soap Flattery.*

Soft touch Someone easily fooled or from whom it is easy to borrow money.*

Soft underbelly A weakness – usually there is the implication that it is a weakness in an otherwise strong system. The image is drawn from a fearsome thick-skinned animal (e.g. a rhino or an alligator) which often has a relatively unprotected stomach area that is accordingly more vulnerable to attack.*

Soften the blow Means the same as *cushion the blow.*

Softly, softly The start of a proverb – 'softly, softly, catchee monkey'. The essence of this is that the best way to accomplish some tasks is by a subtle method that may at times appear as if things are not being done quickly enough.*

Sold out (1) Sold all the copies of a particular item and thus have no more to sell. (2) Abandoned a moral principle for money.*

Soldier on Persevere with something. There is usually the implication that the task is a long or boring one.*

Some of my best friends are... The phrase is completed by the name of a group of people a person is accused of being prejudiced against. For example, if a person is accused of being anti-Semitic, he or she might say 'but some of my best friends are Jewish'. The phrase at one time was meant seriously, but through over-use it has become an unconvincing cliché, and is often used sarcastically (e.g. a man who is being sexist might be told 'I suppose some of your best friends are women, aren't they?').*

Someone up there likes me Said after something fortuitous has occurred. The phrase is perhaps most often said by someone who has just escaped suffering severe misfortune.*

Something else Remarkable (e.g. 'Simon's singing was something else').*

Something fierce Very strongly.*

Something fishy Suspicious or implausible.*

Something nasty in the woodshed Something unpleasant that is kept secret. The phrase comes from the novel *Cold Comfort Farm*, where 'something nasty in the woodshed' is a key reason behind the dysfunctional nature of a rural family.*

Something's up There is a problem.*

Somewhere to the left of... Followed by the name of an extreme left-wing figure (e.g. 'Chairman Mao'). A joking phrase meaning that someone has pronounced left-wing views.*

Somewhere to the right of... Followed by the name of an extreme authoritarian figure (e.g. 'Hitler', 'Attila the Hun'). A joking phrase meaning that someone has extreme right-wing views, or at least is being unreasonably authoritarian.*

Son and heir Jocular term for the eldest boy in a family. The term derives from the fact that in the case of hereditary peerages, the eldest son inherits the father's title upon the latter's death.*

Son of a bitch A term of abuse. The phrase varies in offensiveness between different groups of people, but, to be cautious, its use is not advised. Curiously, it might be supposed that a man being called a *dog* would mean the same as 'son of a bitch' and be considered offensive as well, but this is not true – see *dog*.***

Son of a gun A term of friendly address (e.g. 'how are you, you son of a gun?'). The origin of the phrase refers to an illegitimate child whose father was a sailor or soldier. The modern use of the phrase does not carry this connotation, and can be taken as being harmless.*

Song and dance (1) Unnecessary fuss. (2) Unnecessary length.*

Sore thumb See *stick out like a sore thumb*.

Sort out the men from the boys Discover those who are truly capable and/or skilled.*

Sort out the sheep from the goats Discover what is desirable.*

Sound hollow Appear implausible.*

Sound out Ask the opinion of a person or people, typically with the intent of discovering if they are likely to be in favour or against something.*

Soup to nuts Completely.*

Sour grapes Making unpleasant remarks about something a person is unable to have or, more generally, to make unpleasant remarks about a competitor who has

202 / SOW DRAGON'S TEETH

done better than the speaker. The term comes from one of Aesop's fables, in which a fox, unable to reach a bunch of grapes, decides that they must be sour and thus not worth trying to get anyway.*

Sow dragon's teeth In attempting to solve a problem, accidentally create fresh difficulties.*

Sow wild oats Engage in a promiscuous, carefree lifestyle. The phrase is usually especially applied to young adults.*

Spade work Work that requires considerable effort (usually physical). There is usually an implication that the work is not very intellectually demanding or interesting.*

Spank the monkey Masturbate.***

Spanner in the works Someone or something who mars or completely ruins a plan, process or activity.*

Spare their blushes Prevent someone being embarrassed.*

Sparks fly If 'sparks fly' in a conversation, then it is one that is very lively.*

Speak as they find Only speak about what is personally known to be true (i.e. rather than believe rumour or hearsay).*

Speak from the heart Express sincere opinions.*

Speak the same language Have similar opinions.*

Speak their mind Say what they truly feel and/or believe.*

Speak volumes If something 'speaks volumes', then it is particularly descriptive.*

Spectre at the feast Means the same as *ghost at the feast*.

Spend a penny To use a lavatory. The phrase originates with the fact that many public conveniences in the UK originally required the patron to pay a penny to use them.*

Spend money hand over fist Spend money at a fast rate. There is usually the implication that a person is spending more than they can afford.*

Spend money like water Means the same as *spend money hand over fist*.

Spend the night with The phrase can literally mean to occupy an evening socialising with someone, but is more often a euphemism for having sexual relations with someone.*

Spend time with Be with.*

Spice of life Something that makes a lifestyle enjoyable rather than boring or routine.*

Spike their guns Prevent or weaken a plan from being put into action.*

Spill the beans Reveal a secret.*

Spilled milk American spelling of *spilt milk*.

Spilt milk See *crying over spilt milk*.

Spin a yarn Tell or write a story that is either fictional and lengthy, or claims to be factual, but appears improbable.*

Spin doctor A person responsible for publicising an organisation or government policy. The implication is that the publicity distorts the truth.*

Spirit is willing The rest of the saying is 'but the flesh is weak'. In other words, a person may have good intentions, but a more attractive (but less worthy) option is chosen because of lack of willpower.*

Spit and polish Very neat and tidy.*

Spit feathers Be angry.*

Spit in the eye Express contempt.*

Spit in the face Means the same as *spit in the eye*.

Spit it out An instruction to *get to the point*. The phrase is often used when a person appears embarrassed or nervous about saying something.*

Spit the dummy Become angry.*

* denotes level of impoliteness

Spitting distance See *within spitting distance.*

Spitting image An exact copy. The origins of the phrase are unknown, but it is doubtful if they have anything to do with expectoration.*

Splice the main brace To have an alcoholic drink. The phrase is a British naval expression.*

Split hairs Be pedantic.*

Split the bill Sometimes followed by 'down the middle'. Share the cost of something equally.*

Split their sides Find something very amusing.*

Spoke in their wheel Sabotage a plan.*

Spot it a mile off Means the same as *see it a mile off.*

Sprat to catch a mackerel Something relatively minor or inexpensive used to try to gain something larger and more expensive.*

Spread See *good spread.*

Spread their wings Means the same as *stretch their wings.*

Spread themselves too thin Try to do too many tasks simultaneously.*

Spur of the moment Something done on the 'spur of the moment' is done spontaneously.*

Square away Make tidy.*

Square deal (1) Fair treatment. (2) An equitable arrangement.*

Square eyes A person who has 'square eyes' is said to watch too much television. The phrase is intended as a joke (traditional TV screens are approximately square shaped).*

Square meal Adequate sustenance.*

Square one See *back to square one.*

Square peg in a round hole A person who is unsuitable for the job they are doing.*

Square the circle Attempting to square the circle is to attempt a very difficult or impossible task. The phrase is derived from a mathematical problem of how to calculate the area of a circle (that was not satisfactorily solved until the identity of pi was found).*

Squat See *got squat.*

Squeaky clean Totally well behaved; there is usually the implication that a person who is described as squeaky clean is also very boring.*

Squeeze until the pips squeak Take as much money as possible from someone.*

Stab a person in the back To betray a person.*

Stab at Attempt.*

Stab in the back (1) Betray. (2) Betrayal.*

Stable door See *shut the stable door after the horse has bolted.*

Stake a claim Make a claim of ownership or entitlement.*

Stakes See *raise the stakes.*

Stamp of approval See *seal of approval.*

Stand corrected Accept a correction to an idea or statement.*

Stand it on its head Radically alter the way something is interpreted.*

Stand on ceremony Insist that a rigid protocol is followed. The phrase is more often heard in the negative – 'don't stand on ceremony' is an exhortation to behave in a relaxed, informal manner.*

Stand on dignity Insist upon being treated with a marked degree of respect.*

Stand up and be counted Declare support or allegiance.*

Stand up for themselves Defend themselves from attack and show resilience.*

Stand-up guy A person who is prepared to offer loyal support and has moral integrity.*

Standing See *leave them standing.*

Standing on their head See *do it standing on their head.*

Stands to reason It is logically valid.*

Star is rising See *rising star.*

Staring it in the face Close to something unpleasant (e.g. 'they were staring defeat in the face').*

Staring them in the face Be very obvious. The phrase is often used to describe someone who should have perceived something but has failed to do so (e.g. 'how could she not notice? – it was staring her in the face').*

Stars in their eyes Having unrealistic ambitions.*

Start praying A (usually humorous) comment that what is about to be done has a low probability of success.*

Start the ball rolling Means the same as *set the ball rolling.*

State of nature (1) Nakedness. (2) In a state of moral ignorance.*

State of play What is currently taking place.*

State of repair The condition of a piece of machinery. The term refers as much to how well it has been repaired or serviced in the past, as to the current repairs it may need. *

State of the art The most up-to-date version and thus the most technologically advanced. *

Stay focused Maintain concentration.*

Stay loose Relax.*

Stay out of their hair Means the same as *keep out of their hair.*

Stay put Remain in the same place or position.*

Stay sharp Maintain concentration and/or alertness.*

Stay the course Persevere to the end. The phrase usually denotes persevering to the end of a task that is very demanding or difficult. Thus, someone capable of 'staying the course' has stamina and determination.*

Stay the distance Means the same as *stay the course.*

Steady See *go steady.*

Steady as she goes Move carefully.*

Steady boyfriend A boyfriend with whom there is a (reasonably) long-term relationship.*

Steady girlfriend The female form of *steady boyfriend.*

Steal a march on Gain an advantage over.*

Steal a person's clothes Use another person's ideas or arguments and pretend that they are your own.*

Steal a person's thunder To lessen the impact of another person's actions that were intended to enhance the person's prestige. For example, if preceding a person in a concert recital, playing the piece that they had intended to play, and playing it better than they could.*

Steal the limelight To claim the majority of attention. There is often the implication that this is unfair, because the person was not intended to have that amount of attention. See *in the limelight.*

Steal them blind Means the same as *rob them blind.*

Steam See entry below and: *get up steam, let off steam, run out of steam* and *under their own steam.*

Steam coming out of their ears Be very angry.*

Steer a...course Adopt a particular policy or method. The word in the middle of the phrase indicates what this policy or method is (e.g. 'steer a middle course' means being moderate in opinions and behaviour).*

Steer clear of Avoid.*

Step back (1) Become less involved in something. (2) Permit someone else to take over a job or task.*

---

* *denotes level of impoliteness*

Step into the breach Take over in an emergency.*

Step into their boots Means the same as *fill their shoes.*

Step into their shoes Means the same as *fill their shoes.*

Step on it Hurry up.*

Step out of line Disobey regulations.*

Step up to the crease Means the same as *step up to the plate.*

Step up to the plate Begin to do something. The implication is usually that this will be a demanding task.*

Stew in their own juice Suffer as a result of their own actions.*

Stick See entries below and: *get a lot of stick, in a cleft stick* and *in the sticks.*

Stick at Persevere with.*

Stick in the craw Be a source of irritation. The phrase is often used to describe something objectionable in a situation that is otherwise bearable.*

Stick in the gizzard Means the same as *stick in the craw.*

Stick in the mud A person who is extremely conservative and resistant to change.*

Stick in the throat Means the same as *stick in the craw.*

Stick out like a sore thumb Be very conspicuous.*

Stick their bib in Interfere.*

Stick their neck out Offer an opinion that may be wrong and thus risk criticism or ridicule.*

Stick their nose in Interfere or be over-inquisitive.*

Stick their oar in Means the same as *stick their bib in.*

Stick to (1) Steadfastly maintain the same argument or description (e.g. 'in spite of repeated interrogations, he stuck to his version of events'). (2) Be constantly present. *

Stick to beat them with A piece of evidence or argument that proves very useful in criticising someone.*

Stick to the knitting Maintain a set of familiar and well-practised activities rather than attempting diversification into potentially lucrative (but also risky) new activities.*

Stick to the point (1) Keep the argument centred on the topic (e.g. as opposed to discussing irrelevant details). (2) A demand that a person should confine themselves to the topic – i.e. it is a complaint that a person has started talking about irrelevancies (e.g. 'stick to the point! – we're not interested in trivial details, we just want the main facts').*

Stick to their fingers Steal.*

Stick to their guns Maintain belief and support for an argument in spite of considerable opposition and/or criticism.*

Stick with Maintain contact with or keep supporting.*

Sticky fingered Prone to stealing.*

Sticky wicket A difficult situation.*

Stiff upper lip Deliberately showing no emotion even though a display of emotion might have been expected in the circumstances. The phrase is often used of archetypal British soldiers and dignitaries who maintain a polite, stoical expression even when things are going disastrously wrong. Curiously, several authorities have argued that the phrase is originally American.*

Still waters The start of a proverb that finishes with 'run deep'. In other words, something that appears harmless or placid may in fact be made up of dangerous or more complex components than would at first appear possible.*

Sting in the tail An unexpected conclusion.*

Stir it Encourage dissent or disquiet.*

Stir up a hornets' nest Create trouble. The phrase usually indicates that a previously peaceful situation has been made troublesome. In contrast, *disturb a hornets' nest* also means to create trouble, but usually indicates that a situation that was already potentially troublesome is made far more problematic. See *hornets' nest*.*

Stitch in time The start of a proverb that finishes with 'saves nine'. In other words, fixing a problem when it first appears will save having to do a bigger repair job if the repairs are deferred, because without being fixed the problem will get worse and worse. For example, a loose thread can be quickly mended, but if left, there is a high probability that the garment will get a noticeable hole in it as the stitching weakens. There is nothing particularly meaningful about the number nine in the phrase – it is simply a word that (more or less) rhymes with 'time'.*

Stomach for a fight Willingness to fight or be adversarial.*

Stone See *carved on tablets of stone, fall on stony ground, leave no stone unturned* and *rolling stone.*

Stop a gap Provide a *stop-gap measure.**

Stop at nothing Be undeterred by anything in the pursuit of something.*

Stop-gap measure A procedure that provides a temporary solution to a problem, but is not totally satisfactory and is unlikely to provide a lasting solution.*

Stop the show Do something outstandingly good or praiseworthy. The phrase is usually applied to a theatrical or concert performance.*

Stop their ears Deliberately ignore or refuse to acknowledge.*

Storm force ten With great intensity.*

Storm in a teacup An excessive amount of fuss over a minor incident or problem.*

Story of their life An expression indicating that this is typical of the misfortunes that seem to characterize a particular person's life. It is most often heard in the first person (e.g. 'bad luck like this is the story of my life').*

Stout hearted Courageous.*

Straight and narrow Morally respectable.*

Straight arrow An honest person who can be trusted.*

Straight as a die (1) Completely honest and trustworthy. (2) Physically completely straight.*

Straight away Immediately.*

Straight contest (1) A contest devoid of cheating. (2) A contest between just two opponents.*

Straight fight Means the same as *straight contest.*

Straight from central casting Someone whose behaviour and appearance fit exactly the stereotype of a person with their profession or social background (e.g. a male university professor who is absent-minded, thin, balding and wearing half-moon spectacles).*

Straight from the heart Sincere.*

Straight from the horse's mouth See *horse's mouth.*

Straight off At once.*

Straight talking Honest information and opinions.*

Straight to the heart Appealing to the emotions rather than logic.*

Straight up Honestly. The phrase is often used as an emphatic statement, stressing that something is really true (e.g. 'straight up, that's what happened').*

Straighten up Sometimes followed by 'and fly right'. 'Straighten up' means to cease doing something foolish or wrong and behave in a more sensible way.*

Strain at the leash Show great eagerness to begin to do something, but be currently prevented from doing it.*

Straw See entries below and: *draw the short straw, final straw, grasp at straws* and *make bricks without straw*.

Straw man (1) An argument created with the purpose of being criticized and defeated. This can be created with the purpose of generating ideas, or as a distraction to sidetrack opponents. (2) A person whose abilities are less than they at first appear.*

Straw that broke the camel's back A final event in a series of events that, although in itself slight, is enough to cause something bad to happen. This may be, for example, the failure of a plan or the item, or the last thing that makes a person finally lose their temper after a series of minor annoyances.*

Straws in their hair Eccentric or insane.*

Street cred Something with 'street cred' has a high level of desirability within teenage or young adult culture.*

Streets ahead Considerably superior.*

Strengthen their hand Make a person more powerful.*

Stressed out Experiencing psychological distress to the point of being incapable of functioning normally.*

Stressed up Experiencing psychological distress.*

Stretch See entries below and: *at a stretch, by no stretch of the imagination* and *full stretch*.

Stretch a point (1) Make an argument that uses tenuous logic. The implication is that were the argument any weaker, then it would be false. (2) Interpret a rule in a very lenient manner.*

Stretch the truth Say or write something that, whilst based on truth, is deceptive in the way it is presented.*

Stretch their legs Walk. The phrase is often used to describe a brief walk after sitting for some time.*

Stretch their wings Try something new.*

Stretch to the limit Means the same as *stretch a point*.

Strictly for the birds See *for the birds*.

Strike a blow Do something either in favour of a principle (e.g. 'strike a blow for democracy') or against something (e.g. 'strike a blow against intolerance').*

Strike a chord Generate a feeling of sympathy or of especially deep understanding.*

Strike a false note Do something that appears insincere.*

Strike a note Make a statement.*

Strike at the root Attack the cause or key feature of something.*

Strike home (1) Be accurate. (2) Make a remark that is accurate and makes an argument that a person finds uncomfortable to think about. (3) Make the importance of something apparent.*

Strike it lucky Be fortunate.*

Strike it rich Become wealthy.*

Strike oil Become rich and/or successful.*

Strike sparks off each other Inspire each other.*

Strike while the iron is hot Do something promptly when it is advantageous to do so.*

String See entries below and: *cut the apron strings, hold the purse strings, how long is a ball of string?, on a string, pull strings, pull the strings, second string to their bow* and *tied to the apron strings*.

String along Keep making promises with no intention of ever fulfilling them.*

String them up (1) Execute by hanging. (2) Severely punish.*

String to their bow See *second string to their bow*.

Strings attached Conditions or restrictions. The phrase is often used to describe something that initially appears appealing, but the 'strings attached' make it less so. The opposite – *no strings attached –*

means that there are no conditions or restrictions.*

Stroke of genius A very clever decision, act or thought.*

Stroke of luck Something very fortunate.*

Stroke the wrong way Annoy. The implication is that a different choice of actions or words would not have caused annoyance. There are several variants of the phrase (e.g. 'stroke them up the wrong way', 'stroke their fur the wrong way', etc.).*

Strong See entries below and: *come it strong*, *come on strong* and *going strong*.

Strong arm of the law Means the same as *long arm of the law*.

Strong arm tactics Using force or the threat of force to make someone do something.*

Strong meat Too extreme for most people to find agreeable.*

Strong on (1) Has expertise in. (2) Is obsessed by. (3) Has large quantities of.*

Strong stomach The capacity to witness unpleasant things without feeling nauseous.*

Strut their stuff Make an ostentatious display.*

Stuff to give the troops Something entertaining or morale-boosting.*

Stuffed shirt A pompous, overly formal person.*

Stumbling block A problem that produces errors and either stops or slows up the running of a plan. The phrase comes from the use of 'stumbling blocks' or obstacles to deter invading soldiers.*

Sublime to the ridiculous See *from the sublime to the ridiculous*.

Suck it and see Try it to find out its true qualities. The phrase is often used to describe situations where theoretical analysis cannot reveal the true nature of

something, and only practical experimentation will give a satisfactory result.*

Sugar daddy An older man who buys expensive things for, or otherwise indulges, a younger person who is not related to him. The phrase is often used to describe an older man who expends money on a younger woman in exchange for sexual favours, but note the phrase does not automatically imply this.*

Sugar the pill Make something unpleasant easier to accept.*

Suit their book Be acceptable.*

Sun is over the yardarm A time when it is socially acceptable to be drinking alcoholic drinks.*

Sunday best The smartest set of clothes a person possesses.*

Sunny Jim A phrase used as a slightly hostile or patronising form of address to a person – usually male (e.g. 'what do you have to say for yourself, Sunny Jim?'). The phrase was originally a character used in advertisements for a breakfast cereal.*

Sunny side up (1) A fried egg fried on only one side is 'sunny side up'. (2) The phrase is occasionally used to describe the mood or life of someone who appears cheerful.*

Sup with the Devil Have dealings with an untrustworthy or devious person.*

Sure as eggs is eggs With absolute certainty.*

Sure footed Extremely competent.*

Sure thing (1) As a reply to a request or order, the phrase means 'certainly', and it indicates that something will be done. (2) A 'sure thing' means 'a certainty'.*

Surf the net Means the same as *surf the web*.

Surf the web Explore sites on the Internet.*

Survival of the fittest The argument that only those who are ruthless and cunning are likely to succeed.*

---

* denotes level of impoliteness

Swear blind Insist that something is true.*

Swear up and down Means the same as *swear blind*.

Sweat See entries below and: *by the sweat of their brow* and *no sweat*.

Sweat blood Make a considerable effort. The phrase is a deliberate exaggeration.*

Sweat it out Endure an unpleasant situation.*

Sweat like a pig Profusely sweat.*

Sweep the board In a competition, a person or team that 'sweeps the board' wins everything.*

Sweep under the carpet Ignore or try to forget something because it is embarrassing or it does not suit current policy. The implication is that what is being ignored still exists and has not been destroyed or refuted.*

Sweep under the rug Means the same as *sweep under the carpet*.

Sweet See entries below and: *keep them sweet* and *like a child in a sweet shop*.

Sweet FA See *sweet Fanny Adams*.

Sweet Fanny Adams A derogatory term meaning 'useless' or 'of little value or use'. The phrase originates by a convoluted route from a girl called Fanny Adams who was murdered in the nineteenth century. The term is considered not very polite in the UK, because 'fanny' is sometimes used as slang for a woman's genitals (in US slang it refers to a woman's posterior). The phrase subsequently became shortened to *sweet FA*, which in turn led to the phrase being 're-invented' as *sweet fuck all* (though it still means the same as 'sweet Fanny Adams'). The latter is considered very impolite.** or ***

Sweet fuck all See *sweet Fanny Adams*.

Sweet shop See *like a child in a sweet shop*.

Sweeten the deal Means the same as *sugar the pill*. The phrase is often used with specific reference to a business venture made more attractive by an extra inducement.

Sweeten the pill Means the same as *sugar the pill*.

Swim against the tide See *against the tide*.

Swing See entries below and: *back in the swing of things*, *in full swing* and *no room to swing a cat*.

Swing it (1) Succeed in arranging for something to happen. (2) Persuade someone to be in favour of something.*

Swings and roundabouts Advantages and disadvantages that approximately balance each other out.*

Switch horses in midstream Means the same as *change horses in midstream*.

Sword See *beat swords into ploughshares*, *cross swords*, *double-edged sword*, *he who lives by the sword* and *put to the sword*.

T

T and A Means the same as *tits and ass*.

Tab See *keep tabs on* and *pick up the tab*.

Table a motion (1) In UK English, the phrase means to present something for discussion. (2) In US English, the phrase means to postpone discussion until a later date. See *lay on the table*.*

Tablets of stone See *carved on tablets of stone*.

Tail between their legs Humiliated.*

Tail up An optimistic or cheerful mood.*

Tail wags the dog An undesirable situation where a subordinate part of a larger process is governing what will be done.*

Take See entries below and: *on the take*.

Take a back seat Move to a position with less influence or power.*

Take a bath Lose a lot of money through an unwise investment.*

Take a bead on Take aim at a target.*

Take a bite out of Appreciably reduce in size or quantity.*

Take a bow (1) Gracefully acknowledge praise. (2) In a sentence including someone's name, a statement that the person has performed well (e.g. 'Mike, take a bow for that excellent work on the report').*

Take a dim view Have an unfriendly opinion.*

Take a dive (1) Show a marked decline. (2) *Throw a fight.**

Take a fade Escape.*

Take a flyer Do something risky.*

Take a hammering (1) Suffer a severe defeat. (2) Be physically damaged.*

Take a hand Be partly responsible for.*

Take a hike Fairly impolite way of saying 'go away' or 'leave'.**

Take a knock Receive a setback.*

Take a leaf out of their book Copy or emulate.*

Take a leak Urinate.**

Take a pew An invitation to sit down.*

Take a rain check [or cheque] To postpone something until a later date. The term originally referred to 'rain checks' issued to spectators at baseball games which had to be postponed due to bad weather. The checks could be used to gain free admittance when the game was replayed at a later date.*

Take a ride A demand that someone goes away. Tends to be used in US English.**

Take a running jump A demand that someone goes away. Tends to be used in UK English.**

Take a seat Sit down.*

Take a shine to Become fond of.*

Take a shot at Attempt.*

Take after (1) Resemble. (2) Chase after.*

Take an early bath Finish unexpectedly early.*

Take apart Comprehensively defeat.*

Take as read Assume something to be true without checking.*

Take away When referring to food, means the same as *to go.*

Take by storm Create a strong, favourable impression.*

Take care of number one Means the same as *look after number one.*

Take courage in both hands Prepare to do something requiring considerable courage.*

Take down a peg Means the same as *bring down a peg or two.*

Take five Have a rest.*

Take for a ride Deceive.*

Take-home message The summary of the information contained in something (e.g. a lecture, book, film, etc.).*

Take in their stride Accept and/or deal with without apparent concern.*

Take it easy (1) An instruction to calm down. (2) Engage in a relaxing activity unconnected with work. (3) Perform a task in an unhurried manner.*

Take it from me Accept my advice.*

Take it into their head Decide. There is usually an implication that the decision is impetuous and/or illogical.*

Take it like a man Accept a rebuke or a punishment without complaining about it. The phrase is considered sexist these days, and its use is not recommended.*

Take it lying down Accept a punishment or insult without protest.*

Take it on the chin Accept punishment or a difficult situation without complaint. There is sometimes the implication of admitting responsibility for a mistake or misdeed and accepting the punishment without complaint.*

---

* *denotes level of impoliteness*

Take it or leave it An expression of disinterest, indicating that what is offered is all there is, so it can either be accepted or rejected. The implication is that the speaker is not very interested in whether someone accepts or rejects.*

Take it out on… A simple phrase describing a complex subject. First, someone is made bad-tempered by somebody or something (e.g. an illness or an argument can make someone bad-tempered). The person then behaves unpleasantly to someone or something other than the cause of the anger. The implication is that the victim of the unpleasant behaviour does not deserve to be so harshly treated (e.g. 'Bob took out his anger on the blameless Sue because John had been unpleasant to Bob earlier in the day').*

Take it to court If something can be 'taken to court' then it is reliable.*

Take it up To start a discussion about something (e.g. 'I was worried about the seating arrangements for next week's meeting so I decided to take it up with the manager').*

Take leave of their senses Become insane.*

Take liberties with (1) Behave in a manner with someone that moves beyond proper levels of decorum. (2) Treat something in a manner that was not originally intended (e.g. retell a historical event manipulating the true facts in order to make a more exciting story).*

Take no prisoners Behave in a ruthless, uncharitable manner.*

Take off Mimic.*

Take on board Can have the same meanings as *bring on board*, and also: (1) Understand the information supplied. (2) Accept responsibility for something.*

Take out (1) Take to a restaurant, theatre, concert or something else entertaining, usually as part of dating or courtship. (2) Kill. (3) Remove. The context should indicate which meaning is intended.*

Take pains Make a considerable effort and pay attention to details.*

Take root Become established or immovable.*

Take stock Attempt to comprehend.*

Take the air Go for a walk.*

Take the ball and run with it This has two different meanings. (1) To continue a piece of work started by someone else, and improve it so that it ends up better than it would have done if the person who originally started the work had been doing it. (2) To test a piece of work started by someone else to judge if it is feasible.*

Take the biscuit Usually heard in the phrase 'well that takes the biscuit!' The phrase is an expression of disgust or annoyance at a piece of bad behaviour. It is often used when several pieces of mildly bad behaviour are followed by a very bad piece of behaviour.*

Take the breath away Say or do something that amazes. This can be something pleasant (e.g. 'his new collection of paintings is so wonderful it takes the breath away') or unpleasant (e.g. 'the increase in prices of basic goods took my breath away').*

Take the bull by the horns Deal with a problem directly and decisively.*

Take the cake Means the same as *take the biscuit*.

Take the chequered flag Win a race. The phrase derives from the waving of a black and white chequered flag to indicate that a motor race has finished.*

Take the count Be unconscious or defeated (see *out for the count*).*

Take the cue (1) Copy what someone else is doing. The phrase is nearly always used in a situation where a person is unsure what to do and so copies ('takes the cue from') others. (2) Obey the advice of someone.*

Take the easy way out (1) Choose to end something by the method requiring the least work. The phrase is usually derogatory, and implies that there is a better solution that is morally more acceptable, but which requires more work. (2) Commit suicide. *

Take the edge off Make less. The phrase can refer to level of interest, sensation, pain or other things, depending upon context. The phrase nearly always implies that something is made less unpleasant.*

Take the fall Receive punishment or criticism.*

Take the fifth Means the same as *plead the fifth*.

Take the floor (1) Give a presentation at a public meeting. (2) Dance at a disco or a ballroom dancing event.*

Take the gilt off the gingerbread Make less appealing.*

Take the heat (1) Receive punishment. (2) Withstand an unpleasant situation without weakening.*

Take the lead (1) Move into first place. (2) If someone 'takes the lead' from another person, then they are copying them (e.g. 'Brian took the lead from Sue and stood up as well').*

Take the liberty Do something without permission.*

Take the lid off Uncover secrets (typically scandals).*

Take the mickey To make fun of, or tease, someone.*

Take the money and run To accept what is on offer without argument.*

Take the piss Means the same as *take the mickey*.***

Take the pledge Promise to be teetotal.*

Take the plunge Commit to doing something.*

Take the rap Means the same as *take the fall*.

Take the shine off Reduce the level of excitement or enjoyment.*

Take the starch out (1) Weaken. (2) Make less formal and pompous.*

Take the waters Undertake a combined holiday and therapeutic treatment.*

Take their eye off the ball See *keep their eye on the ball*.

Take their life in their hands Engage in a dangerous activity.*

Take their lumps Be punished.*

Take their point Accept the validity of an argument.*

Take them back Be reminded of something that happened a long time ago (e.g. 'hearing the song took me back to a time when it was first released and in the hit parade').*

Take to Like or find attractive.*

Take to heart Believe.*

Take to task Criticize and/or punish.*

Take to the cleaners (1) Take a lot of money off someone. It is usually implied that this was done by trickery. (2) Defeat someone in a comprehensive manner.*

Take to the grave Die without revealing a particular secret.*

Take to the hills Hide.*

Take to the road Begin a journey.*

Take to their heels Escape.*

Take under their wing Offer protection and guidance.*

Take up (1) Begin to study or participate in (e.g. 'take up golf'). (2) Level of response to something (e.g. 'what's the take up on the new course?').*

Take up cudgels Begin to support a cause.*

Take up the gauntlet See *throw down the gauntlet*.

Take up the slack Make good use of a surplus or something unproductive.*

---

* denotes level of impoliteness

Take up with Begin courting or dating.*

Take with a pinch of salt Be sceptical.*

Take words out of their mouth Say the exact words or a paraphrase of something that someone else was contemplating saying.*

Take years off Feel and/or look far younger than the actual age.*

Take you home See *wrap you up and take you home*. The phrase can also be used as a polite rebuke when someone is too drunk or is misbehaving at a social gathering (e.g. 'I think someone had better take Jessica home').*

Takes all sorts An expression of the belief that people differ enormously in personality and taste. The phrase is sometimes used in a dismissive fashion to indicate that the speaker doesn't share someone else's tastes (e.g. 'you like Led Zeppelin? It takes all sorts I suppose').*

Talent will out If somebody has a talent for something, then it will display itself in some form or another.*

Talk a blue streak Talk for a long time.*

Talk about... Indicate that something is being done excessively or unreasonably (e.g. 'talk about being unreasonable – did you see what he did?').*

Talk dirty Talk about sex in a lascivious way.**

Talk down (1) Refute an argument. (2) Talk in a patronising manner.*

Talk in riddles Use ambiguous or garbled expressions.*

Talk of the Devil A phrase said when someone or something being discussed suddenly appears (e.g. 'talk of the Devil – we were just discussing you').*

Talk shop Discuss work activities or business matters. The phrase tends to be used in two different ways. (1) A request such as 'let's talk shop' means that someone wants to talk about work or a business matter. It is usually used in conversations after an initial phase of talking about harmless 'conversational openers' such as the weather. (2) As a description of an activity (e.g. 'they talked shop') it can be a simple description (i.e. it means nothing more than 'they discussed business matters') or it can be a complaint that the conversation was dull (i.e. it means 'all they did was talk about business').*

Talk the hind leg off a donkey Very talkative.*

Talk the talk Say the appropriate or expected things. The phrase is often used as the start of a longer question – 'you can talk the talk, but can you walk the walk?' – and means that someone can say the right things, but are they capable of putting them into practice? See *walk the walk*.*

Talk to the hand (1) Talk on the phone. (2) A phrase indicating lack of interest in, and/or rejection of a criticism or comment. This is often accompanied by a hand gesture imitating talking on the phone or, more emphatically, a hand extended palm outwards.**

Talk turkey Discuss business matters.*

Talking heads People who offer their opinions on the television and radio. The implication is that the opinions are of little value.*

Talking shop (1) A different grammatical construction of *talk shop*. (2) A contemptuous term for an organisation or activity that discusses things and makes grand gestures without ever doing anything of practical value.*

Tall and short of it Means the same as *long and the short of it*.

Tall order A difficult or preposterous task.*

Tall story An implausible story.*

Tangled web (1) Something that is difficult. (2) A lie, especially one that has become more complex with retelling.*

Tango See *it takes two to tango.*

Tap into Make use of.*

Tar with the same brush Decide that everyone belonging to a particular group has the same attributes, regardless of differences between individuals within the group. The phrase is often used to describe how a person can be unfairly discriminated against because others in his or her group are seen as unpleasant.*

Taste See entries below and: *bad taste in the mouth.*

Taste blood Means the same as *scent blood.*

Taste of their own medicine A person receiving a 'taste of their own medicine' experiences the same harm or discomfort that he or she has inflicted on other people.*

Tea and sympathy Consolation and sympathetic treatment offered by someone untrained in therapeutic methods. The phrase derives from the widespread habit of offering cups of tea to people who appear distressed.*

Tea in China See *not for all the tea in China.*

Teach granny to suck eggs Telling someone something that they already know.*

Teach them a lesson Punish.*

Tear ass Move quickly.**

Tear limb from limb Destroy violently. The phrase is nearly always used as an exaggerated threat.*

Tear off a strip Tell off severely.*

Tear their hair out Become very annoyed or frustrated.*

Tear to pieces Heavily criticize.*

Tear to ribbons Means the same as *cut to shreds.*

Tear to shreds Means the same as *cut to shreds.*

Technicolour yawn Vomit.**

Teed off Annoyed.*

Telephone number figures Large numbers.*

Tell it a mile off Means the same as *see it a mile off.*

Tell it to the Marines An expression of disbelief. The phrase usually indicates that the speaker finds something preposterous rather than simply surprising but plausible.*

Tell me something I don't know A retort that means that what has just been said was already known.**

Tell tales out of school (1) Reveal secrets about another person. (2) Gossip.*

Tell them where they get off Means the same as *tell them where to get off.*

Tell them where to get off Rebuke someone. It is often implied that the rebuke is for being over-presumptive.*

Tells it like it is Is truthful; usually with the implication that there is no attempt to use euphemisms.*

Tempt fate Express optimism at a point in the proceedings when something can still go wrong. Whether or not it will go wrong is unlikely to be affected by what is said, but given the record of sports commentators (e.g. 'at this stage in the game they cannot lose' is practically a guarantee that they will) one may speculate.*

Ten a penny Commonly occurring.*

Ten out of ten Utterly correct or successful.*

Tent pissing out See *in the tent pissing out.*

Terribly... Used by British people from some social groups as a synonym for 'very'. Thus, 'it's terribly charming' means 'it's very charming'.*

Test the water Make a preliminary investigation. The phrase usually describes attempting to gauge the worth of something by presenting it to a small sample of people, rather than the general public.*

---

* *denotes level of impoliteness*

Thanks for nothing An expression of annoyance that someone has failed to do something that they were meant to do (e.g. 'so you failed to wash the dishes as I asked you to – thanks for nothing').*

That figures That appears logically plausible.*

That good? Usually followed by 'eh' or 'huh'. An ironic expression given in response to a description of something that was patently not very enjoyable.*

That makes two of us An expression of allegiance, sympathy or solidarity with another person because they hold the same opinions or are experiencing the same problems. *

That'll be the day An expression of incredulity in reply to a statement.*

That's all he [or she] wrote Indicating the end of the story – i.e. there is no more to tell.*

That's all folks A light-hearted way of announcing the end of a presentation. The phrase is a quotation from a popular movie cartoon series that often ended with the announcement 'that's all folks!'*

That's the pinch That is the problem.*

That's the way the cookie crumbles The phrase expresses the argument that some things end badly, but this is what should have been expected. It is often used as a reply when someone describes how something turned out less well than they expected or hoped.*

Their own worst enemy A person who is 'their own worst enemy' is more likely to inflict damage on themselves than to other people. The phrase is often used of someone who is too self-critical.*

Their pigeon Their concern.*

Their shout Their turn to buy a round of drinks.*

Them as wants it A deliberately ungrammatical phrase used to describe something that appeals to some people, but by no means everybody. There is usually an implication that the speaker or writer does not themselves like it (e.g. 'there's a Sondheim musical at the local theatre for them as wants it').*

There again In some contexts, the phrase means 'alternatively' (e.g. 'but there again, this might happen').*

There's...for you The phrase is nearly always used sarcastically, so that the opposite of the word inserted in the phrase is usually intended. Thus, 'there's gratitude for you' means 'look at that ungrateful behaviour'.*

There's no telling (1) It is impossible to give an accurate account of what happened. (2) It is impossible to predict what will happen.*

There's one born every minute A phrase expressing the belief that there are plenty of gullible people. The phrase is usually said when describing someone who has become, or is about to become, the victim of a fraudulent plan.*

There's the rub There is the problem.*

Thereby hangs a tale Phrase indicating that following on from whatever is being discussed is another story or explanation.*

They should get out more They should be less insular and more aware of current news and fashions.*

They'll be sunk They will fail or encounter difficulties.*

They'll live The phrase can be used when someone is making too much fuss about a minor injury or illness. Thus, a retort of 'they'll live' or 'you'll live' means that the situation is not serious and there is no reason for the level of complaint.*

They've made their bed they'd better lie in it The phrase means that if a person has done something, then they must accept responsibility for what happens as a result of their actions. There are several permutations of this phrase.*

Thick See entries below and: *bit thick, blood is thicker than water, give them a thick ear, in the thick of it, lay it on thick, plot thickens* and *through thick and thin.*

Thick and fast Describes the movement of something in large quantities and/or large numbers of something moving in rapid succession.*

Thick as... The phrase normally means 'stupid' when followed by a word or phrase describing something thick in size (e.g. 'thick as two short planks', 'thick as a docker's butty', 'thick as a brick').* or ** or *** (depends on word used)

Thick as thieves Describes people who have strong allegiances to each other and are secretive about their activities.*

Thick on the ground Plentiful.*

Thick skinned Unbothered by criticism.*

Thin end of the wedge (1) The most minor features of a problem. (2) The initial signs that there is a problem.*

Thin on the ground Rare.*

Thin on top Bald or balding.*

Thin times Unpleasant events.*

Things that go bump in the night Ghosts. The phrase is often used as a joking explanation of noises heard at night-time.*

Think of England See *close your eyes and think of England.*

Think on their feet A person who can 'think on their feet' is able to analyse a problem or do other mental tasks immediately, without initial planning.*

Thinking cap See *put on their thinking cap.*

Third degree (1) Intense questioning. (2) Describes something that is very serious.*

This bites This is of poor quality or is uninspiring.*

This sucks This is of poor quality or is unfair.**

Thorn in their side A constant annoyance.*

Thousand and one reasons Lots of reasons.*

Three guesses A phrase used sarcastically or jokingly to indicate that something very predictable has occurred. For example, if Tom was expected to fail badly at an exam, a person who has found out that Tom in fact did fail badly might ask another person who is aware of Tom's likely chances, but who does not yet know the result, 'Do you know what Tom did in his exam? Three guesses.' *

Three-ring circus (1) A lot of activity, usually with the implication of chaotic, rather than organized, activity. (2) An ostentatious event, sometimes implying that there is a lot of display but little of actual worth.*

Three Rs The fundamental subjects taught in school – reading, writing and arithmetic (all begin with 'r' if the first letters are taken off the latter two words and a Cockney accent is used).*

Three sheets to the wind Inebriated. Numbers other than 'three' are sometimes used in this phrase.*

Thrills and spills Excitement. The phrase is generally used to describe the excitement gained by watching a spectacular movie or other entertainment.*

Throat See *at each other's throats, force down their throat, frog in the throat, jump down their throat, lump in the throat* and *stick in the throat.*

Through the ceiling See *go through the ceiling.*

Through the mill Treated harshly.*

Through the roof See *go through the roof.*

Through thick and thin In all situations, whether pleasant or unpleasant, easy or difficult.*

Throw a fight In boxing, deliberately losing a match to benefit an illegal betting syndicate. By extension, deliberately performing badly for illicit gain.*

Throw a lifeline Offer assistance.*

Throw a wobbly Have a temper tantrum.*

Throw-away remark Means the same as *off the cuff remark*.

Throw back in their face Reject something in a forceful way. The phrase often is used to describe an act of ingratitude.*

Throw caution to the wind Do something without thinking of possible bad consequences.*

Throw down the gauntlet To challenge someone to do something. The phrase comes from a medieval method of challenging an opponent to a fight by throwing a glove down on the ground in front of them. If the person picked up the glove, then they accepted the challenge. Hence, *take up the gauntlet* means to accept a challenge.*

Throw for a loop Astonish.*

Throw good money after bad Foolishly spend more money on something that has already had money spent on it and is already clearly a failure and/or waste of time.*

Throw in Include.*

Throw in the sponge Means the same as *throw in the towel*.

Throw in the towel Give up. The term comes from boxing, where the trainer of a boxer obviously losing the fight would throw a towel into the ring to stop the fight and save the boxer further injury.*

Throw money at Attempt to solve a problem by spending money on it.*

Throw mud Make accusations and/or spread rumours which have the effect of discrediting someone or something.*

Throw off balance Create uncertainty.*

Throw off the scent Prevent from finding.*

Throw overboard Abandon or discard.*

Throw stones Make accusations.*

Throw the baby out with the bath water To remove or destroy not only the bad bits of something, but also the good things that were worth saving. The phrase indicates that this is a foolish thing to do.*

Throw the book at them Punish someone for every law and rule they have broken.*

Throw their hat into the ring Offer to take part in a contest.*

Throw their weight about Be aggressive or bullying.*

Throw them Confuse them.*

Throw to the dogs (1) Remove the protection afforded someone so that they can be attacked. (2) Discard. (3) Place in danger.*

Throw to the lions Means the same as *throw to the dogs*.

Throw to the wolves (1) Can mean the same as *throw to the dogs*. (2) More specifically, the phrase can mean to place one member of a group in danger so that the other members of the group stand a better chance of survival.*

Thrown in at the deep end Placed in a situation for which a person has little prior experience, and which is very demanding.*

Thumbs down Disapproval.*

Thumbs up Approval.*

Thunder See *steal a person's thunder*.

Tickets on himself [or herself] A person with a very high opinion of their own merits.*

Tickle their fancy Amuse them.*

Tickled pink Very pleased.*

Tie hand and foot Limit activities and/or freedom of movement.*

Tie the knot Get married.*

Tie themselves in knots Become confused. The phrase usually indicates someone who through their own actions makes things more complicated than they should be.*

Tied to the apron strings Derogatory term for a person who is over-reliant on their parents at an age when they are capable of being independent. Note that this does not apply to people who remain at home because of, for example, physical or mental health problems or because they cannot financially afford to leave the family home. *

Tiger See *easy tiger, have a tiger by the tail* and *paper tiger.*

Tight corner Difficult situation.*

Tight ship See *run a tight ship.*

Tight spot Means the same as *tight corner.*

Tighten the screw Make even more unpleasant and/or threatening.*

Tighten their belt Adopt economy measures to save money (typically in response to a loss of earnings).*

Tightly strung Having very repressed emotions but permanently anxious or wary.*

Tilt at windmills A person who 'tilts at windmills' feels they must attack (or create defences against) an enemy that they believe to be real, but in fact does not exist. There is often an implication that the person does this for what they believe to be the best of motives. The phrase is derived from *Don Quixote*, in which the eponymous hero attacks windmills, believing them to be ferocious giants.*

Time and tide The start of a proverb that concludes with 'wait for no man'. In other words, some things will inevitably change or happen regardless of what a person thinks will or should happen. The phrase generally carries the implication that some things have to be done when the opportunity is there, and that waiting or delaying will result in the opportunity being lost.*

Time out Temporarily stop an activity to rest and/or contemplate. The phrase is often used to suggest that people stop arguing before tempers are lost. The phrase is derived from various US sports where a 'time out' (break in play) is permitted for teams to discuss tactics.*

Time out of mind A long time.*

Time will tell An expression used when the importance of something is uncertain at the present time. 'Time will tell' means that in the future it may be possible to better appreciate it (e.g. 'only time will tell whether the pop music of today will remain popular in the future').*

Tin ear No musical ability or ability to appreciate music.*

Tinder box A situation which could very easily become problematic unless great care is taken.*

Tip of the iceberg Something that seems in itself to be a major issue, but is in fact just the most noticeable feature of something far larger. The term is nearly always used to describe something that presents a considerable problem in itself but is in reality symptomatic of something larger and more serious.*

Tip of the tongue (1) Something on the 'tip of the tongue' is something that can almost, but not quite, be recalled. (2) Something that someone is about to say and then represses it.*

Tip the balance (1) Weigh (e.g. 'it tips the balance at 54 kilos'). (2) Be the deciding factor in an argument (e.g. 'the final piece of evidence tipped the balance in favour of the defence').*

Tip the scales Means the same as *tip the balance*, particularly definition 1.

Tire out Make exhausted or become exhausted.*

Tired and emotional Drunk. Derived from a frequently used euphemism in the

British media to refer to inebriated people.*

Tit for tat An argument or dispute in which the attacks of one opponent are responded to with counter-attacks of the same strength and type.*

Tits and ass A blatant (and perhaps exploitative) use of feminine physical sex appeal.***

To a fare-you-well Completely.*

To a fault Generously.*

To a T If something is done to a T, it is exactly correct.*

To a tee Means the same as *to a T*.

To a turn Exactly right. The phrase is most often used to describe a piece of food cooked exactly the right length of time.*

To all intents and purposes By reasonable, rather than utterly precise, argument. The phrase is usually used to indicate that something is sufficiently similar to the desired result for it to be acceptable (e.g. 'to all intents and purposes they are the same').*

To be frank Means the same as *to be honest*.

To be honest A statement emphasising that what follows should be attended to (e.g. 'to be honest, I'm not sure we can do anything more'). It does not mean that the rest of the time the speaker is being dishonest.*

To bits Placed after a phrase to indicate that the sentiment expressed is meant very strongly (e.g. 'I love him to bits').*

To boot In addition (e.g. 'as well as the damage there was the inconvenience and upset to boot').*

To die for Something that is 'to die for' is seen as highly desirable. The phrase is an exaggeration – the desired item in question is usually very appealing but not worth risking life in order to acquire it.*

To-do An argument. See *bit of a to-do*.*

To go Food 'to go' is food to be eaten off the premises where it was prepared.*

To hand Available straight away.*

To hell and back A period of considerable hardship and/or suffering.*

To say the least Attached to a criticism, the phrase means that the criticism offered is the mildest that can be offered, and implies that an accurate criticism would probably be much harsher.*

To the core If something has an attribute 'to the core' then it is full of that attribute (e.g. 'rotten to the core' means it is thoroughly rotten, 'good to the core' that it is thoroughly good, etc.). The phrase is derived from an image of an apple – does it only look good on the outside, or is it the same through to its centre (i.e. core)?*

To the full As much as possible. The phrase is often used in the form *live life to the full*. A person who 'lives life to the full' has a life that is full of activity and experiences.*

To the good (1) In profit. (2) Good.*

To the heart's content To the complete satisfaction (e.g. 'having moved out of the family home into his own house, Laurence was able to play loud music to his heart's content without fearing his parents' complaints').*

To the hilt As far as it is possible.*

To the letter Every detail correct.*

To the manner born Well suited to a particular situation, as if genetically predestined for it.*

To the marrow Totally.*

To the max To the most extreme.*

To the skies With enthusiasm (e.g. 'praise to the skies').*

To the teeth Possessing a lot of something (e.g. 'armed to the teeth' means 'possessing a lot of weapons').*

To their bootstraps Someone who is said to be something 'to their bootstraps' is a very characteristic example (e.g. 'Susan was an annoying person to her bootstraps; everybody found her annoying'.*

To their dying day For the whole of the rest of the lifespan.*

To their fingertips Totally.*

Toast See *on toast.*

Toe See the entries below and: *catch them on their toes, dip their toes in, make their toes curl, on their toes* and *turn up their toes.*

Toe in the door Initial access. Typically the phrase refers to the early stages of an activity that has the aim of attaining something desirable.*

Toe the line Obey regulations and/or orders.*

Toffee See entry below and: *for toffee.*

Toffee-nosed Snobbish.*

Tom, Dick and Harry Ordinary people (e.g. 'this is the sort of thing that would appeal to any Tom, Dick and Harry' means that it is the sort of thing that most people would find appealing). The phrase is often used to denote exclusivity – or lack of it (e.g. 'we don't want just any Tom, Dick and Harry joining the club').*

Ton of bricks See *come down like a ton of bricks.*

Tongue hanging out Showing great eagerness and/or interest.*

Tongue in cheek Something that is 'tongue in cheek' may appear to be meant seriously, but is in reality intended to be humorous.*

Tons of Lots of.*

Too big for their boots Conceited.*

Too big for their britches Means the same as *too big for their boots.*

Too clever by half Derogatory phrase for someone felt to be 'too intelligent'. It is often used to describe someone who displays intelligence but lacks the ability to make any practical use of their skills.**

Too clever for their own good Means the same as *too clever by half.*

Too close for comfort Typically refers to a situation in which something nearly hit someone (e.g. 'the enemy gunners were getting more accurate, and the last volley of shells missed us, but was too close for comfort, so we withdrew'). It can also refer to a criticism or comment that nearly uncovers something a person wants to be kept secret.*

Too close to call If nearing the end of a competition, and it is difficult to predict who will win, then it can be said to be 'too close to call'.*

Too many chiefs and not enough Indians Too many managers and administrators and not enough people actually doing work.*

Too many cooks The phrase refers to the saying *too many cooks spoil the broth,* and means that too many people are involved in something.*

Too many cooks in the kitchen Means the same as *too many cooks spoil the broth.*

Too many cooks spoil the broth A saying expressing the belief that too many people can be involved in an activity, thereby making the finished product of the activity worse than if a smaller number had been involved.*

Too many for Cleverer than.*

Too right An emphatic expression of agreement.*

Too true Means the same as *too right.*

Top and bottom of it The most important or salient features of something.*

Top and tail (1) Clean the extremities. The phrase is particularly used of cleaning a child. (2) Remove the top and bottom of those vegetables or fruit which have inedible or less palatable extremities.*

Top banana (1) The person in charge. (2) The person with the best abilities.*

Top brass Originally meant the senior officers in the armed services (see *brass hats*). Is now used also for the most senior members of any company or government.*

Top dog Means the same as *top banana*.

Top drawer Best quality.*

Top gun Means the same as *top banana*.

Top of the heap At the most powerful and/or prestigious position.*

Top of the ladder Means the same as *top of the heap*.

Top of the morning Traditional Irish greeting.*

Top of the pile Means the same as *top of the heap*.

Top of the tree The most important, successful or senior status.*

Top of the world See *on top of the world*.

Top off Kill.*

Top rung Means the same as *top of the heap*.

Top the bill Means the same as *head the bill*.

Torch See entry below and: *carry a torch* and *hand on the torch*.

Torch song A song of unrequited love.*

Toss off (1) Produce effortlessly and/or carelessly. (2) Masturbate.* (1) or *** (2)

Touch a chord Means the same as *strike a chord*.

Touch a raw nerve Do something that is physically or psychologically painful.*

Touch all the bases To deal with all aspects of the matter.*

Touch and go If something is 'touch and go' then its outcome is uncertain.*

Touch base Make contact.*

Touch bottom Reach the worst and/or most depressing stage.*

Touch on the raw Means the same as *touch a raw nerve*.

Touch their forelock Means the same as *tug their forelock*.

Touch wood An expression of hope that something will happen. Originally, people would also make an earnest effort to touch a piece of wood, but this appears to be becoming a less frequent action.*

Tough act to follow Means the same as *hard act to follow*.

Tough as old boots Resilient.*

Tough cookie A resilient person.*

Tough love Caring in a way that may appear harsh but is advantageous (e.g. making a diabetic child not eat sweets even though they want to).*

Tower of strength Means the same as *pillar of strength*.

Town on fire See *set the town on fire*.

Toy boy (1) A younger man involved in a sexual relationship with an older partner. (2) A younger man whom a woman has a sexual relationship with solely because of his physical attractiveness.*

Tracks See *cover their tracks* and *make tracks*.

Trail their coat Be eager to start an argument.*

Train wreck A very bad failure.*

Tread on air Means the same as *walk on air*.

Tread on their toes (1) Offend them. (2) Do something that is someone else's right or privilege to do.*

Tread water Make no progress.*

Treat like dirt Behave in a very unpleasant manner towards someone.*

Tree See *barking up the wrong tree*.

Trembling in their beds Nervous.*

Trial and error Something calculated by 'trial and error' is done by trying out various methods until the correct one is found.*

Trick in the book See *every trick in the book* and *oldest trick in the book*.

Trick of the trade An advantageous working practice that is well known within a profession or trade but largely unknown by the general public.*

Trifling sum A very small amount (usually money).*

Trim their sails Make adjustments to cope with new conditions. The phrase nearly always implies that the new conditions are less favourable.*

Trip down memory lane Reminisce.*

Trip the light fantastic Have a dance. The phrase is invariably used in a joking manner, or sarcastically to describe someone who is very bad at dancing.*

Trojan Horse (1) An attractive gift that is destructive. (2) A person who, whilst ostensibly working for a group, deliberately weakens or destroys it. (3) A malicious computer program that enters a computer by appearing to be an innocuous file and then causes damage to the computer.*

Troops See *stuff to give the troops.*

Trouble and strife Cockney rhyming slang for 'wife'. Potentially offensive and should be avoided.*

Trouble at mill A joking way of saying that there is a problem. Derives from the clichéd use of the phrase in historical dramas about life in Lancashire or Yorkshire mill towns.*

Trousers See *all mouth and no trousers* and *wear the trousers.*

Truck with See *have no truck with.*

True blue Patriotic or loyal.*

True colours See *show their true colours.*

True grit Fortitude.*

Trumps See *come up trumps.*

Try it on (1) Test something (e.g. 'the dress looked very elegant so I asked to try it on to see if it would fit'). (2) Do something naughty or offensive to see if it will be punished. (3) Do something to see what the reaction will be. (4) Attempt to deceive.*

Try to fit a quart into a pint pot See *get a quart in a pint pot.*

Try to see it my way A request that a person tries to recognize that the speaker has a different *point of view*. In other words, the speaker wants someone to change their opinion.*

Tug and liner A physically unattractive person with a physically attractive friend.*

Tug of love A 'tug of love' legal case involves two divorcing parents disputing who should have custody of their children.*

Tug their forelock Indicate obedience to a social superior. The phrase is often used sarcastically.*

Tummies tickled See *roll over and have their tummies tickled.*

Turkey shoot A very easy task.*

Turkeys waiting for Christmas (1) An improbable event. (2) Foolish or illogical behaviour. Both meanings of the phrase are explained by the thought that it is unlikely that turkeys, if they knew their fate, would look forward to Christmas.*

Turn a blind eye to Ignore. The phrase is often to indicate deliberately ignoring something that should, strictly speaking, be punished, but is not either out of indulgence, because of bribery or because it is not felt worthwhile.*

Turn a deaf ear to Ignore.*

Turn a trick A prostitute who 'turns a trick' has a session with a customer.**

Turn an honest penny Earn money in a morally respectable way.*

Turn cat in pan Become a traitor.*

Turn down Refuse to do something. The phrase is often used to describe rejection of a request (e.g. 'she turned down my application for promotion').*

Turn full circle Means the same as *come full circle*.

Turn heads Attract interest.*

Turn in their grave The phrase has various permutations, most of them following the format 'it's enough to have...turning in their grave' (e.g. 'your proposal to alter the running of the family firm is enough to have grandfather turning in his grave'). The concept being expressed is that if the person mentioned were alive, then he or she would object to the topic under discussion.*

Turn it on its head Radically alter the way something is interpreted.*

Turn of events A sequence of events that together form a story.*

Turn of phrase A phrase; there is usually the implication that the phrase is, if interpreted literally, rather nonsensical (i.e. like most of the phrases in this book).*

Turn of the screw Something that makes an unpleasant situation even more unpleasant.*

Turn of the tide A change in fortunes such that the side that was winning now begins to move towards defeat.*

Turn off (1) As a verb, the phrase means to destroy interest in something (e.g. 'his poor teaching turned off my interest in geography'). (2) As a noun, the phrase means something that destroys interest (e.g. 'the lecture was a turn off'). The phrase (both as a noun and a verb) is often used to describe something that lowers sexual arousal. *Turn on* means the exact opposite of 'turn off' and thus means to raise interest in something or describes something that raises interest. 'Turn on' is generally used to describe the raising of sexual arousal.* or ** (if referring to sexual arousal)

Turn on See *turn off.*

Turn on its head Regard from a radically different perspective.*

Turn out (1) Switch off (e.g. 'turn out the light'). (2) Remove from a building (e.g. 'the dog was turned out of doors'). (3) A group attending an event ('the turn out at the speech day was larger than last year'). (4) Means the same as 'transpire' (e.g. 'how does the story turn out?').*

Turn over a new leaf Change behaviour and/or working practices.*

Turn over in their grave Means the same as *turn in their grave.*

Turn the clock back Restore to an earlier period of time. This obviously cannot be literally done, but refers to either the wish that things could be returned to an earlier time (e.g. 'I wish I could turn the clock back and not make the mistakes I've made') or to remembering what things used to be like (e.g. 'turn the clock back – tell me what you remember about your childhood').*

Turn the corner Begin to recover from a serious illness or problem.*

Turn the heat down Make less exciting.*

Turn the heat on Increase the level of criticism and/or harassment.

Turn the heat up (1) Increase the level of criticism and/or harassment. (2) Make more exciting.*

Turn the other cheek Respond to aggression by refusing to retaliate.*

Turn the tables Change what was an advantage into a disadvantage (or vice versa).*

Turn their back on... (1) When talking about a person, the phrase means to refuse to help someone. (2) When talking about something rather than someone (e.g. 'I turned my back on the whole affair'), the phrase means to refuse to spend any more time talking or thinking about it.*

Turn their hand to Take part in an activity not attempted before.*

Turn their head Alter their belief or behaviour. The phrase usually denotes a change for the worse, such as making a person conceited or believing in impractical schemes.*

Turn their nose up Reject as being of inferior quality.*

Turn them off Destroy their interest. The phrase nearly always refers to sexual interest.*

Turn them on Arouse their interest. The phrase nearly always refers to sexual interest.*

Turn to ashes Be very disappointing. The phrase is sometimes used in a longer version – 'turn to ashes in the mouth'.*

Turn turtle Turn upside-down.*

Turn up (1) Arrival (e.g. 'Jim turned up yesterday with a bunch of flowers'). (2) An event; the phrase is usually reserved for describing an unexpected event (e.g. 'we never expected that turn up').*

Turn up for the books An unexpected event (e.g. 'the meteorite landing in our garden was a turn up for the books').*

Turn up like a bad penny The belief that someone unpleasant will always come back.*

Turn up their toes Die.*

Turning point A moment when something can change (e.g. a turning point in a story occurs when there is a major development in the plot).*

Turns them on See *whatever turns them on*.

Twain See *never the twain shall meet*.

Twenty-four carat Completely.*

Twenty-four hour culture An environment in which there is access to shopping and entertainment twenty-four hours a day. The phrase usually refers to cities with a perceived vibrant cultural life as opposed to 24-hour supermarkets and late night television.*

Twiddle their fingers (1) Be bored because there is nothing to do. (2) Have

nothing to do because no activities are available.*

Twiddle their thumbs Means the same as *twiddle their fingers*.

Twig something Understand something.*

Twinkle in their eye (1) A genial expression. (2) If something is 'just a twinkle in their eye' then it is solely an idea that has yet to be acted upon.*

Twinkling of an eye See *in the twinkling of an eye*.

Twist round their little finger See *wrap round their little finger*.

Twist the knife In an argument or in telling someone off, be more unpleasant than necessary by making a further unpleasant comment that is even more hurtful than what has already been said.*

Twist their arm Persuade someone to do something they at first were unwilling to do.*

Two a penny Means the same as *ten a penny*.

Two bites of the cherry Means the same as *second bite at the cherry*.

Two can play at that game If one person can do something, then it is justifiable for another person to do it as well. The phrase is often used to justify retaliating against an aggressive act.*

Two cents' worth Means the same as *two pennyworth*.

Two heads are better than one The opinion that two people working at the same problem can be more effective than one person.*

Two left feet Clumsy.*

Two of us See *that makes two of us*.

Two pennyworth A person's opinion on a matter, usually unasked for (e.g. 'if I could put in my two pennyworth on this matter I'd say that...').*

Two pint screamer A person (usually a teenager unused to drinking) who gets argumentative or even violent after a small amount of alcohol.*

Two sides of the same coin Things that are different in many respects but still related in some manner (e.g. two lecturers may both work on the same area of research, but have radically different methods of conducting their studies).*

Two ticks A short period of time.*

Two-way street A situation involving two people or groups in which both must contribute to something.*

U

Ugandan discussions Sexual intercourse. The phrase, made popular by the UK magazine *Private Eye*, derives from a supposedly true diplomatic incident involving a Ugandan government representative found in a sexually compromising situation.**

Ugly duckling (1) An unattractive child who becomes attractive when they become an adult. (2) Something that appears unattractive but develops into something attractive.*

Unbalanced personality Describes a person who behaves in a very unusual way. Almost always the term describes someone who not only behaves in an unusual way, but is also a danger to others (e.g. a mentally ill murderer). The term is the opposite of *balanced personality*.*

Uncle Tom Originally, an African-American who showed subservience to white people and/or attempted to integrate into white culture whilst denying their African-American heritage. The phrase is now applied in other contexts to denote a member of a minority group who is over-ingratiating towards members of the majority group.**

Uncle Tom Cobley and all Meaning 'a lot of people'. The phrase is usually added on to the end of a spoken list of people to indicate that a lot of other people are on the list, but they are not of interest. The phrase comes from a folk song that has a chorus that gets increasingly long with a list of names, but always finishes with 'old Uncle Tom Cobley and all'.*

Under a cloud In disgrace or disapproved of.*

Under fire (1) Shot at. (2) Criticized.*

Under par To feel unwell or to describe someone who is not performing up to the expected standard ('par' means 'normal'). Very confusingly, in golf being 'under par' means playing well.*

Under pressure Being compelled or coerced into doing something that is difficult and/or stressful. The phrase is often used to describe a situation in which a person is being asked to do too many things in too short a time.*

Under protest Unwillingly.*

Under the banner of... Supporting or representing a cause (e.g. 'I offer my services under the banner of liberty and freedom').*

Under the belt Describes something already achieved or acquired. Contrast with *below the belt*.*

Under the counter See *over the counter*.

Under the gun Means the same as *under pressure*.

Under the hammer Means the same as *on the block*.

Under the hatches Kept secret.*

Under the heel of Controlled by. The phrase usually implies that control is done through intimidation.*

Under the influence Intoxicated.*

Under the microscope Under scrutiny.*

Under the radar Something that gets 'under the radar' is something that has escaped detection.*

Under the skin Something that gets 'under the skin' (1) causes an irritation;

(2) is pervasive; or (3) shows an especially profound level of understanding.*

Under the sun A property of everything that exists on the Earth, since everything is 'under the sun'. See *nothing new under the sun*.*

Under the table (1) Something done illegally or with deception. (2) Very inebriated.*

Under the weather Feeling unwell.*

Under their nose If something is done 'under a person's nose', then it is done in a way that the person should have detected, but failed to do so.*

Under their own steam By their own efforts.*

Under their thumb Controlled by them.*

University of life A person who claims to have been to 'the university of life' did not attend university. The implication is that by working in the 'real world', rather than reading books, he or she has learnt more about what the world is really like.*
Note: The phrase is considered by many people to be rather self-pitying and should be avoided.

Unknown country Something about which a person lacks expertise.*

Unstaked territory Something that has yet to be explored or claimed.*

Until hell freezes over Since hell is notoriously hot, its freezing over seems improbable. Thus, the phrase means that something is never going to happen.*

Until the cows come home For a very long time.*

Up See the entries below and: *ace up their sleeve, act up, all ends up, all up with, back up, bail up, balloon's gone up, barking up the wrong tree, blood is up, blow up in their face, bottoms up, bring up short, bring up to code, bring up to speed, buck up their ideas, came up, clean up their act, clear up, clued up, come up against a brick wall, come up and see me sometime, come up and see my etchings, come up dry, come up roses, come up smelling of roses,* come up smiling, come up to scratch, come up trumps, come up with the goods, conjure up, couldn't organize a piss-up in a brewery, cover up, crack up, cracked up to be, cut up rough, dead from the neck up, death warmed up, dig up dirt, disappear up their own fundament, don't give up the day job, dressed up to the nines, drive up the wall, dukes up, earth swallow me up, end up, everything's coming up roses, fed up, fed up to the back teeth, fired up and ready to go, first up, game is up, get their back up, get their dander up, get them up, get up and go, get up steam, get up their nose, give it up, give it up for..., give up, give up the ghost, go up in smoke, had it up to here, ham it up, hang up, hang up their..., jumping up and down, keep their end up, keep up with the Joneses, keep your chin up, keep their pecker up, kick up a fuss, kick up a stink, kick up dust, kick up the backside, kick up their heels, kiss and make up, knock up, lair it up, lathered up, laugh up their sleeve, lead up the garden path, leg up, let the earth swallow me up, let up, like death warmed up, lit up, live it up, look up, make their mind up, make up for lost time, make up leeway, not all it's cracked up to be, number is up, on the up and up, own up, pick up, pick up on, pick up some slack, pick up the ball and run with it, pick up the baton, pick up the bill, pick up the pieces, pick up the tab, pick up the thread, pick you up, play up, point up, prick up their ears, prop up the bar, pull their socks up, pull themselves up by their bootstraps, pull up stakes, pull up stumps, pushing up daisies, put their feet up, put their hands up, put up, put up job, put up or shut up, read up, right up their street, roll up their sleeves, rub up the wrong way, run it up the flagpole, sharpen up, show up, shut up, shut up shop, sit up, someone up there likes me, something's up, stand up and be counted, stand up for themselves, stir up a hornets' nest, straight up, straighten up, stressed up, sunny side up, swear up and down, tail up, take it up, take up, take up cudgels, take up the gauntlet, take up the slack, thumbs up, turn the heat up, turn their nose up, turn up, turn up for the books, turn up like a bad penny, turn up their toes, wait up, wake up and smell the..., what's up?* and *wrap you up and take you home.*

Up a gum tree Experiencing a problem with few or no solutions.*

Up a tree Means the same as *up a gum tree.*

Up against the wall In a difficult situation.*

Up and running Completed and operational.*

Up for grabs Available. There is often an implication that the first person to apply will get it.*

Up for it Willing to do it.*

Up hill, down dale An arduous journey.*

Up in arms To be annoyed or angry about something. The phrase usually is used to describe a group of people protesting against something (e.g. 'the whole workforce is up in arms about the proposed redundancies').*

Up in the air To be in a state of uncertainty (e.g. 'nobody knows if the new hospital wing will be built – it's up in the air at the moment and we won't know until the planning committee meets next week').*

Up in the world Raised socio-economic status.*

Up on (1) Ahead of. (2) Have extensive knowledge of.*

Up shit creek Ruder form of *up the creek without a paddle.****

Up the... (1) An expression of support (e.g. '"up the Liberals," he cried enthusiastically'). (2) An expression of hostility akin to *up yours.** (1) or ** (2)

Up the ante (1) To increase the size of a demand or to make things more difficult for a competitor. (2) The phrase can also mean to increase the value or appeal of something. Both uses of the phrase are taken from the card game poker, in which the 'ante' is the money a player must bet to remain in the game.*

Up the boo-eye Utterly incorrect.*

Up the creek Can mean the same as *up the creek without a paddle*, but may also mean 'ruined' or 'damaged beyond repair'.*

Up the creek without a paddle In a difficult situation.*

Up the dose Increase the quantity.*

Up the duff Pregnant.**

Up the spout (1) Having no useful function through bad design or through being broken. (2) Pregnant.* (1) or ** (2)

Up their alley Means the same as *right up their alley.*

Up their sleeve If someone has something 'up their sleeve', then they have a secret plan.*

Up their street Means the same as *right up their street.*

Up to here Means the same as *up to the eyeballs.*

Up to no good Misbehaving.*

Up to par Of an acceptable standard.*

Up to scratch Of the required standard.*

Up to snuff Means the same as *up to scratch.*

Up to speed (1) Fully informed about something. (2) At the expected standard.*

Up to the armpits See *up to the eyeballs.*

Up to the ears Means the same as *up to the eyeballs.*

Up to the elbows Deeply involved.*

Up to the eyeballs An expression used to indicate having too much of something. For example, 'I've had it up to the eyeballs with this problem' means 'I've spent too much time and energy on this problem', whilst 'I'm up to my eyeballs in work' means 'I've got too much work to do'. There are similar phrases such as *up to the armpits* that mean the same thing. The phrase is presumably meant to give the impression of a person standing in a room that has flooded, so that water has reached up to eyeball level.*

Up to the hilt Utterly.*

Up to the mark Means the same as *up to scratch.*

Up to the neck Means the same as *up to the eyeballs.*

Up with the lark Very early morning.*

Up yours An impolite response to something the speaker disagrees with.***

Upper crust The upper social classes.*

Upright citizen A respectable person. The implication is usually that they appear to be rather dull.*

Upset the applecart To disrupt something to a serious extent. The phrase is often used to describe a situation in which a person reveals a carefully guarded secret to a person who was not meant to know, and who in turn causes trouble over it (e.g. 'Janice upset the applecart when she told Mary about the affair between Mary's husband and Elizabeth').*

Upwardly mobile Rising in socio-economic status.*

Use a sledgehammer to crack a nut Use too much energy or expense to achieve something that could have been achieved at far lower cost.*

V

V sign A gesture made by curling up all but the first and second fingers, which are spread slightly apart in a 'V' shape. (1) In the UK, if the hand is held in the air in a stationary position with the palm towards the recipient of the gesture, then it means 'V for victory', and thus is an indication that something has been successful. (2) In the UK, if the same gesture is made with the outside of the hand facing towards the recipient of the gesture (and often done in an upwards motion of the arm and hand), then it is offensive. It is important that in making a hand gesture indicating two of something that this gesture is not used (it is the UK equivalent of the US *give the finger*). The phrase describing either gesture is polite.*

Vaccinated with a gramophone needle Over-talkative.*

Vanilla version The *bare bones* version of something. There is usually the implication that it is boring or uninteresting without the extras (e.g. 'you can buy the DVD in a vanilla version with no extras or the super deluxe version with director's commentary and deleted scenes'). Named because ice cream is usually seen as 'unflavoured' if it has vanilla in it (this is perverse, because vanilla is a flavouring, and as any one with an ice cream maker knows, ice cream without vanilla tastes like frozen cream).*

Veins See ... *in their* veins.

Vicar of Bray A person who changes allegiances to suit his or her own best interests rather than having a rigid moral code or loyalty. Named after a vicar (church minister) of a village in Berkshire, England, who was attributed (probably falsely) of altering his faith between Protestantism and Catholicism as dictated by the different religious policies of the Tudor monarchs of Edward, Mary and Elizabeth.*

Vicious circle A problem that appears to get worse by trying to solve it, since any attempt to work on the problem creates more problems, and makes the original problem even harder to solve.*

Villain of the piece The person principally responsible.*

Viper in the bosom A person who shows ingratitude to their benefactors.*

Virgin territory Means the same as *unstaked territory.*

Voice in the wilderness A single person or group expressing an opinion that is different from that of the majority, and which is being ignored.*

Vote with their feet Indicate approval or disapproval through action (e.g. if a new theatre show is popular, then people are said to 'vote with their feet' by going to the theatre to see the show).*

W

Wait on them hand and foot Be extremely attentive to their needs.*

Wait 'til I get my hands on you A threat of punishment.*

Wait until I get you home (1) A threat of punishment (usually made by a parent to a child) for misbehaviour. The threat is made when the people concerned are in public, and thus administering punishment there and then might not be expedient. (2) When in public, an expression of hoping for engaging in sexual activity upon returning home. The context and tone of voice in which the phrase is said should be sufficient to indicate which meaning is meant.*

Wait up (1) Stay awake rather than go to bed at the usual time and wait for something (typically, waiting for someone to return). (2) A colloquial phrase meaning 'stop!' It's typically addressed to a person walking away.*

Waiting in the wings Something that is about to happen.*

Wake up and smell the... A demand to attend to what is really happening. The phrase is usually used as a rebuke to a person who has an unrealistically over-optimistic attitude towards a particular situation. The most commonly used version is *wake up and smell the coffee.* or **
or ***

Note: politeness level depends on the word at the end of the phrase.

Wake up and smell the coffee See *wake up and smell the....* *

Wake-up call An event that stops a person being complacent about something and makes them do something to change the situation (e.g. 'September 11th was a wake-up call to countries that had grown complacent about airport security').*

Walk a mile in another person's shoes Try to understand how another person thinks or feels about something. See *put yourself in my shoes.* *

Walk down memory lane Reminisce.*

Walk it Do it without any appreciable effort.*

Walk on air Be in a state of great happiness.*

Walk on eggshells Behave carefully in a situation where there is a danger of causing offence.*

Walk the plank (1) Be expelled from a group. (2) Lose a job.*

Walk the walk A person who can 'walk the walk' can do what they say they can do (i.e. they are not just saying they can do things).*

Walk them off their feet Make them exhausted through too much walking.*

Walls have ears A warning to be more careful about what is being said because there is a danger of being overheard.*

Waltz Matilda Travel with all possessions carried in a bag.*

Wank The word means 'masturbate' in British slang. It is considered rude and caution should be applied in using it. The word appears to be used as a rather milder (but less frequent) swear word in US English.***

Want jam on it Have unreasonable and/or unrealistic expectations.*

War room A meeting place where senior members of an organisation meet to make strategic decisions.*

Warm the cockles The start of a longer phrase – 'warm the cockles of the heart'. If something warms the cockles, then it creates a feeling of great contentment.*

Wars See *been in the wars.*

Warts and all Refers to a complete description, including unflattering details. The implication is that a complete and accurate description is given. The phrase comes from Oliver Cromwell's instruction to a portrait painter to produce an accurate, rather than flattering, portrait, that should include 'warts and all' (i.e. rather than give a more flattering but inaccurate depiction of a smooth complexion).*

Wash dirty linen in public Divulge secrets that should have been prudently hidden. The phrase can describe both the deliberate revealing of such information, or arguing in public during which such secrets are revealed.*

Wash their hands of… Refuse to accept responsibility for.*

Waste their breath Argue something with no effect. Hence the advice *don't waste your breath*, indicating that any argument will have no effect.*

Watch it Be careful.*

Watch like a hawk Observe very carefully. There is usually an implication that the watching is being done to detect signs of wrongdoing.*

Watch their back Use caution.*

Watch this space There are likely to be further developments.*

Watched kettle The start of a proverb that finishes with 'never boils'. In other words, something that is being observed too intently never seems to finish.*

Water under the bridge Something that happened in the past, and whose implications are being ignored.*

Wavelength See *on the same wavelength*.

Wax lyrical Talk animatedly.*

Way of all flesh Death or decay.*

Way to go (1) A term of praise (e.g. 'way to go! – that was a brilliant piece of playing'). (2) Used ironically, it means 'you really did that badly' (e.g. 'way to go! – you managed to offend just about everybody'). Contrast with *what a way to go.*

Weak at the knees Feel enfeebled because of strong emotions.*

Wear and tear The minor damage and changes created through normal use of something.*

Wear the trousers Be the dominant partner in a relationship.*

Wear their fingers to the bone Work very hard.*

Wear their heart on their sleeve Make no attempt to hide their emotional feelings.*

Weather for ducks Heavy rain with waterlogged conditions.*

Wee small hours Late at night and very early in the morning.*

Weigh in the balance Carefully consider the alternatives.*

Weight See entry below and: *above their weight* and *worth their weight in gold*.

Weight off their mind A feeling of relief.*

Welcome to their world Experience for the first time something that is a routine experience for someone else.*

Well I never An expression of surprise.*

Welly See *give it some welly* and *green welly brigade*.

Went out with the ark Joking term for something that is very old-fashioned or is now outmoded (e.g. 'high Internet connection charges went out with the ark – modern customers expect a low flat-rate connection fee').*

Wet behind the ears Inexperienced.*

Wet blanket (1) A person who finds something to be miserable about, thereby spoiling everyone else's enjoyment. (2) Something that spoils the enjoyment of an event (e.g. 'the poor weather threw a wet blanket over the event').*

Whale of a… An especially impressive quantity or magnitude of… *

What a way to go A term used to express amazement at the manner in which someone died. It is usually reserved for someone who died doing something they enjoyed (e.g. it might be said of a keen golfer who died from shock after scoring a hole in one). Contrast with *way to go.**

What are they driving at? An expression of incomprehension; a paraphrase is 'what are they trying to say? – I don't understand'.*

What are you looking at? An aggressive question implying that someone is being nosey.**
Note: this can be used by some very aggressive people as a ploy to start a fight. Very carefully attend to tone of voice and the context in which it is said.

What are you? My analyst? A phrase indicating that someone is making unwanted statements about a person's behaviour.*

What are you? My mother? A phrase indicating that someone is being too fussy and/or over-cautious.*

What can I do you for? A deliberate (and supposedly humorous) alteration of the phrase 'what can I do for you?' It means the same as 'what can I do for you?'*

What do you expect? A rhetorical question indicating that what happened could have been easily predicted. The phrase is thus a criticism implying that it is foolish to be surprised about something that should have been anticipated.*

What do you expect from a pig but a grunt? A comment passed on hearing about bad behaviour. The phrase means that the person is known to have unappealing attributes, so why be surprised when they do something unappealing? *

What have you When used at the end of a spoken description, the phrase often means 'whatever' (e.g. 'there were various expensive cars there, such as Volvos, Lexuses, Mercedes or what have you').*

What it takes See *got what it takes.*

What kept you? A gently sarcastic question asked when someone does something far faster than expected. The response expected is an explanation of why something was done so quickly.*

What thought did See *you know what thought did.*

What's bred in the bone The phrase in essence means that what is genetically inherited cannot be suppressed by education, training in etiquette and manners, etc.*

What's eating them? What is annoying them? *

What's it worth? (1) A serious response to a request indicating that a person won't comply unless rewarded (e.g. 'what's it worth for me to keep quiet?'). (2) A joking response to a request indicating that the person will comply, but that they are only doing it to please the person who made the request (e.g. 'will you baby-sit for us tomorrow night?' – 'what's it worth?'). Whether meaning 1 or 2 is implied depends on the context, the tone of the voice and similar indications.*

What's sauce for the goose The start of a proverb that finishes with 'is sauce for the gander'. In other words, what is appropriate for a woman is appropriate for a man as well.*

What's the big deal? See *big deal.*

What's the big idea? Means the same as *what's this in aid of?*

What's the damage? How much does this cost? *

What's the magic word? If someone asks for something but does not say 'please' (i.e. is being ill-mannered), then they might get the reply 'what's the magic word?' (meaning 'you didn't say please'). The phrase is more often used by teachers and parents training children to be polite, but can sometimes be used (usually jokingly) by adults.*

What's their game? A question indicating grievance at an observed behaviour. A paraphrase might be 'why are they doing that, 'cause I don't like it'.*

What's this in aid of? What is the purpose of this? **

What's up? What is happening? The phrase nearly always is used when the person asking the question thinks that there is something wrong.*

Whatever gets you through the night Means the same as *whatever turns them on.*

Whatever lights their candle Means the same as *whatever turns them on.*

Whatever turns them on An expression of bemused tolerance. The expression is usually used jokingly.*

Wheat from the chaff See *separate the wheat from the chaff.*

Wheel has come full circle The phrase generally means that a situation has returned to how it was at the start after a rise and fall in fortunes. The phrase comes from William Shakespeare's play *King Lear.*

Wheeling and dealing Engaged in important business transactions.*

Whelk stall See *couldn't run a whelk stall.*

When a person's back is turned If something is done 'when a person's back is turned' then it is done without the person knowing about it. The term is often used to describe a situation where a person is guarding or watching over something.*

When all is said and done What ultimately matters.*

When hell freezes over Means the same as *until hell freezes over.*

When in Rome This is the shortened form of a longer saying – 'when in Rome, do as the Romans do'. In fact, this in turn is a shortened form of an even longer proverb, that in essence advises that when in Rome, act like a Roman; when elsewhere, act according to the local customs. Thus, the phrase simply means 'do whatever seems to be the normal behaviour for where you are'.*

When Methuselah was a boy Joking phrase meaning 'a very long time ago' (e.g. 'his clothes were last in fashion when Methuselah was a boy'). Methuselah is the longest-living person in the Bible and in any case lived a long time ago.*

When Nelson gets his eye back Phrase indicating that something is felt to be impossible or will never happen (e.g. 'lecturers will get a good salary when Nelson gets his eye back'). Admiral Nelson commanded the British fleet during the early part of the Napoleonic Wars, and had only one eye.*

When push comes to shove When the theoretical discussions must stop and the task be done.*

When…sneezes…catches a cold The phrase expresses the idea that what happens to one person or thing will inevitably happen to another person or thing if the first person or thing is important enough (e.g. 'when America sneezes, the world catches a cold').*

When the band begins to play When the situation becomes serious.*

When the cat's away The start of a longer saying – 'when the cat's away, the mice will play'. It means that if the person in charge is away (e.g. on holiday) the people they normally control are likely to misbehave and/or not work as hard.*

When the chips are down See *chips are down.*

When the dust settles At a time after an event when there is less excitement about it.*

When the going gets tough When the situation or something becomes difficult. The phrase is sometimes followed by 'then the tough get going', meaning that difficult situations require tough, resolute people to deal with them.*

When the shit hits the fan In other words, when there is trouble (if excrement is thrown at an electric fan, the effect can be readily imagined to be unpleasant).***

Where it's at (1) Description of a fashionable place or activity (i.e. if it's 'where it's at' then it is fashionable). (2) In some forms of colloquial English, a way of saying 'where it is'.*

Where the action is (1) Where the most important things are done in an organisation. (2) The liveliest, most socially desirable parts of a town or city (generally refers specifically to nightclubs, bars, discos, etc.).*

Where there's muck The start of a longer proverb that finishes with 'there's brass'. The proverb expresses the view that money can often be made from dealing with unpleasant things.*

Where's the beef? The phrase essentially asks the question 'where is there anything of substance or importance?' The phrase was originally used in a television advert for a hamburger company (the question addressed the relative smallness of the meat component in rival companies' burgers), and was later used by US politicians to query whether their opponents had policies or just effective-sounding (but ultimately vacuous) speeches.*

Where's the fire? A question asking why someone is running or otherwise behaving in a frantic, harassed manner.*

Which way the cat jumps See *see which way the cat jumps.*

While the going is good During good or advantageous conditions.*

Whip into shape Improve performance.*

Whip their ass Defeat someone very convincingly.**

Whipping boy A person blamed for a mishap (regardless of whether they were truly to blame). Refers to the historical custom of educating a boy along with a prince or nobleman's son – if the prince/nobleman's son misbehaved, the other boy (the 'whipping boy') was punished, since the tutors were not allowed to punish the 'socially superior' prince/nobleman's son.*

Whistle Dixie Waste time daydreaming.*

Whistle for it Have no possibility of success. Often used as a retort (e.g. 'if you think you are having any more ice cream you can whistle for it, because there's none left').*

White bread Very mundane and unexciting.*

White elephant A useless item.*

White elephant sale A sale of items of bric-a-brac. Such a sale is a traditional feature of UK village and church fêtes and similar fund-raising activities.*

White man's burden Phrase expressing the Victorian belief (now seen as racist and hopelessly inaccurate) that it was the sacred duty of white Europeans to introduce 'civilized values' to the rest of the world. The phrase should be used with very great care. **

Whited sepulchre A hypocritical person.*

Who are you looking at? Means the same as *what are you looking at?*

Who are you? My analyst? Means the same as *what are you? My analyst?*

Who are you? My mother? Means the same as *what are you? My mother?*

Who ate all the pies? A supposedly humorous question indicating that someone is overweight. Should be avoided – the speaker is in fact indicating that they are uncouth.***

Who goes there? Means the same as *halt, who goes there?*

Who he? [who she?] A question indicating that a person just mentioned is unfamiliar (i.e. what is meant is 'who is he?' or 'who is she?'). The lack of correct grammar is supposed to make it sound amusing.*

Who opened their lunch? Means 'who farted?'**

Who rattled its cage? A joking remark, meaning 'who made them lose their temper?' The phrase uses the image of a caged, bad-tempered animal provoked into an aggressive display by having its cage rattled.*

Who split the cheese? Means the same as *who opened their lunch?*

Who was your servant last half year? A response to a demand or request for assistance that implies that what is being asked for is excessive.*

Who's...when they're at home? A question asking 'who is this person?' and simultaneously indicating that the speaker has never heard of them before. There is often an implied contempt that because the person has not been heard of, then they are probably not very good at what they do.*

Whole ball of wax Means the same as the *whole caboodle.*

Whole caboodle The complete thing.*

Whole cloth Something made of 'whole cloth' is untrue.*

Whole enchilada The complete thing or situation.*

Whole hog Everything.*

Whole kit and caboodle Means the same as *whole caboodle.*

Whole new ball game Means the same as *new ball game.*

Whole person A person who has all the skills necessary to function without help from others, and whose behaviour is seen as 'normal'.*

Whole shebang Everything.*

Whole shooting match Everything.*

Wide blue yonder (1) Far away. (2) The sea or sky.*

Wide boy Someone who is eager to acquire money and is unscrupulous about how they do it. The phrase generally implies rather outlandish manners and tastes.*

Wide of the mark Inaccurate.*

Wide-eyed and bushy tailed Eager and enthusiastic.*

Wide-eyed and legless Inebriated.*

Widow's mite A small sum that is a disproportionately large amount to a poor person. The phrase is used particularly to describe contributions to charity and other similar morally good acts.*

Wild card An unpredictable person or thing. In some games of cards, certain cards ('wild cards') can assume any value the player chooses.*

Wild goose chase A task that cannot possibly succeed and is time-consuming and frustrating.*

Wild horses wouldn't... The phrase typically finishes with a phrase like 'drag it from them' or similar. The phrase indicates that a person is not going to reveal a secret they know.*

...will out See *blood will out* and *talent will out.*

Willies See *gave me the willies.*

Win by a... Followed by a word indicating the margin of victory. For example, 'landslide' or 'mile' indicates an overwhelming win, whilst 'squeak', 'canvas', 'whisker' or 'neck' indicates a narrow victory. Several other words can be used.*

Win on points Gain victory by having some superior features rather than being overwhelmingly better at everything.*

Win the day Win. The phrase often implies that the victory has been gained after a debate.*

Wind them up Tease them or lead them to believe a false story.*

Wind up (1) Means the same as *wind them up.* (2) A 'wind up' is a deliberate deception.*

Window of opportunity An opportunity that will only be available for a short period of time.*

Winds of change A movement for reform. The phrase is often used for major changes in administration or politics.*

---

* denotes *level of impoliteness*

Wipe the slate clean Forget or deliberately ignore everything that happened before. The phrase is normally used to describe the forgiveness of past misdemeanours.*

Wisdom of Solomon Someone with the 'wisdom of Solomon' is very wise. Solomon was an Old Testament king and reputedly wise.*

Wise after the event Capable of understanding the problem after it has had its effect. The implication is usually that this is not a difficult skill – anticipating and avoiding the problem so it never happened would have been more desirable.*

Wish them joy Wish them success. The phrase is nearly always used sarcastically.*

With a capital... Used in a phrase such as 'psychology with a capital P', 'business with a capital B', etc., the intention is to indicate that the most important or serious aspects of the matter are being discussed. See *life with a capital L* for an illustration.*

With all guns blazing With great enthusiasm, and in an unsubtle manner.*

With apologies to... When included in the title of a piece of art or writing, the phrase means that what follows is a parody or pastiche of the work of the person whose name is mentioned (e.g. 'the title of this article on cookery is "The Ancient Marinader, with apologies to Coleridge"').*

With bated breath In a state of anxiety and/or great curiosity, waiting to see what will happen next (e.g. 'we awaited the result of the trial with bated breath').*

With bells on With enthusiasm.*

With child Pregnant.*

With closed eyes Means the same as *with eyes closed.*

With eyes closed Unaware or only partly aware. It is usually implied that this (partial or total) ignorance is deliberate.*

With eyes open Fully aware.*

With flying colours Something done 'with flying colours' is done very successfully. 'Colours' are flags that were often displayed on naval sailing ships.*

With forked tongue Deceitful.*

With gloves off Especially unpleasant or unrestrained.*

With knobs on Phrase sometimes added at the end of a statement to emphasize the strength of feeling. The phrase is most often used as a reply to an insult (e.g. 'the same to you with knobs on').*

With open arms The phrase is used to describe a greeting or acceptance that is offered without question or restrictions (e.g. 'the proposed improvements to working conditions were met with open arms by the staff').*

With open eyes Means the same as *with eyes open.*

With the best will in the world Meaning 'with the best of intentions'. The phrase is usually used in a sentence indicating that something cannot be done even though it is strongly desired (e.g. 'with the best will in the world, I don't think we can do this').*

With the flies To do something 'with the flies' is to do it alone.*

With you When used as a response to an explanation, 'with you' indicates that the speaker understands the explanation.*

Wither on the vine Fail because of neglect or absence of action.*

Within an ace Almost succeeding in doing something (but nonetheless failing).*

Within an inch of their life Receiving a serious physical punishment.*

Within coo-ee A short distance away.*

Within distance Attainable.*

Within spitting distance Means the same as *within coo-ee*.

Within striking distance Means the same as *within distance*.

Within the meaning of the act As is usually understood or accepted.*

Without fail Reliably.*

Without number A large quantity.*

Without rhyme or reason Without any logical or moral justification.*

Without tears Without difficulty.*

Wolf in sheep's clothing Someone or something dangerous but who appears harmless.*

Woman of letters An educated woman.*

Women and children first A phrase used in earlier generations to indicate that, in the case of a major accident requiring evacuation (e.g. a sinking ship), women and children should be allowed to flee first. The phrase is these days more likely to be heard as a joking comment on receipt of bad (but not disastrous) news affecting a group of people.*

Won't take no for an answer See *no for an answer*.

Wood for the trees See *can't see the wood for the trees*.

Wooden spoon A 'prize' for the worst performance.*

Woodwork See *crawl out of the woodwork*.

Wool over their eyes See *pull the wool over their eyes*.

Woolly thinking Vague or unintelligent thought or behaviour.*

Word See entries below and: *a word, actions speak louder than words, by word of mouth, can't get a word in edgeways, don't mince words, drop a word in their ear, famous last words, from the word go, have the last word, last word, lost for words, mark my words, mince words, mum's the word, not know the meaning of the word, put words into their mouth, say the word, take words out of their mouth* and *what's the magic word?*

Word in edgeways See *can't get a word in edgeways*.

Word in their ear To have 'a word in someone's ear' is to tell them something in private.*

Word on everyone's lips The currently most-discussed person or issue.*

Word on the street The current gossip.*

Word to the wise A brief piece of advice.*

Word up A phrase indicating particularly strong agreement.*

Words of one syllable Very simple language. It is not a requirement that every word is literally one syllable long.*

Work cut out See *have their work cut out*.

Work into the ground Make exhausted through over-work.*

Work their fingers to the bone Work very hard.*

Work their...off Work extremely hard at something. The phrase varies in politeness according to the word used in the phrase (e.g. 'work their bottom off' is relatively innocuous, whilst 'work their balls off' is less widely socially acceptable).* or ** or ***

Work their passage Offer labour instead of money as payment for a service. The phrase originally referred to working as a ship's labourer in exchange for a free sea voyage. However, more generally it can refer to, for example, working to pay for college tuition fees and similar.*

Work their ticket Gain permission to leave.*

World and his wife In other words, everybody. The term is now in decline because it is seen as sexist.*

World doesn't owe them a living See *owe them a living*.

World is their oyster There are lots of opportunities.*

---

* *denotes level of impoliteness*

World of difference A very large difference.*

World on their shoulders A person with the 'world on their shoulders' has problems that preoccupy them and are causing a feeling of depression.*

World revolves around them People who think that the 'world revolves around them' are very self-centred in their beliefs.*

Worm has turned A previously meek person or group has rebelled.*

Worm's-eye view The opinion or perspective of an ordinary person or part of the general (as opposed to the managerial) workforce.*

Worried over Concerned about.*

Worried sick Very concerned.*

Worse than death See *fate worse than death.*

Worse things happen at sea Said in consolation after a mishap or other unpleasant event. The intention of the phrase is to indicate that, although things may appear bad, there are worse fates which could have happened (e.g. drowning, being eaten alive by a shark). There are of course much nicer things as well, which rather weakens the argument, at least in this author's view.*

Worth their salt Useful and/or competent.*

Worth their weight in gold Very useful and/or competent.*

Worthy See *I am not worthy.*

Would skin a flea for a halfpenny Would do anything to earn money.*

Would you cocoa An expression of disbelief.*

Wouldn't be seen dead in... An expression of strong disapproval of something, indicating that the speaker wouldn't do it (e.g. 'I wouldn't be seen dead in one of those new cars').*

Wouldn't give them the time of day Treat with disdain and aloofness. The phrase is often used to describe good-looking and/or rich people who cannot be bothered to show even basic courtesy to people who are less attractive and/or rich.*

Wouldn't hurt a fly Is incapable of doing harm.*

Wouldn't kick out of bed (1) Would be willing to have sexual intercourse with. (2) Would be willing to consider.** (2) or *** (1)

Wouldn't say boo to a goose Is very timid.*

Wouldn't say no In other words, 'yes'.*

Wouldn't touch them with a bargepole An expression of extreme dislike (e.g. 'I wouldn't touch her with a bargepole'). A bargepole is a long pole used by bargees; if someone is unwilling to be even the distance of a bargepole from them, then they clearly are not very fond of them. The phrase is sometimes slightly embellished (e.g. 'wouldn't touch them with a ten foot bargepole').*

Wrap in cotton wool Be over-protective.*

Wrap in the flag Show patriotic behaviour to an excessive degree. There is often an inference that this is being done hypocritically.*

Wrap round their little finger Easily control someone.*

Wrap you up and take you home The phrase, usually preceded by 'I could...', is a term of praise and simply means that the speaker thinks someone is a useful worker or otherwise is appealing. It is a relatively mild term of praise and should not be interpreted more literally.*

Wrapped too tight Too emotionally repressed and concerned with correct protocol.*

Wrench in the works Means the same as *spanner in the works.*

Write off Dismiss as unimportant or no longer worthy of consideration.*

Write-off Totally destroyed. The phrase comes from the idea that a badly damaged item will be 'written off' (i.e. erased from the inventory of working items) because it either cannot be repaired or would be too costly to repair.*

Writes itself Very predictable.*

Writing on the wall A forewarning of disaster. The phrase refers to the story of Belshazzar in the Old Testament, who was warned of the collapse of his kingdom by the appearance of magical handwriting on the wall.*

Wrong box See *in the wrong box.*

Wrong end of the stick An incorrect interpretation of something.*

Wrong side of the bedsheets Born out of wedlock.*

Wrong side of the tracks From a socially 'inferior' area or group.*

X

X marks the spot In popular fiction, the location of buried treasure was marked by an 'X' on a map. By extension, whatever is the desired object or location might be described as 'X marks the spot'.*

Y

Yanking the chain Telling a lie (e.g. 'I don't believe you – I think you're yanking my chain').*

Yarn See *spin a yarn.*

Yea and nay (1) Indecision. (2) Can mean the same as *yes and no.**

Year dot A date that is not precisely known, but is believed to be a very long time ago.

Thus, if something has been done a particular way 'since the year dot', it means it has been done that way for a very long time.*

Yell bloody murder Means the same as *yell blue murder.*

Yell blue murder Loudly protest.*

Yes and no If something is 'yes and no' it is partly correct and partly incorrect.*

Yesterday's man [or woman] A person who is no longer as influential or important as they once were.*

Yesterday's news Something no longer of interest. The phrase can apply to people (e.g. an actor no longer popular might be called 'yesterday's news'), things (e.g. 'yo-yos are yesterday's news') or information (e.g. 'the evidence of Andrew's lying was yesterday's news').*

You ain't seen nothing yet Something even better or more surprising than what has just been witnessed is about to be revealed.*

You and whose army? A response to a threat implying that the person making the threat is incapable of carrying out what he or she is threatening.*

You and yours Closest members of the family and close friends.*

You can say that again An expression of agreement. It is not necessary to repeat what has been said.*

You can't beat the system See *beat the system.*

You can't win Being in a helpless situation in which something must be done, but every course of action has disadvantages.*

You don't keep a dog and bark yourself In other words, there is no point in employing someone or something to do a job and then do it yourself.*

You forgot to say please The phrase, as used to children, is literally a reminder that they have been impolite because they forgot to say 'please' when making a request. In the case of adults, the phrase can be used in a more jovial sense to indicate that what has been asked for is unrealistic (e.g. 'I'd like a pay rise of a hundred per cent' – 'you forgot to say please').*

You know what thought did The rest of the proverb is ' – it followed a muck cart and thought it was a wedding'. The phrase is used as a criticism of someone who says 'I thought...' followed by an inaccurate statement.*

You name it Anything. The phrase is often used to emphasize how wide-ranging something is (e.g. 'I've done lots of jobs – you name it, and I've probably done it').*

You pays your money and takes your choice All the available options are of approximately the same quality.*

You scratch my back and I'll scratch yours An expression meaning that if you help a person do something, they will help you do something else. The phrase is often used where either person has something the other wants. For example, one person might have paint brushes and no paint and another person has lots of paint. The person with the paint brushes might offer to loan them to the other person in return for some of the paint. In suggesting this, the person with the paint brushes might say 'you scratch my back and I'll scratch yours'.*

You should see mine A response made when someone apologizes that something is of poor quality, untidy or similar. The response of 'you should see mine' or similar is intended to mean 'it's alright, mine is far poorer/more untidy' (or whatever is appropriate) and thus is a polite way of telling someone that there is no need to apologize or feel awkward.*

You want fries with that? In a setting other than a café or restaurant, a facetious response implying that someone is making unrealistic demands.*

You wish A response indicating that what has just been said is hopelessly beyond what the speaker is capable of accomplishing (e.g. 'when I'm a millionaire' leading to the reply 'you wish!').*

You're telling me A phrase that indicates emphatic agreement (e.g. 'Hitler was a bad person' – 'you're telling me').*

Young blood (1) Younger members of a team or organisation. There is often the implication that the young blood will be better at producing fresh new ideas. (2) An over-confident young adult; generally there is an implication that they are rich and part of fashionable society.*

Young Turk A young person with a strong desire to reform (e.g. politics, workplace practices, a field of study, etc.). The phrase is derived from an influential group of reformers in Turkey in the early twentieth century. However, the phrase applies to people of any nationality, not just Turks.*

Your mileage may vary Your opinions may differ from the one expressed.*

Z

Zapped out Produced.*

Zero sum game A situation in which if one person or group gains something, another person or group loses the same amount.*

Zs See *catch some zs*.

---

101 If something is '101' then it is very elementary. The phrase is derived from the observation that many introductory university courses have the coding of '101'.*

24/7 Stands for '24 hours per day, 7 days a week'. In other words, continuously (e.g. 'I want her to be under surveillance 24/7').*

9/11 The terrorist attack on the Twin Towers and the Pentagon on 11 September 2001. The ordering of the numbers is the American habit of placing the month before the date (i.e. the reverse of the UK method).*

denotes level of impoliteness